HARLEY QUINN

VOLUME 3

KISS KISS BANG STAB

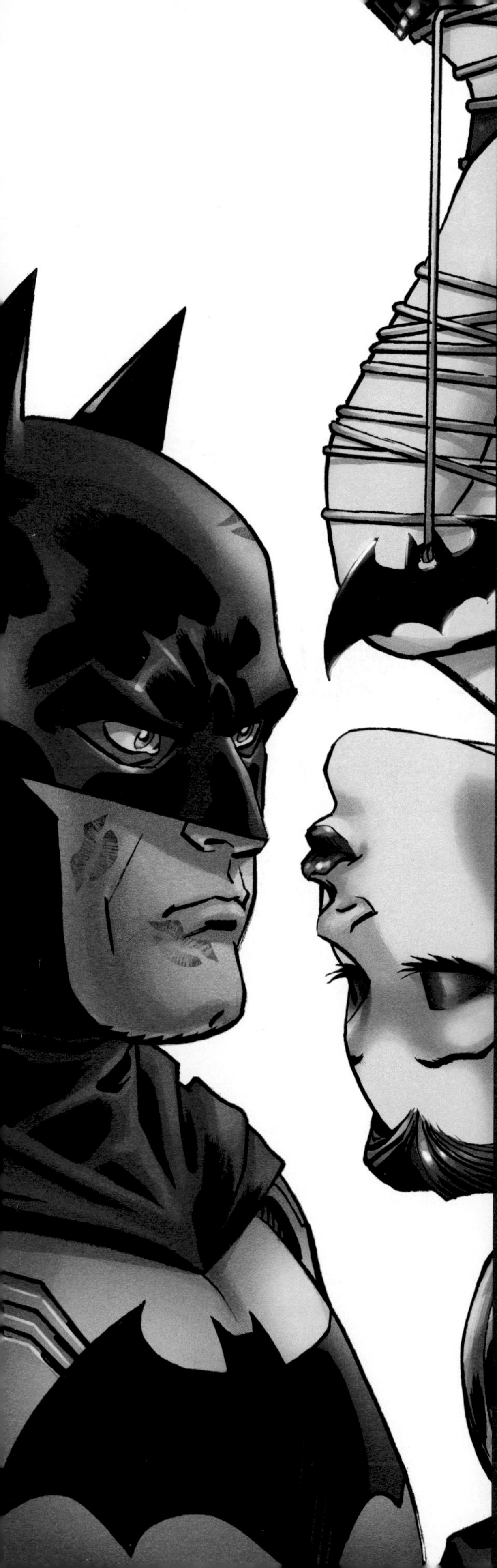

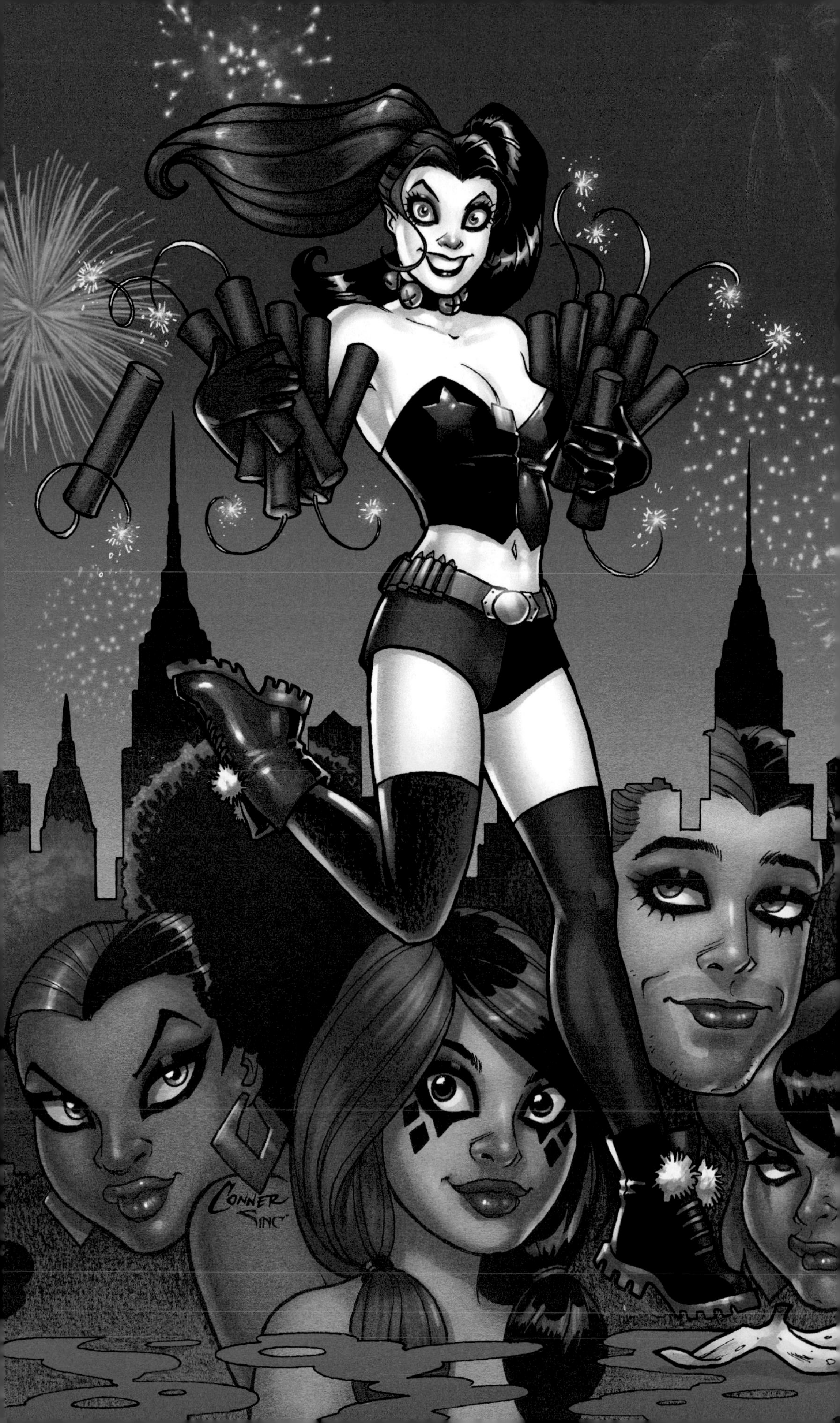
CONNER
SINC'

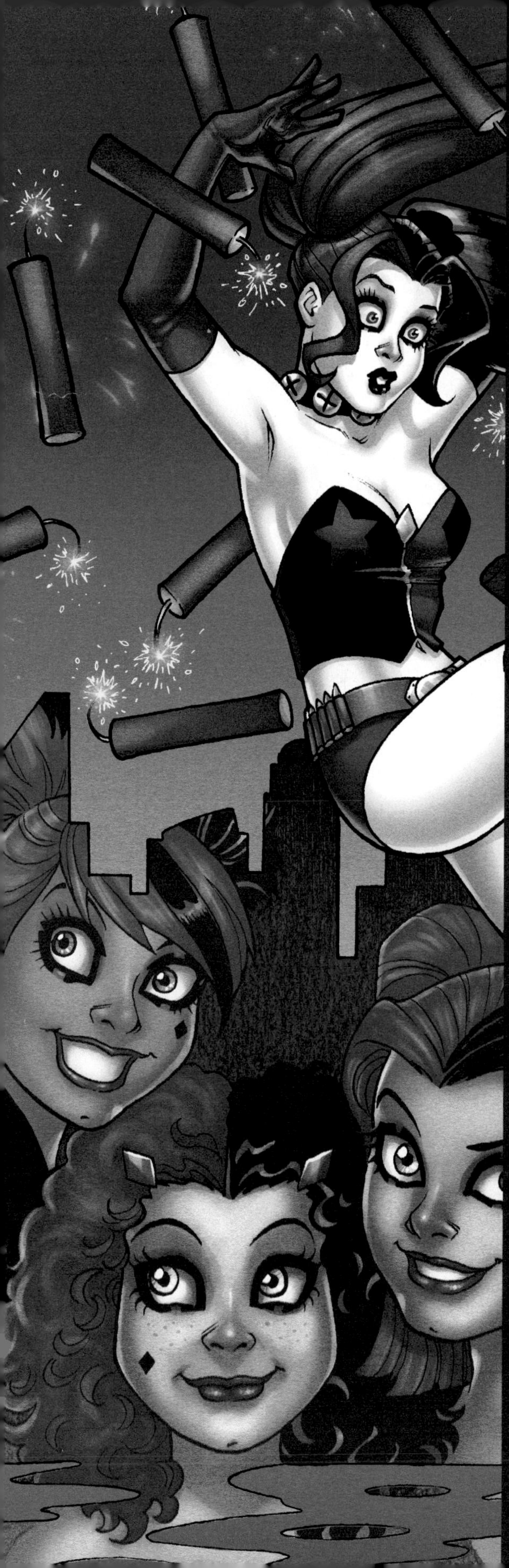

VOLUME 3
KISS KISS BANG STAB

WRITTEN BY
AMANDA CONNER
JIMMY PALMIOTTI

ART BY
CHAD HARDIN
JOHN TIMMS
STJEPAN ŠEJIĆ
JOE QUINONES
BEN CALDWELL
KELLEY JONES
MAURICET
BRANDT PETERS
AMANDA CONNER
DARWYN COOKE
AARON CAMPBELL
THONY SILAS

COLOR BY
ALEX SINCLAIR
PAUL MOUNTS
STJEPAN ŠEJIĆ
JOE QUINONES
RICO RENZI
MICHELLE MADSEN
DAVE McCAIG
DAVE STEWART
HI-FI

LETTERS BY
JOHN J. HILL

COLLECTION COVER ARTISTS
AMANDA CONNER &
ALEX SINCLAIR

HARLEY QUINN CREATED BY
PAUL DINI & BRUCE TIMM

BATMAN CREATED BY
BOB KANE

CHRIS CONROY Editor – Original Series
DAVE WIELGOSZ Assistant Editor – Original Series
ROBIN WILDMAN Editor – Collected Edition
JEB WOODARD Group Editor – Collected Editions
DAMIAN RYLAND Publication Design

BOB HARRAS Senior VP – Editor-in-Chief, DC Comics

DIANE NELSON President
DAN DIDIO and JIM LEE Co-Publishers
GEOFF JOHNS Chief Creative Officer
AMIT DESAI Senior VP – Marketing & Global Franchise Management
NAIRI GARDINER Senior VP – Finance
SAM ADES VP – Digital Marketing
BOBBIE CHASE VP –Talent Development
MARK CHIARELLO Senior VP – Art, Design & Collected Editions
JOHN CUNNINGHAM VP – Content Strategy
ANNE DEPIES VP – Strategy Planning & Reporting
DON FALLETTI VP – Manufacturing Operations
LAWRENCE GANEM VP – Editorial Administration & Talent Relations
ALISON GILL Senior VP – Manufacturing & Operations
HANK KANALZ Senior VP – Editorial Strategy & Administration
JAY KOGAN VP – Legal Affairs
DEREK MADDALENA Senior VP – Sales & Business Development
JACK MAHAN VP – Business Affairs
DAN MIRON VP – Sales Planning & Trade Development
NICK NAPOLITANO VP – Manufacturing Administration
CAROL ROEDER VP – Marketing
EDDIE SCANNELL VP – Mass Account & Digital Sales
COURTNEY SIMMONS Senior VP – Publicity & Communications
JIM (SKI) SOKOLOWSKI VP – Comic Book Specialty & Newsstand Sales
SANDY YI Senior VP – Global Franchise Management

HARLEY QUINN VOLUME 3: KISS KISS BANG STAB

DC Comics, 4000 Warner Blvd., Burbank, CA 91522
A Warner Bros. Entertainment Company.
Printed by RR Donnelley, Salem, VA, USA. 11/6/15. First Printing.
ISBN: 978-1-4012-5764-4

Library of Congress Cataloging-in-Publication Data

Conner, Amanda, author.
Harley Quinn. Volume 3, Kiss kiss bang stab / Amanda Conner, Jimmy Palmiotti ; illustrated by Chad Hardin.
pages cm
ISBN 978-1-4012-5764-4 (hardback)
1. Graphic novels. I. Palmiotti, Jimmy, author. II. Hardin, Chad, illustrator. III. Title. IV. Title: Kiss kiss bang stab.
PN6728.H367C68 2015
741.5'973—dc23
2015031185

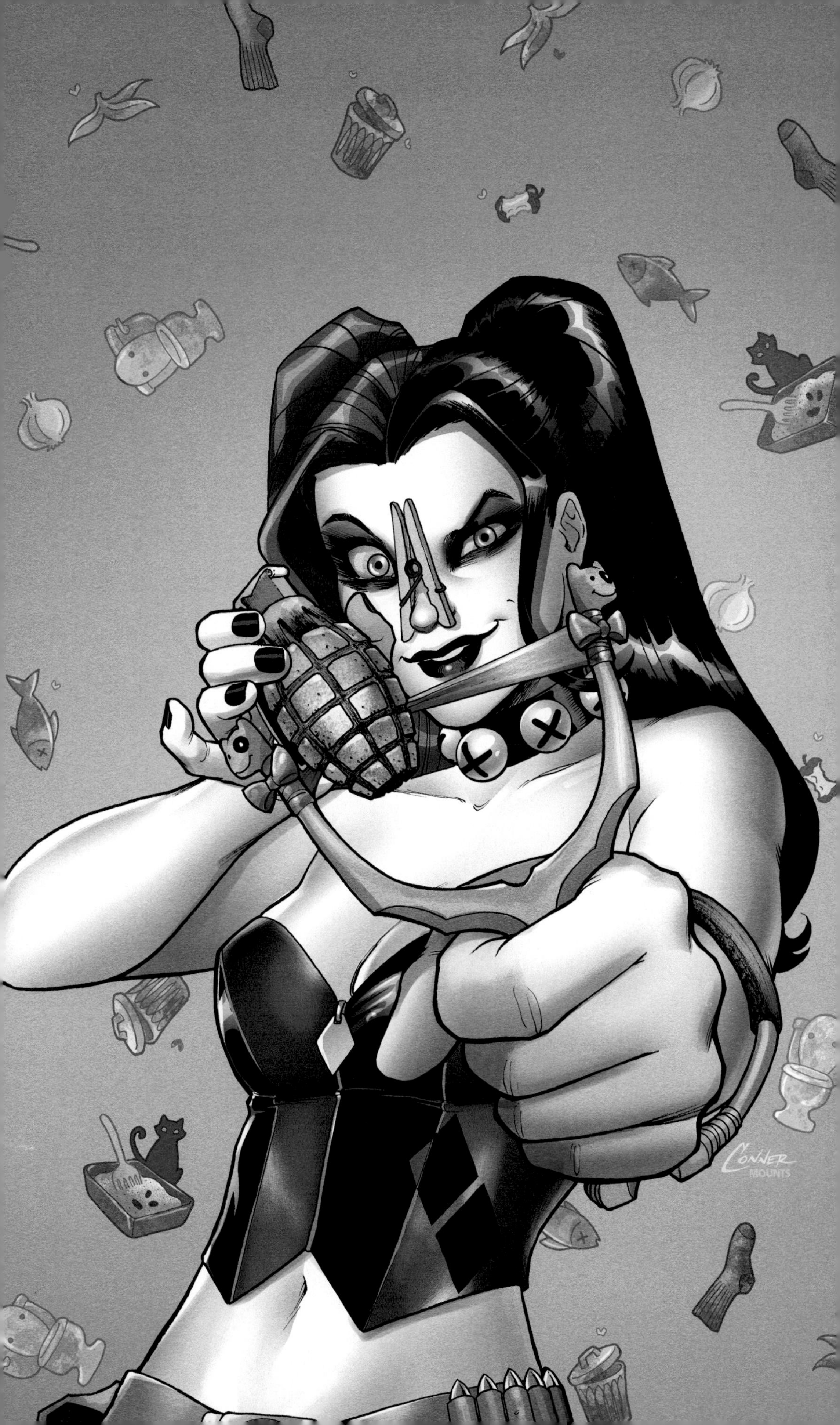
CONNER
MOUNTS

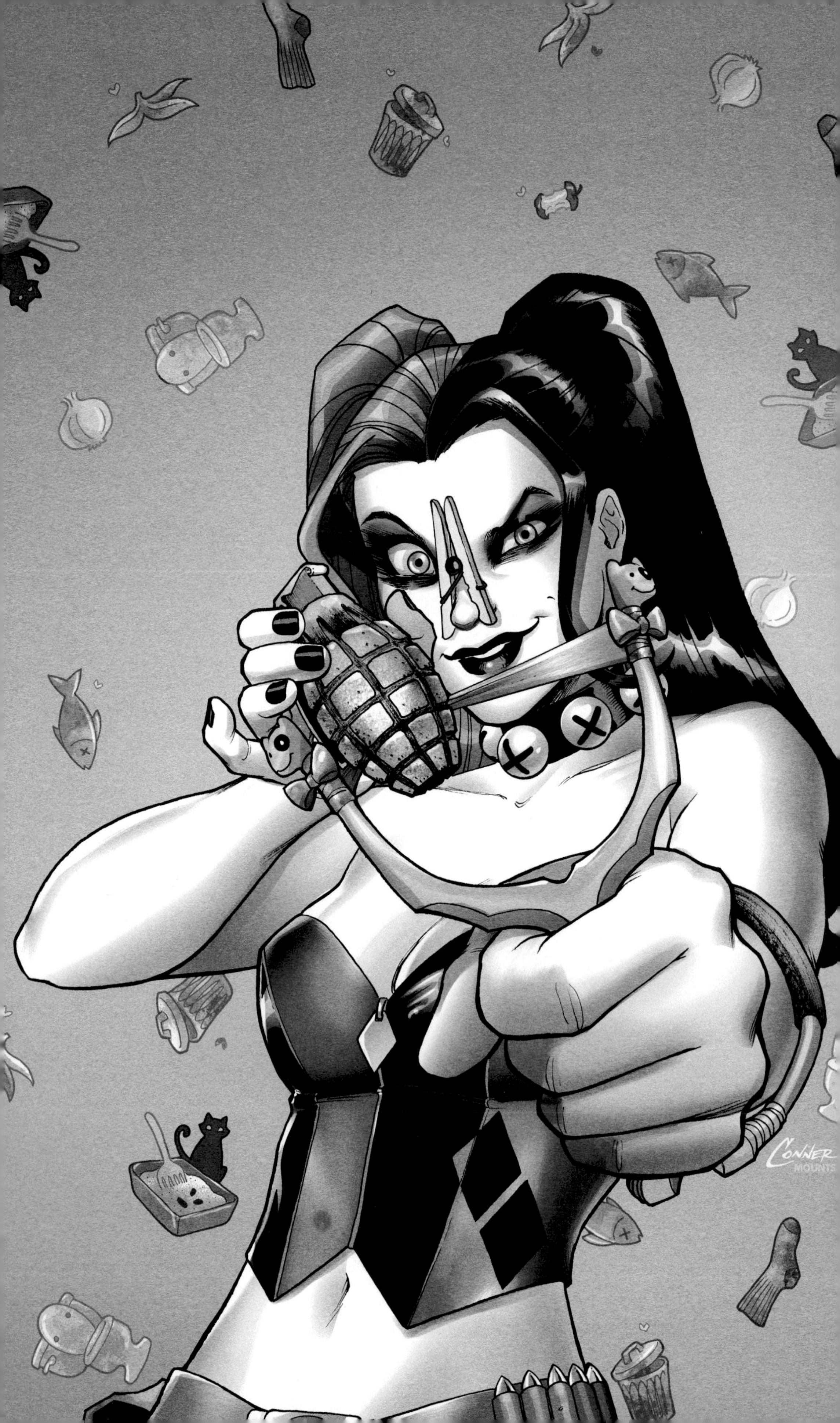
CONNER
MOUNTS

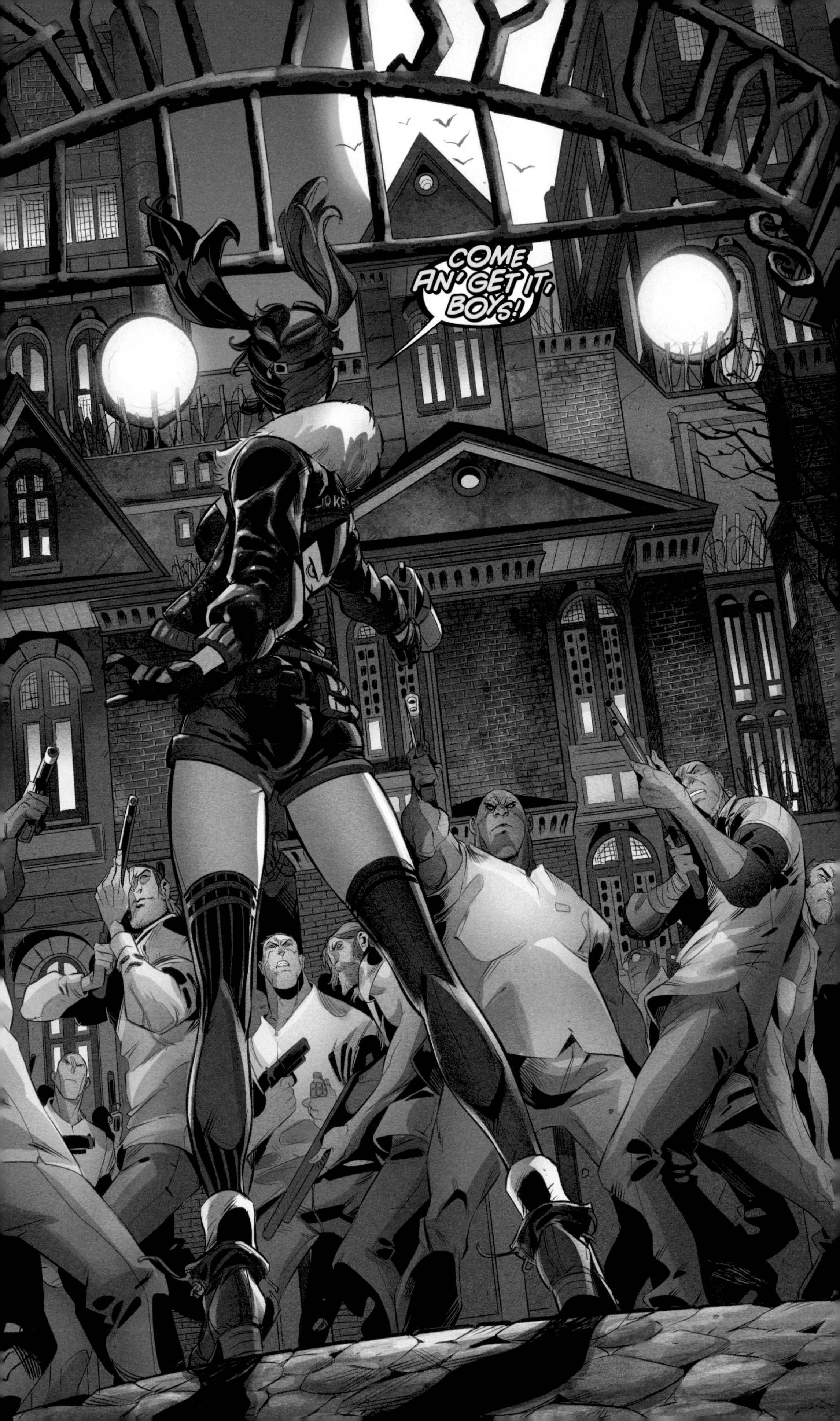
COME AN' GET IT, BOYS!

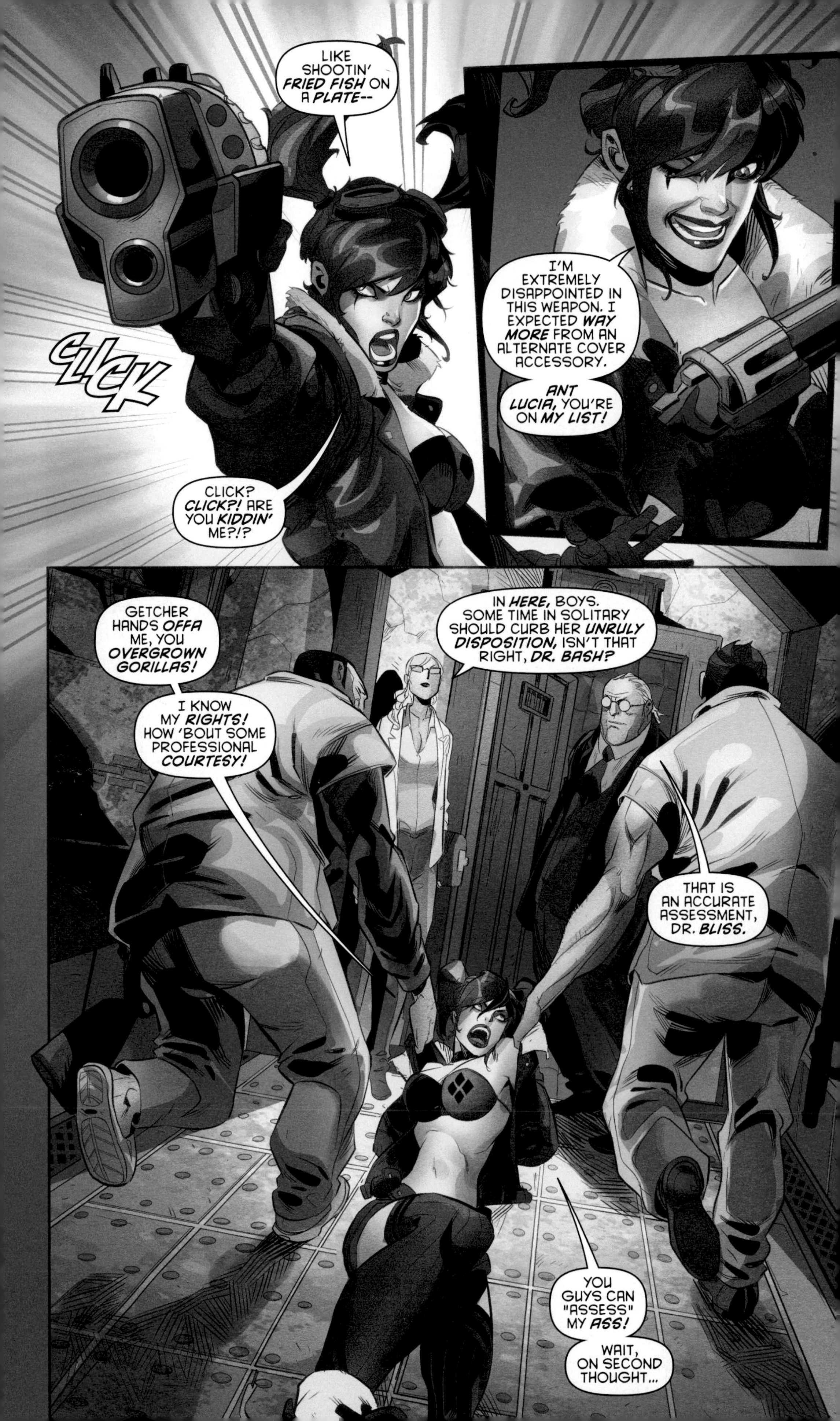
LIKE SHOOTIN' FRIED FISH ON A PLATE--
CLICK
CLICK? CLICK?! ARE YOU KIDDIN' ME?!?
I'M EXTREMELY DISAPPOINTED IN THIS WEAPON. I EXPECTED WAY MORE FROM AN ALTERNATE COVER ACCESSORY.
ANT LUCIA, YOU'RE ON MY LIST!
GETCHER HANDS OFFA ME, YOU OVERGROWN GORILLAS!
I KNOW MY RIGHTS! HOW 'BOUT SOME PROFESSIONAL COURTESY!
IN HERE, BOYS. SOME TIME IN SOLITARY SHOULD CURB HER UNRULY DISPOSITION, ISN'T THAT RIGHT, DR. BASH?
THAT IS AN ACCURATE ASSESSMENT, DR. BLISS.
YOU GUYS CAN "ASSESS" MY ASS!
WAIT, ON SECOND THOUGHT...

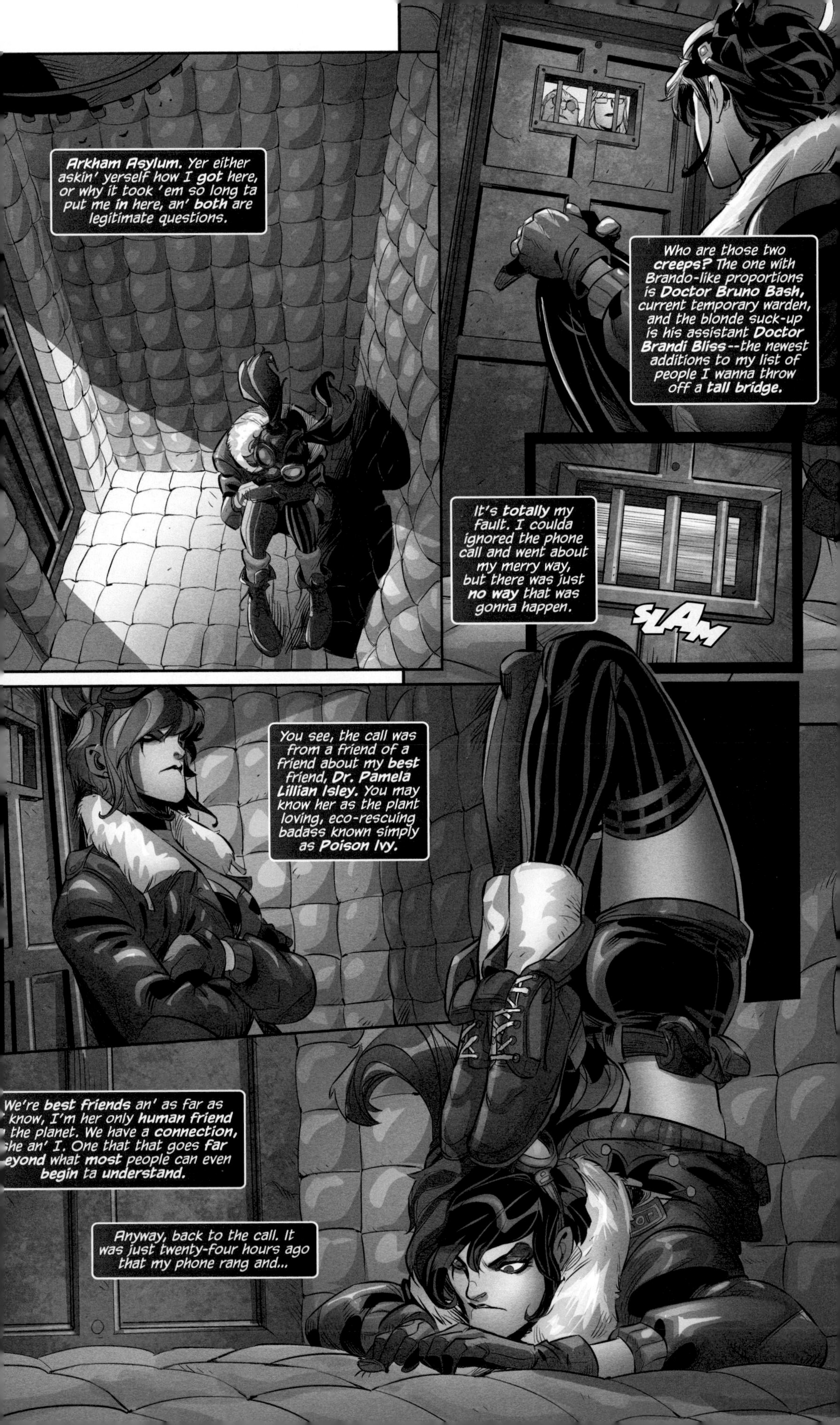

Arkham Asylum. Yer either askin' yerself how I got here, or why it took 'em so long ta put me in here, an' both are legitimate questions.
Who are those two creeps? The one with Brando-like proportions is Doctor Bruno Bash, current temporary warden, and the blonde suck-up is his assistant Doctor Brandi Bliss--the newest additions to my list of people I wanna throw off a tall bridge.
It's totally my fault. I coulda ignored the phone call and went about my merry way, but there was just no way that was gonna happen.
SLAM
You see, the call was from a friend of a friend about my best friend, Dr. Pamela Lillian Isley. You may know her as the plant loving, eco-rescuing badass known simply as Poison Ivy.
We're best friends an' as far as know, I'm her only human friend the planet. We have a connection, he an' I. One that that goes far eyond what most people can even begin ta understand.
Anyway, back to the call. It was just twenty-four hours ago that my phone rang and...

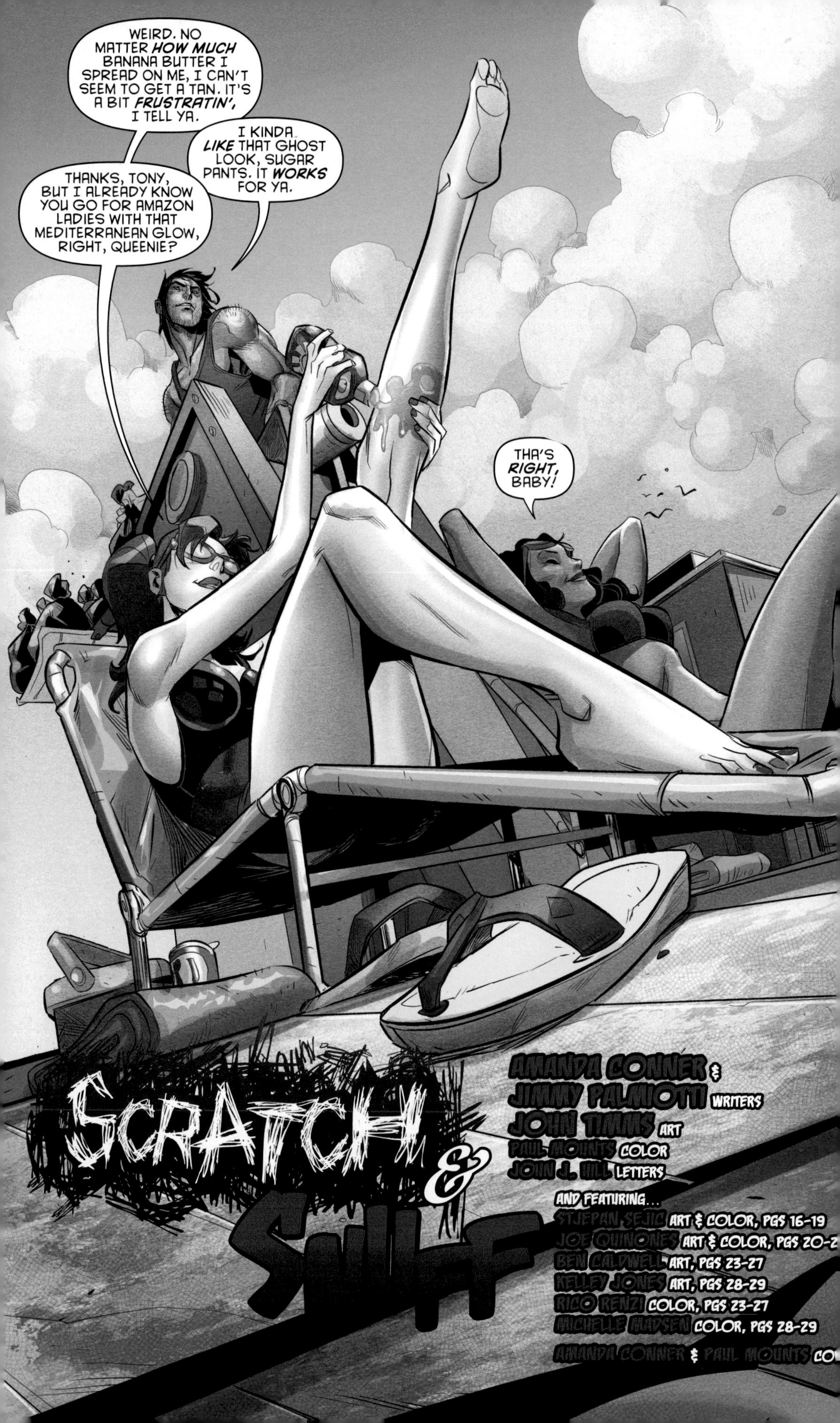
WEIRD. NO MATTER *HOW MUCH* BANANA BUTTER I SPREAD ON ME, I CAN'T SEEM TO GET A TAN. IT'S A BIT *FRUSTRATIN'*, I TELL YA.
I KINDA *LIKE* THAT GHOST LOOK, SUGAR PANTS. IT *WORKS* FOR YA.
THANKS, TONY, BUT I ALREADY KNOW YOU GO FOR AMAZON LADIES WITH THAT MEDITERRANEAN GLOW, RIGHT, QUEENIE?
THA'S *RIGHT*, BABY!
SCRATCH & SNIFF
AMANDA CONNER & JIMMY PALMIOTTI WRITERS
JOHN TIMMS ART
PAUL MOUNTS COLOR
JOHN J. HILL LETTERS
AND FEATURING...
STJEPAN SEJIC ART & COLOR, PGS 16-19
JOE QUINONES ART & COLOR, PGS 20-2
BEN CALDWELL ART, PGS 23-27
KELLEY JONES ART, PGS 28-29
RICO RENZI COLOR, PGS 23-27
MICHELLE MADSEN COLOR, PGS 28-29
AMANDA CONNER & PAUL MOUNTS CO

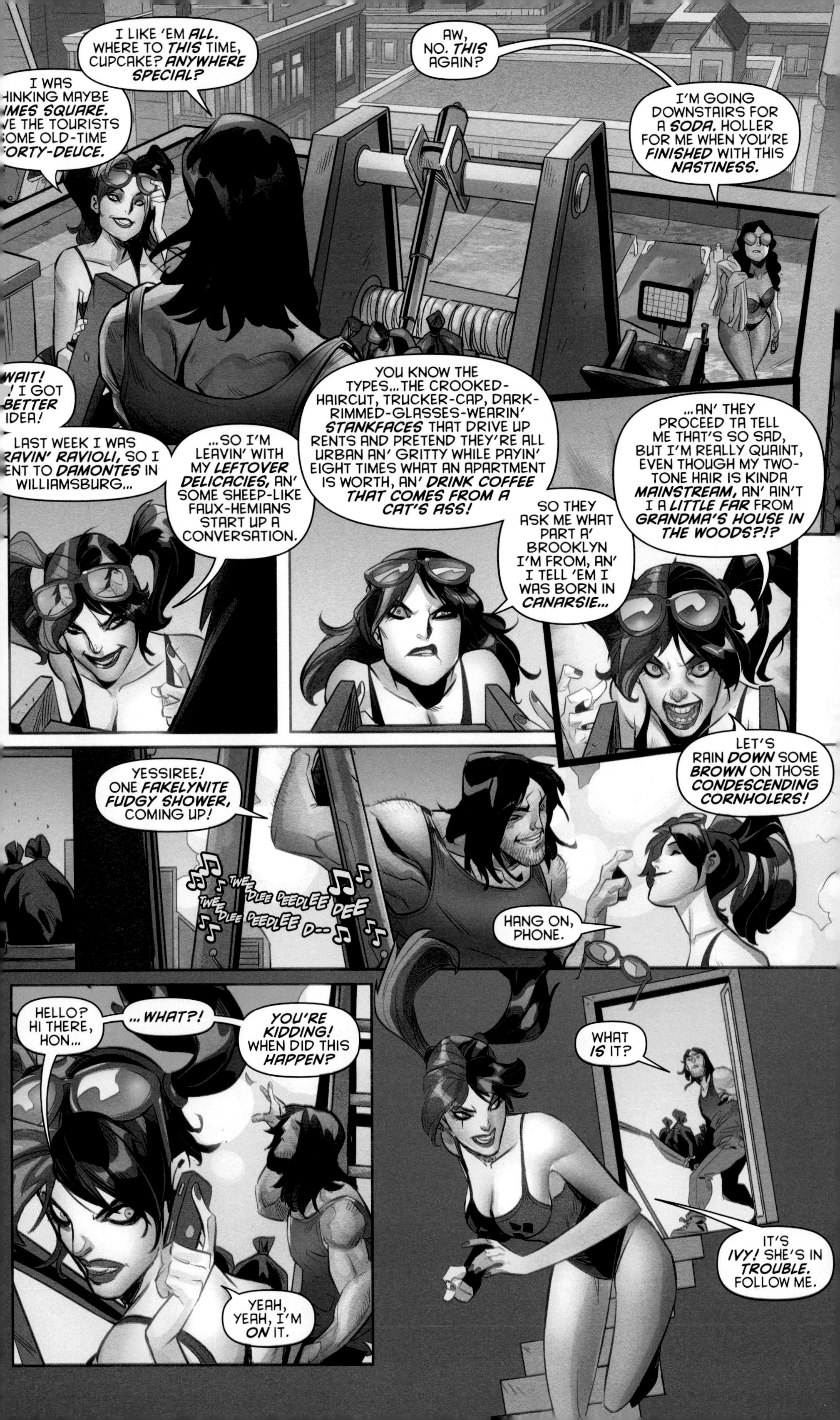
I WAS HINKING MAYBE IMES SQUARE. VE THE TOURISTS OME OLD-TIME ORTY-DEUCE.
I LIKE 'EM ALL. WHERE TO THIS TIME, CUPCAKE? ANYWHERE SPECIAL?
AW, NO. THIS AGAIN?
I'M GOING DOWNSTAIRS FOR A SODA. HOLLER FOR ME WHEN YOU'RE FINISHED WITH THIS NASTINESS.
AIT! I GOT BETTER IDEA!
LAST WEEK I WAS AVIN' RAVIOLI, SO I ENT TO DAMONTES IN WILLIAMSBURG...
...SO I'M LEAVIN' WITH MY LEFTOVER DELICACIES, AN' SOME SHEEP-LIKE FAUX-HEMIANS START UP A CONVERSATION.
YOU KNOW THE TYPES... THE CROOKED-HAIRCUT, TRUCKER-CAP, DARK-RIMMED-GLASSES-WEARIN' STANKFACES THAT DRIVE UP RENTS AND PRETEND THEY'RE ALL URBAN AN' GRITTY WHILE PAYIN' EIGHT TIMES WHAT AN APARTMENT IS WORTH, AN' DRINK COFFEE THAT COMES FROM A CAT'S ASS!
SO THEY ASK ME WHAT PART A' BROOKLYN I'M FROM, AN' I TELL 'EM I WAS BORN IN CANARSIE...
...AN' THEY PROCEED TA TELL ME THAT'S SO SAD, BUT I'M REALLY QUAINT, EVEN THOUGH MY TWO-TONE HAIR IS KINDA MAINSTREAM, AN' AIN'T I A LITTLE FAR FROM GRANDMA'S HOUSE IN THE WOODS?!?
LET'S RAIN DOWN SOME BROWN ON THOSE CONDESCENDING CORNHOLERS!
YESSIREE! ONE FAKELYNITE FUDGY SHOWER, COMING UP!
TWEEDLEE DEEDLEE DEE
TWEEDLEE DEEDLEE D--
HANG ON, PHONE.
HELLO? HI THERE, HON...
...WHAT?!
YOU'RE KIDDING! WHEN DID THIS HAPPEN?
YEAH, YEAH, I'M ON IT.
WHAT IS IT?
IT'S IVY! SHE'S IN TROUBLE. FOLLOW ME.

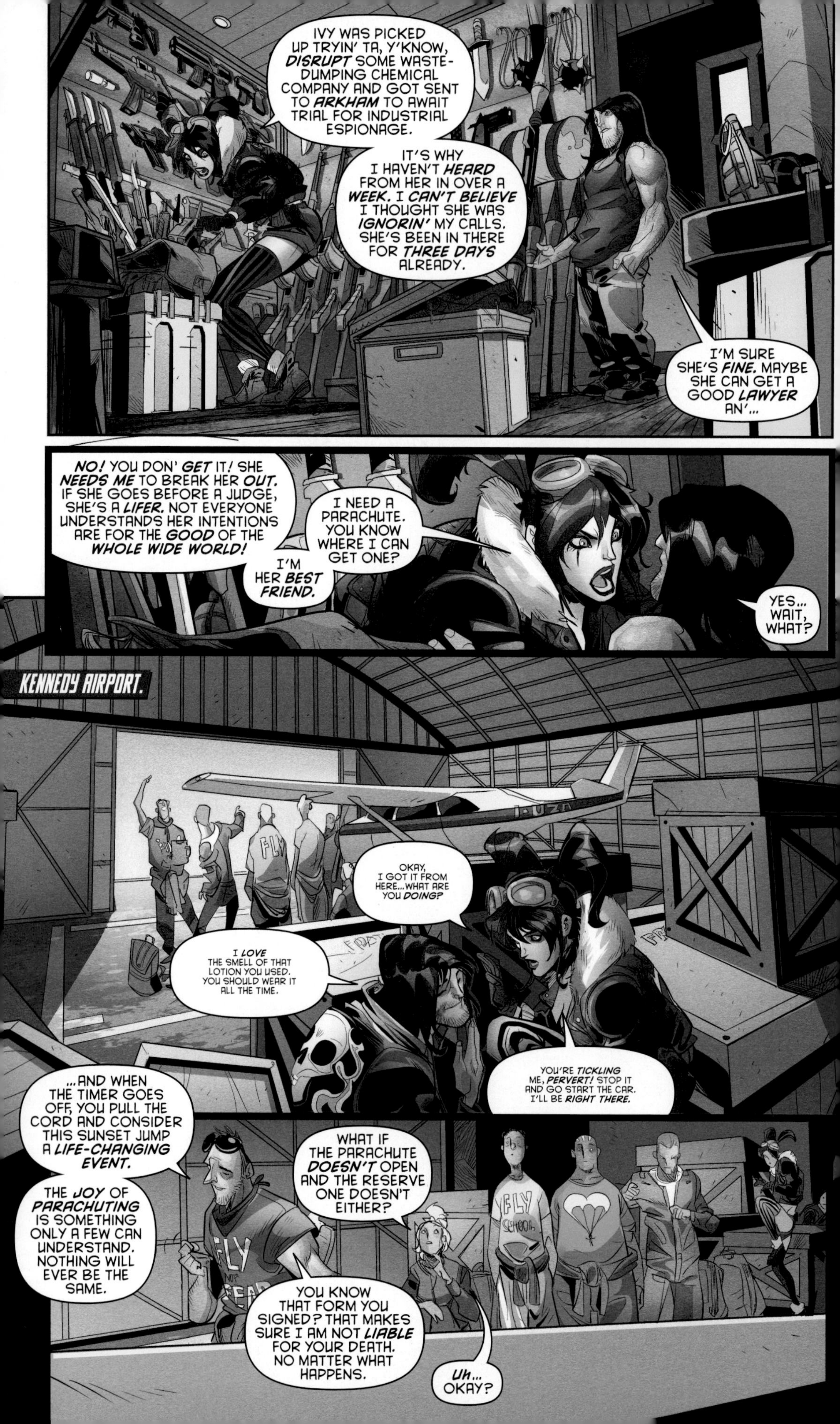
IVY WAS PICKED UP TRYIN' TA, Y'KNOW, DISRUPT SOME WASTE-DUMPING CHEMICAL COMPANY AND GOT SENT TO ARKHAM TO AWAIT TRIAL FOR INDUSTRIAL ESPIONAGE.
IT'S WHY I HAVEN'T HEARD FROM HER IN OVER A WEEK. I CAN'T BELIEVE I THOUGHT SHE WAS IGNORIN' MY CALLS. SHE'S BEEN IN THERE FOR THREE DAYS ALREADY.
I'M SURE SHE'S FINE. MAYBE SHE CAN GET A GOOD LAWYER AN'...
NO! YOU DON' GET IT! SHE NEEDS ME TO BREAK HER OUT. IF SHE GOES BEFORE A JUDGE, SHE'S A LIFER. NOT EVERYONE UNDERSTANDS HER INTENTIONS ARE FOR THE GOOD OF THE WHOLE WIDE WORLD!
I'M HER BEST FRIEND.
I NEED A PARACHUTE. YOU KNOW WHERE I CAN GET ONE?
YES... WAIT, WHAT?
KENNEDY AIRPORT.
OKAY, I GOT IT FROM HERE...WHAT ARE YOU DOING?
I LOVE THE SMELL OF THAT LOTION YOU USED. YOU SHOULD WEAR IT ALL THE TIME.
YOU'RE TICKLING ME, PERVERT! STOP IT AND GO START THE CAR. I'LL BE RIGHT THERE.
...AND WHEN THE TIMER GOES OFF, YOU PULL THE CORD AND CONSIDER THIS SUNSET JUMP A LIFE-CHANGING EVENT.
THE JOY OF PARACHUTING IS SOMETHING ONLY A FEW CAN UNDERSTAND. NOTHING WILL EVER BE THE SAME.
WHAT IF THE PARACHUTE DOESN'T OPEN AND THE RESERVE ONE DOESN'T EITHER?
YOU KNOW THAT FORM YOU SIGNED? THAT MAKES SURE I AM NOT LIABLE FOR YOUR DEATH. NO MATTER WHAT HAPPENS.
Uh... OKAY?

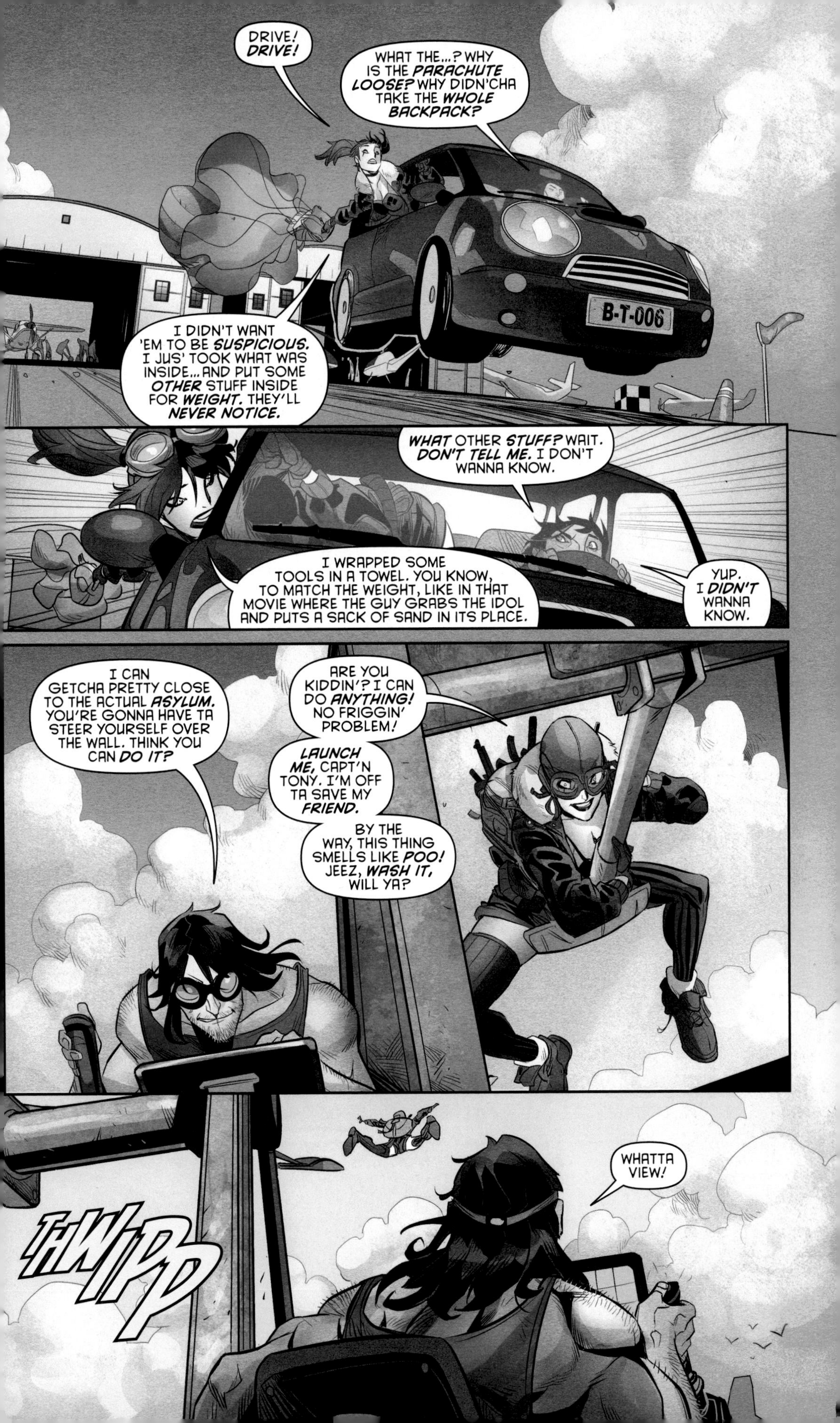
DRIVE! DRIVE!
WHAT THE...? WHY IS THE PARACHUTE LOOSE? WHY DIDN'CHA TAKE THE WHOLE BACKPACK?
B-T-006
I DIDN'T WANT 'EM TO BE SUSPICIOUS. I JUS' TOOK WHAT WAS INSIDE... AND PUT SOME OTHER STUFF INSIDE FOR WEIGHT. THEY'LL NEVER NOTICE.
WHAT OTHER STUFF? WAIT. DON'T TELL ME. I DON'T WANNA KNOW.
I WRAPPED SOME TOOLS IN A TOWEL. YOU KNOW, TO MATCH THE WEIGHT, LIKE IN THAT MOVIE WHERE THE GUY GRABS THE IDOL AND PUTS A SACK OF SAND IN ITS PLACE.
YUP. I DIDN'T WANNA KNOW.
I CAN GETCHA PRETTY CLOSE TO THE ACTUAL ASYLUM. YOU'RE GONNA HAVE TA STEER YOURSELF OVER THE WALL. THINK YOU CAN DO IT?
ARE YOU KIDDIN'? I CAN DO ANYTHING! NO FRIGGIN' PROBLEM!
LAUNCH ME, CAPT'N TONY. I'M OFF TA SAVE MY FRIEND.
BY THE WAY, THIS THING SMELLS LIKE POO! JEEZ, WASH IT, WILL YA?
THWIPP
WHATTA VIEW!

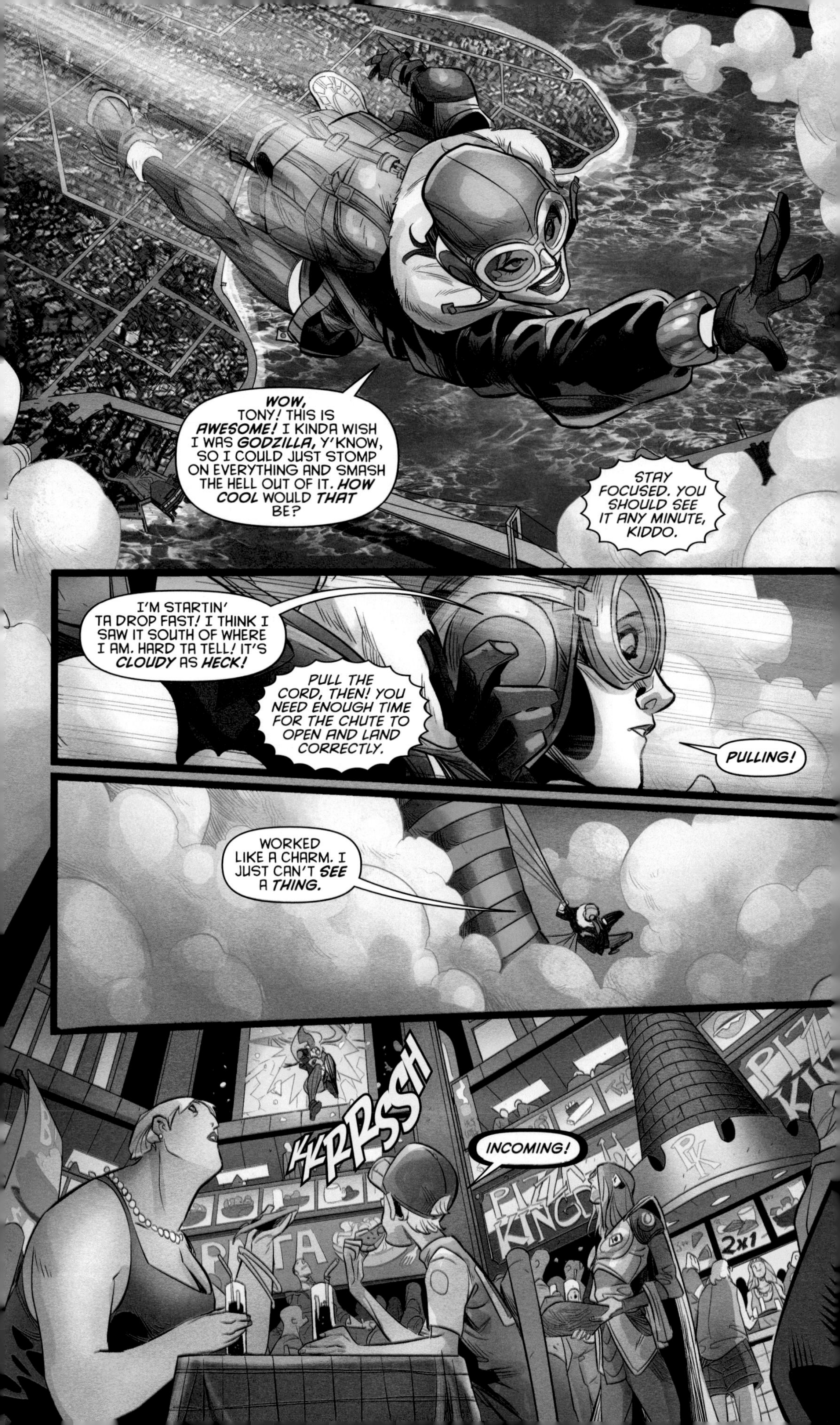
WOW, TONY! THIS IS AWESOME! I KINDA WISH I WAS GODZILLA, Y'KNOW, SO I COULD JUST STOMP ON EVERYTHING AND SMASH THE HELL OUT OF IT. HOW COOL WOULD THAT BE?
STAY FOCUSED. YOU SHOULD SEE IT ANY MINUTE, KIDDO.
I'M STARTIN' TA DROP FAST! I THINK I SAW IT SOUTH OF WHERE I AM. HARD TA TELL! IT'S CLOUDY AS HECK!
PULL THE CORD, THEN! YOU NEED ENOUGH TIME FOR THE CHUTE TO OPEN AND LAND CORRECTLY.
PULLING!
WORKED LIKE A CHARM. I JUST CAN'T SEE A THING.
KLRRSSH
INCOMING!
PIZZA KINGDOM
PK
2x1

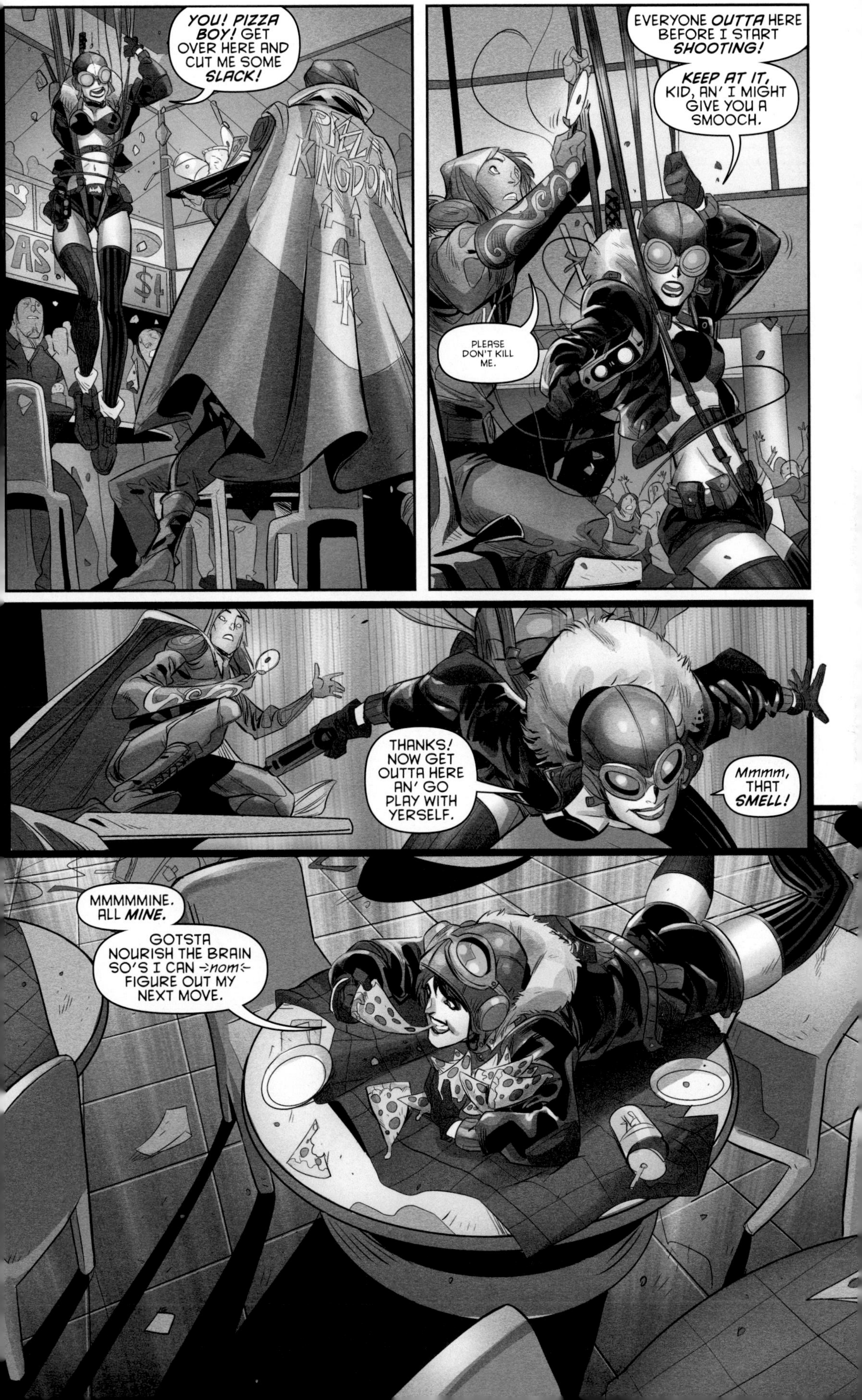
YOU! PIZZA BOY! GET OVER HERE AND CUT ME SOME SLACK!
PIZZA KINGDOM
$1
EVERYONE OUTTA HERE BEFORE I START SHOOTING!
KEEP AT IT, KID, AN' I MIGHT GIVE YOU A SMOOCH.
PLEASE DON'T KILL ME.
THANKS! NOW GET OUTTA HERE AN' GO PLAY WITH YERSELF.
Mmmm, THAT SMELL!
MMMMMINE. ALL MINE.
GOTSTA NOURISH THE BRAIN SO'S I CAN ~nom~ FIGURE OUT MY NEXT MOVE.

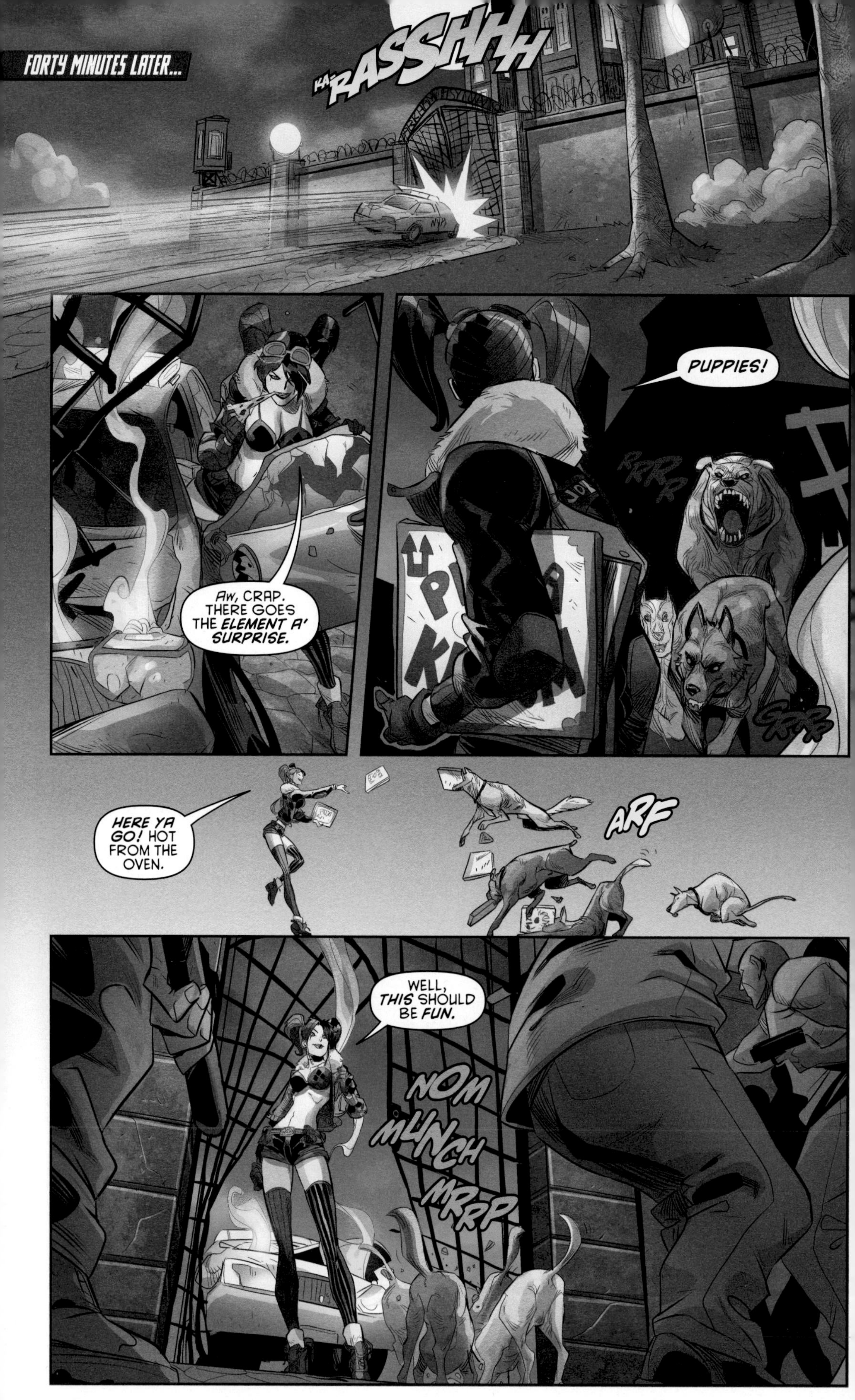

FORTY MINUTES LATER...
KA-RASSHHH
AW, CRAP. THERE GOES THE ELEMENT A' SURPRISE.
PUPPIES!
RRRR
GRRR
HERE YA GO! HOT FROM THE OVEN.
ARF
WELL, THIS SHOULD BE FUN.
NOM
MUNCH
MRRP

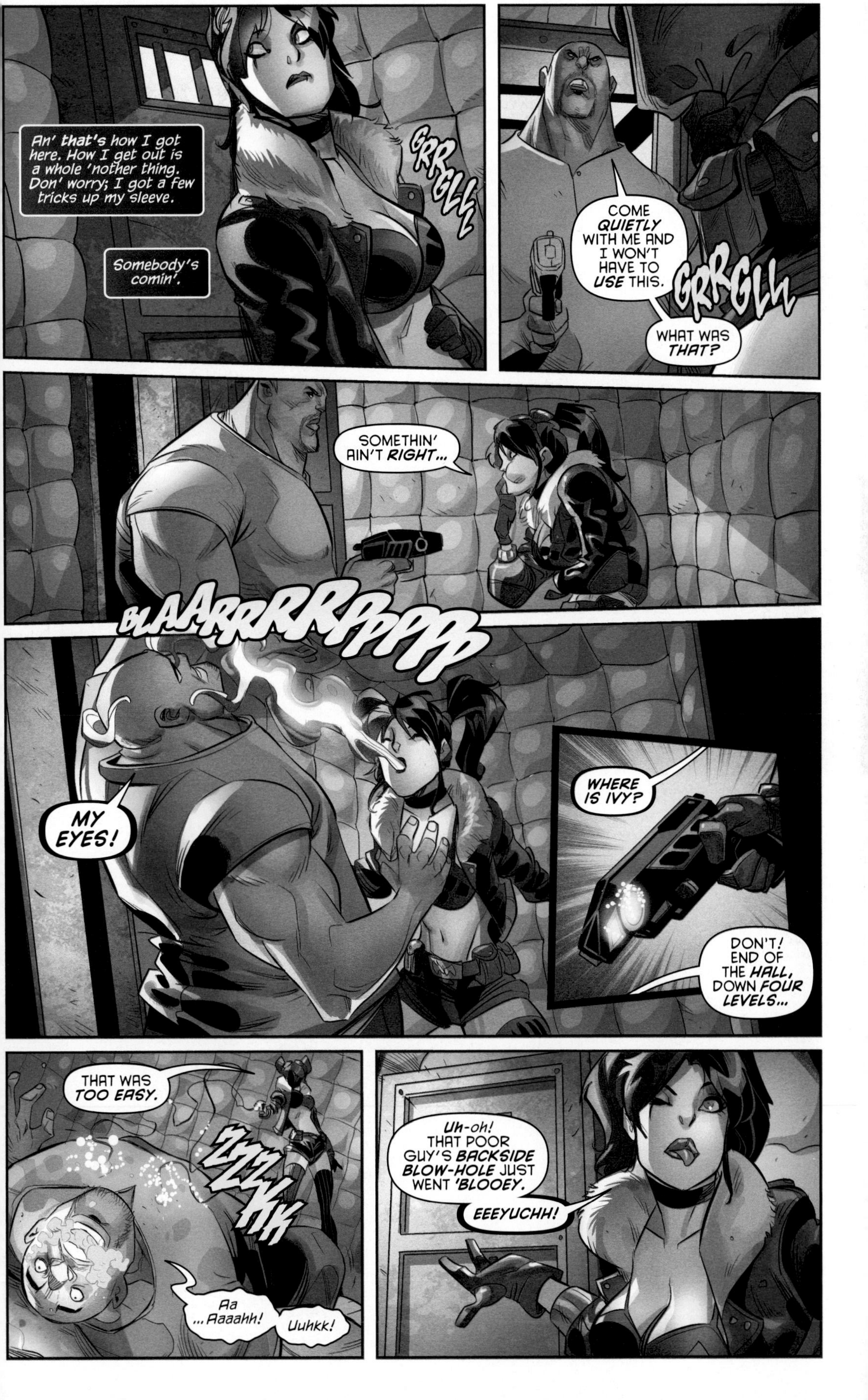

An' that's how I got here. How I get out is a whole 'nother thing. Don' worry; I got a few tricks up my sleeve.
Somebody's comin'.
GRRGLL
COME QUIETLY WITH ME AND I WON'T HAVE TO USE THIS.
GRRGLL
WHAT WAS THAT?
SOMETHIN' AIN'T RIGHT...
BLAARRRRPPPP
MY EYES!
WHERE IS IVY?
DON'T! END OF THE HALL, DOWN FOUR LEVELS...
THAT WAS TOO EASY.
ZZZKK
Aa ...Aaaahh!
Uuhkk!
Uh-oh! THAT POOR GUY'S BACKSIDE BLOW-HOLE JUST WENT 'BLOOEY.
EEEYUCHH!

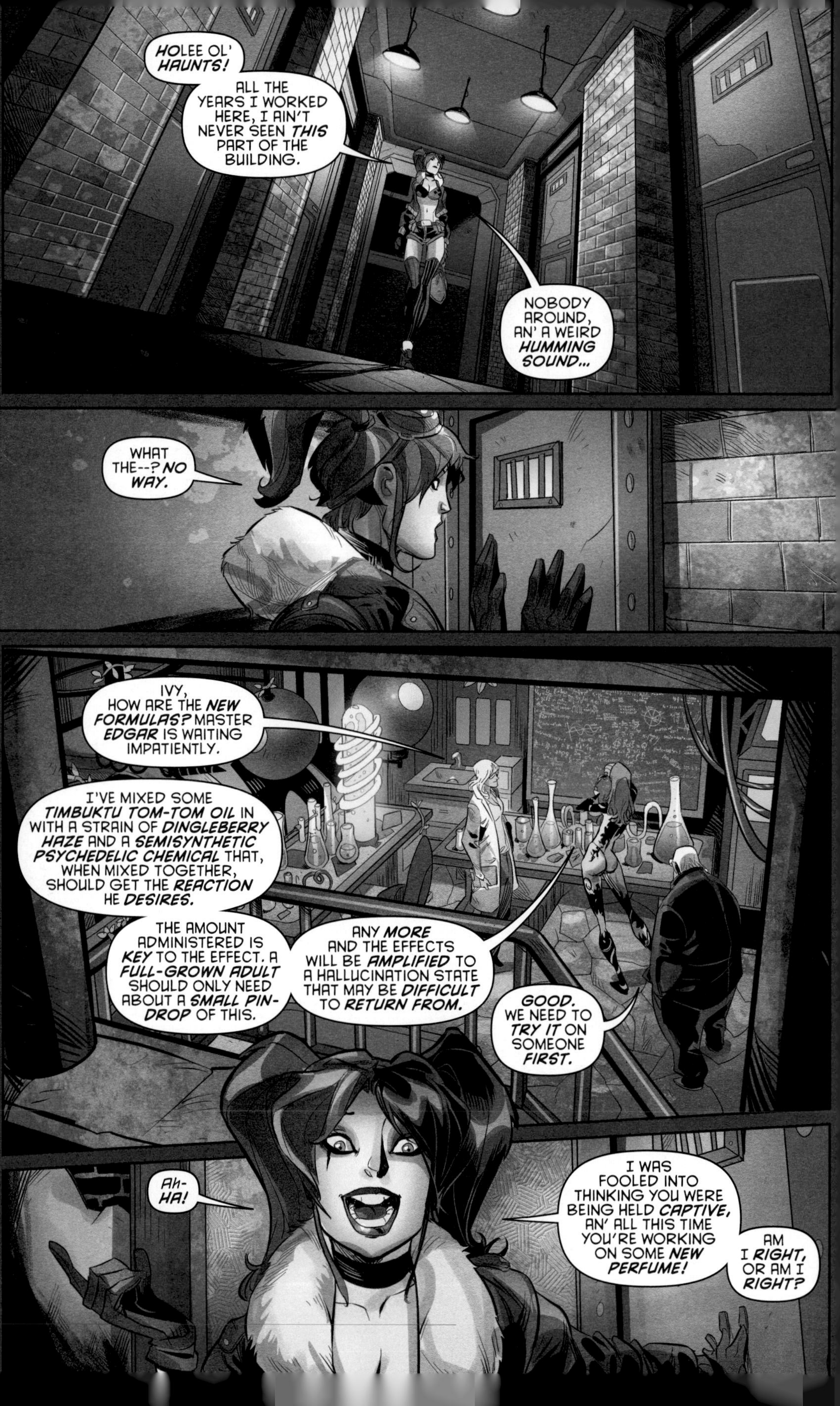
HOLEE OL' HAUNTS!
ALL THE YEARS I WORKED HERE, I AIN'T NEVER SEEN THIS PART OF THE BUILDING.
NOBODY AROUND, AN' A WEIRD HUMMING SOUND...
WHAT THE--? NO WAY.
IVY, HOW ARE THE NEW FORMULAS? MASTER EDGAR IS WAITING IMPATIENTLY.
I'VE MIXED SOME TIMBUKTU TOM-TOM OIL IN WITH A STRAIN OF DINGLEBERRY HAZE AND A SEMISYNTHETIC PSYCHEDELIC CHEMICAL THAT, WHEN MIXED TOGETHER, SHOULD GET THE REACTION HE DESIRES.
THE AMOUNT ADMINISTERED IS KEY TO THE EFFECT. A FULL-GROWN ADULT SHOULD ONLY NEED ABOUT A SMALL PIN-DROP OF THIS.
ANY MORE AND THE EFFECTS WILL BE AMPLIFIED TO A HALLUCINATION STATE THAT MAY BE DIFFICULT TO RETURN FROM.
GOOD. WE NEED TO TRY IT ON SOMEONE FIRST.
AH-HA!
I WAS FOOLED INTO THINKING YOU WERE BEING HELD CAPTIVE, AN' ALL THIS TIME YOU'RE WORKING ON SOME NEW PERFUME!
AM I RIGHT, OR AM I RIGHT?

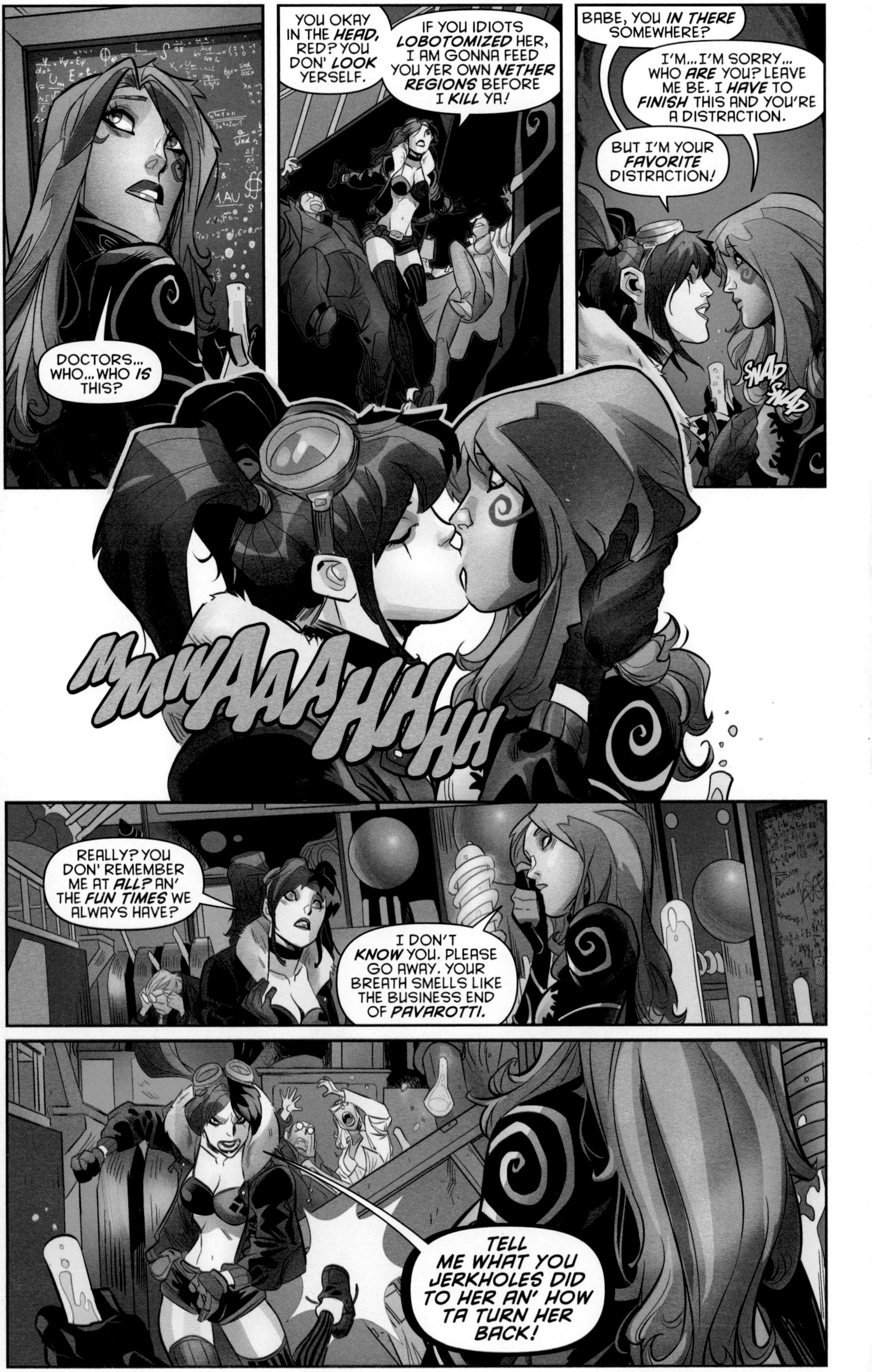
DOCTORS... WHO... WHO IS THIS?
YOU OKAY IN THE HEAD, RED? YOU DON' LOOK YERSELF.
IF YOU IDIOTS LOBOTOMIZED HER, I AM GONNA FEED YOU YER OWN NETHER REGIONS BEFORE I KILL YA!
BABE, YOU IN THERE SOMEWHERE?
I'M... I'M SORRY... WHO ARE YOU? LEAVE ME BE. I HAVE TO FINISH THIS AND YOU'RE A DISTRACTION.
BUT I'M YOUR FAVORITE DISTRACTION!
SNAP SNAP
MMWAAAAHHHH
REALLY? YOU DON' REMEMBER ME AT ALL? AN' THE FUN TIMES WE ALWAYS HAVE?
I DON'T KNOW YOU. PLEASE GO AWAY. YOUR BREATH SMELLS LIKE THE BUSINESS END OF PAVAROTTI.
TELL ME WHAT YOU JERKHOLES DID TO HER AN' HOW TA TURN HER BACK!

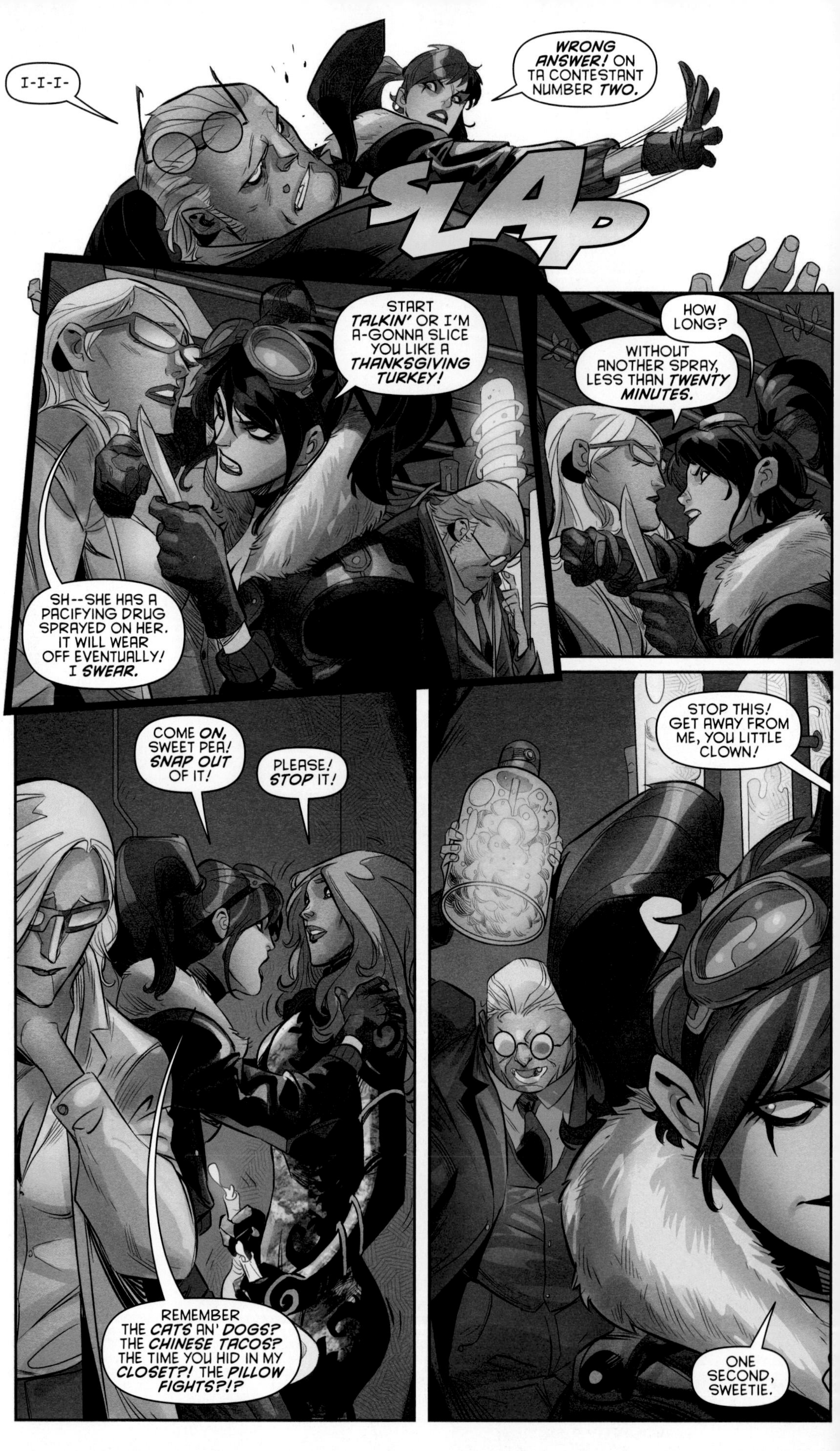
I-I-I-
WRONG ANSWER! ON TA CONTESTANT NUMBER TWO.
SLAP
START TALKIN' OR I'M A-GONNA SLICE YOU LIKE A THANKSGIVING TURKEY!
SH--SHE HAS A PACIFYING DRUG SPRAYED ON HER. IT WILL WEAR OFF EVENTUALLY! I SWEAR.
HOW LONG?
WITHOUT ANOTHER SPRAY, LESS THAN TWENTY MINUTES.
COME ON, SWEET PEA! SNAP OUT OF IT!
PLEASE! STOP IT!
REMEMBER THE CATS AN' DOGS? THE CHINESE TACOS? THE TIME YOU HID IN MY CLOSET?! THE PILLOW FIGHTS?!?
STOP THIS! GET AWAY FROM ME, YOU LITTLE CLOWN!
ONE SECOND, SWEETIE.

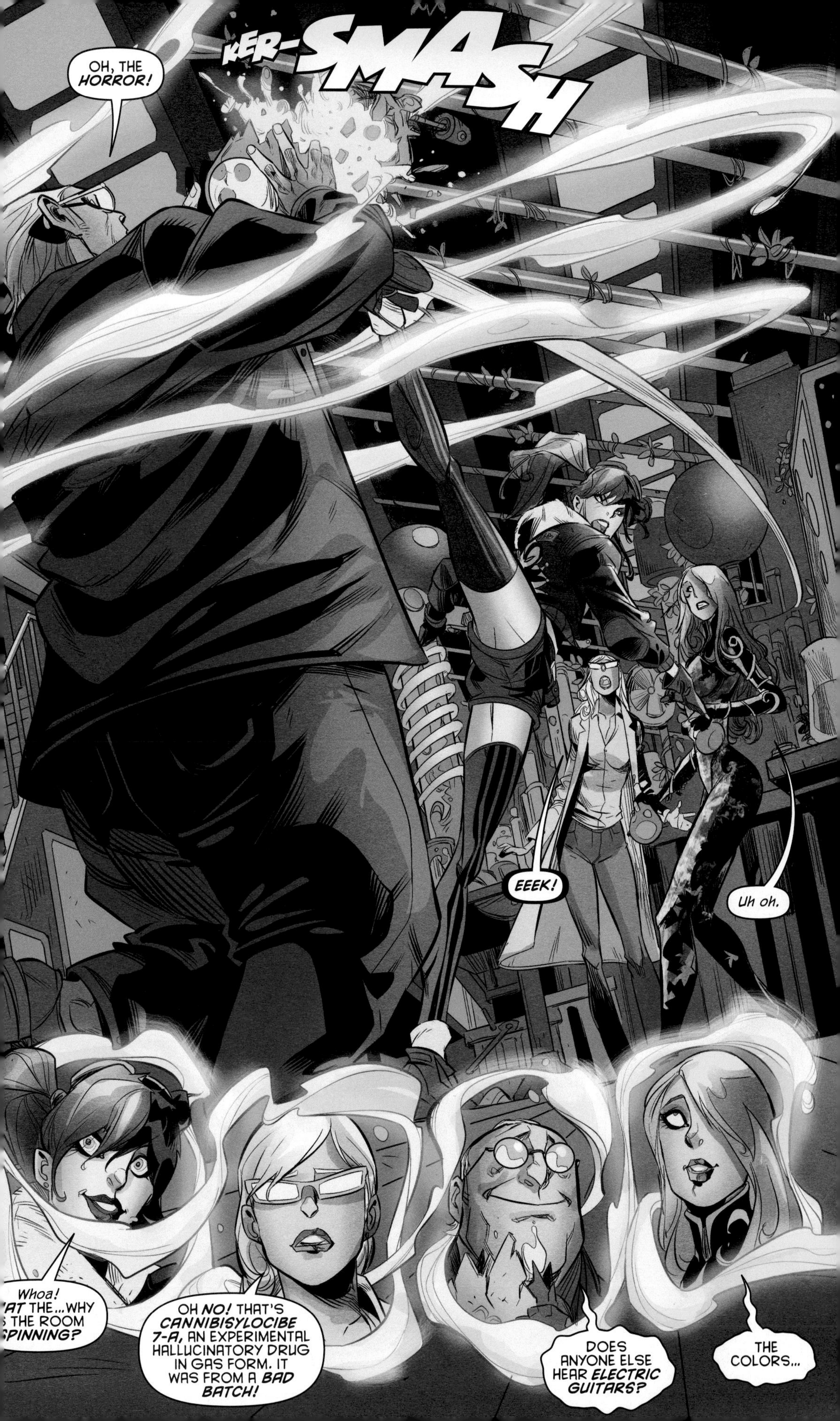
KER-SMASH
OH, THE HORROR!
EEEK!
Uh oh.
Whoa! AT THE... WHY S THE ROOM SPINNING?
OH NO! THAT'S CANNIBISYLOCIBE 7-A, AN EXPERIMENTAL HALLUCINATORY DRUG IN GAS FORM. IT WAS FROM A BAD BATCH!
DOES ANYONE ELSE HEAR ELECTRIC GUITARS?
THE COLORS...

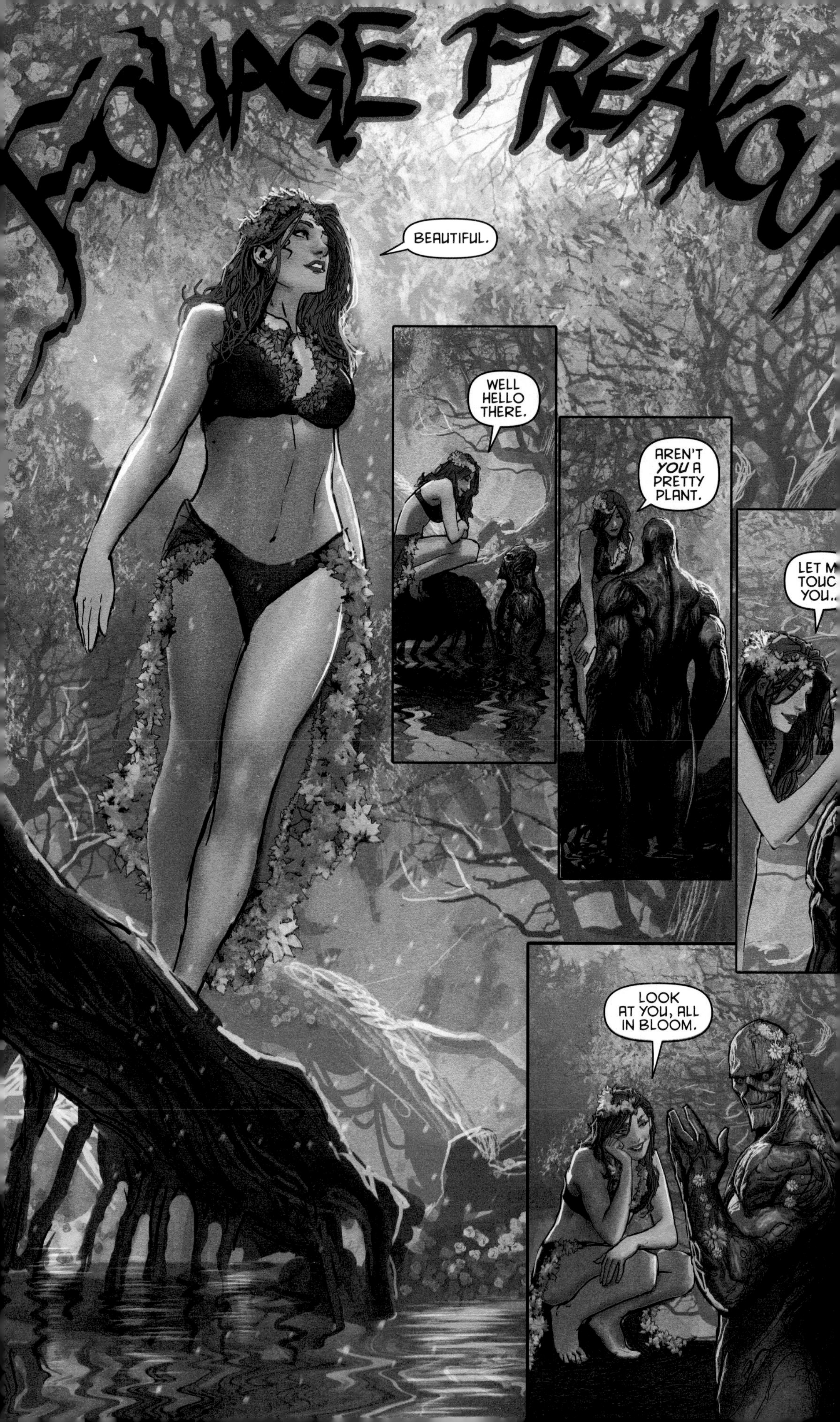
FOLIAGE FREAKOUT
BEAUTIFUL.
WELL HELLO THERE.
AREN'T *YOU* A PRETTY PLANT.
YOU...
LOOK AT YOU, ALL IN BLOOM.

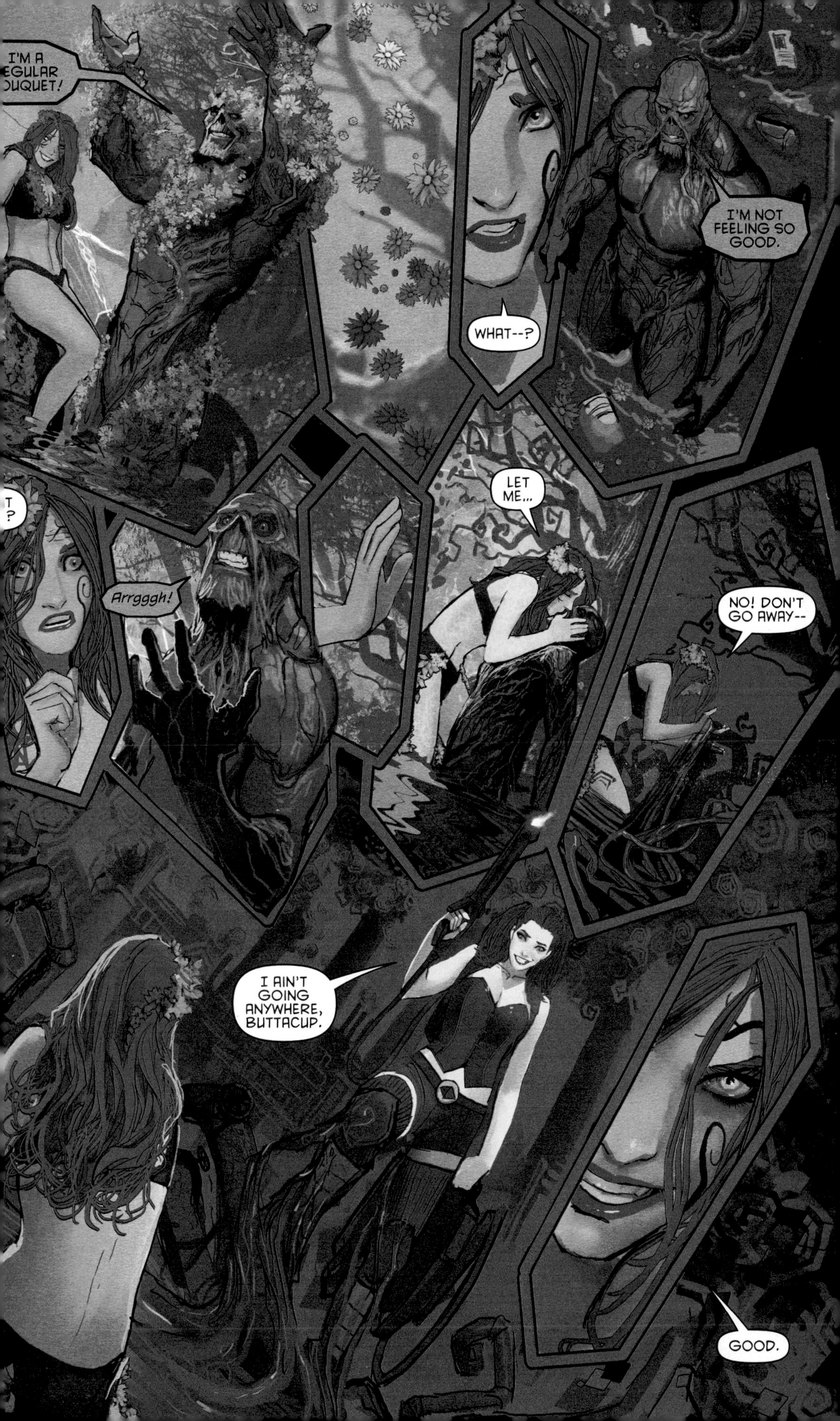

I'M A EGULAR OUQUET!
WHAT--?
I'M NOT FEELING SO GOOD.
Arrgggh!
LET ME...
NO! DON'T GO AWAY--
I AIN'T GOING ANYWHERE, BUTTACUP.
GOOD.

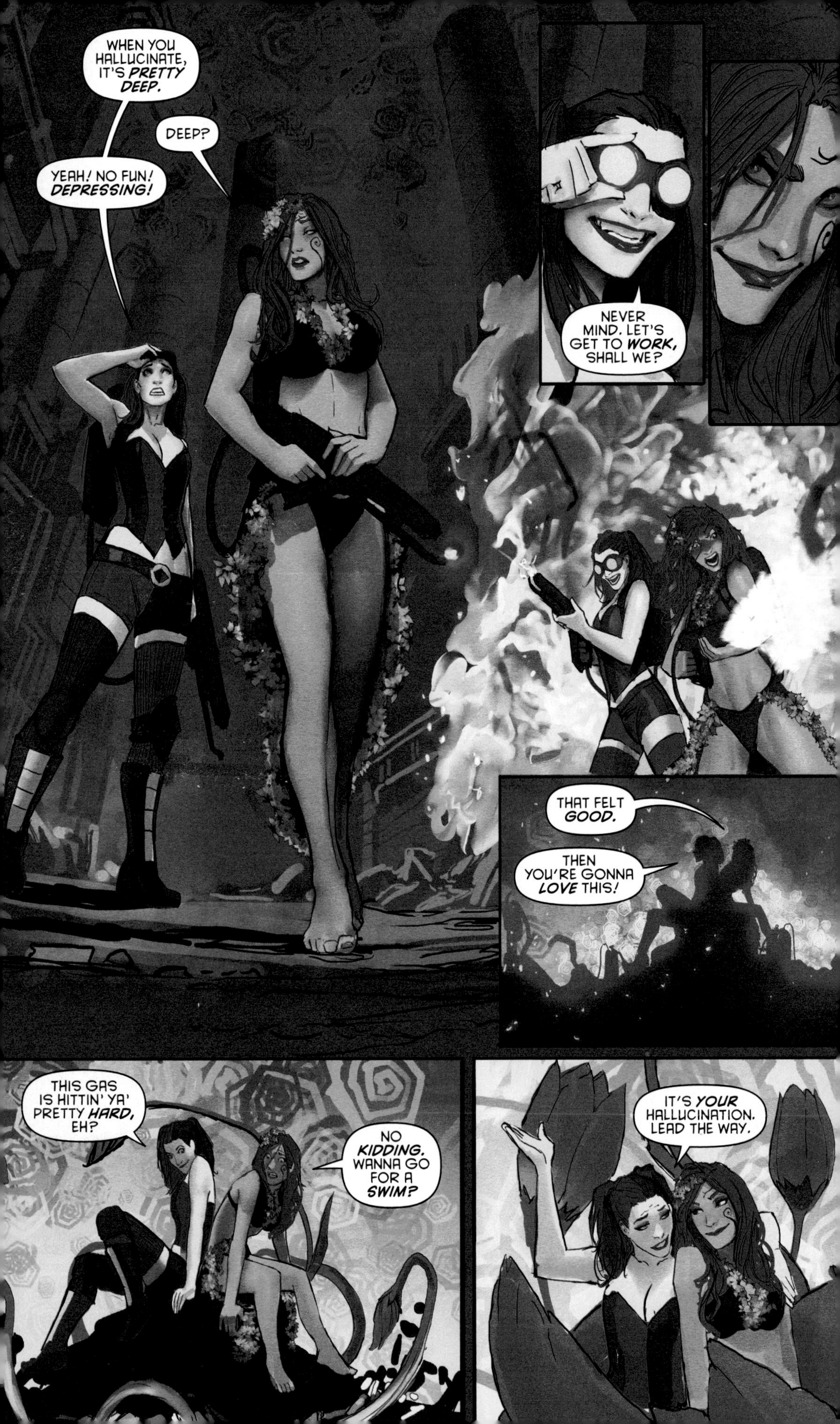
WHEN YOU HALLUCINATE, IT'S *PRETTY DEEP.*
DEEP?
YEAH! NO FUN! *DEPRESSING!*
NEVER MIND. LET'S GET TO *WORK,* SHALL WE?
THAT FELT *GOOD.*
THEN YOU'RE GONNA *LOVE* THIS!
THIS GAS IS HITTIN' YA' PRETTY *HARD,* EH?
NO *KIDDING.* WANNA GO FOR A *SWIM?*
IT'S *YOUR* HALLUCINATION. LEAD THE WAY.

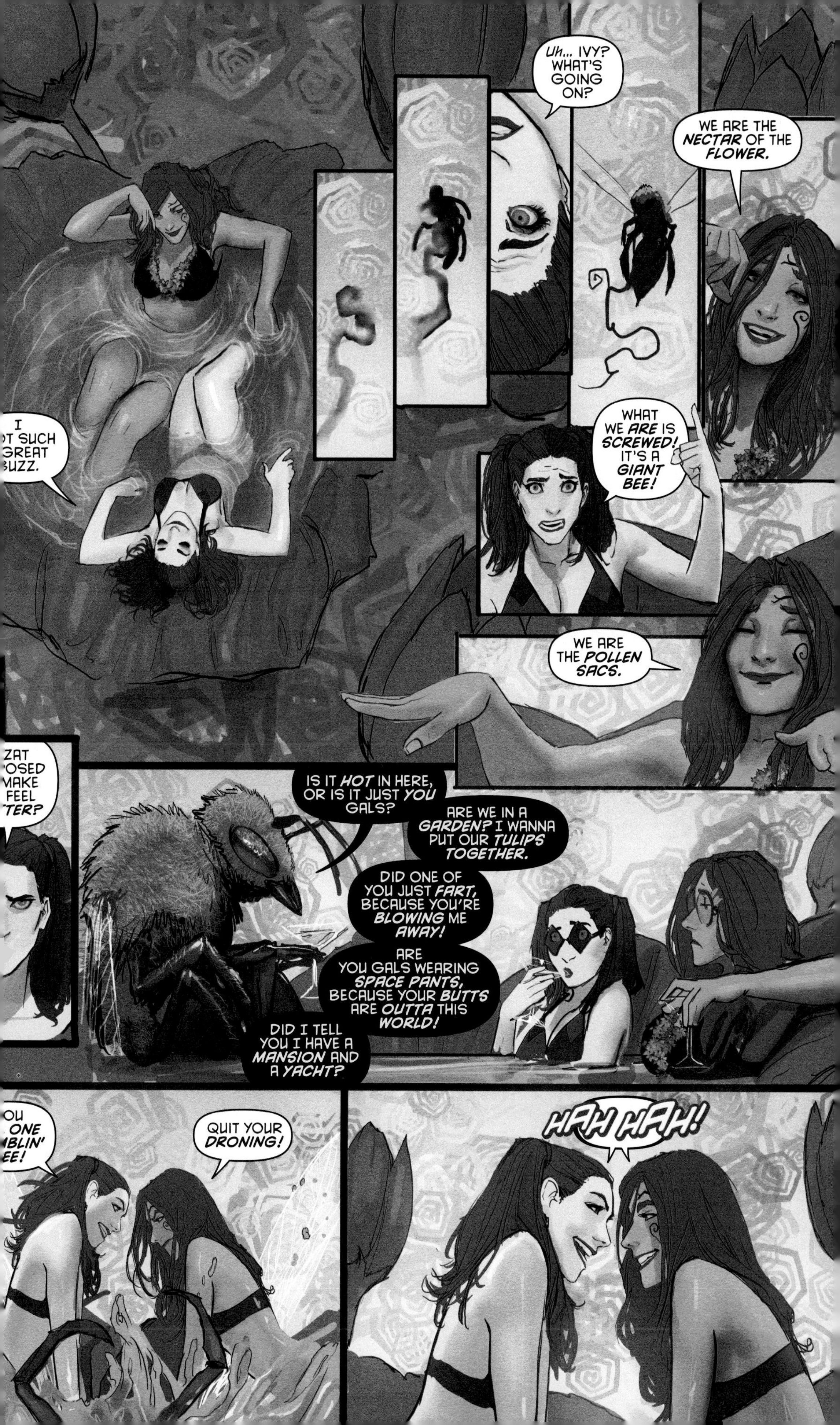

UH... IVY? WHAT'S GOING ON?
WE ARE THE NECTAR OF THE FLOWER.
I OT SUCH GREAT UZZ.
WHAT WE ARE IS SCREWED! IT'S A GIANT BEE!
WE ARE THE POLLEN SACS.
ZAT POSED MAKE FEEL TER?
IS IT HOT IN HERE, OR IS IT JUST YOU GALS?
ARE WE IN A GARDEN? I WANNA PUT OUR TULIPS TOGETHER.
DID ONE OF YOU JUST FART, BECAUSE YOU'RE BLOWING ME AWAY!
ARE YOU GALS WEARING SPACE PANTS, BECAUSE YOUR BUTTS ARE OUTTA THIS WORLD!
DID I TELL YOU I HAVE A MANSION AND A YACHT?
OU ONE MBLIN' EE!
QUIT YOUR DRONING!
HAH HAH!

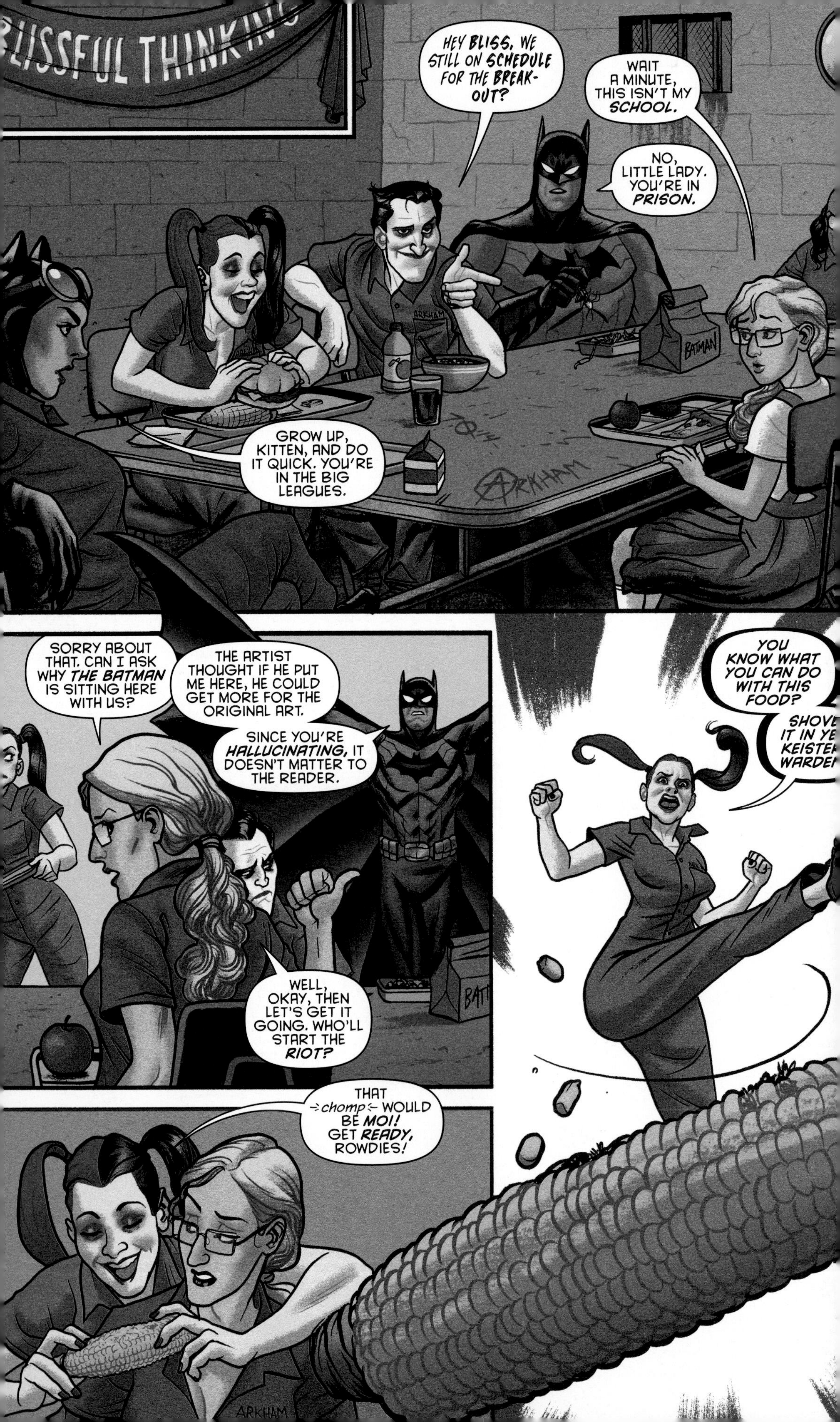
BLISSFUL THINKING
HEY BLISS, WE STILL ON SCHEDULE FOR THE BREAK-OUT?
WAIT A MINUTE, THIS ISN'T MY SCHOOL.
NO, LITTLE LADY. YOU'RE IN PRISON.
BATMAN
ARKHAM
GROW UP, KITTEN, AND DO IT QUICK. YOU'RE IN THE BIG LEAGUES.
ARKHAM
SORRY ABOUT THAT. CAN I ASK WHY THE BATMAN IS SITTING HERE WITH US?
THE ARTIST THOUGHT IF HE PUT ME HERE, HE COULD GET MORE FOR THE ORIGINAL ART.
SINCE YOU'RE HALLUCINATING, IT DOESN'T MATTER TO THE READER.
WELL, OKAY, THEN LET'S GET IT GOING. WHO'LL START THE RIOT?
THAT -chomp- WOULD BE MOI! GET READY, ROWDIES!
ARKHAM
YOU KNOW WHAT YOU CAN DO WITH THIS FOOD?

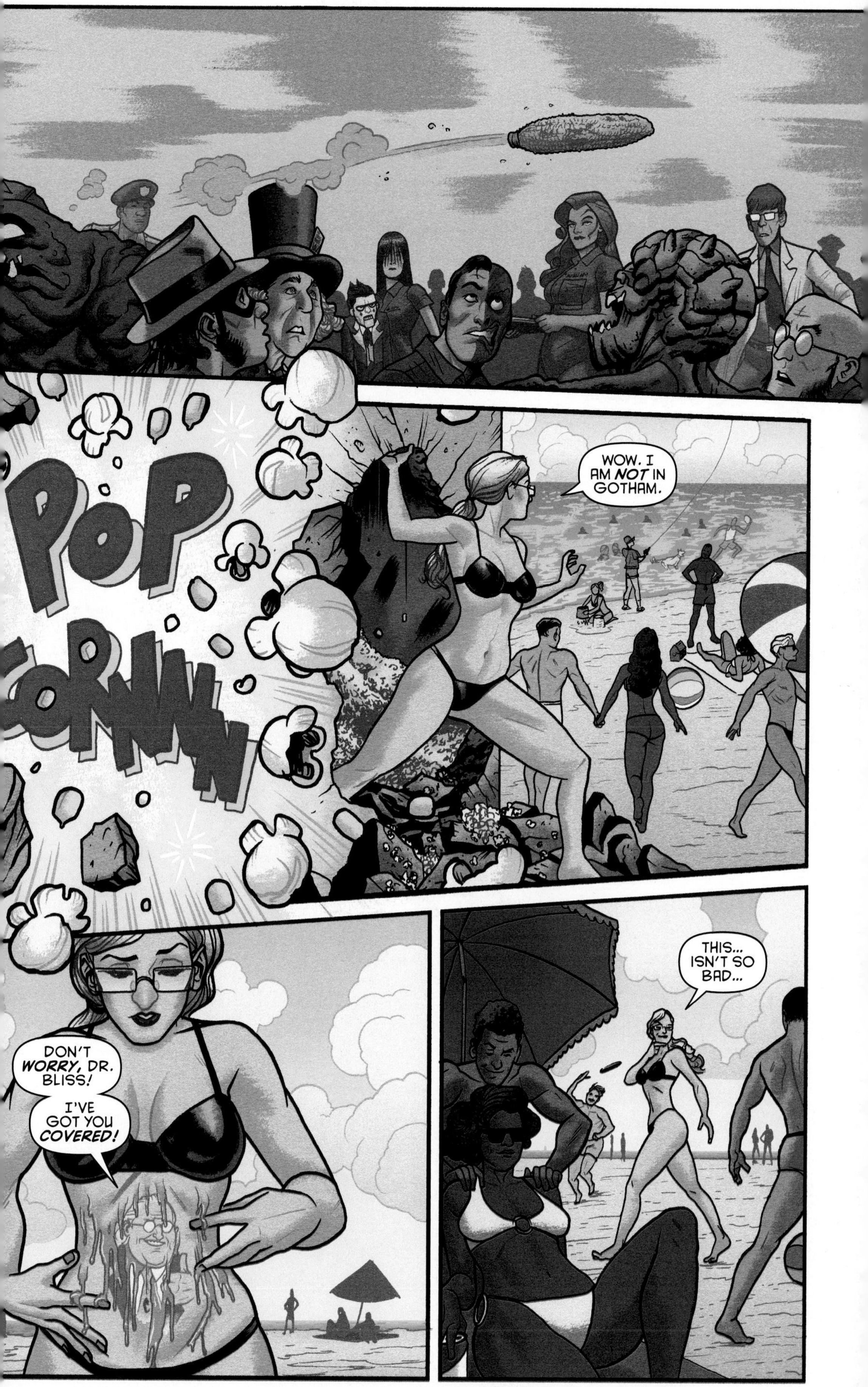
POP
CORNNN
WOW. I AM NOT IN GOTHAM.
DON'T WORRY, DR. BLISS!
I'VE GOT YOU COVERED!
THIS... ISN'T SO BAD...

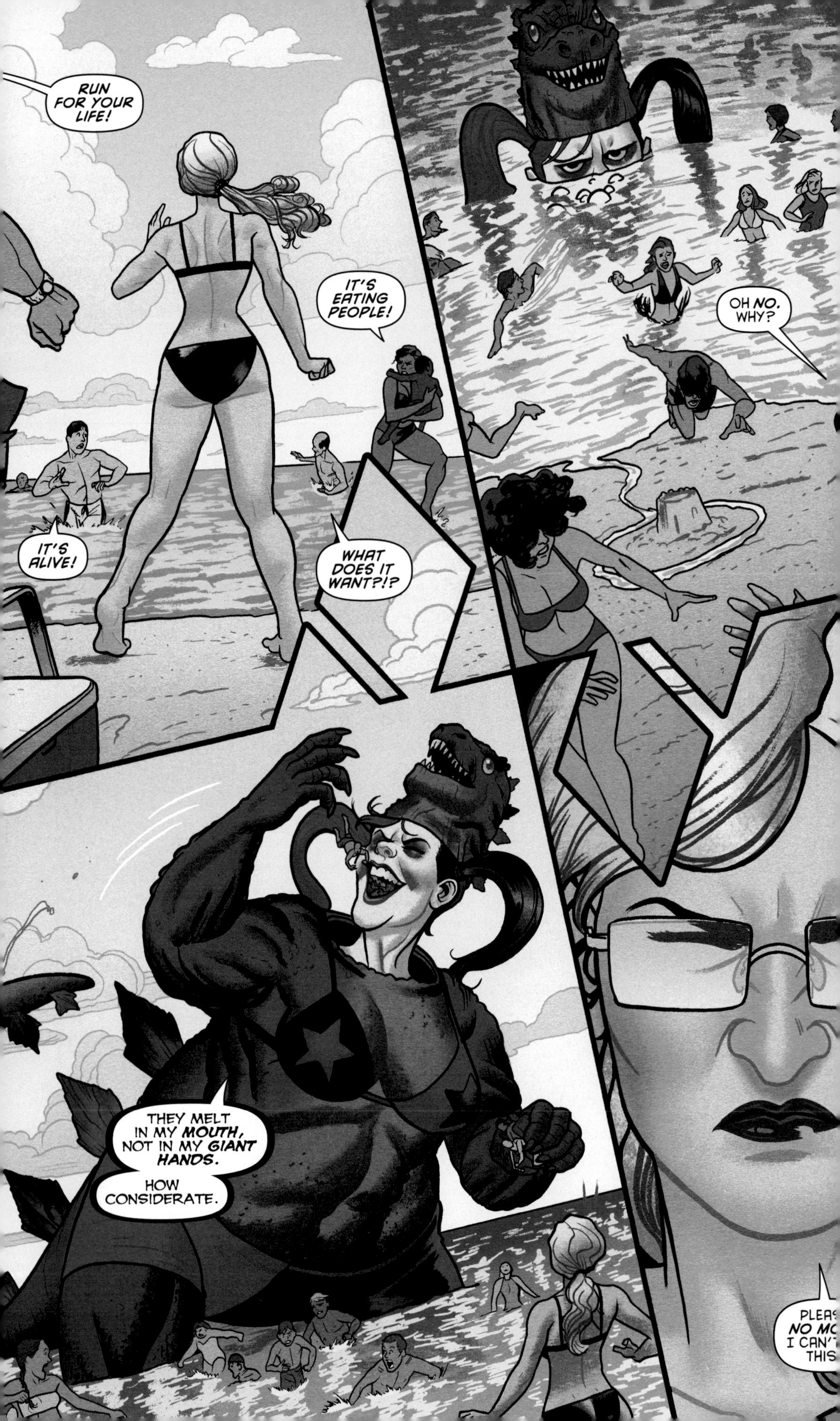
RUN FOR YOUR LIFE!
IT'S EATING PEOPLE!
IT'S ALIVE!
WHAT DOES IT WANT?!?
OH NO. WHY?
THEY MELT IN MY MOUTH, NOT IN MY GIANT HANDS.
HOW CONSIDERATE.
PLEAS
NO MO
I CAN'
THIS

STUPOR-HERO TEAM UP!

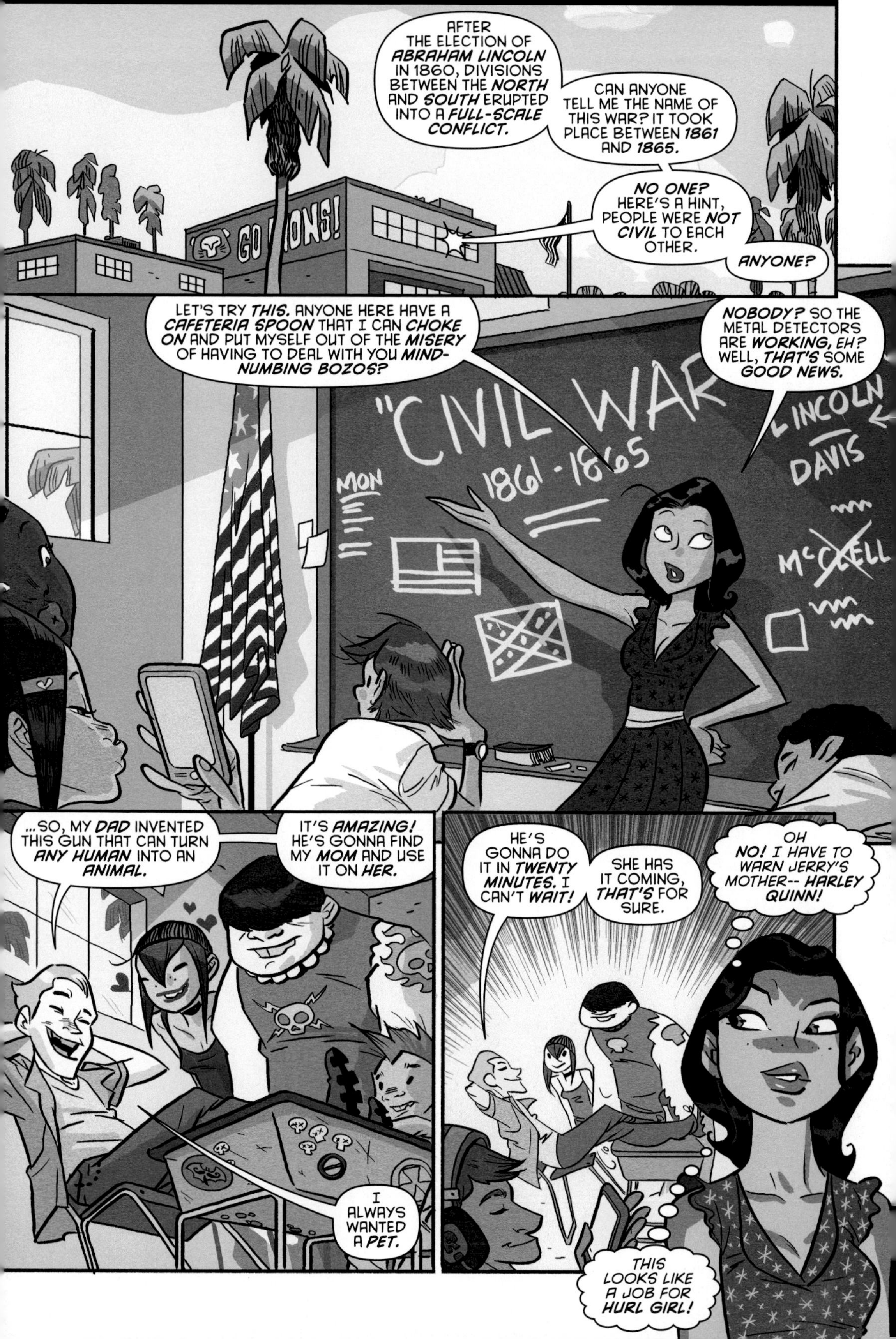

AFTER THE ELECTION OF ABRAHAM LINCOLN IN 1860, DIVISIONS BETWEEN THE NORTH AND SOUTH ERUPTED INTO A FULL-SCALE CONFLICT.
CAN ANYONE TELL ME THE NAME OF THIS WAR? IT TOOK PLACE BETWEEN 1861 AND 1865.
NO ONE? HERE'S A HINT, PEOPLE WERE NOT CIVIL TO EACH OTHER.
ANYONE?
GO LIONS!
LET'S TRY THIS. ANYONE HERE HAVE A CAFETERIA SPOON THAT I CAN CHOKE ON AND PUT MYSELF OUT OF THE MISERY OF HAVING TO DEAL WITH YOU MIND-NUMBING BOZOS?
NOBODY? SO THE METAL DETECTORS ARE WORKING, EH? WELL, THAT'S SOME GOOD NEWS.
"CIVIL WAR"
1861 - 1865
MON
LINCOLN
DAVIS
McCLELL
...SO, MY DAD INVENTED THIS GUN THAT CAN TURN ANY HUMAN INTO AN ANIMAL.
IT'S AMAZING! HE'S GONNA FIND MY MOM AND USE IT ON HER.
I ALWAYS WANTED A PET.
HE'S GONNA DO IT IN TWENTY MINUTES. I CAN'T WAIT!
SHE HAS IT COMING, THAT'S FOR SURE.
OH NO! I HAVE TO WARN JERRY'S MOTHER-- HARLEY QUINN!
THIS LOOKS LIKE A JOB FOR HURL GIRL!

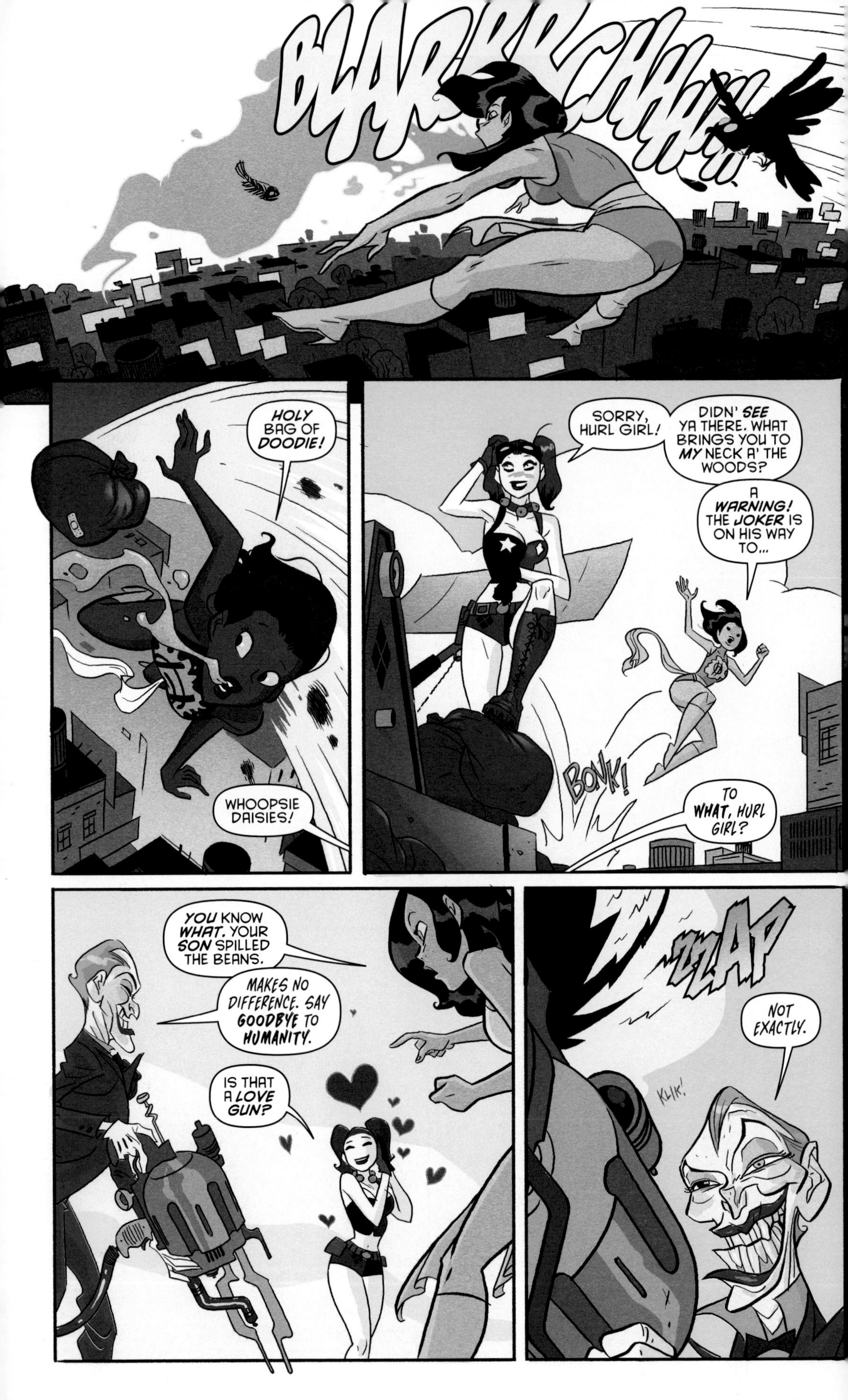
BLARRRCHHH!
HOLY BAG OF DOODIE!
WHOOPSIE DAISIES!
SORRY, HURL GIRL!
DIDN' SEE YA THERE. WHAT BRINGS YOU TO MY NECK A' THE WOODS?
A WARNING! THE JOKER IS ON HIS WAY TO...
BONK!
TO WHAT, HURL GIRL?
YOU KNOW WHAT. YOUR SON SPILLED THE BEANS.
MAKES NO DIFFERENCE. SAY GOODBYE TO HUMANITY.
IS THAT A LOVE GUN?
ZZAP
NOT EXACTLY.
KLIK!

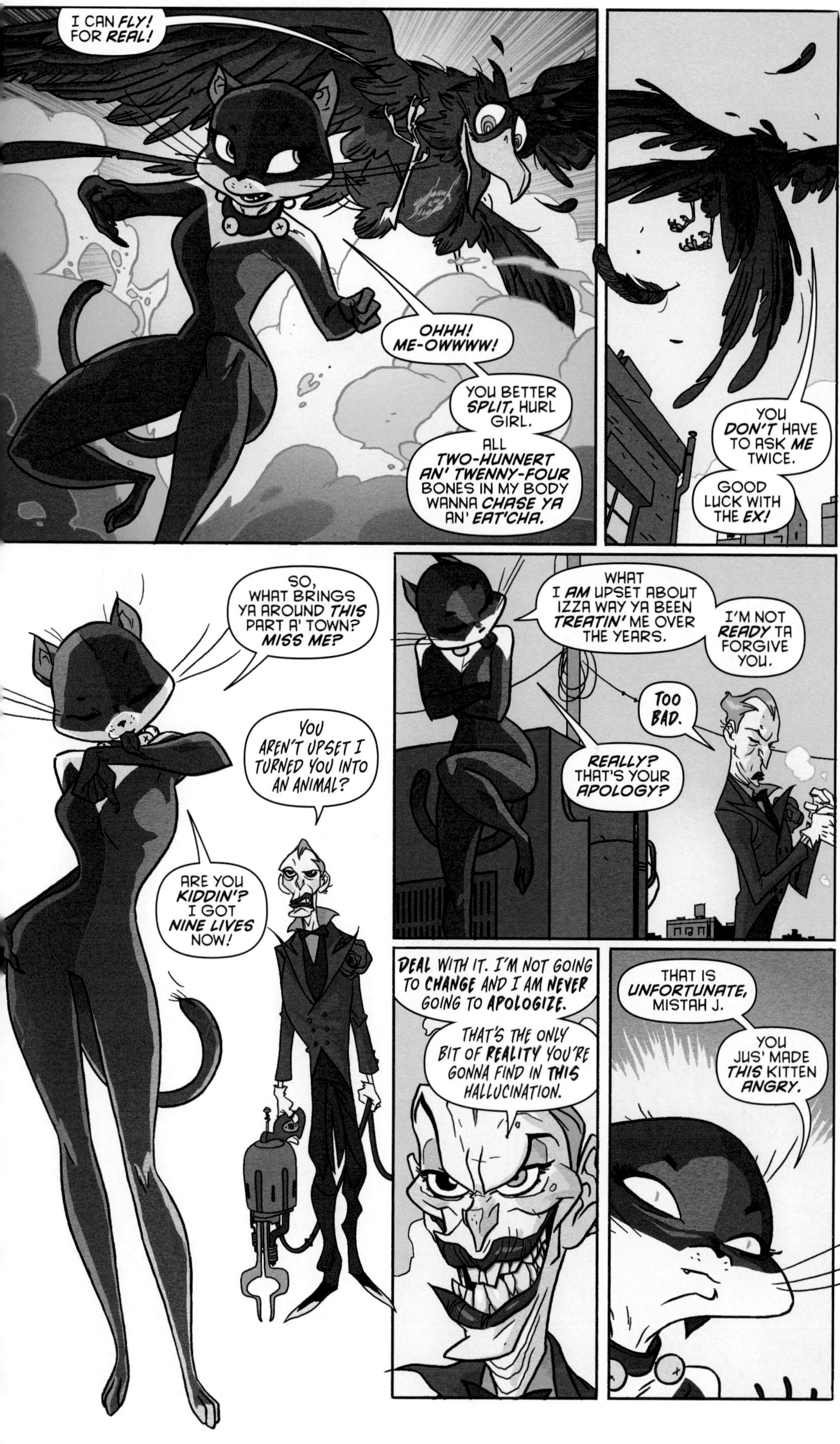
I CAN FLY! FOR REAL!
OHHH! ME-OWWWW!
YOU BETTER SPLIT, HURL GIRL.
ALL TWO-HUNNERT AN' TWENNY-FOUR BONES IN MY BODY WANNA CHASE YA AN' EAT'CHA.
YOU DON'T HAVE TO ASK ME TWICE.
GOOD LUCK WITH THE EX!
SO, WHAT BRINGS YA AROUND THIS PART A' TOWN? MISS ME?
YOU AREN'T UPSET I TURNED YOU INTO AN ANIMAL?
ARE YOU KIDDIN'? I GOT NINE LIVES NOW!
WHAT I AM UPSET ABOUT IZZA WAY YA BEEN TREATIN' ME OVER THE YEARS.
I'M NOT READY TA FORGIVE YOU.
TOO BAD.
REALLY? THAT'S YOUR APOLOGY?
DEAL WITH IT. I'M NOT GOING TO CHANGE AND I AM NEVER GOING TO APOLOGIZE.
THAT'S THE ONLY BIT OF REALITY YOU'RE GONNA FIND IN THIS HALLUCINATION.
THAT IS UNFORTUNATE, MISTAH J.
YOU JUS' MADE THIS KITTEN ANGRY.

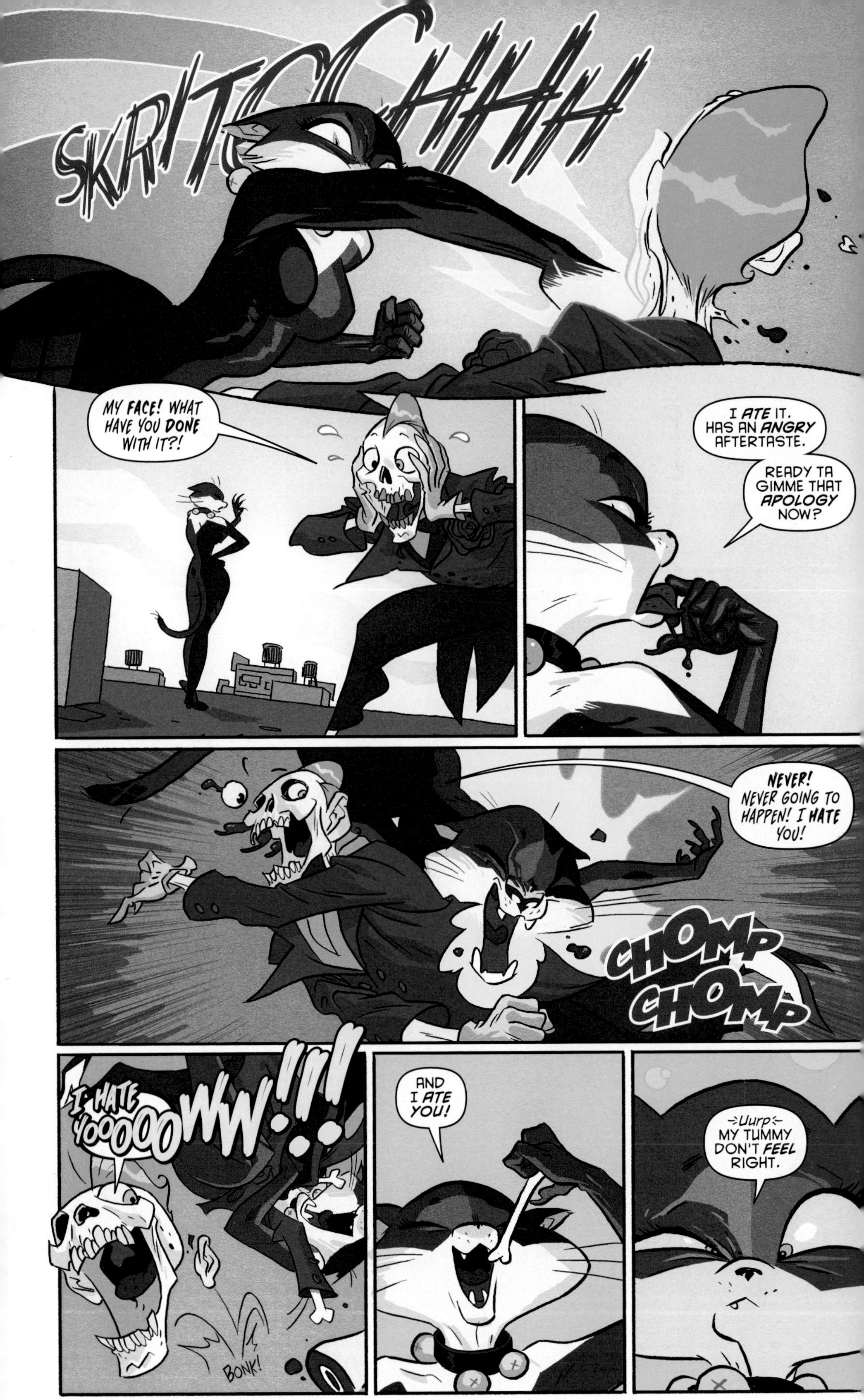
SKRITCCHHH
MY FACE! WHAT HAVE YOU DONE WITH IT?!
I ATE IT. HAS AN ANGRY AFTERTASTE.
READY TA GIMME THAT APOLOGY NOW?
NEVER! NEVER GOING TO HAPPEN! I HATE YOU!
CHOMP CHOMP
I HATE YOOOOOWW!!!
BONK!
AND I ATE YOU!
Uurp MY TUMMY DON'T FEEL RIGHT.

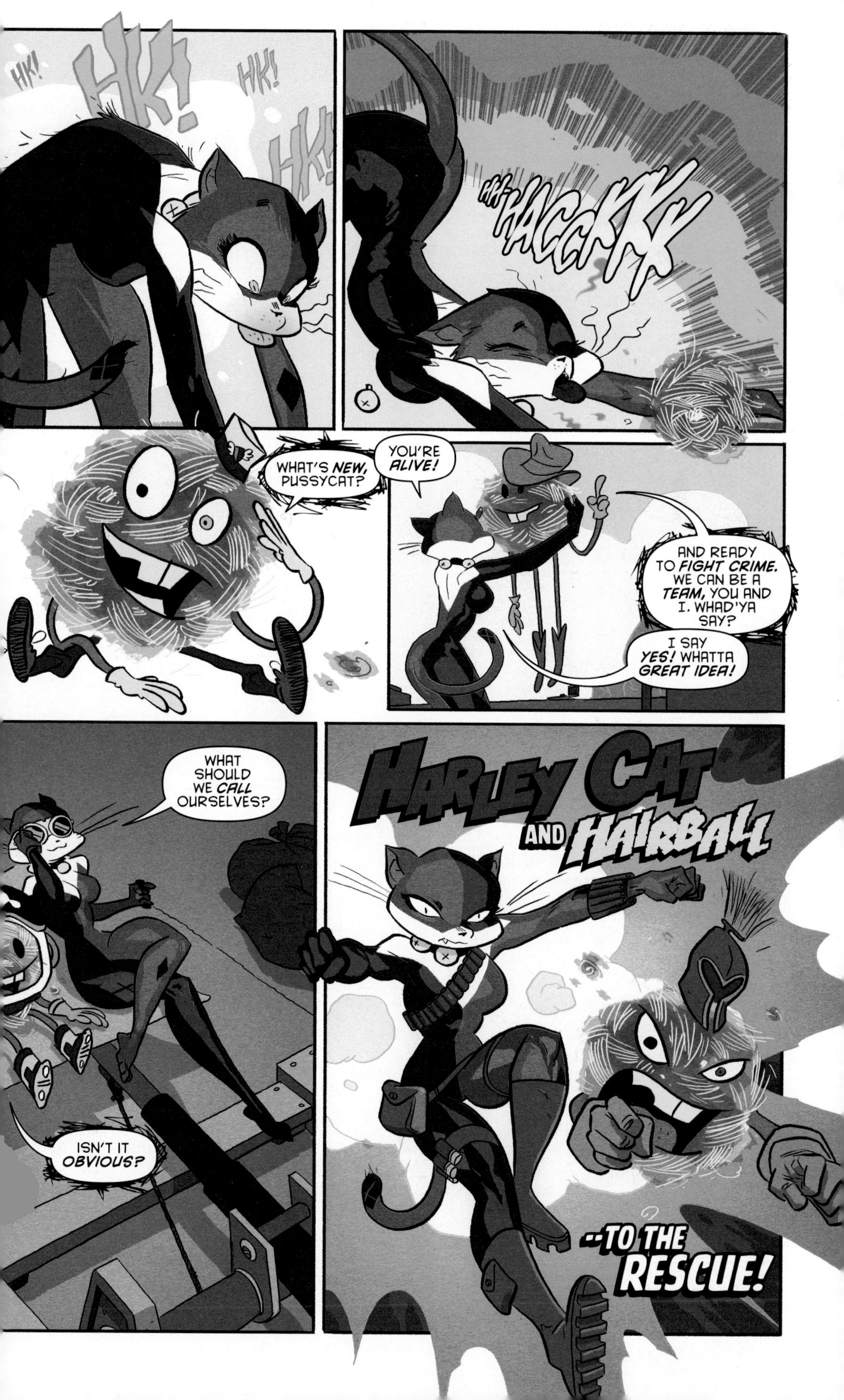
HK!
HK!
HK!
HK!
HK-HACCKKK
WHAT'S NEW, PUSSYCAT?
YOU'RE ALIVE!
AND READY TO FIGHT CRIME. WE CAN BE A TEAM, YOU AND I. WHAD'YA SAY?
I SAY YES! WHATTA GREAT IDEA!
WHAT SHOULD WE CALL OURSELVES?
ISN'T IT OBVIOUS?
HARLEY CAT AND HAIRBALL
--TO THE RESCUE!

A STUDY IN HARLEY

FUNNY... I CAN'T REMEMBER IF I *READ* THIS BOOK OR NOT.

HOW *SPLENDID* WOULD THIS ROOM LOOK WITH A LAVA LAMP IN IT?

DR. BELL, IT SEEMS LIKE THE *RIPPER* IS AT IT *AGAIN.* WE FOUND *ANOTHER BODY* DOWN AT THE END OF *BAKER STREET.* SEEMS *SCOTLAND YARD* HASN'T A *CLUE.*

IT'S DR. BASH, WATSON. AND FOR THE RECORD, SCOTLAND YARD IS UTTERLY *INADEQUATE.*

WE HAVE TO DO THIS *OURSELVES* AND I KNOW *EXACTLY* WHERE TO LOOK. *FOLLOW ME...* AFTER I FINISH THIS *WONDERFUL SMOKE.*

I JUST CAN'T GET ENOUGH OF THIS WACKY STUFF.

THE KILLER IS *HERE,* IN *WHITECHAPEL.* ALL THE EVIDENCE I'VE GATHERED LEADS ME TO BELIEVE THAT HE IS GOING TO *STRIKE AGAIN,* IN THIS *PRECISE LOCATION,* THIS *VERY NIGHT!*

ALL WE MUST DO IS STEER CLEAR OF THE LIGHT AND KEEP AN *EYE OUT.* ONCE THE KILLER MAKES HIMSELF *KNOWN,* WE WILL HAVE THE *ADVANTAGE.*

I'M CRAVING SOME *FISH AND CHIPS.*

WE MUST OBTAIN SOMETHING *FRIED* AFTER THIS.

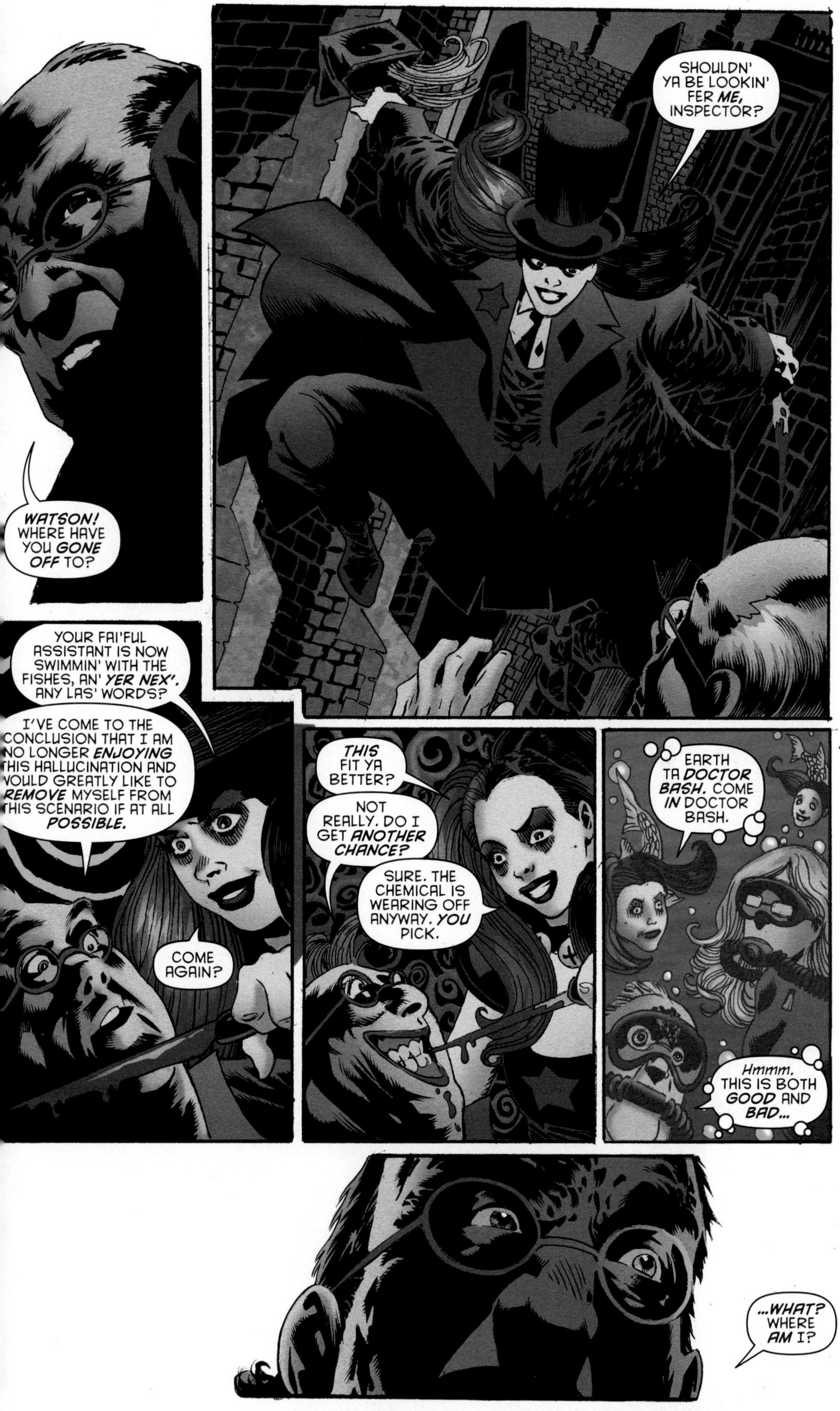
SHOULDN' YA BE LOOKIN' FER ME, INSPECTOR?
WATSON! WHERE HAVE YOU GONE OFF TO?
YOUR FAI'FUL ASSISTANT IS NOW SWIMMIN' WITH THE FISHES, AN' YER NEX'. ANY LAS' WORDS?
I'VE COME TO THE CONCLUSION THAT I AM NO LONGER ENJOYING THIS HALLUCINATION AND WOULD GREATLY LIKE TO REMOVE MYSELF FROM THIS SCENARIO IF AT ALL POSSIBLE.
COME AGAIN?
THIS FIT YA BETTER?
NOT REALLY. DO I GET ANOTHER CHANCE?
SURE. THE CHEMICAL IS WEARING OFF ANYWAY. YOU PICK.
EARTH TA DOCTOR BASH. COME IN DOCTOR BASH.
Hmmm. THIS IS BOTH GOOD AND BAD...
...WHAT? WHERE AM I?

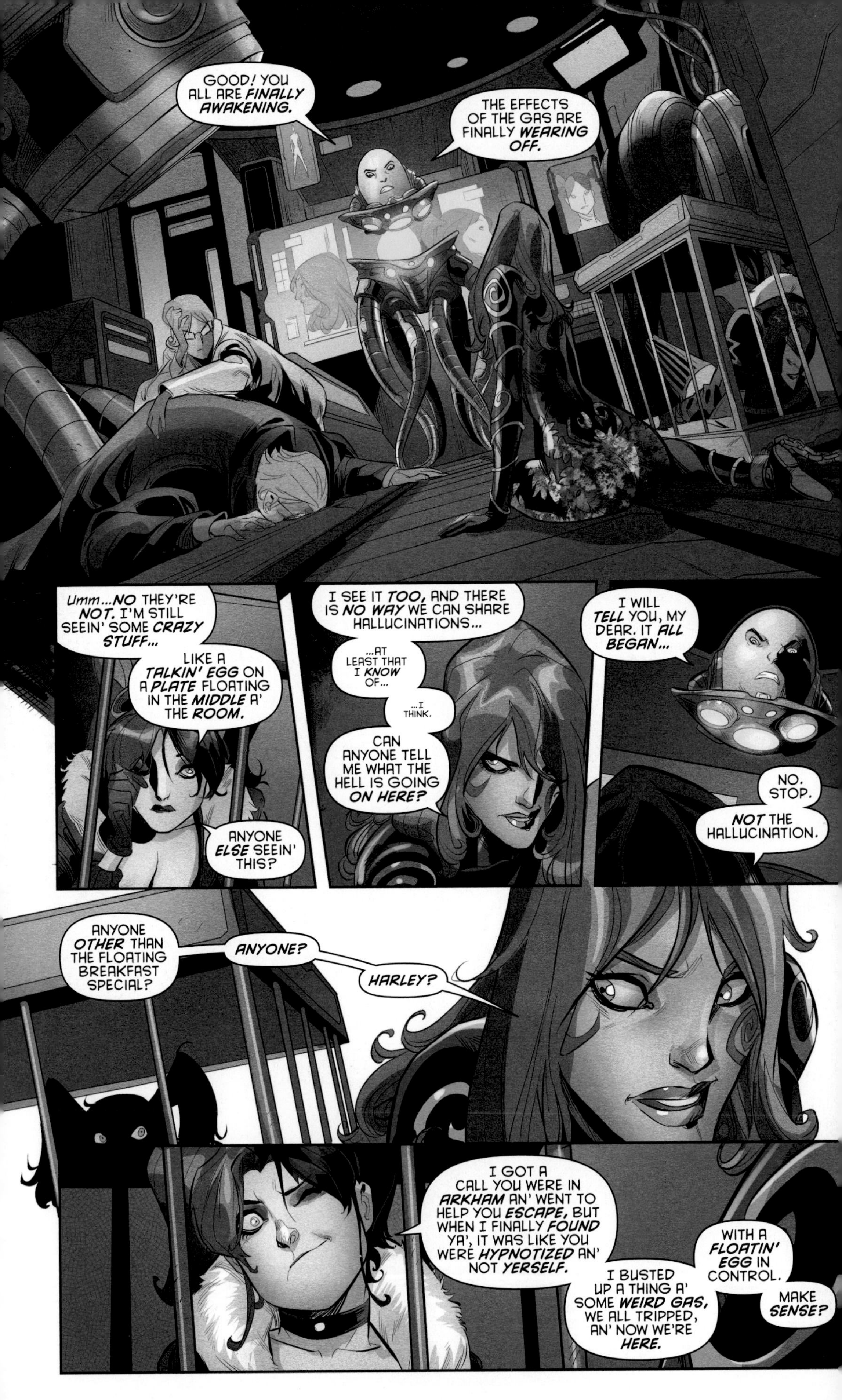
GOOD! YOU ALL ARE FINALLY AWAKENING.
THE EFFECTS OF THE GAS ARE FINALLY WEARING OFF.
Umm...NO THEY'RE NOT. I'M STILL SEEIN' SOME CRAZY STUFF...
LIKE A TALKIN' EGG ON A PLATE FLOATING IN THE MIDDLE A' THE ROOM.
ANYONE ELSE SEEIN' THIS?
I SEE IT TOO, AND THERE IS NO WAY WE CAN SHARE HALLUCINATIONS...
...AT LEAST THAT I KNOW OF...
...I THINK.
CAN ANYONE TELL ME WHAT THE HELL IS GOING ON HERE?
I WILL TELL YOU, MY DEAR. IT ALL BEGAN...
NO. STOP.
NOT THE HALLUCINATION.
ANYONE OTHER THAN THE FLOATING BREAKFAST SPECIAL?
ANYONE?
HARLEY?
I GOT A CALL YOU WERE IN ARKHAM AN' WENT TO HELP YOU ESCAPE, BUT WHEN I FINALLY FOUND YA', IT WAS LIKE YOU WERE HYPNOTIZED AN' NOT YERSELF.
I BUSTED UP A THING A' SOME WEIRD GAS, WE ALL TRIPPED, AN' NOW WE'RE HERE.
WITH A FLOATIN' EGG IN CONTROL.
MAKE SENSE?

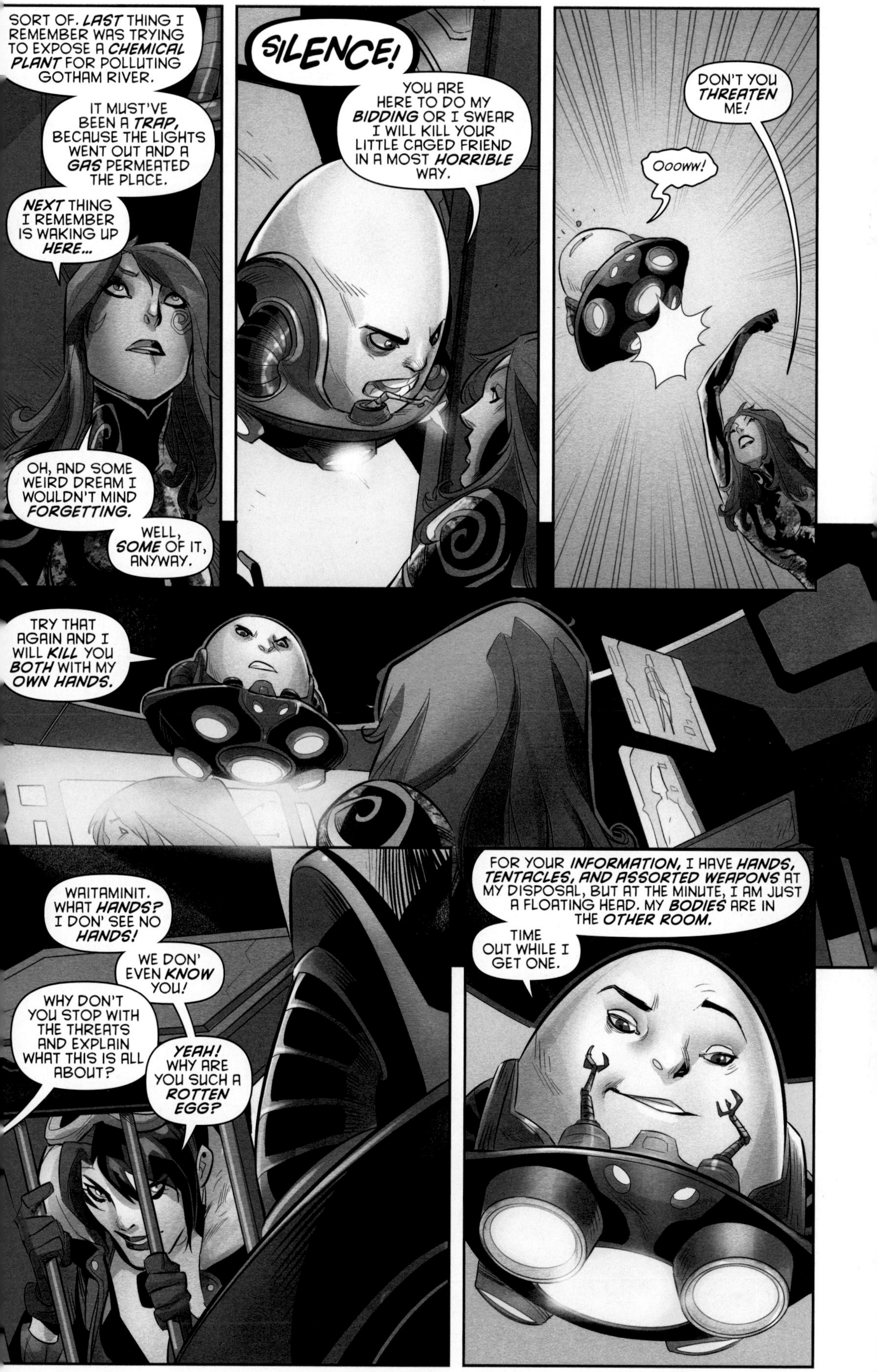

SORT OF. LAST THING I REMEMBER WAS TRYING TO EXPOSE A CHEMICAL PLANT FOR POLLUTING GOTHAM RIVER.
IT MUST'VE BEEN A TRAP, BECAUSE THE LIGHTS WENT OUT AND A GAS PERMEATED THE PLACE.
NEXT THING I REMEMBER IS WAKING UP HERE...
OH, AND SOME WEIRD DREAM I WOULDN'T MIND FORGETTING.
WELL, SOME OF IT, ANYWAY.
SILENCE!
YOU ARE HERE TO DO MY BIDDING OR I SWEAR I WILL KILL YOUR LITTLE CAGED FRIEND IN A MOST HORRIBLE WAY.
DON'T YOU THREATEN ME!
Oooww!
TRY THAT AGAIN AND I WILL KILL YOU BOTH WITH MY OWN HANDS.
WAITAMINIT. WHAT HANDS? I DON' SEE NO HANDS!
WE DON' EVEN KNOW YOU!
WHY DON'T YOU STOP WITH THE THREATS AND EXPLAIN WHAT THIS IS ALL ABOUT?
YEAH! WHY ARE YOU SUCH A ROTTEN EGG?
FOR YOUR INFORMATION, I HAVE HANDS, TENTACLES, AND ASSORTED WEAPONS AT MY DISPOSAL, BUT AT THE MINUTE, I AM JUST A FLOATING HEAD. MY BODIES ARE IN THE OTHER ROOM.
TIME OUT WHILE I GET ONE.

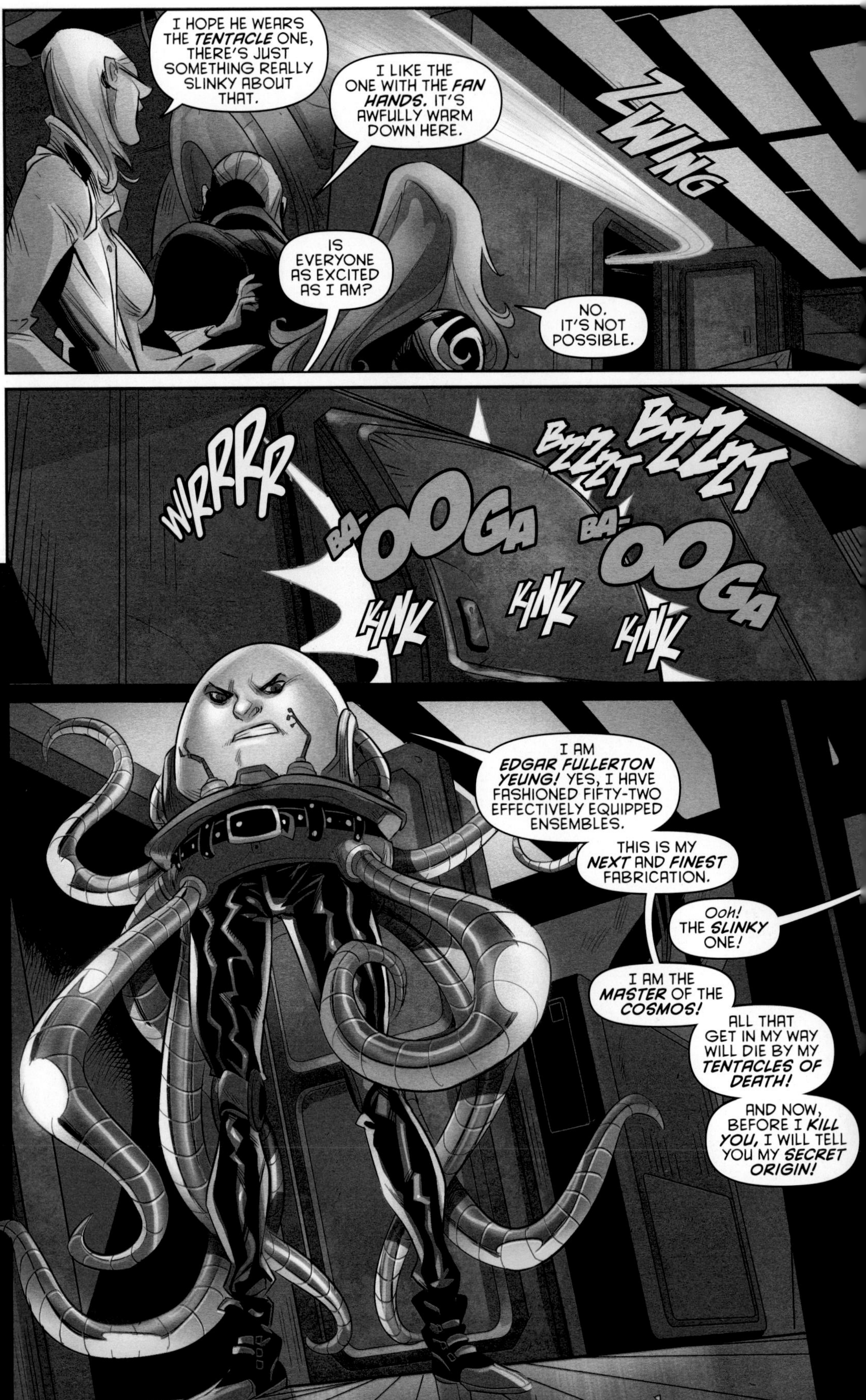
I HOPE HE WEARS THE *TENTACLE* ONE, THERE'S JUST SOMETHING REALLY SLINKY ABOUT THAT.
I LIKE THE ONE WITH THE *FAN HANDS.* IT'S AWFULLY WARM DOWN HERE.
ZZWING
IS EVERYONE AS EXCITED AS I AM?
NO. IT'S NOT POSSIBLE.
WIRRRR
BZZZZT BZZZZT
BA-OOGA BA-OOGA
KLINK KLINK KLINK
I AM *EDGAR FULLERTON YEUNG!* YES, I HAVE FASHIONED FIFTY-TWO EFFECTIVELY EQUIPPED ENSEMBLES.
THIS IS MY *NEXT* AND *FINEST* FABRICATION.
Ooh! THE *SLINKY* ONE!
I AM THE *MASTER* OF THE *COSMOS!*
ALL THAT GET IN MY WAY WILL DIE BY MY *TENTACLES OF DEATH!*
AND NOW, BEFORE I *KILL YOU,* I WILL TELL YOU MY *SECRET ORIGIN!*

OH NO. NOT A *SECRET ORIGIN*. WHY DON'CHA *JUST* KILL US INSTEAD?

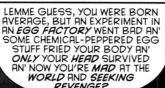

LEMME GUESS, YOU WERE BORN AVERAGE, BUT AN EXPERIMENT IN AN *EGG FACTORY* WENT BAD AN' SOME CHEMICAL-PEPPERED EGG STUFF FRIED YOUR BODY AN' *ONLY* YOUR *HEAD* SURVIVED AN' NOW YOU'RE *MAD* AT THE *WORLD* AND *SEEKING REVENGE*?

IS IT POSSIBLE YOU WERE ONE OF FIVE CHILDREN BORN WITH AN ODD BIRTH DEFECT WHERE ONLY YOUR *HEAD* SURVIVED?

IN ORDER TO KEEP YOUR HEAD ALIVE, SCIENTISTS KEPT YOU INCUBATED ON A GIANT FRYING PAN.

WHEN YOU WERE READY TO MOVE ON, THEY MADE A BED OF HOME FRIES FOR YOU TO LIE IN.

EVENTUALLY YOU GOT A JOB AT A *CIRCUS* WHERE YOU WERE ABUSED BY THE *BEARDED LADY,* AND YOU EXPLODED INTO PIECES IN HER BEARD AND SHE SHAVED YOU OFF, DROPPED YOU AND THE BEARD DOWN A SINK, AND YOU WASHED UP *HERE*, IN THE BASEMENT OF *ARKHAM*, AWAITING THE TIME YOU CAN TAKE *REVENGE* ON PEOPLE YOU *DON'T EVEN KNOW.*

CLOSE?

IT'S *MY* TURN, CORRECT? I THINK YOU COME FROM AN *ALIEN PLANET* FULL OF CREATURES LIKE YOU AND YOUR PLANET WAS *DYING.*

YOUR PARENTS SENT YOU HERE IN A SHIP TO LIVE THE *REST* OF *YOUR LIFE* AMONG *HUMANS.*

DAMN, THAT'S SO *UNORIGINAL.* I THINK I VOTE FOR POISON IVY'S STORY.

I THINK I HAVE A *GOOD* ONE.

YOUR MOTHER PROCREATED WITH A *GIANT ALIEN CHICKEN* AND--

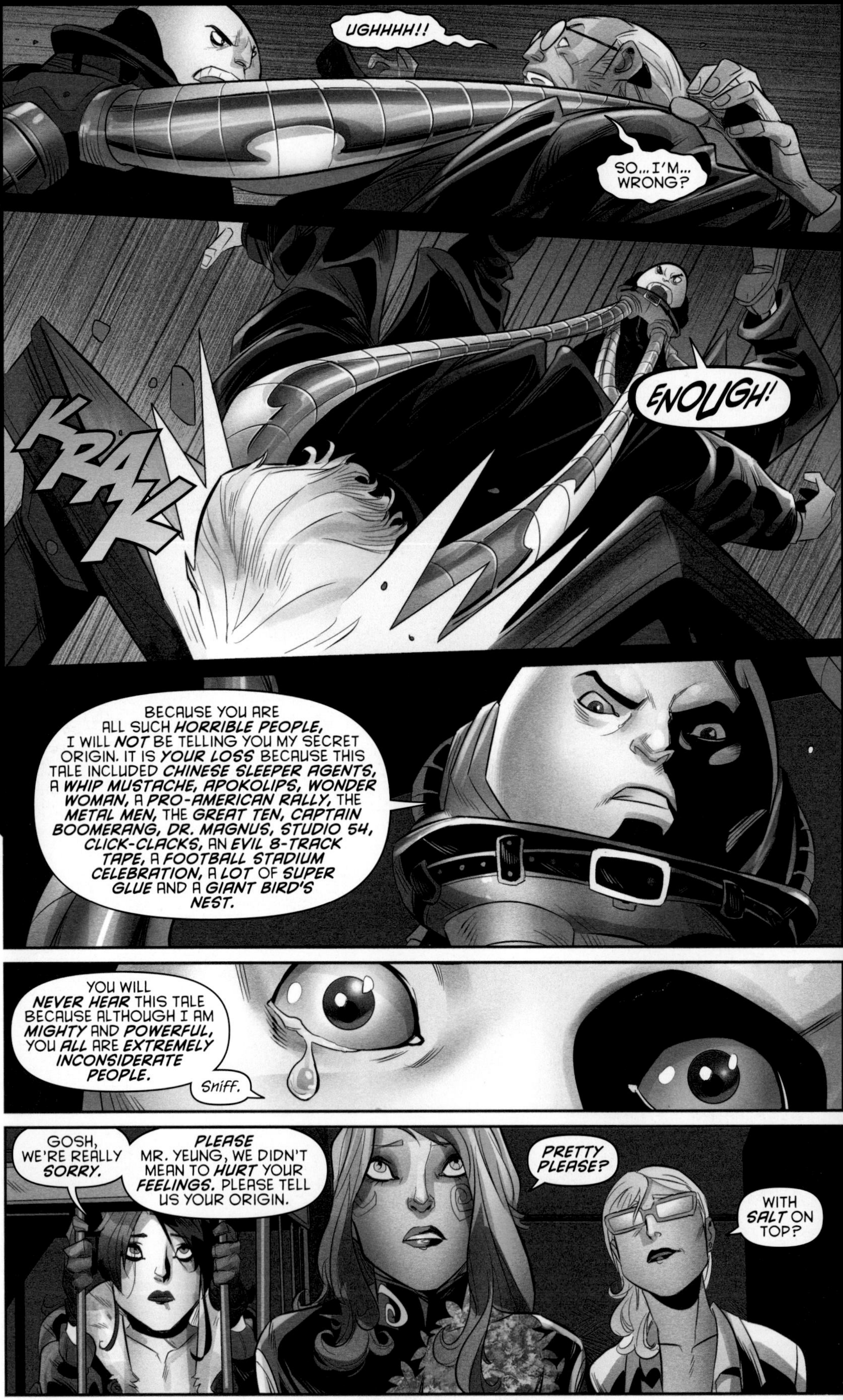
UGHHHH!!
SO... I'M... WRONG?
KRAK
ENOUGH!
BECAUSE YOU ARE ALL SUCH HORRIBLE PEOPLE, I WILL NOT BE TELLING YOU MY SECRET ORIGIN. IT IS YOUR LOSS BECAUSE THIS TALE INCLUDED CHINESE SLEEPER AGENTS, A WHIP MUSTACHE, APOKOLIPS, WONDER WOMAN, A PRO-AMERICAN RALLY, THE METAL MEN, THE GREAT TEN, CAPTAIN BOOMERANG, DR. MAGNUS, STUDIO 54, CLICK-CLACKS, AN EVIL 8-TRACK TAPE, A FOOTBALL STADIUM CELEBRATION, A LOT OF SUPER GLUE AND A GIANT BIRD'S NEST.
YOU WILL NEVER HEAR THIS TALE BECAUSE ALTHOUGH I AM MIGHTY AND POWERFUL, YOU ALL ARE EXTREMELY INCONSIDERATE PEOPLE.
Sniff.
GOSH, WE'RE REALLY SORRY.
PLEASE MR. YEUNG, WE DIDN'T MEAN TO HURT YOUR FEELINGS. PLEASE TELL US YOUR ORIGIN.
PRETTY PLEASE?
WITH SALT ON TOP?

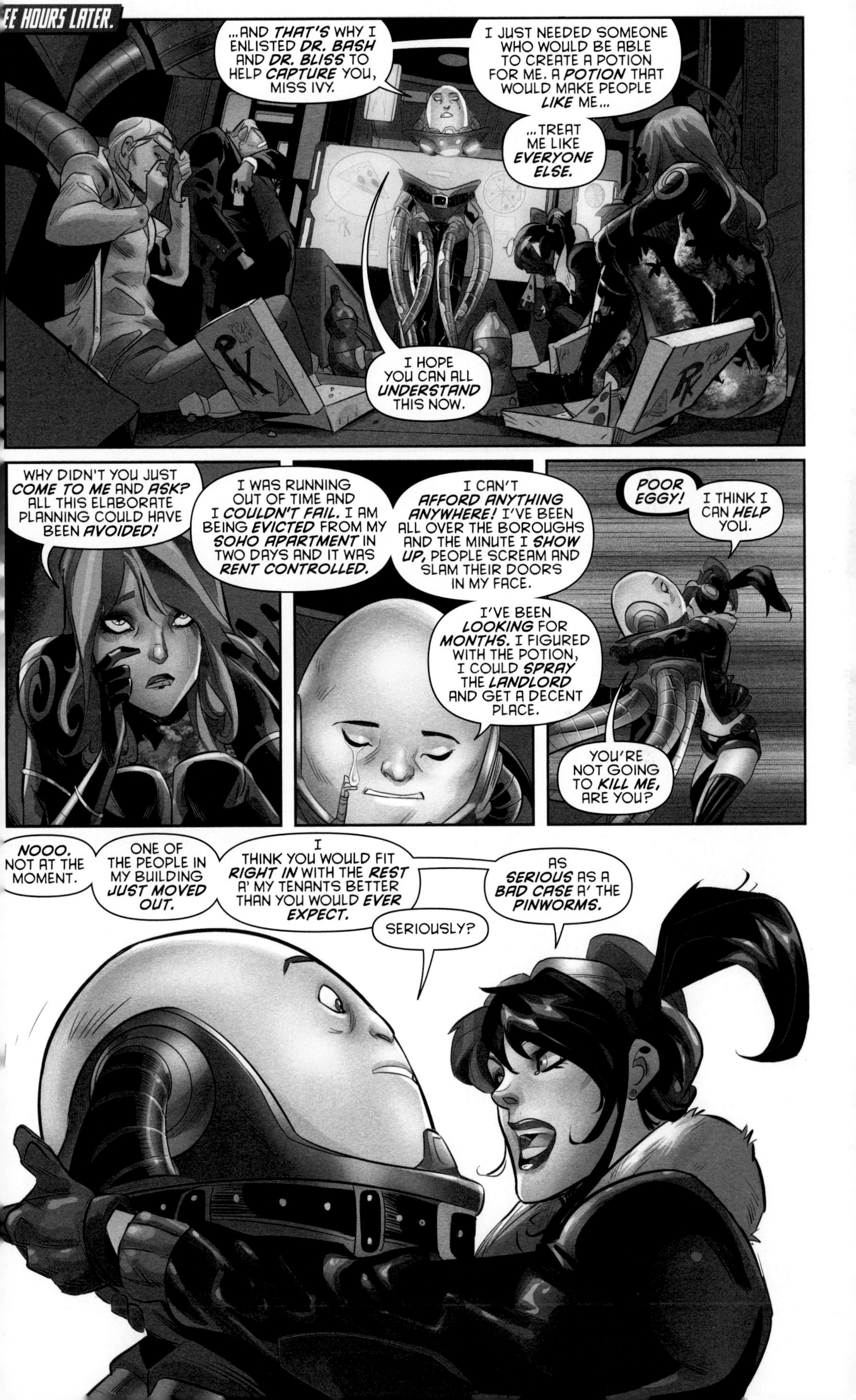
EE HOURS LATER.
...AND THAT'S WHY I ENLISTED DR. BASH AND DR. BLISS TO HELP CAPTURE YOU, MISS IVY.
I JUST NEEDED SOMEONE WHO WOULD BE ABLE TO CREATE A POTION FOR ME. A POTION THAT WOULD MAKE PEOPLE LIKE ME...
...TREAT ME LIKE EVERYONE ELSE.
I HOPE YOU CAN ALL UNDERSTAND THIS NOW.
WHY DIDN'T YOU JUST COME TO ME AND ASK? ALL THIS ELABORATE PLANNING COULD HAVE BEEN AVOIDED!
I WAS RUNNING OUT OF TIME AND I COULDN'T FAIL. I AM BEING EVICTED FROM MY SOHO APARTMENT IN TWO DAYS AND IT WAS RENT CONTROLLED.
I CAN'T AFFORD ANYTHING ANYWHERE! I'VE BEEN ALL OVER THE BOROUGHS AND THE MINUTE I SHOW UP, PEOPLE SCREAM AND SLAM THEIR DOORS IN MY FACE.
I'VE BEEN LOOKING FOR MONTHS. I FIGURED WITH THE POTION, I COULD SPRAY THE LANDLORD AND GET A DECENT PLACE.
POOR EGGY!
I THINK I CAN HELP YOU.
YOU'RE NOT GOING TO KILL ME, ARE YOU?
NOOO. NOT AT THE MOMENT.
ONE OF THE PEOPLE IN MY BUILDING JUST MOVED OUT.
I THINK YOU WOULD FIT RIGHT IN WITH THE REST A' MY TENANTS BETTER THAN YOU WOULD EVER EXPECT.
SERIOUSLY?
AS SERIOUS AS A BAD CASE A' THE PINWORMS.

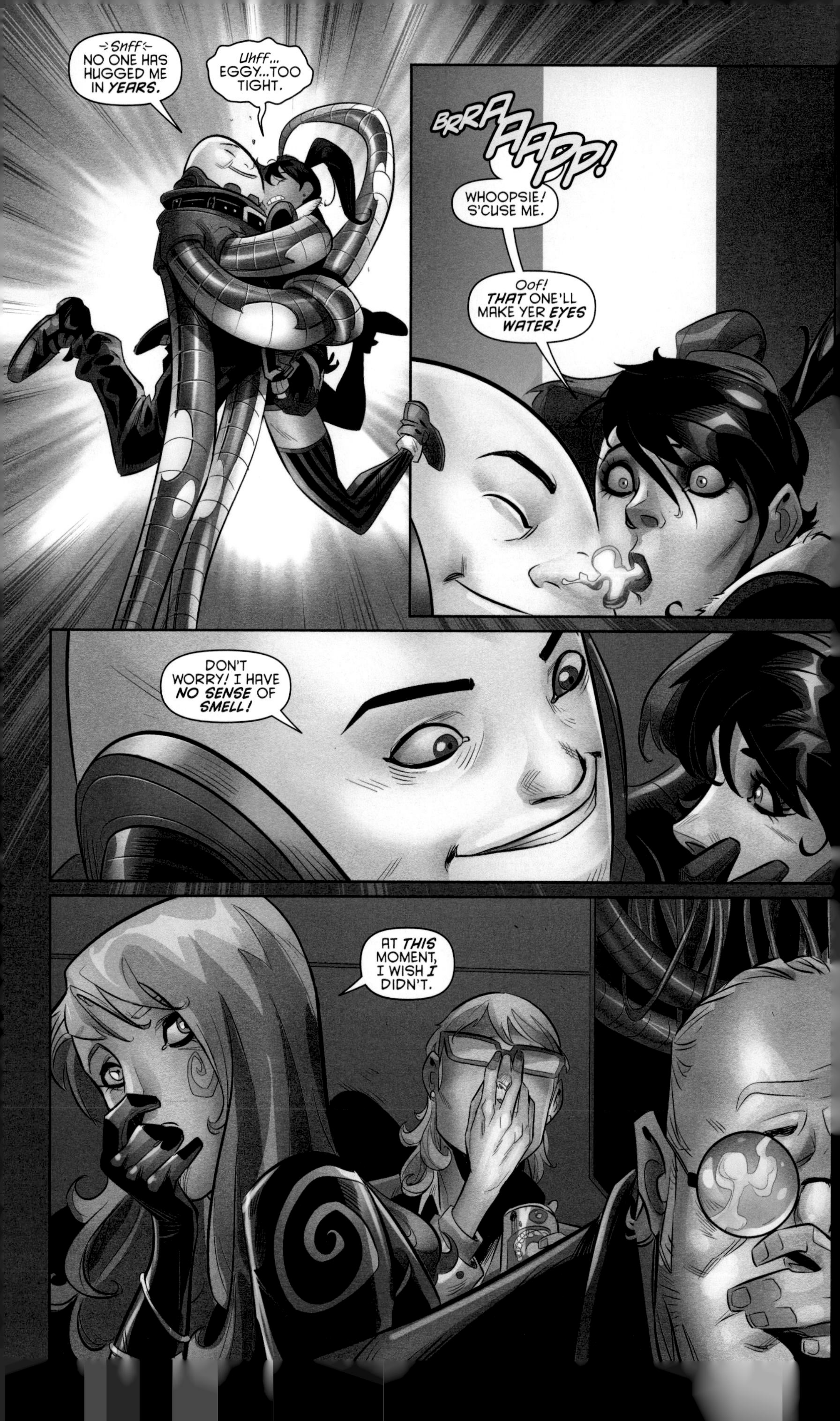

-SNFF- NO ONE HAS HUGGED ME IN YEARS.
UHFF... EGGY...TOO TIGHT.
BRRAAAPP!
WHOOPSIE! S'CUSE ME.
OOF! THAT ONE'LL MAKE YER EYES WATER!
DON'T WORRY! I HAVE NO SENSE OF SMELL!
AT THIS MOMENT, I WISH I DIDN'T.

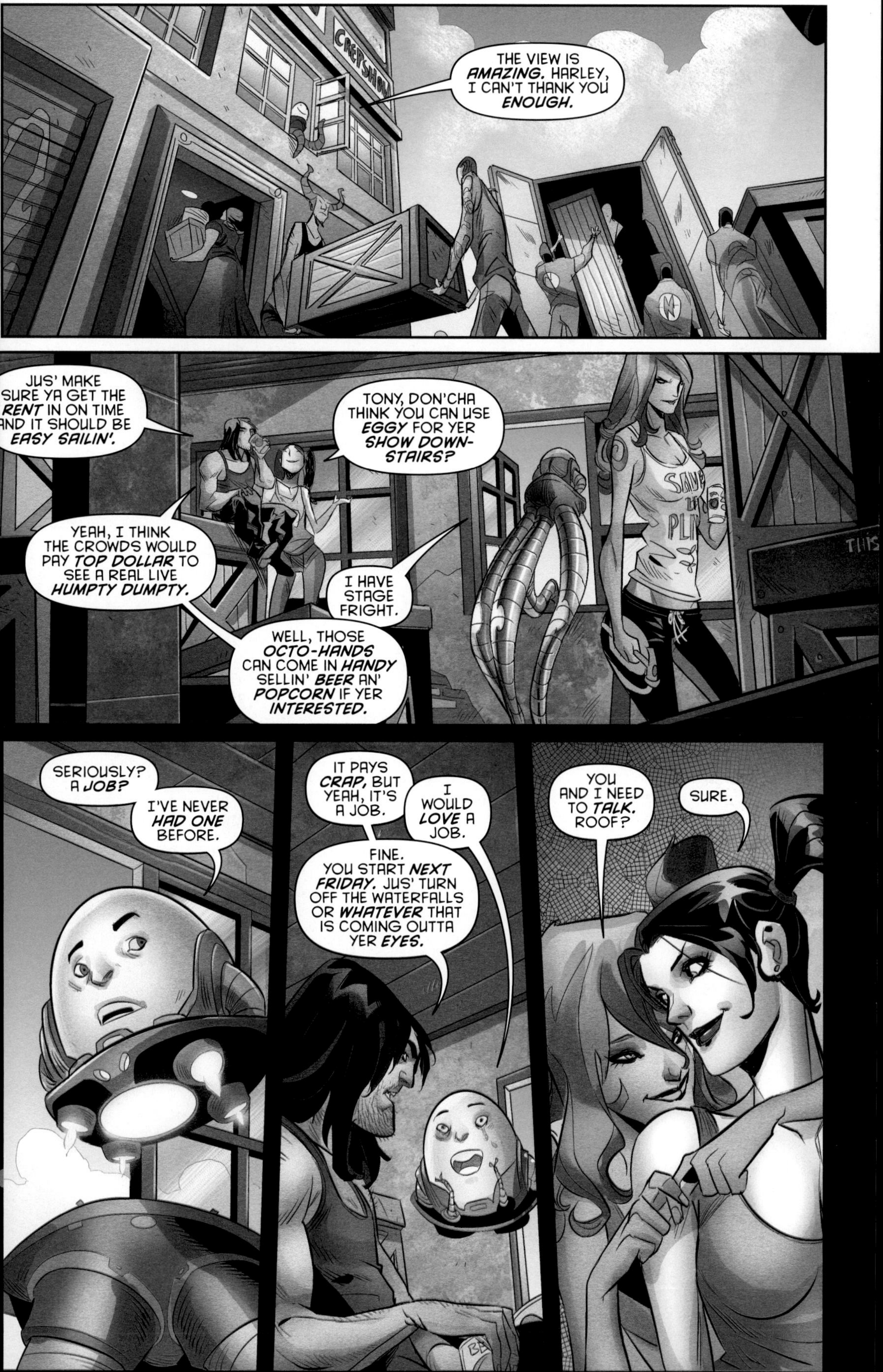

CREPSHOW
THE VIEW IS AMAZING. HARLEY, I CAN'T THANK YOU ENOUGH.
JUS' MAKE SURE YA GET THE RENT IN ON TIME AND IT SHOULD BE EASY SAILIN'.
TONY, DON'CHA THINK YOU CAN USE EGGY FOR YER SHOW DOWN-STAIRS?
YEAH, I THINK THE CROWDS WOULD PAY TOP DOLLAR TO SEE A REAL LIVE HUMPTY DUMPTY.
I HAVE STAGE FRIGHT.
WELL, THOSE OCTO-HANDS CAN COME IN HANDY SELLIN' BEER AN' POPCORN IF YER INTERESTED.
THIS
SERIOUSLY? A JOB?
I'VE NEVER HAD ONE BEFORE.
IT PAYS CRAP, BUT YEAH, IT'S A JOB.
I WOULD LOVE A JOB.
FINE. YOU START NEXT FRIDAY. JUS' TURN OFF THE WATERFALLS OR WHATEVER THAT IS COMING OUTTA YER EYES.
YOU AND I NEED TO TALK. ROOF?
SURE.

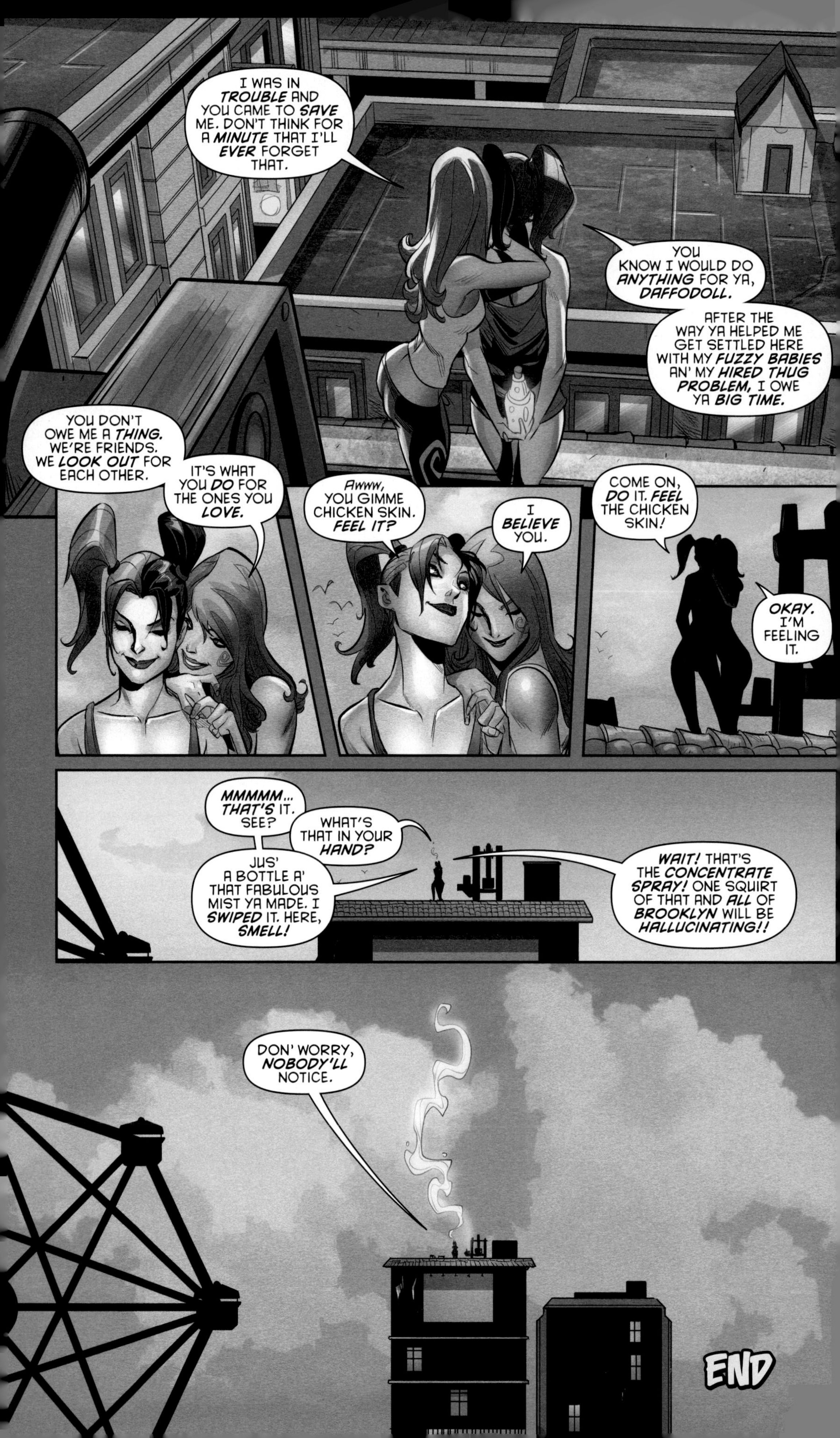
I WAS IN *TROUBLE* AND YOU CAME TO *SAVE* ME. DON'T THINK FOR A *MINUTE* THAT I'LL *EVER* FORGET THAT.
YOU KNOW I WOULD DO *ANYTHING* FOR YA, *DAFFODOLL.*
AFTER THE WAY YA HELPED ME GET SETTLED HERE WITH MY *FUZZY BABIES* AN' MY *HIRED THUG PROBLEM,* I OWE YA *BIG TIME.*
YOU DON'T OWE ME A *THING.* WE'RE FRIENDS. WE *LOOK OUT* FOR EACH OTHER.
IT'S WHAT YOU *DO* FOR THE ONES YOU *LOVE.*
Awww, YOU GIMME CHICKEN SKIN. *FEEL IT?*
I *BELIEVE* YOU.
COME ON, *DO* IT. *FEEL* THE CHICKEN SKIN!
OKAY. I'M FEELING IT.
MMMMM... THAT'S IT. SEE?
WHAT'S THAT IN YOUR *HAND?*
JUS' A BOTTLE A' THAT FABULOUS MIST YA MADE. I *SWIPED* IT. HERE, *SMELL!*
WAIT! THAT'S THE *CONCENTRATE SPRAY!* ONE SQUIRT OF THAT AND *ALL* OF *BROOKLYN* WILL BE *HALLUCINATING!!*
DON' WORRY, *NOBODY'LL* NOTICE.
END

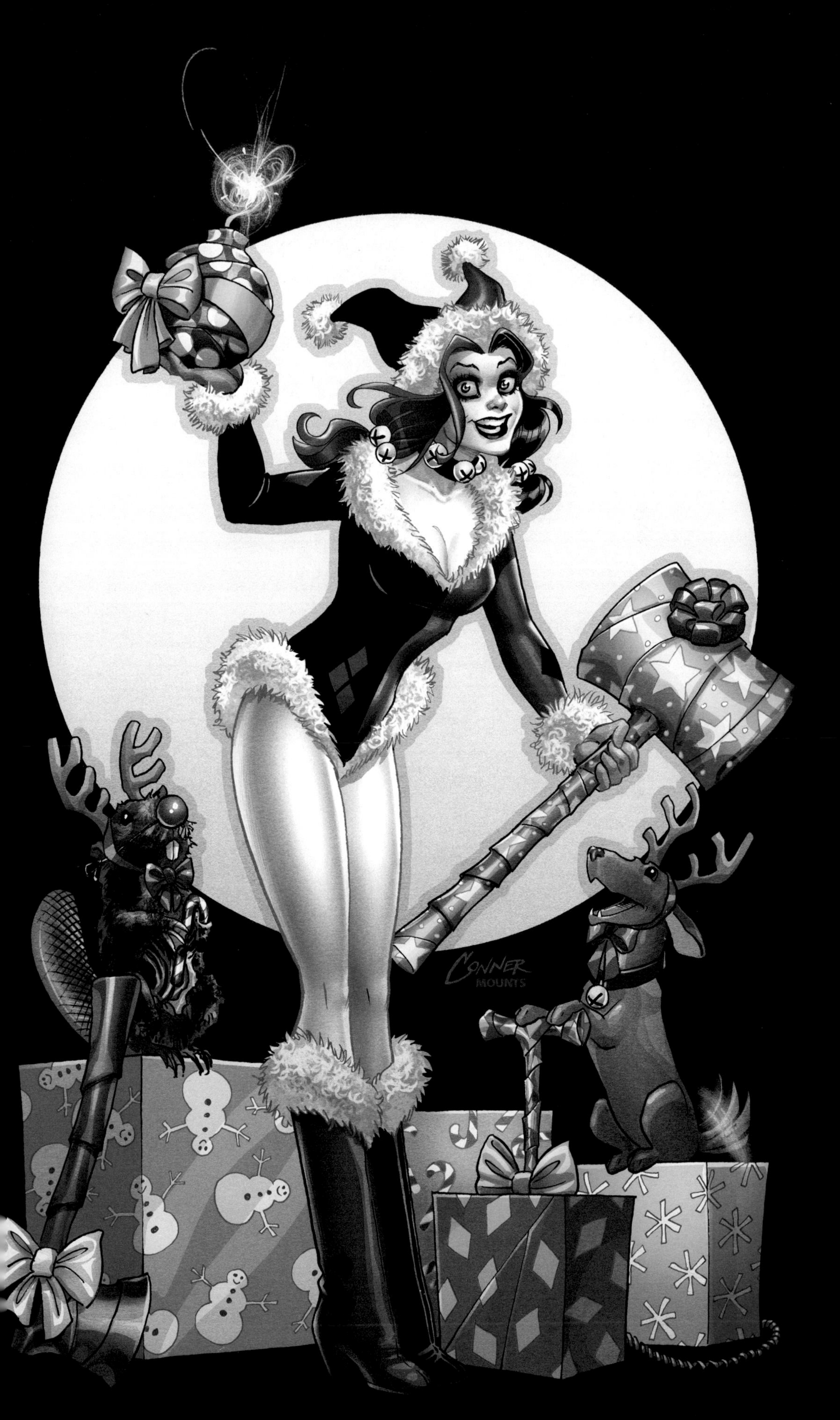
CONNER
MOUNTS

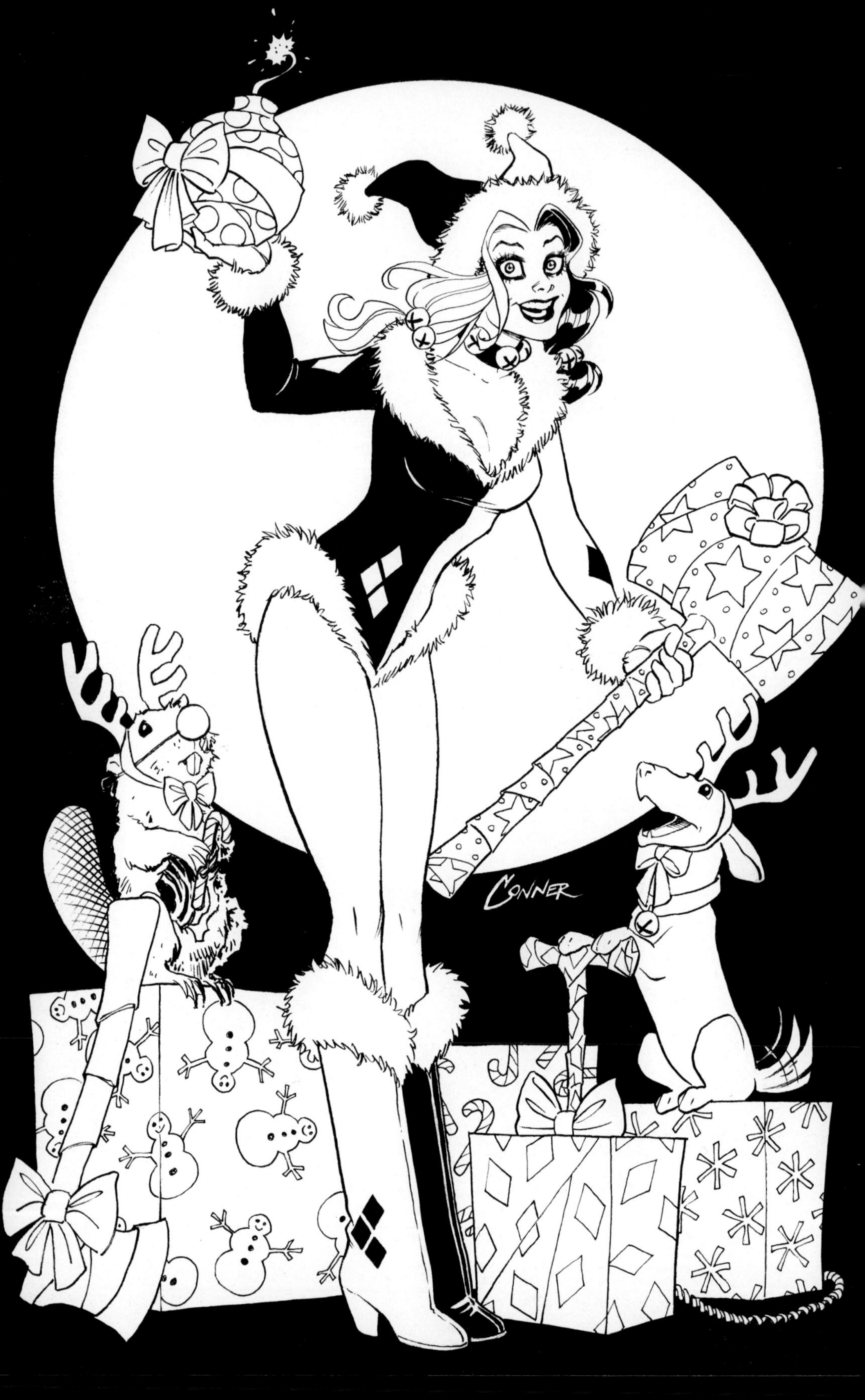
CONNER

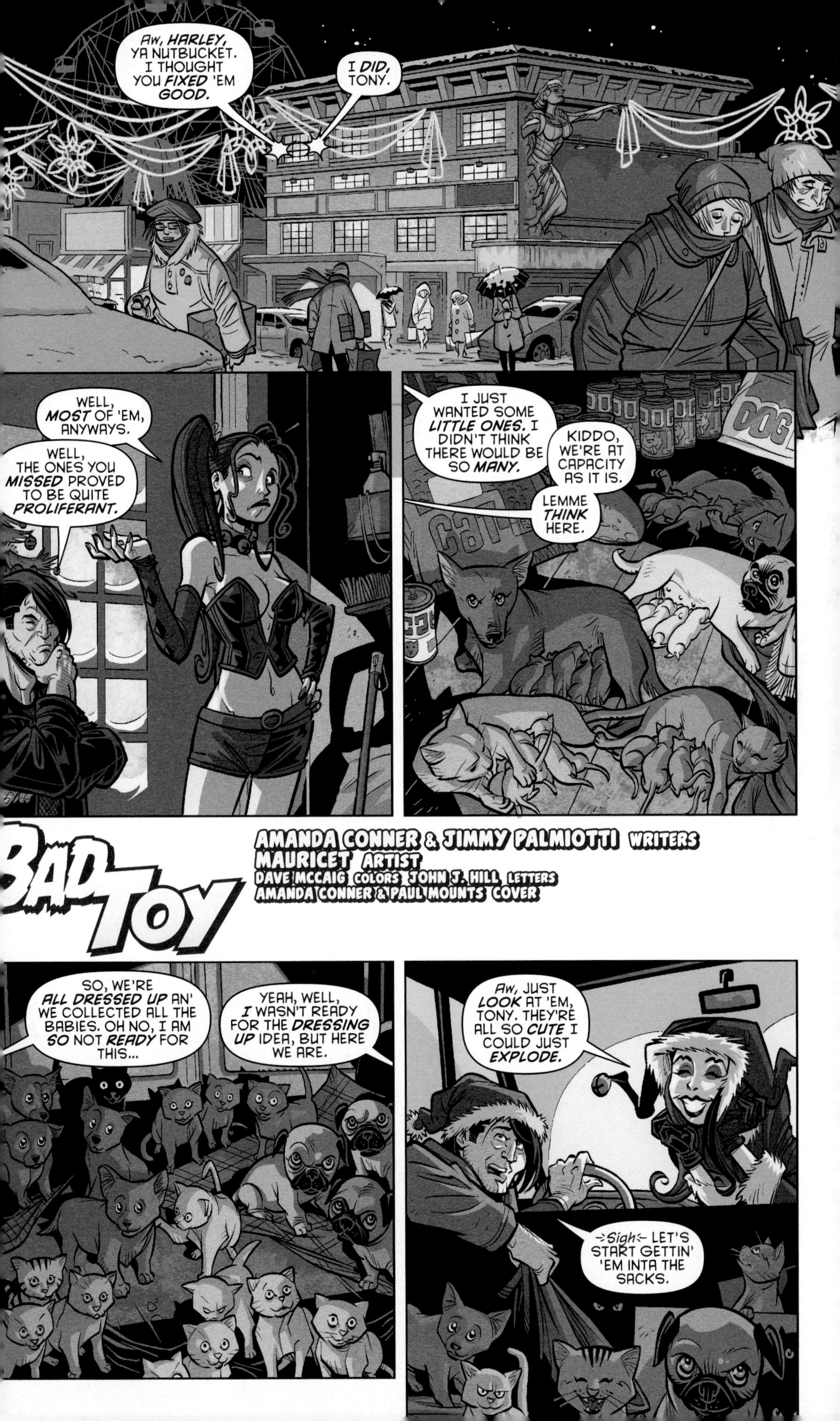

AW, HARLEY, YA NUTBUCKET. I THOUGHT YOU FIXED 'EM GOOD.
I DID, TONY.
WELL, MOST OF 'EM, ANYWAYS.
WELL, THE ONES YOU MISSED PROVED TO BE QUITE PROLIFERANT.
I JUST WANTED SOME LITTLE ONES. I DIDN'T THINK THERE WOULD BE SO MANY.
KIDDO, WE'RE AT CAPACITY AS IT IS.
LEMME THINK HERE.
DOG
BAD TOY
AMANDA CONNER & JIMMY PALMIOTTI WRITERS
MAURICET ARTIST
DAVE MCCAIG COLORS JOHN J. HILL LETTERS
AMANDA CONNER & PAUL MOUNTS COVER
SO, WE'RE ALL DRESSED UP AN' WE COLLECTED ALL THE BABIES. OH NO, I AM SO NOT READY FOR THIS...
YEAH, WELL, I WASN'T READY FOR THE DRESSING UP IDEA, BUT HERE WE ARE.
AW, JUST LOOK AT 'EM, TONY. THEY'RE ALL SO CUTE I COULD JUST EXPLODE.
SIGH LET'S START GETTIN' 'EM INTA THE SACKS.

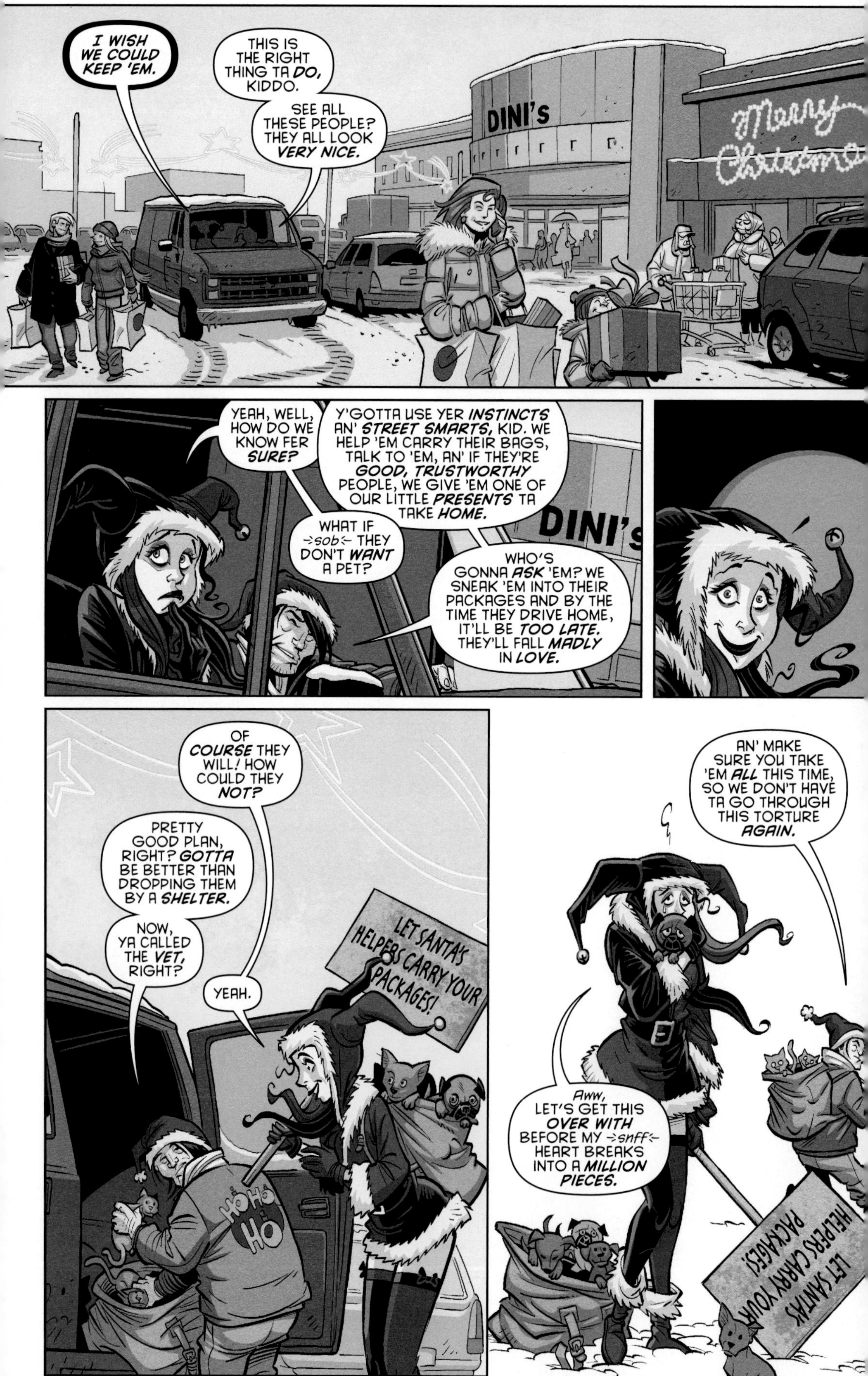
I WISH WE COULD KEEP 'EM.
THIS IS THE RIGHT THING TA DO, KIDDO.
SEE ALL THESE PEOPLE? THEY ALL LOOK VERY NICE.
DINI'S
Merry Christmas
YEAH, WELL, HOW DO WE KNOW FER SURE?
Y'GOTTA USE YER INSTINCTS AN' STREET SMARTS, KID. WE HELP 'EM CARRY THEIR BAGS, TALK TO 'EM, AN' IF THEY'RE GOOD, TRUSTWORTHY PEOPLE, WE GIVE 'EM ONE OF OUR LITTLE PRESENTS TA TAKE HOME.
WHAT IF ⇒sob⇐ THEY DON'T WANT A PET?
WHO'S GONNA ASK 'EM? WE SNEAK 'EM INTO THEIR PACKAGES AND BY THE TIME THEY DRIVE HOME, IT'LL BE TOO LATE. THEY'LL FALL MADLY IN LOVE.
DINI'S
OF COURSE THEY WILL! HOW COULD THEY NOT?
PRETTY GOOD PLAN, RIGHT? GOTTA BE BETTER THAN DROPPING THEM BY A SHELTER.
NOW, YA CALLED THE VET, RIGHT?
YEAH.
LET SANTA'S HELPERS CARRY YOUR PACKAGES!
HO HO HO
AN' MAKE SURE YOU TAKE 'EM ALL THIS TIME, SO WE DON'T HAVE TA GO THROUGH THIS TORTURE AGAIN.
Aww, LET'S GET THIS OVER WITH BEFORE MY ⇒snff⇐ HEART BREAKS INTO A MILLION PIECES.
LET SANTA'S HELPERS CARRY YOUR PACKAGES!

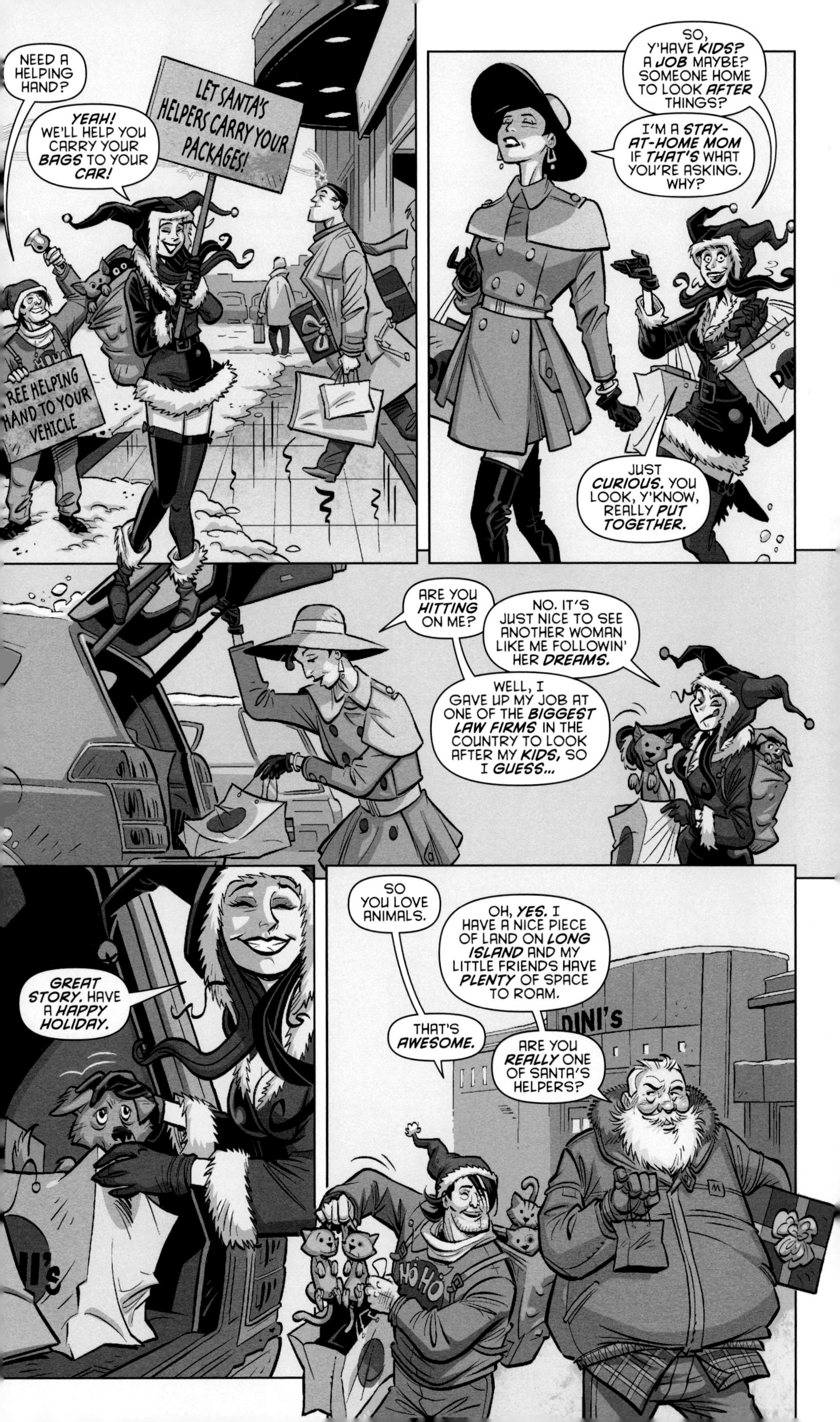
NEED A HELPING HAND?
YEAH! WE'LL HELP YOU CARRY YOUR BAGS TO YOUR CAR!
LET SANTA'S HELPERS CARRY YOUR PACKAGES!
REE HELPING HAND TO YOUR VEHICLE
SO, Y'HAVE KIDS? A JOB MAYBE? SOMEONE HOME TO LOOK AFTER THINGS?
I'M A STAY-AT-HOME MOM IF THAT'S WHAT YOU'RE ASKING. WHY?
JUST CURIOUS. YOU LOOK, Y'KNOW, REALLY PUT TOGETHER.
ARE YOU HITTING ON ME?
NO. IT'S JUST NICE TO SEE ANOTHER WOMAN LIKE ME FOLLOWIN' HER DREAMS.
WELL, I GAVE UP MY JOB AT ONE OF THE BIGGEST LAW FIRMS IN THE COUNTRY TO LOOK AFTER MY KIDS, SO I GUESS...
GREAT STORY. HAVE A HAPPY HOLIDAY.
SO YOU LOVE ANIMALS.
OH, YES. I HAVE A NICE PIECE OF LAND ON LONG ISLAND AND MY LITTLE FRIENDS HAVE PLENTY OF SPACE TO ROAM.
THAT'S AWESOME.
ARE YOU REALLY ONE OF SANTA'S HELPERS?
DINI'S
HO HO

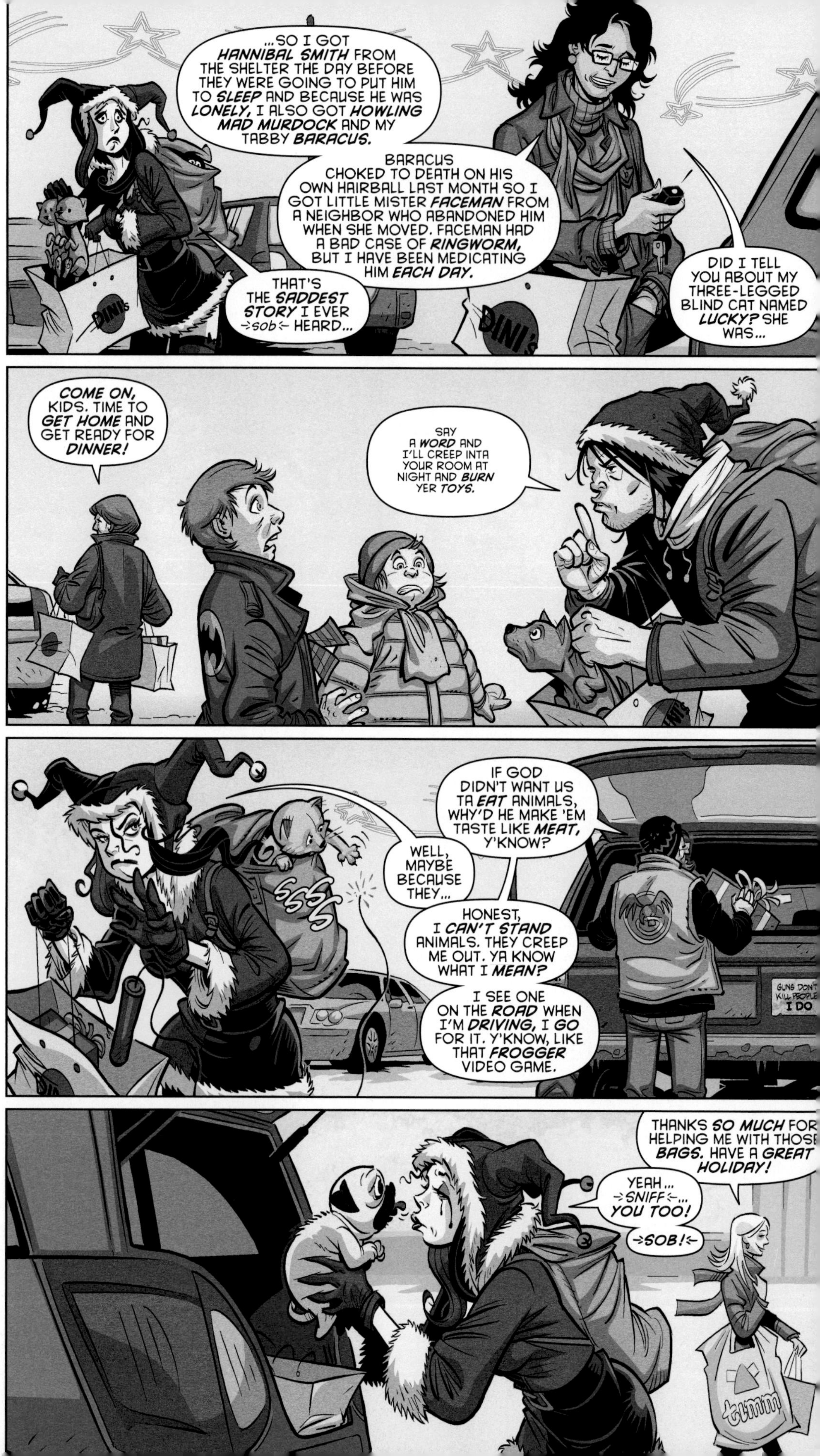
...SO I GOT HANNIBAL SMITH FROM THE SHELTER THE DAY BEFORE THEY WERE GOING TO PUT HIM TO SLEEP AND BECAUSE HE WAS LONELY, I ALSO GOT HOWLING MAD MURDOCK AND MY TABBY BARACUS.
BARACUS CHOKED TO DEATH ON HIS OWN HAIRBALL LAST MONTH SO I GOT LITTLE MISTER FACEMAN FROM A NEIGHBOR WHO ABANDONED HIM WHEN SHE MOVED. FACEMAN HAD A BAD CASE OF RINGWORM, BUT I HAVE BEEN MEDICATING HIM EACH DAY.
THAT'S THE SADDEST STORY I EVER >sob< HEARD...
DINI's
DINI's
DID I TELL YOU ABOUT MY THREE-LEGGED BLIND CAT NAMED LUCKY? SHE WAS...
COME ON, KIDS. TIME TO GET HOME AND GET READY FOR DINNER!
SAY A WORD AND I'LL CREEP INTA YOUR ROOM AT NIGHT AND BURN YER TOYS.
IF GOD DIDN'T WANT US TA EAT ANIMALS, WHY'D HE MAKE 'EM TASTE LIKE MEAT, Y'KNOW?
WELL, MAYBE BECAUSE THEY...
HONEST, I CAN'T STAND ANIMALS. THEY CREEP ME OUT. YA KNOW WHAT I MEAN?
I SEE ONE ON THE ROAD WHEN I'M DRIVING, I GO FOR IT. Y'KNOW, LIKE THAT FROGGER VIDEO GAME.
GUNS DON'T KILL PEOPLE I DO
THANKS SO MUCH FOR HELPING ME WITH THOSE BAGS. HAVE A GREAT HOLIDAY!
YEAH... >SNIFF<... YOU TOO!
>SOB!<
timm

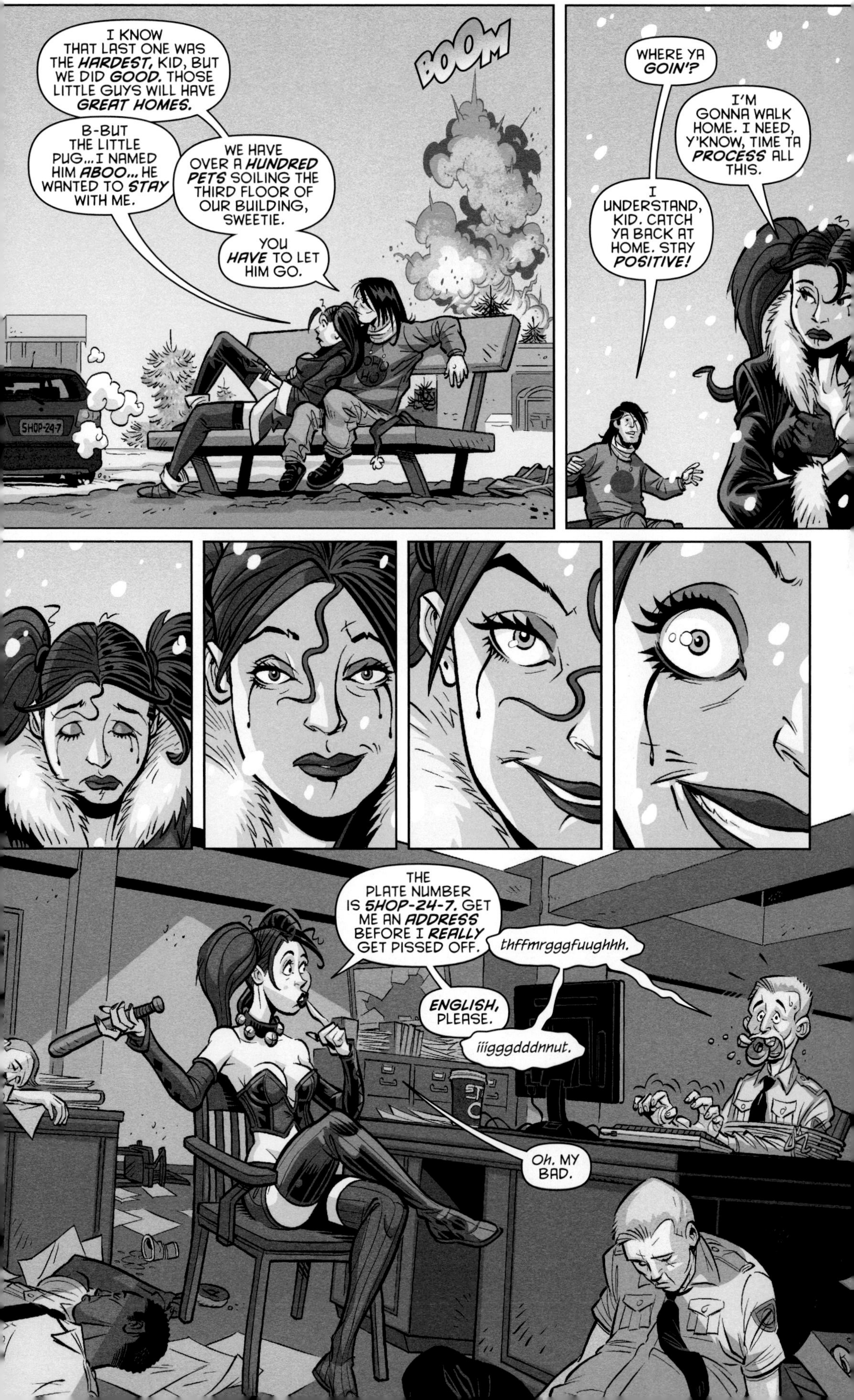
BOOM
I KNOW THAT LAST ONE WAS THE *HARDEST*, KID, BUT WE DID *GOOD*. THOSE LITTLE GUYS WILL HAVE *GREAT HOMES.*
B-BUT THE LITTLE PUG... I NAMED HIM *ABOO*... HE WANTED TO *STAY* WITH ME.
WE HAVE OVER A *HUNDRED PETS* SOILING THE THIRD FLOOR OF OUR BUILDING, SWEETIE.
YOU *HAVE* TO LET HIM GO.
SHOP-24-7
WHERE YA *GOIN'?*
I'M GONNA WALK HOME. I NEED, Y'KNOW, TIME TA *PROCESS* ALL THIS.
I UNDERSTAND, KID. CATCH YA BACK AT HOME. STAY *POSITIVE!*
THE PLATE NUMBER IS *SHOP-24-7*. GET ME AN *ADDRESS* BEFORE I *REALLY* GET PISSED OFF.
thffmrgggfuughhh.
ENGLISH, PLEASE.
iiigggdddnnut.
Oh. MY BAD.

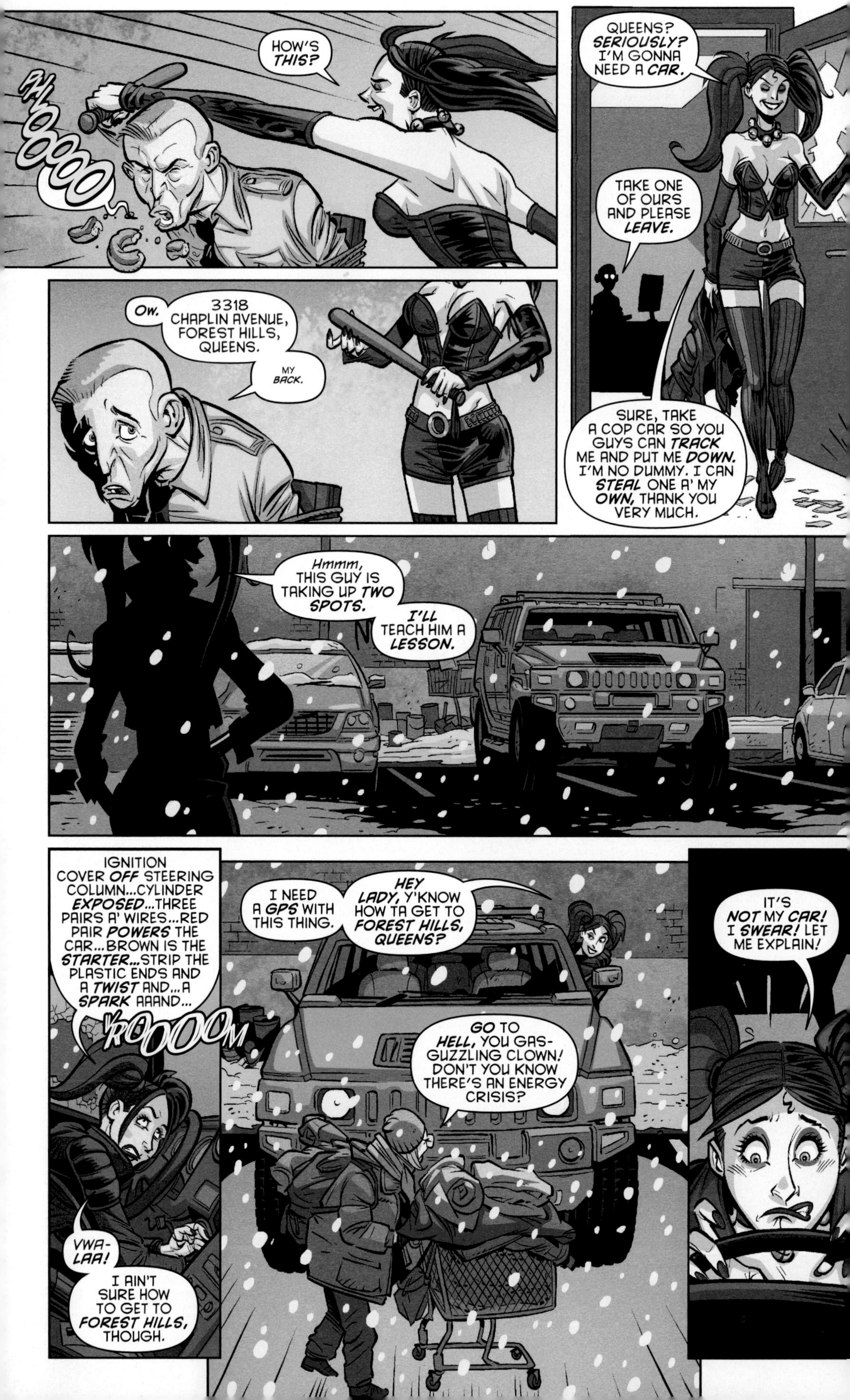
HOW'S THIS?
AHOOOOOO
Ow.
3318 CHAPLIN AVENUE, FOREST HILLS, QUEENS.
MY BACK.
QUEENS? SERIOUSLY? I'M GONNA NEED A CAR.
TAKE ONE OF OURS AND PLEASE LEAVE.
SURE, TAKE A COP CAR SO YOU GUYS CAN TRACK ME AND PUT ME DOWN. I'M NO DUMMY. I CAN STEAL ONE A' MY OWN, THANK YOU VERY MUCH.
Hmmm, THIS GUY IS TAKING UP TWO SPOTS.
I'LL TEACH HIM A LESSON.
IGNITION COVER OFF STEERING COLUMN...CYLINDER EXPOSED...THREE PAIRS A' WIRES...RED PAIR POWERS THE CAR...BROWN IS THE STARTER...STRIP THE PLASTIC ENDS AND A TWIST AND...A SPARK AAAND...
VROOOOOM
VWA-LAA!
I AIN'T SURE HOW TO GET TO FOREST HILLS, THOUGH.
I NEED A GPS WITH THIS THING.
HEY LADY, Y'KNOW HOW TA GET TO FOREST HILLS, QUEENS?
GO TO HELL, YOU GAS-GUZZLING CLOWN! DON'T YOU KNOW THERE'S AN ENERGY CRISIS?
IT'S NOT MY CAR! I SWEAR! LET ME EXPLAIN!

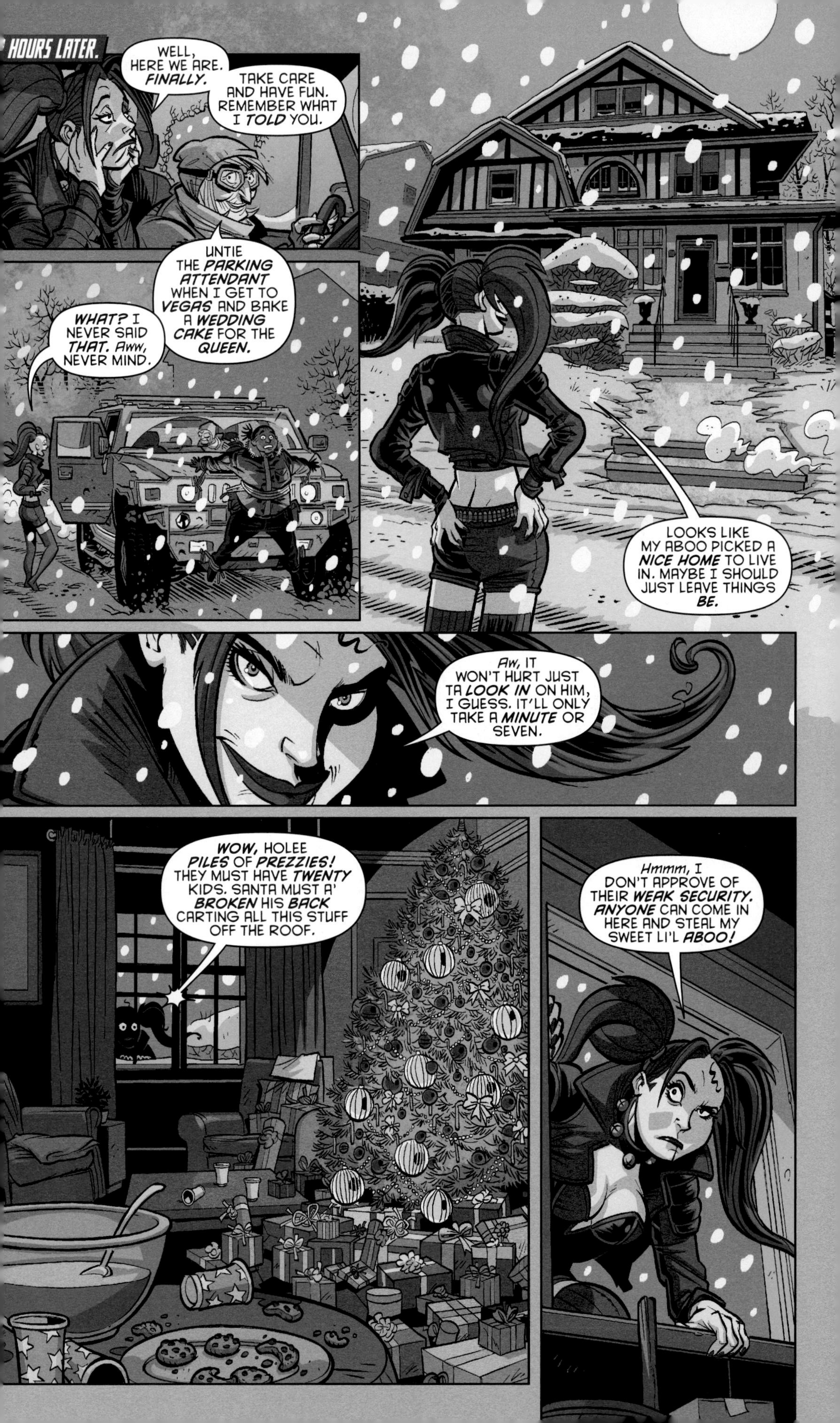
HOURS LATER.
WELL, HERE WE ARE. FINALLY.
TAKE CARE AND HAVE FUN. REMEMBER WHAT I TOLD YOU.
UNTIE THE PARKING ATTENDANT WHEN I GET TO VEGAS AND BAKE A WEDDING CAKE FOR THE QUEEN.
WHAT? I NEVER SAID THAT. Aww, NEVER MIND.
LOOKS LIKE MY ABOO PICKED A NICE HOME TO LIVE IN. MAYBE I SHOULD JUST LEAVE THINGS BE.
Aw, IT WON'T HURT JUST TA LOOK IN ON HIM, I GUESS. IT'LL ONLY TAKE A MINUTE OR SEVEN.
WOW, HOLEE PILES OF PREZZIES! THEY MUST HAVE TWENTY KIDS. SANTA MUST A' BROKEN HIS BACK CARTING ALL THIS STUFF OFF THE ROOF.
Hmmm, I DON'T APPROVE OF THEIR WEAK SECURITY. ANYONE CAN COME IN HERE AND STEAL MY SWEET LI'L ABOO!

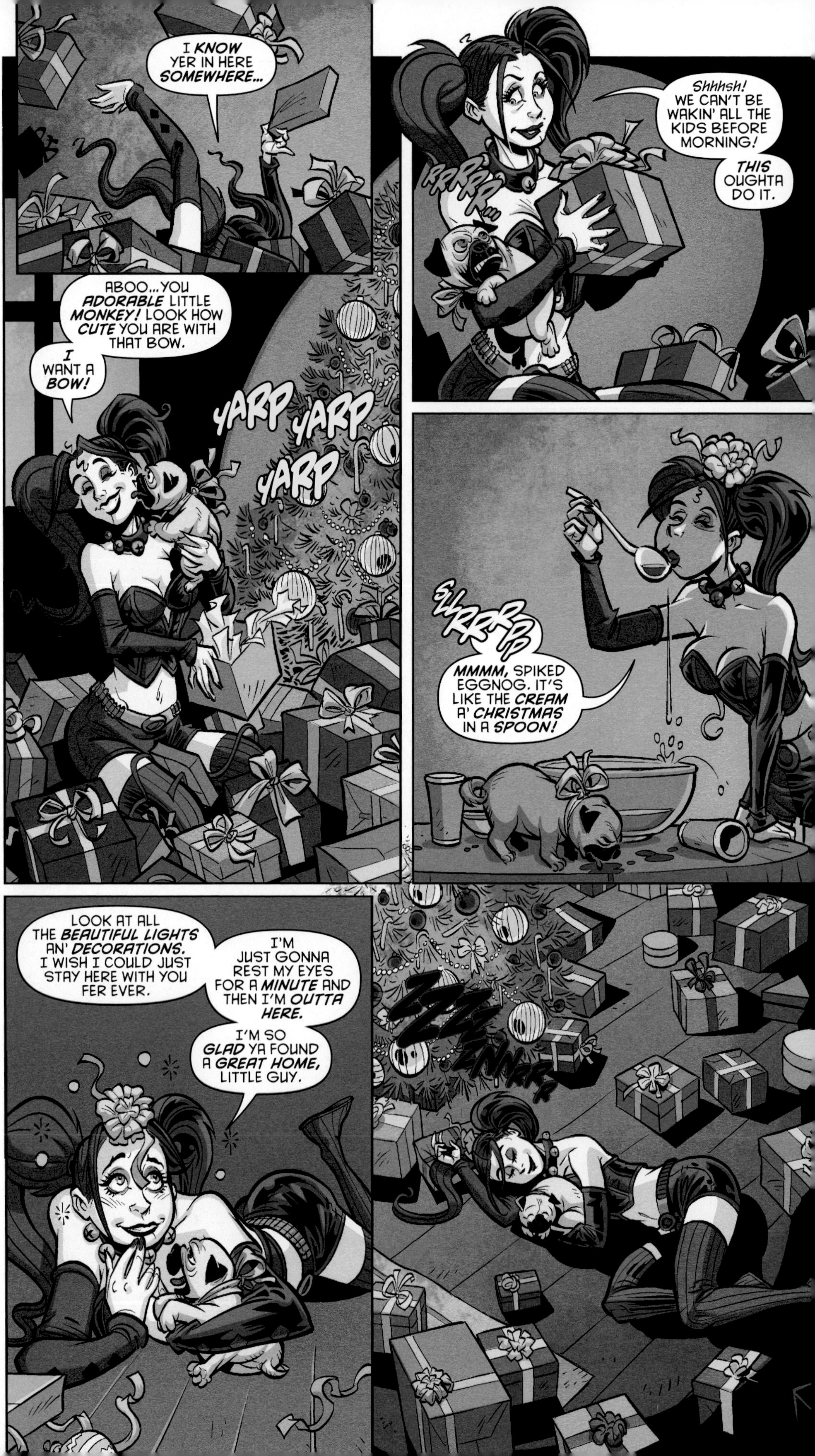
I KNOW YER IN HERE SOMEWHERE...
RRRRR...
Shhhsh! WE CAN'T BE WAKIN' ALL THE KIDS BEFORE MORNING!
THIS OUGHTA DO IT.
ABOO...YOU ADORABLE LITTLE MONKEY! LOOK HOW CUTE YOU ARE WITH THAT BOW.
I WANT A BOW!
YARP YARP YARP
SLURRRP
MMMM, SPIKED EGGNOG. IT'S LIKE THE CREAM A' CHRISTMAS IN A SPOON!
LOOK AT ALL THE BEAUTIFUL LIGHTS AN' DECORATIONS. I WISH I COULD JUST STAY HERE WITH YOU FER EVER.
I'M JUST GONNA REST MY EYES FOR A MINUTE AND THEN I'M OUTTA HERE.
I'M SO GLAD YA FOUND A GREAT HOME, LITTLE GUY.

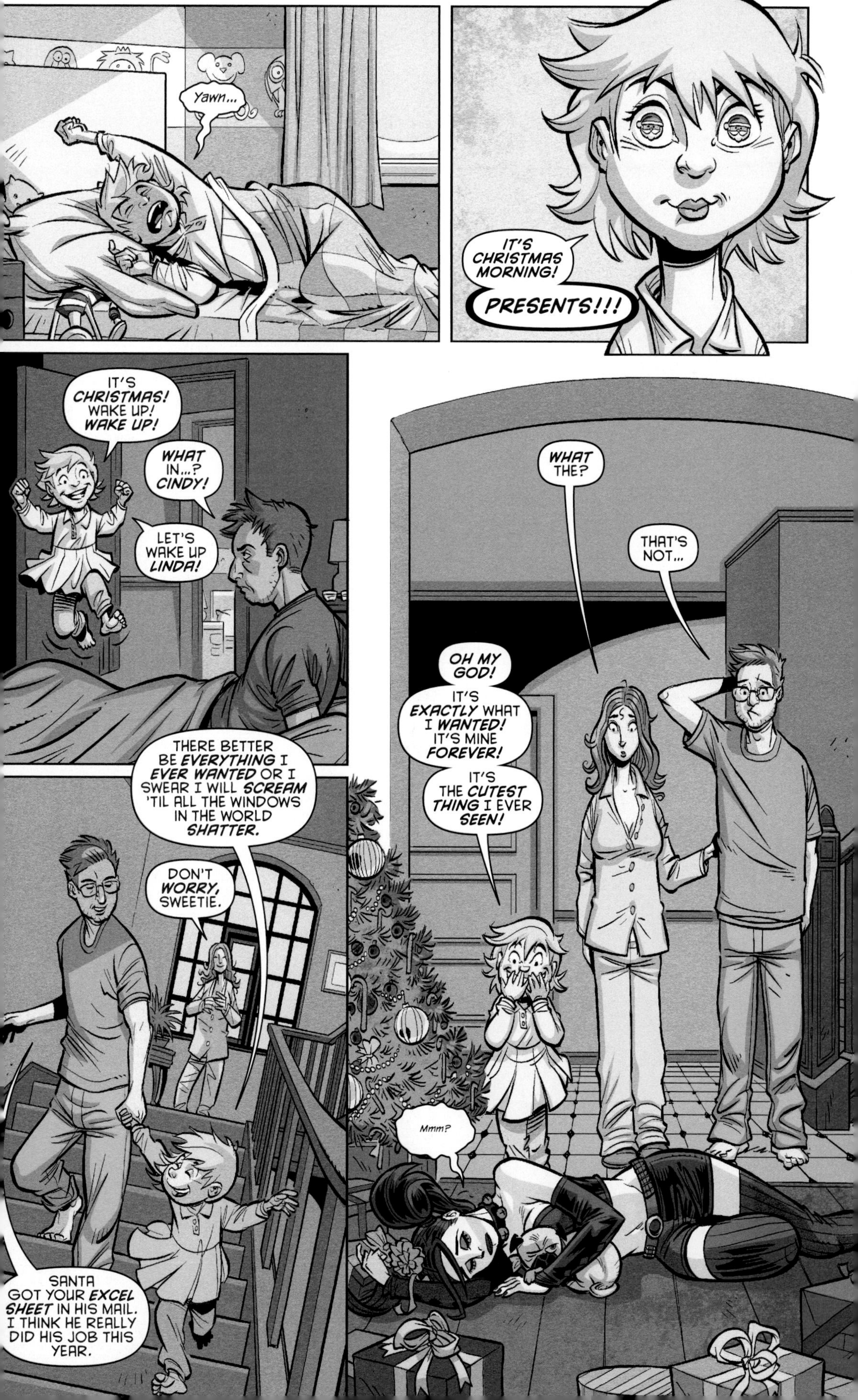
Yawn...
IT'S CHRISTMAS MORNING!
PRESENTS!!!
IT'S CHRISTMAS! WAKE UP! WAKE UP!
WHAT IN...? CINDY!
LET'S WAKE UP LINDA!
THERE BETTER BE EVERYTHING I EVER WANTED OR I SWEAR I WILL SCREAM 'TIL ALL THE WINDOWS IN THE WORLD SHATTER.
DON'T WORRY, SWEETIE.
SANTA GOT YOUR EXCEL SHEET IN HIS MAIL. I THINK HE REALLY DID HIS JOB THIS YEAR.
WHAT THE?
THAT'S NOT...
OH MY GOD!
IT'S EXACTLY WHAT I WANTED! IT'S MINE FOREVER!
IT'S THE CUTEST THING I EVER SEEN!
Mmm?

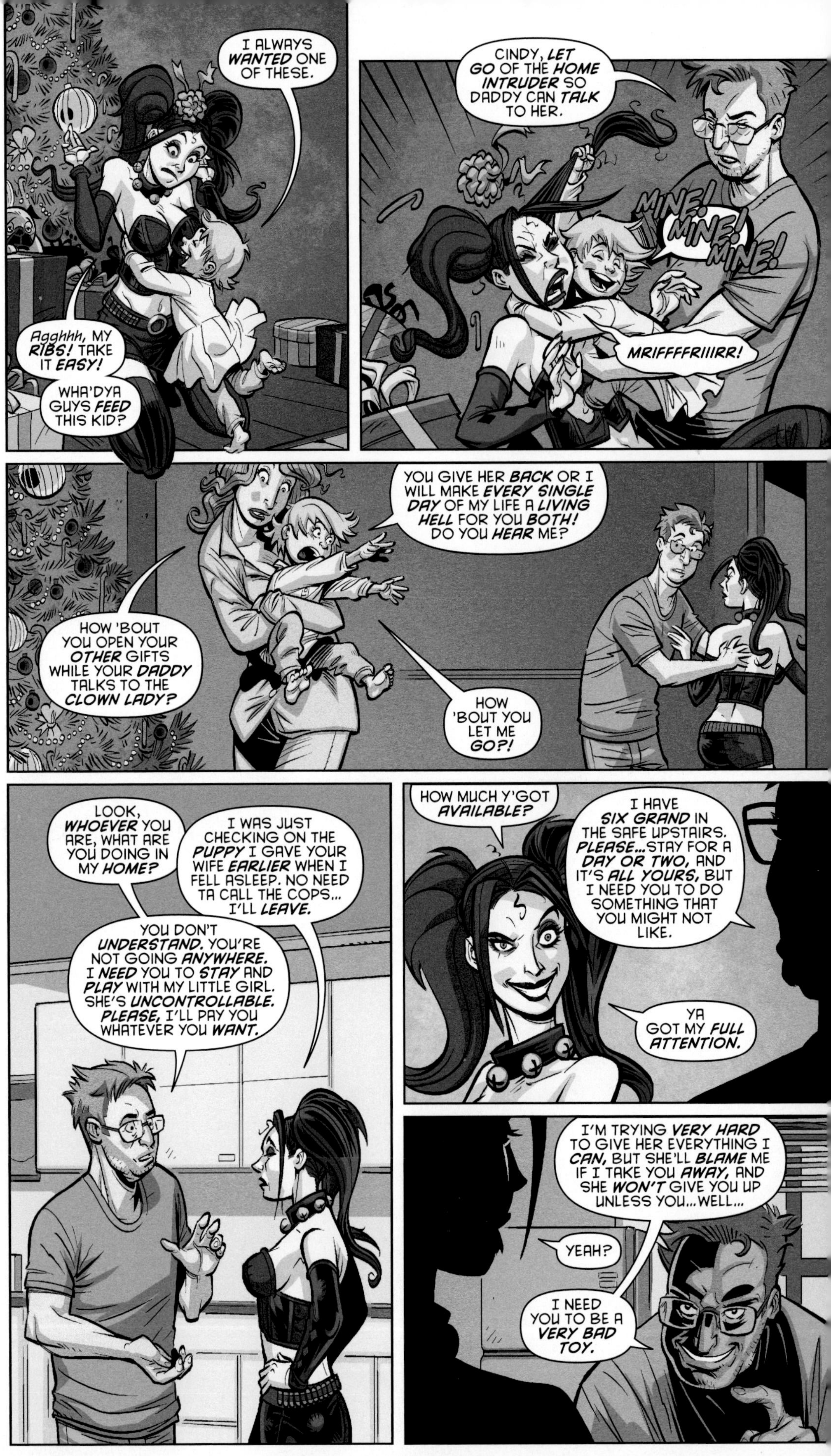
I ALWAYS WANTED ONE OF THESE.
Agghhh, MY RIBS! TAKE IT EASY!
WHA'DYA GUYS FEED THIS KID?
CINDY, LET GO OF THE HOME INTRUDER SO DADDY CAN TALK TO HER.
MINE! MINE! MINE!
MRIFFFFRIIIRR!
YOU GIVE HER BACK OR I WILL MAKE EVERY SINGLE DAY OF MY LIFE A LIVING HELL FOR YOU BOTH! DO YOU HEAR ME?
HOW 'BOUT YOU OPEN YOUR OTHER GIFTS WHILE YOUR DADDY TALKS TO THE CLOWN LADY?
HOW 'BOUT YOU LET ME GO?!
LOOK, WHOEVER YOU ARE, WHAT ARE YOU DOING IN MY HOME?
I WAS JUST CHECKING ON THE PUPPY I GAVE YOUR WIFE EARLIER WHEN I FELL ASLEEP. NO NEED TA CALL THE COPS... I'LL LEAVE.
YOU DON'T UNDERSTAND. YOU'RE NOT GOING ANYWHERE. I NEED YOU TO STAY AND PLAY WITH MY LITTLE GIRL. SHE'S UNCONTROLLABLE. PLEASE, I'LL PAY YOU WHATEVER YOU WANT.
HOW MUCH Y'GOT AVAILABLE?
I HAVE SIX GRAND IN THE SAFE UPSTAIRS. PLEASE...STAY FOR A DAY OR TWO, AND IT'S ALL YOURS, BUT I NEED YOU TO DO SOMETHING THAT YOU MIGHT NOT LIKE.
YA GOT MY FULL ATTENTION.
I'M TRYING VERY HARD TO GIVE HER EVERYTHING I CAN, BUT SHE'LL BLAME ME IF I TAKE YOU AWAY, AND SHE WON'T GIVE YOU UP UNLESS YOU...WELL...
YEAH?
I NEED YOU TO BE A VERY BAD TOY.

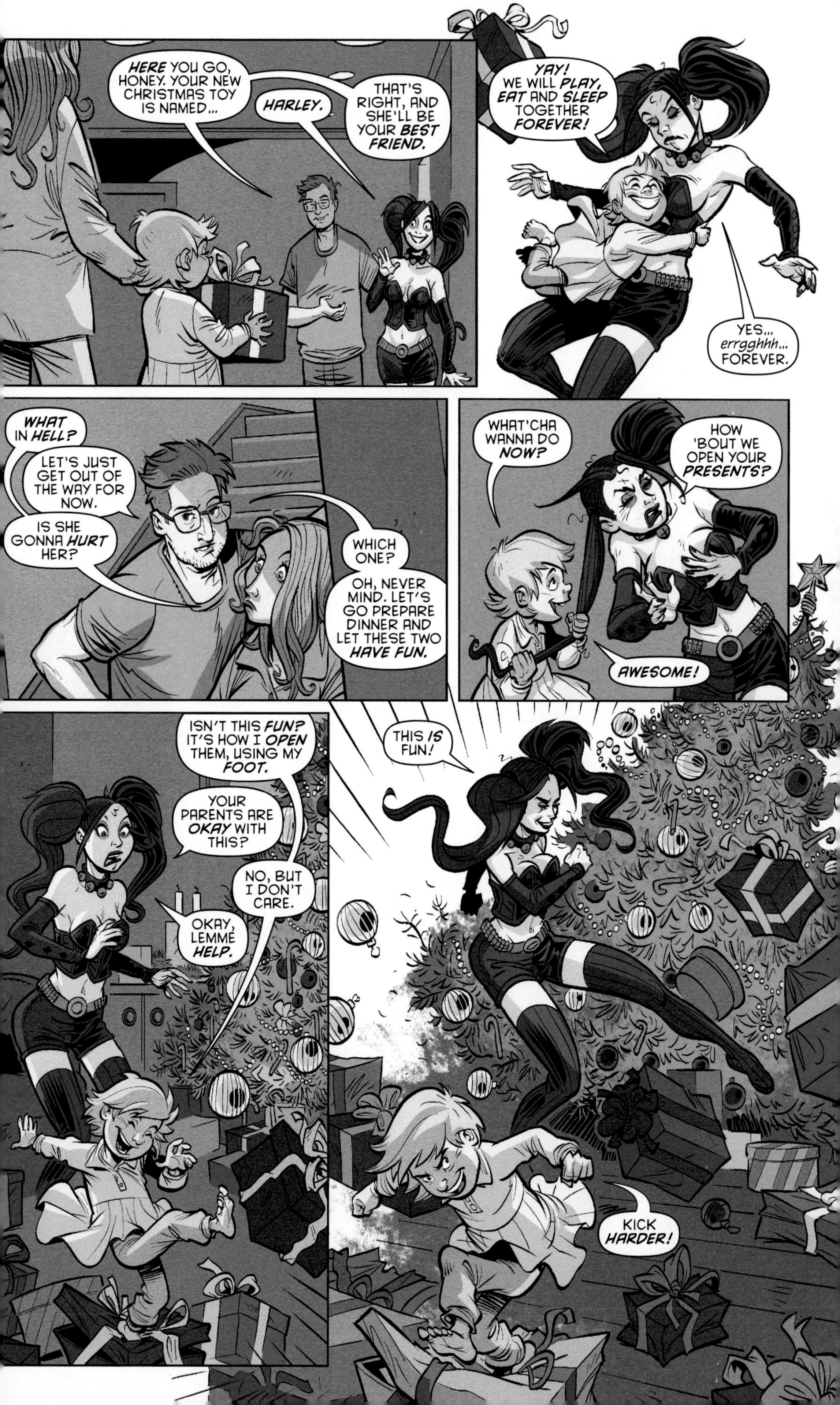
HERE YOU GO, HONEY. YOUR NEW CHRISTMAS TOY IS NAMED...
HARLEY.
THAT'S RIGHT, AND SHE'LL BE YOUR BEST FRIEND.
YAY! WE WILL PLAY, EAT AND SLEEP TOGETHER FOREVER!
YES... errgghhh... FOREVER.
WHAT IN HELL?
LET'S JUST GET OUT OF THE WAY FOR NOW.
IS SHE GONNA HURT HER?
WHICH ONE?
OH, NEVER MIND. LET'S GO PREPARE DINNER AND LET THESE TWO HAVE FUN.
WHAT'CHA WANNA DO NOW?
HOW 'BOUT WE OPEN YOUR PRESENTS?
AWESOME!
ISN'T THIS FUN? IT'S HOW I OPEN THEM, USING MY FOOT.
YOUR PARENTS ARE OKAY WITH THIS?
NO, BUT I DON'T CARE.
OKAY, LEMME HELP.
THIS IS FUN!
KICK HARDER!

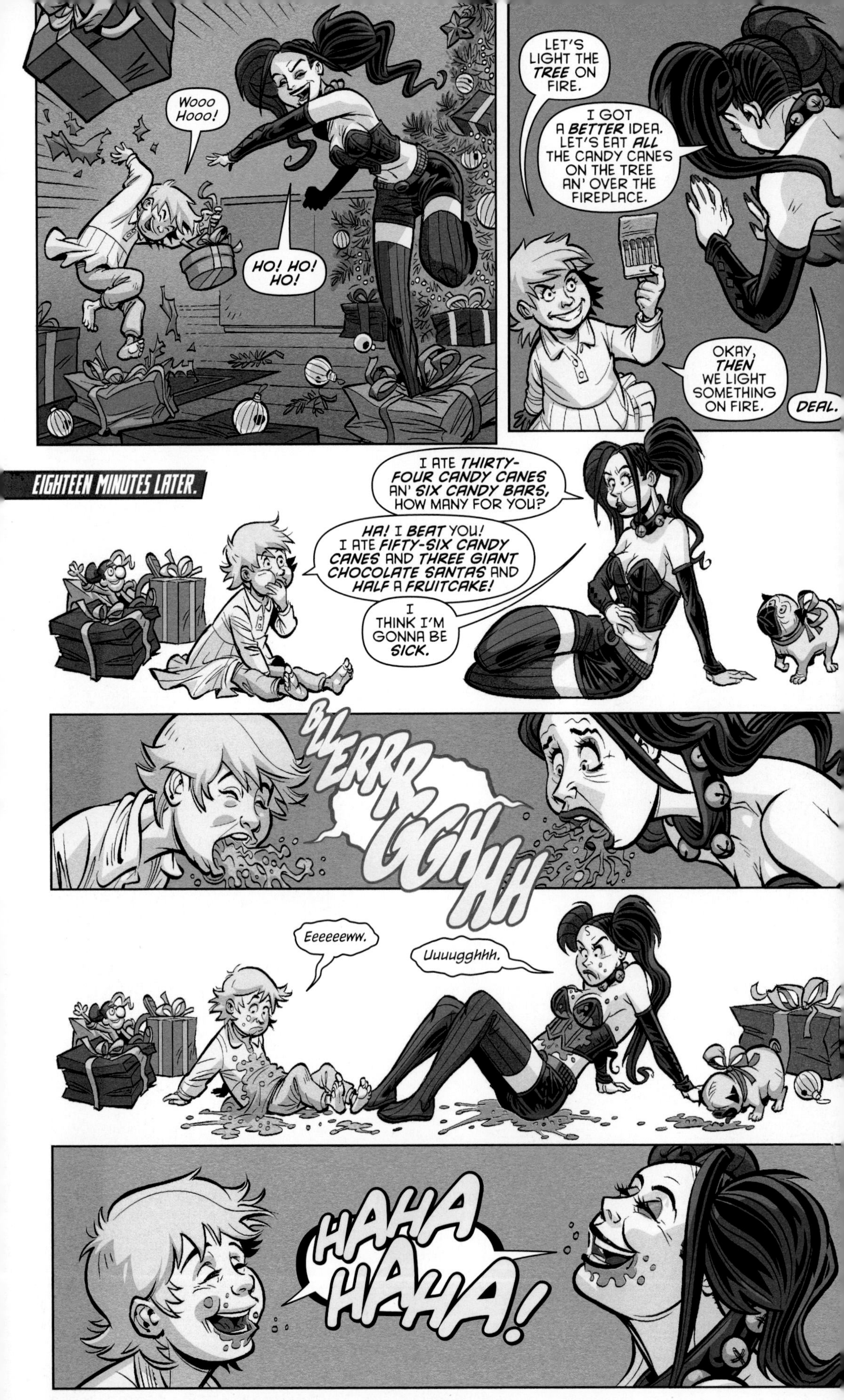
Wooo Hooo!
HO! HO! HO!
LET'S LIGHT THE *TREE* ON FIRE.
I GOT A *BETTER* IDEA. LET'S EAT *ALL* THE CANDY CANES ON THE TREE AN' OVER THE FIREPLACE.
OKAY, *THEN* WE LIGHT SOMETHING ON FIRE.
DEAL.
EIGHTEEN MINUTES LATER.
I ATE *THIRTY-FOUR CANDY CANES* AN' *SIX CANDY BARS*, HOW MANY FOR YOU?
HA! I *BEAT* YOU! I ATE *FIFTY-SIX CANDY CANES* AND *THREE GIANT CHOCOLATE SANTAS* AND *HALF* A *FRUITCAKE!*
I THINK I'M GONNA BE *SICK.*
BLEERRRGGHHH
Eeeeeeww.
Uuuugghhh.
HAHA HAHA!

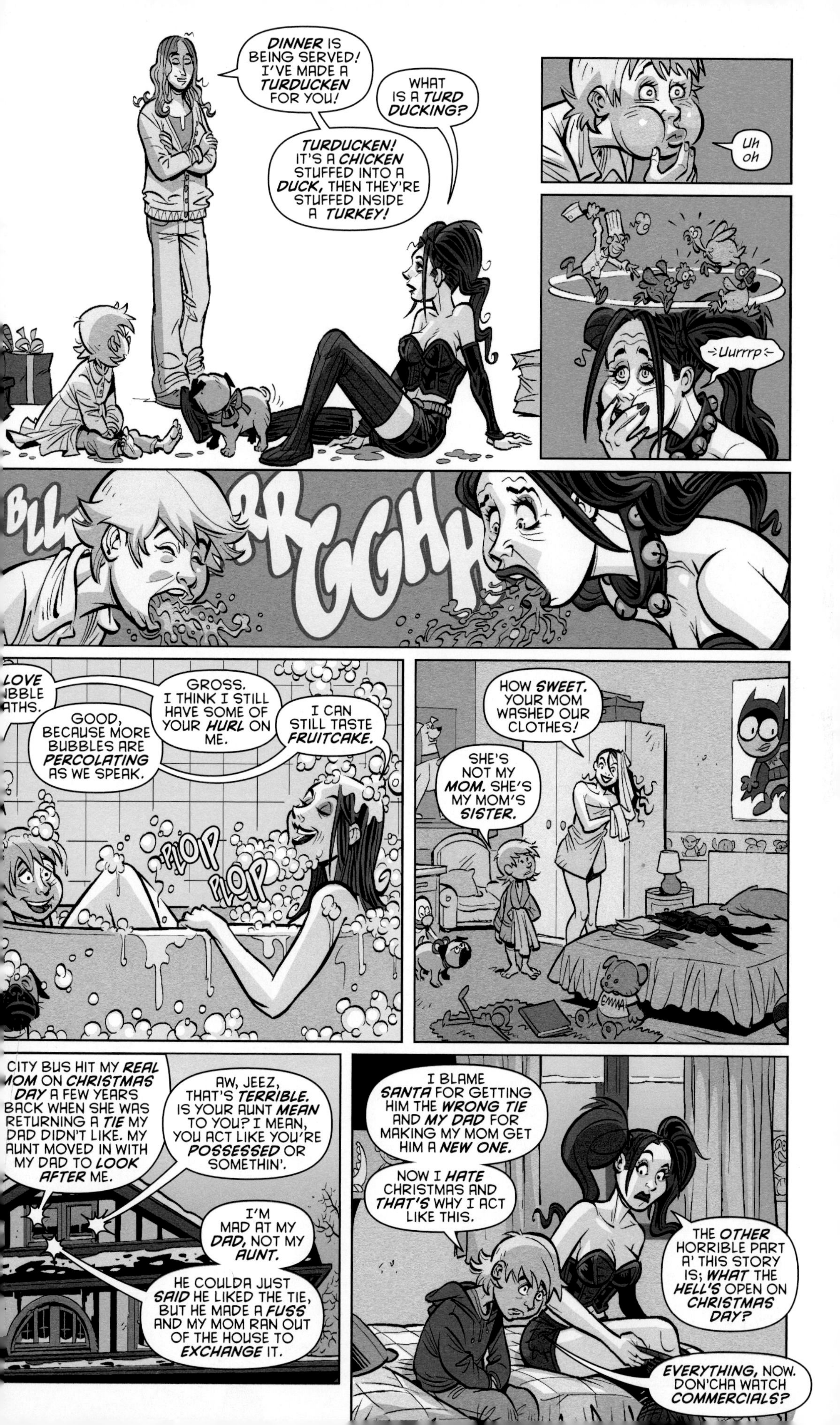
DINNER IS BEING SERVED! I'VE MADE A TURDUCKEN FOR YOU!
WHAT IS A TURD DUCKING?
TURDUCKEN! IT'S A CHICKEN STUFFED INTO A DUCK, THEN THEY'RE STUFFED INSIDE A TURKEY!
Uh oh
Uurrrp
BLURRRGGHH
LOVE BUBBLE BATHS.
GROSS. I THINK I STILL HAVE SOME OF YOUR HURL ON ME.
GOOD, BECAUSE MORE BUBBLES ARE PERCOLATING AS WE SPEAK.
I CAN STILL TASTE FRUITCAKE.
PLOIP
PLOIP
HOW SWEET. YOUR MOM WASHED OUR CLOTHES!
SHE'S NOT MY MOM. SHE'S MY MOM'S SISTER.
EMMA
CITY BUS HIT MY REAL MOM ON CHRISTMAS DAY A FEW YEARS BACK WHEN SHE WAS RETURNING A TIE MY DAD DIDN'T LIKE. MY AUNT MOVED IN WITH MY DAD TO LOOK AFTER ME.
AW, JEEZ, THAT'S TERRIBLE. IS YOUR AUNT MEAN TO YOU? I MEAN, YOU ACT LIKE YOU'RE POSSESSED OR SOMETHIN'.
I'M MAD AT MY DAD, NOT MY AUNT.
HE COULDA JUST SAID HE LIKED THE TIE, BUT HE MADE A FUSS AND MY MOM RAN OUT OF THE HOUSE TO EXCHANGE IT.
I BLAME SANTA FOR GETTING HIM THE WRONG TIE AND MY DAD FOR MAKING MY MOM GET HIM A NEW ONE.
NOW I HATE CHRISTMAS AND THAT'S WHY I ACT LIKE THIS.
THE OTHER HORRIBLE PART A' THIS STORY IS; WHAT THE HELL'S OPEN ON CHRISTMAS DAY?
EVERYTHING, NOW. DON'CHA WATCH COMMERCIALS?

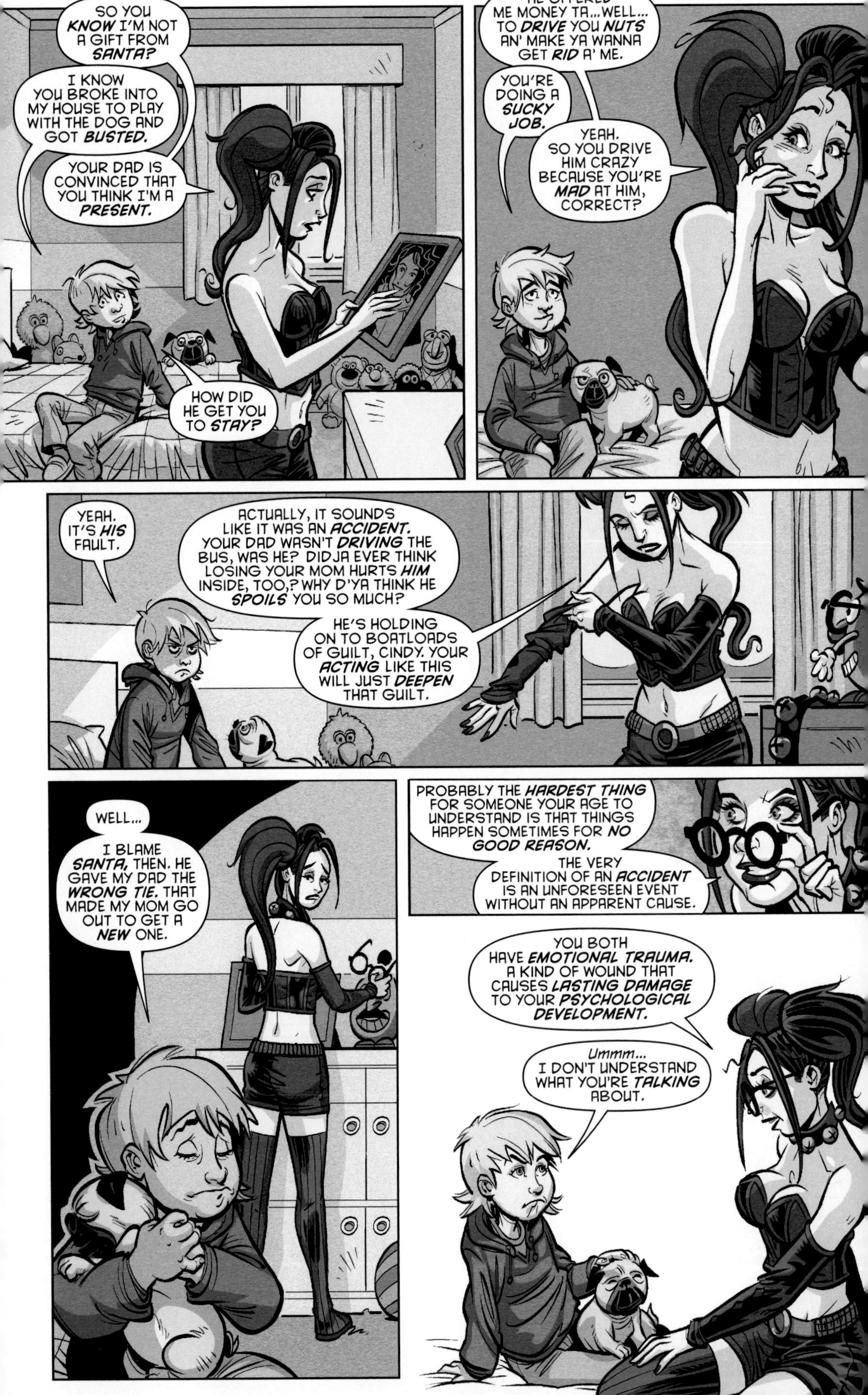
SO YOU KNOW I'M NOT A GIFT FROM SANTA?
I KNOW YOU BROKE INTO MY HOUSE TO PLAY WITH THE DOG AND GOT BUSTED.
YOUR DAD IS CONVINCED THAT YOU THINK I'M A PRESENT.
HOW DID HE GET YOU TO STAY?
HE OFFERED ME MONEY TA...WELL... TO DRIVE YOU NUTS AN' MAKE YA WANNA GET RID A' ME.
YOU'RE DOING A SUCKY JOB.
YEAH.
SO YOU DRIVE HIM CRAZY BECAUSE YOU'RE MAD AT HIM, CORRECT?
YEAH. IT'S HIS FAULT.
ACTUALLY, IT SOUNDS LIKE IT WAS AN ACCIDENT. YOUR DAD WASN'T DRIVING THE BUS, WAS HE? DIDJA EVER THINK LOSING YOUR MOM HURTS HIM INSIDE, TOO,? WHY D'YA THINK HE SPOILS YOU SO MUCH?
HE'S HOLDING ON TO BOATLOADS OF GUILT, CINDY. YOUR ACTING LIKE THIS WILL JUST DEEPEN THAT GUILT.
WELL...
I BLAME SANTA, THEN. HE GAVE MY DAD THE WRONG TIE. THAT MADE MY MOM GO OUT TO GET A NEW ONE.
PROBABLY THE HARDEST THING FOR SOMEONE YOUR AGE TO UNDERSTAND IS THAT THINGS HAPPEN SOMETIMES FOR NO GOOD REASON.
THE VERY DEFINITION OF AN ACCIDENT IS AN UNFORESEEN EVENT WITHOUT AN APPARENT CAUSE.
YOU BOTH HAVE EMOTIONAL TRAUMA. A KIND OF WOUND THAT CAUSES LASTING DAMAGE TO YOUR PSYCHOLOGICAL DEVELOPMENT.
Ummm... I DON'T UNDERSTAND WHAT YOU'RE TALKING ABOUT.

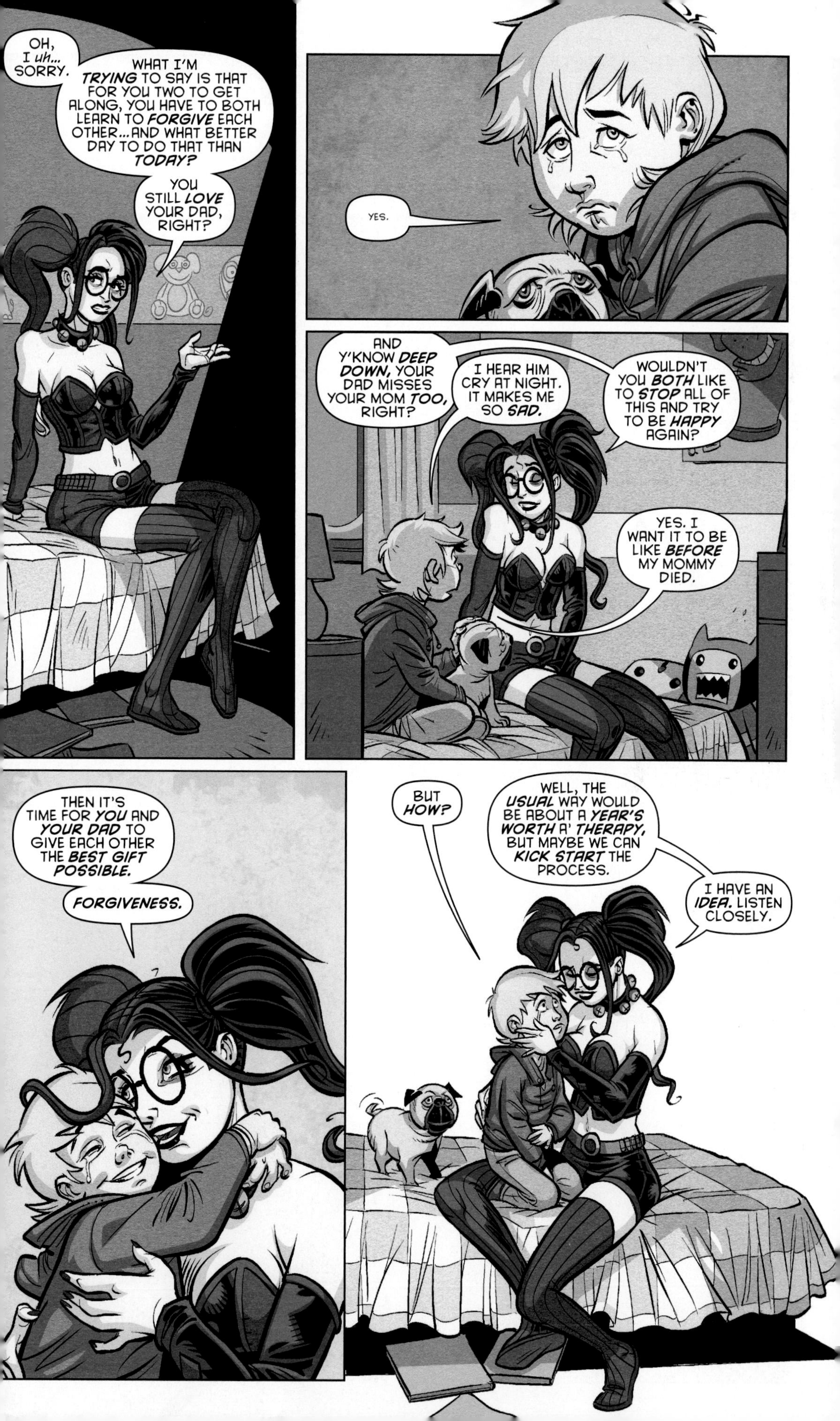
OH, I uh... SORRY.
WHAT I'M TRYING TO SAY IS THAT FOR YOU TWO TO GET ALONG, YOU HAVE TO BOTH LEARN TO FORGIVE EACH OTHER... AND WHAT BETTER DAY TO DO THAT THAN TODAY?
YOU STILL LOVE YOUR DAD, RIGHT?
YES.
AND Y'KNOW DEEP DOWN, YOUR DAD MISSES YOUR MOM TOO, RIGHT?
I HEAR HIM CRY AT NIGHT. IT MAKES ME SO SAD.
WOULDN'T YOU BOTH LIKE TO STOP ALL OF THIS AND TRY TO BE HAPPY AGAIN?
YES. I WANT IT TO BE LIKE BEFORE MY MOMMY DIED.
THEN IT'S TIME FOR YOU AND YOUR DAD TO GIVE EACH OTHER THE BEST GIFT POSSIBLE.
FORGIVENESS.
BUT HOW?
WELL, THE USUAL WAY WOULD BE ABOUT A YEAR'S WORTH A' THERAPY, BUT MAYBE WE CAN KICK START THE PROCESS.
I HAVE AN IDEA. LISTEN CLOSELY.

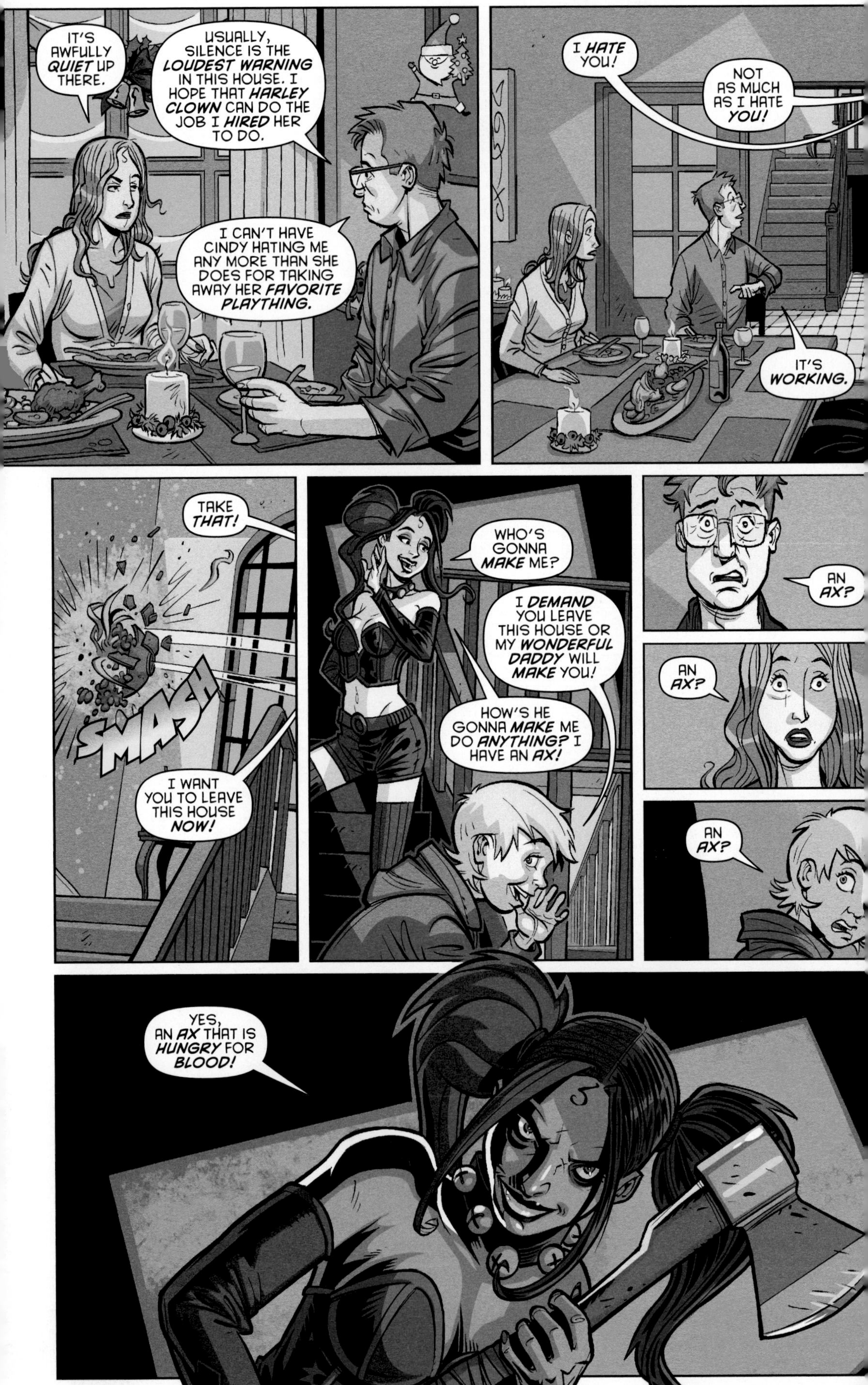
IT'S AWFULLY QUIET UP THERE.
USUALLY, SILENCE IS THE LOUDEST WARNING IN THIS HOUSE. I HOPE THAT HARLEY CLOWN CAN DO THE JOB I HIRED HER TO DO.
I CAN'T HAVE CINDY HATING ME ANY MORE THAN SHE DOES FOR TAKING AWAY HER FAVORITE PLAYTHING.
I HATE YOU!
NOT AS MUCH AS I HATE YOU!
IT'S WORKING.
TAKE THAT!
SMASH
I WANT YOU TO LEAVE THIS HOUSE NOW!
WHO'S GONNA MAKE ME?
I DEMAND YOU LEAVE THIS HOUSE OR MY WONDERFUL DADDY WILL MAKE YOU!
HOW'S HE GONNA MAKE ME DO ANYTHING? I HAVE AN AX!
AN AX?
AN AX?
AN AX?
YES, AN AX THAT IS HUNGRY FOR BLOOD!

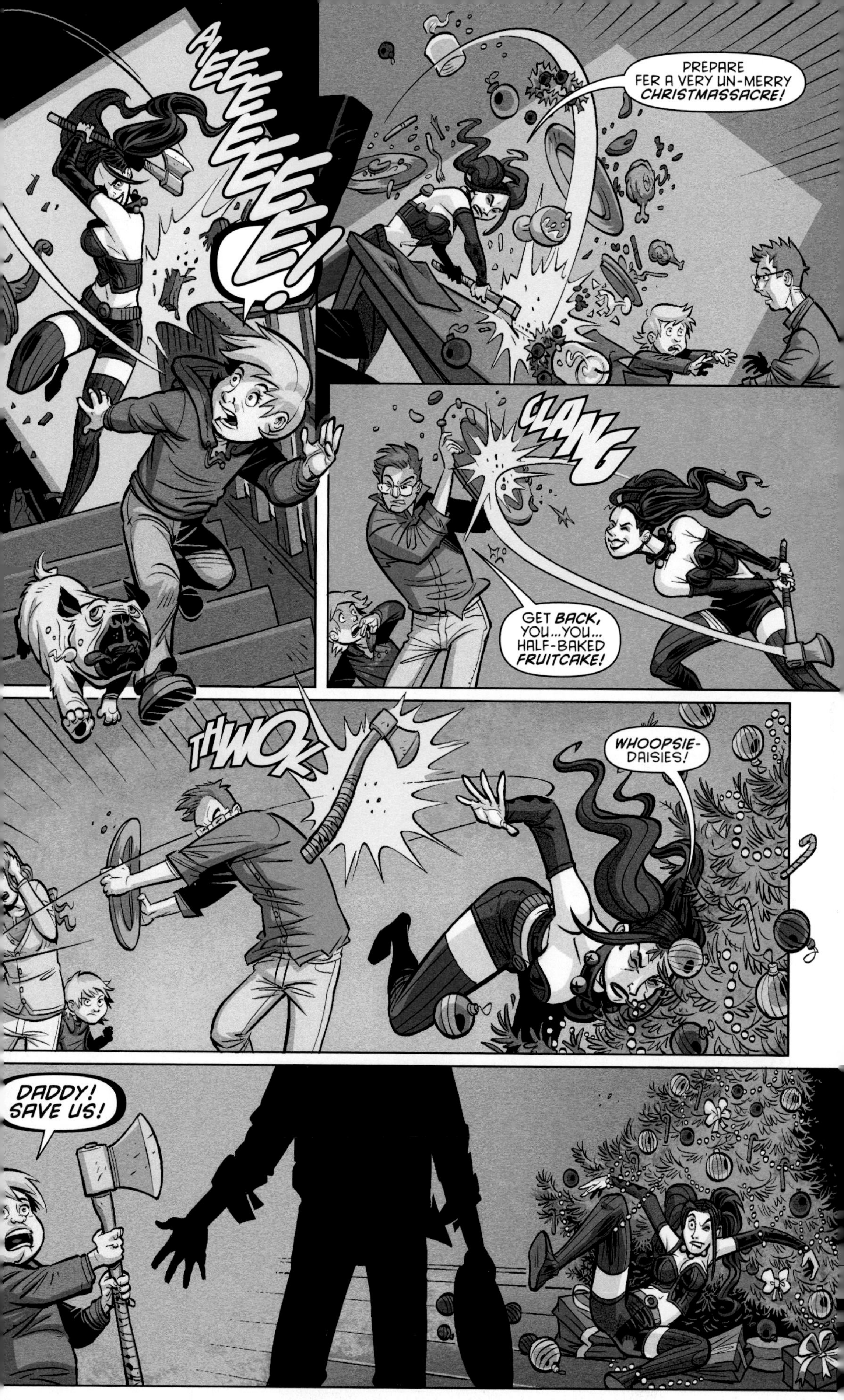
AEEEEEEEE!
PREPARE FER A VERY UN-MERRY CHRISTMASSACRE!
CLANG
GET BACK, YOU...YOU... HALF-BAKED FRUITCAKE!
THWOK
WHOOPSIE-DAISIES!
DADDY! SAVE US!

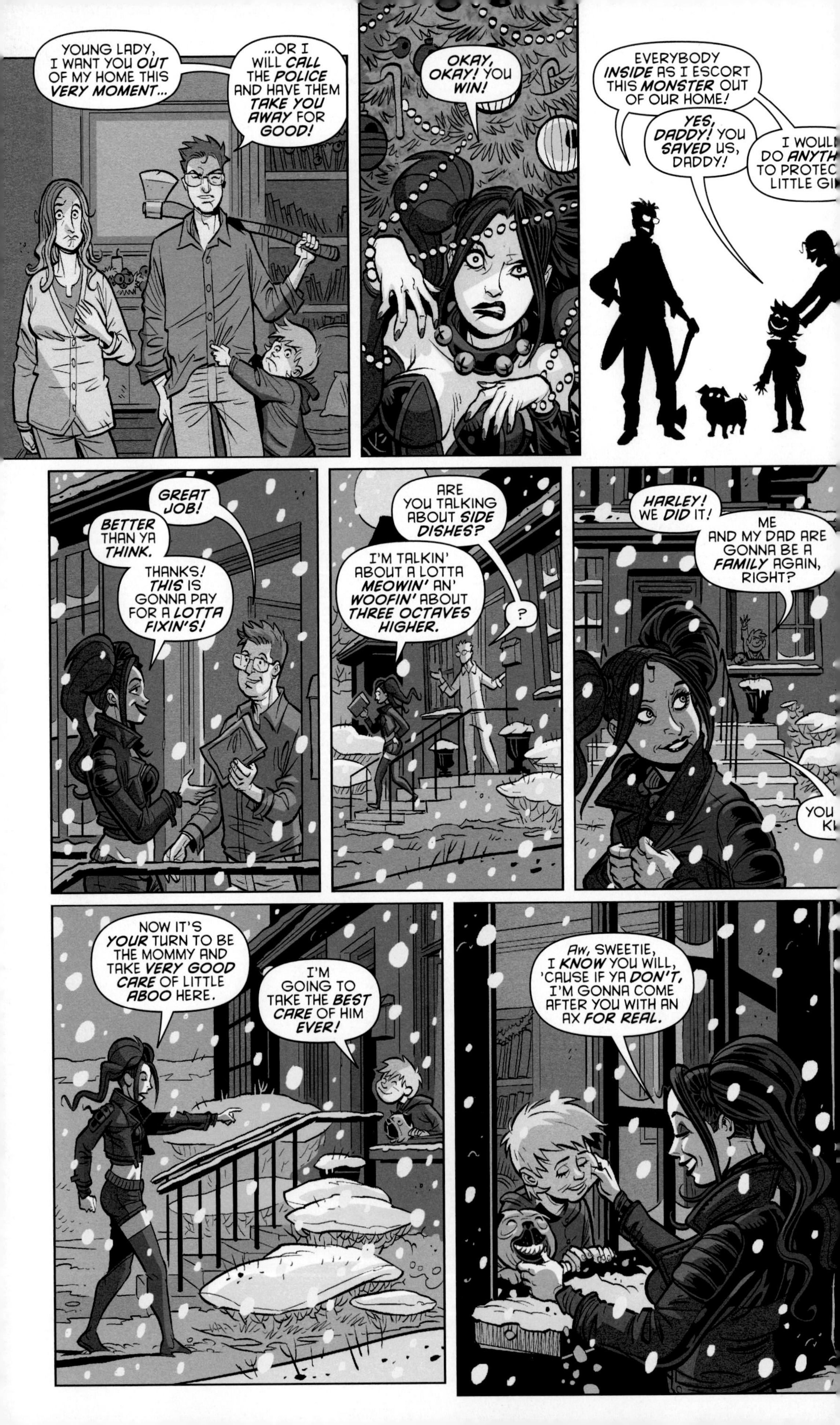
YOUNG LADY, I WANT YOU OUT OF MY HOME THIS VERY MOMENT...
...OR I WILL CALL THE POLICE AND HAVE THEM TAKE YOU AWAY FOR GOOD!
OKAY, OKAY! YOU WIN!
EVERYBODY INSIDE AS I ESCORT THIS MONSTER OUT OF OUR HOME!
YES, DADDY! YOU SAVED US, DADDY!
I WOUL DO ANYTH TO PROTEC LITTLE GI
GREAT JOB!
BETTER THAN YA THINK.
THANKS! THIS IS GONNA PAY FOR A LOTTA FIXIN'S!
ARE YOU TALKING ABOUT SIDE DISHES?
I'M TALKIN' ABOUT A LOTTA MEOWIN' AN' WOOFIN' ABOUT THREE OCTAVES HIGHER.
?
HARLEY! WE DID IT!
ME AND MY DAD ARE GONNA BE A FAMILY AGAIN, RIGHT?
YOU
NOW IT'S YOUR TURN TO BE THE MOMMY AND TAKE VERY GOOD CARE OF LITTLE ABOO HERE.
I'M GOING TO TAKE THE BEST CARE OF HIM EVER!
AW, SWEETIE, I KNOW YOU WILL, 'CAUSE IF YA DON'T, I'M GONNA COME AFTER YOU WITH AN AX FOR REAL.

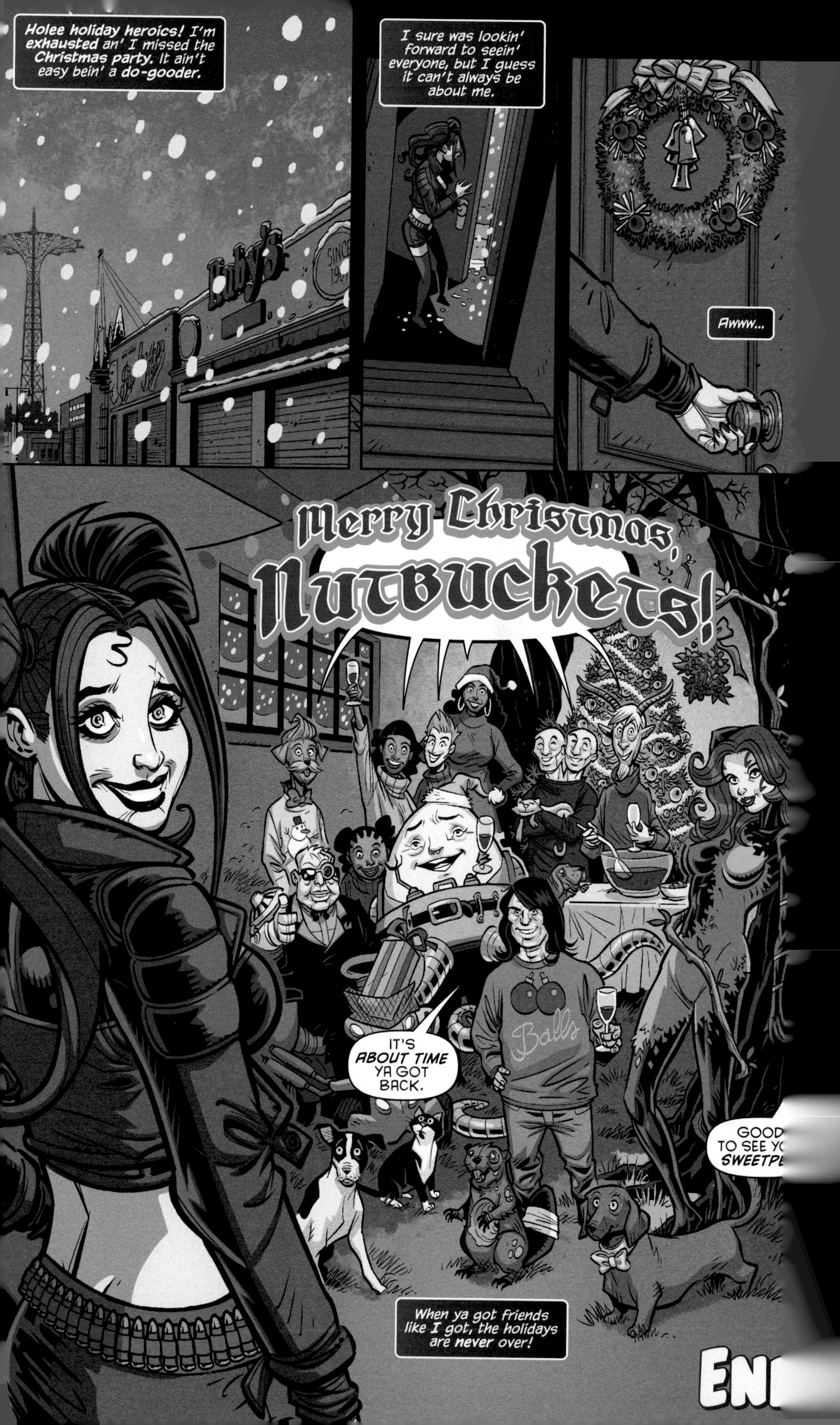

Holee holiday heroics! I'm exhausted an' I missed the Christmas party. It ain't easy bein' a do-gooder.
I sure was lookin' forward to seein' everyone, but I guess it can't always be about me.
Awww...
Merry Christmas, Nutbuckets!
IT'S ABOUT TIME YA GOT BACK.
Balls
GOOD TO SEE YO SWEETPE
When ya got friends like I got, the holidays are never over!

PIN-UP B
BILLY TUCC
WITH HI-F

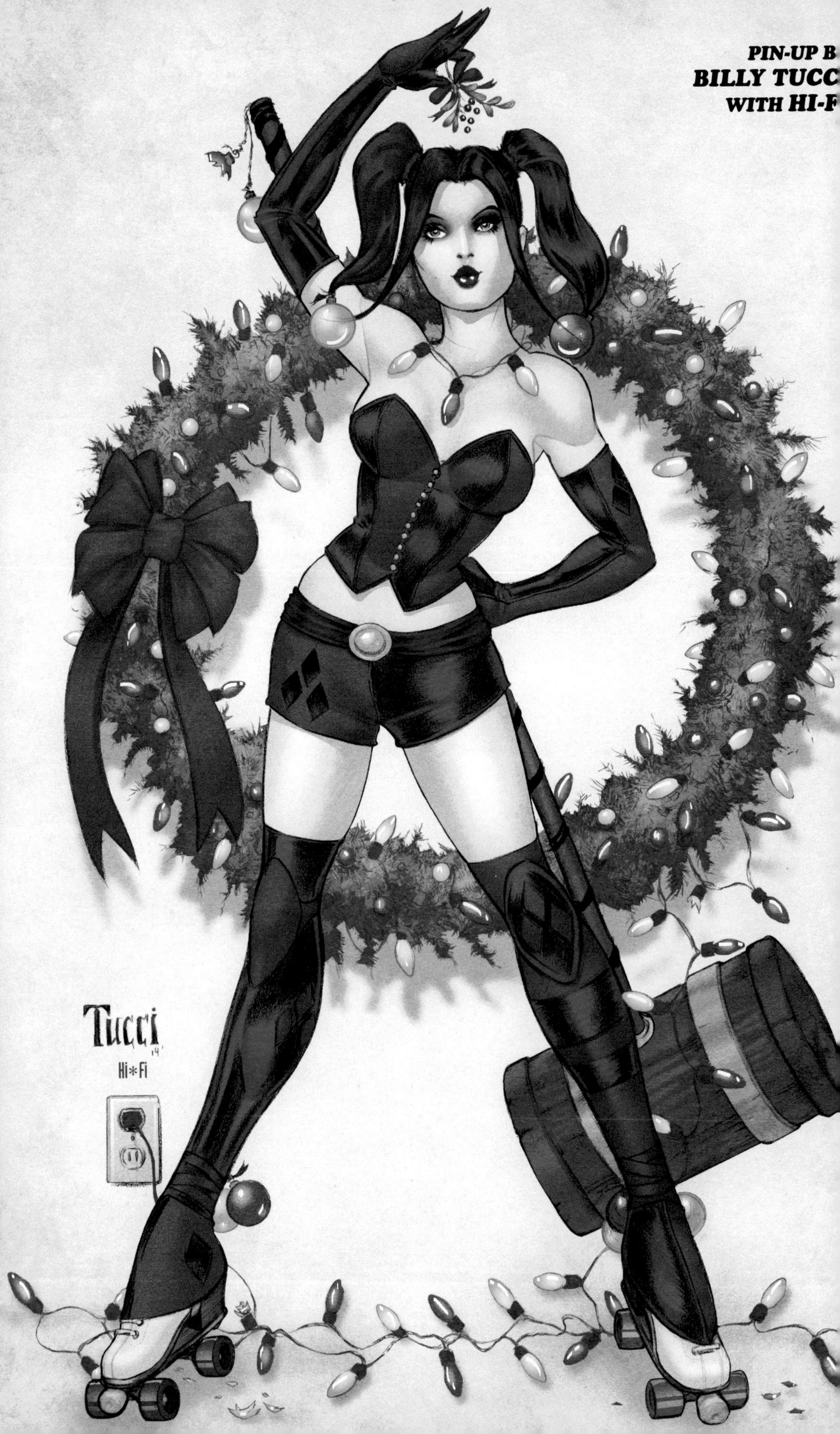
Tucci
'14
Hi*Fi

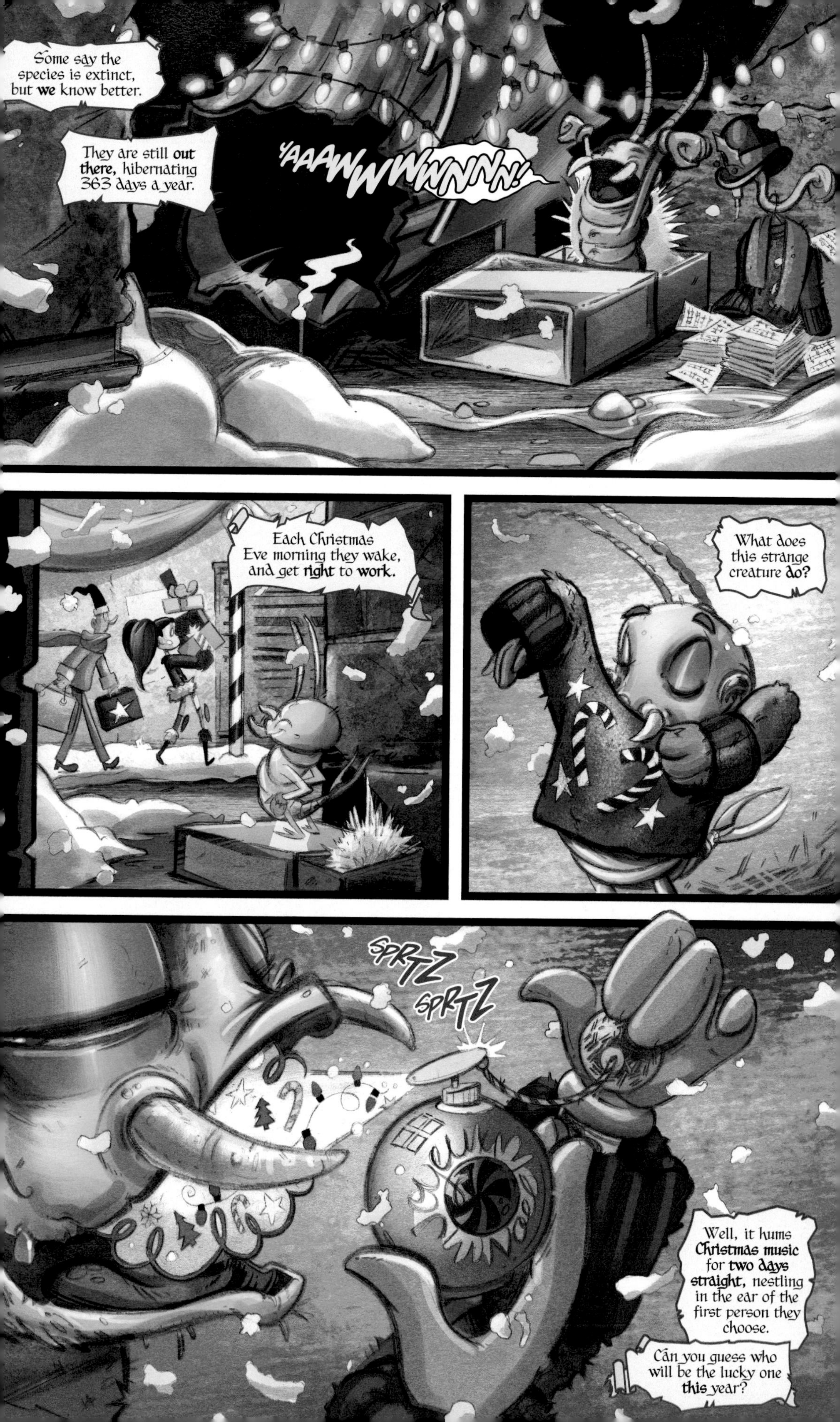
Some say the species is extinct, but we know better.
They are still out there, hibernating 363 days a year.
YAAAWWWNNNH!
Each Christmas Eve morning they wake, and get right to work.
What does this strange creature do?
SPRTZ
SPRTZ
Well, it hums Christmas music for two days straight, nestling in the ear of the first person they choose.
Can you guess who will be the lucky one this year?

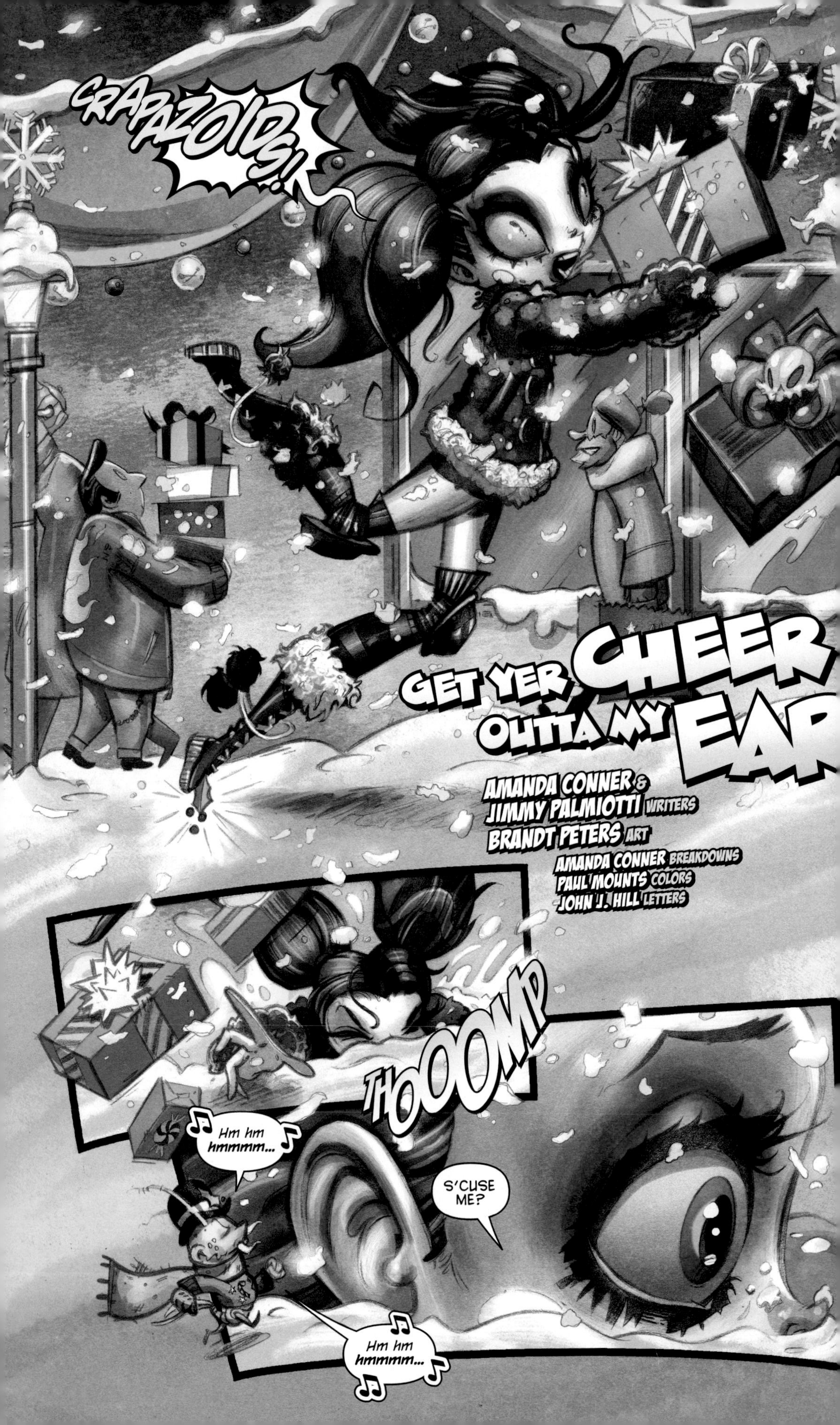
CRAPAZOIDS!
GET YER CHEER OUTTA MY EAR
AMANDA CONNER & JIMMY PALMIOTTI WRITERS
BRANDT PETERS ART
AMANDA CONNER BREAKDOWNS
PAUL MOUNTS COLORS
JOHN J. HILL LETTERS
THOOOMP
Hm hm hmmmm...
S'CUSE ME?
Hm hm hmmmm...

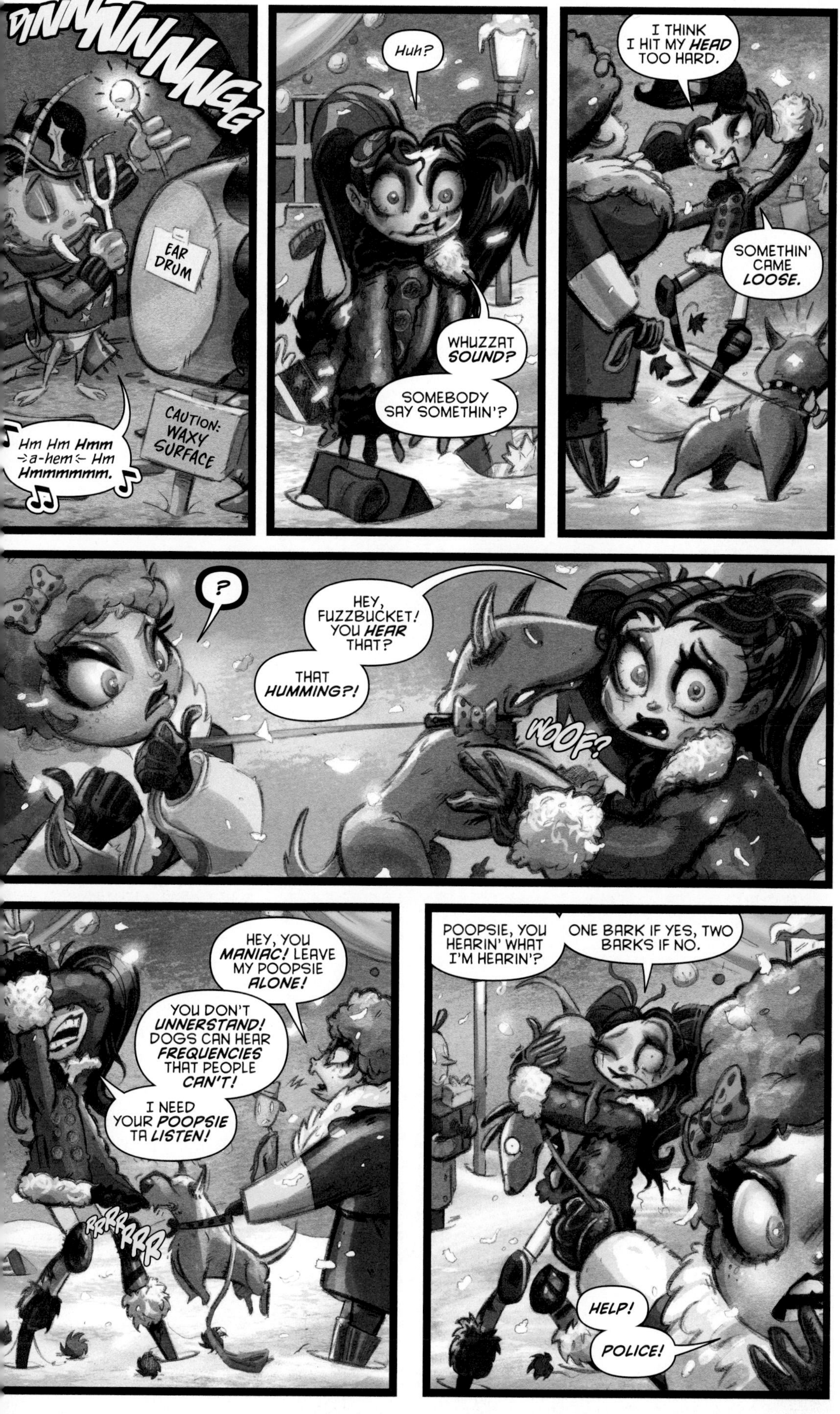
DINNNNNNNGG
EAR DRUM
CAUTION: WAXY SURFACE
Hm Hm Hmm →a-hem← Hm Hmmmmmm.
Huh?
WHUZZAT SOUND?
SOMEBODY SAY SOMETHIN'?
I THINK I HIT MY HEAD TOO HARD.
SOMETHIN' CAME LOOSE.
?
HEY, FUZZBUCKET! YOU HEAR THAT?
THAT HUMMING?!
WOOF?
HEY, YOU MANIAC! LEAVE MY POOPSIE ALONE!
YOU DON'T UNNERSTAND! DOGS CAN HEAR FREQUENCIES THAT PEOPLE CAN'T!
I NEED YOUR POOPSIE TA LISTEN!
RRRRRRR
POOPSIE, YOU HEARIN' WHAT I'M HEARIN'?
ONE BARK IF YES, TWO BARKS IF NO.
HELP!
POLICE!

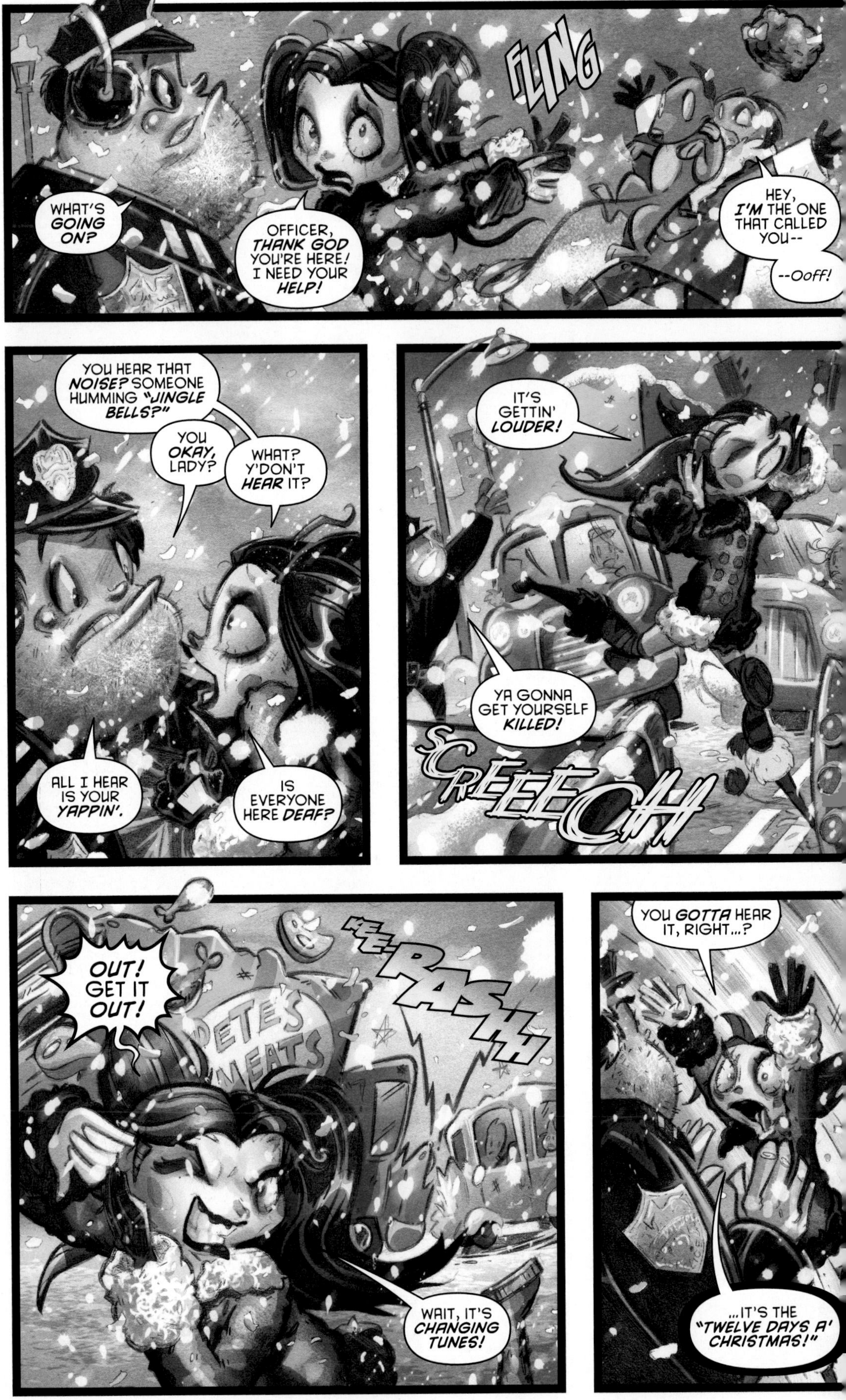

FLING
WHAT'S GOING ON?
OFFICER, THANK GOD YOU'RE HERE! I NEED YOUR HELP!
HEY, I'M THE ONE THAT CALLED YOU--
--Ooff!
YOU HEAR THAT NOISE? SOMEONE HUMMING "JINGLE BELLS?"
YOU OKAY, LADY?
WHAT? Y'DON'T HEAR IT?
ALL I HEAR IS YOUR YAPPIN'.
IS EVERYONE HERE DEAF?
IT'S GETTIN' LOUDER!
YA GONNA GET YOURSELF KILLED!
SCREEECH
OUT! GET IT OUT!
KE-RASHH
PETE'S MEATS
WAIT, IT'S CHANGING TUNES!
YOU GOTTA HEAR IT, RIGHT...?
...IT'S THE "TWELVE DAYS A' CHRISTMAS!"

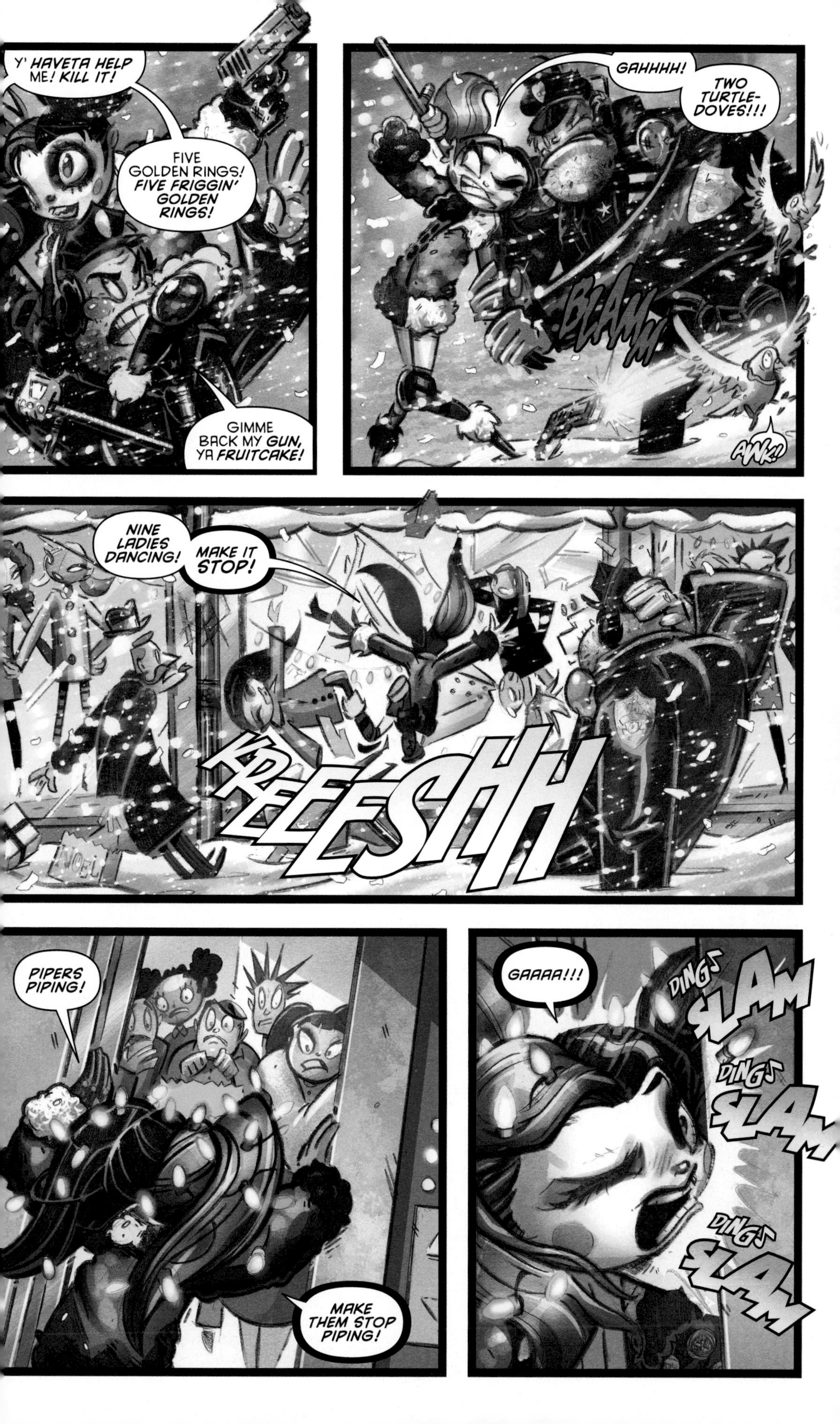

Y' HAVETA HELP ME! KILL IT!
FIVE GOLDEN RINGS! FIVE FRIGGIN' GOLDEN RINGS!
GIMME BACK MY GUN, YA FRUITCAKE!
GAHHHH!
TWO TURTLE-DOVES!!!
BLAM
AWK!
NINE LADIES DANCING!
MAKE IT STOP!
KREEESHH
NOEL
PIPERS PIPING!
MAKE THEM STOP PIPING!
GAAAA!!!
DING SLAM
DING SLAM
DING SLAM

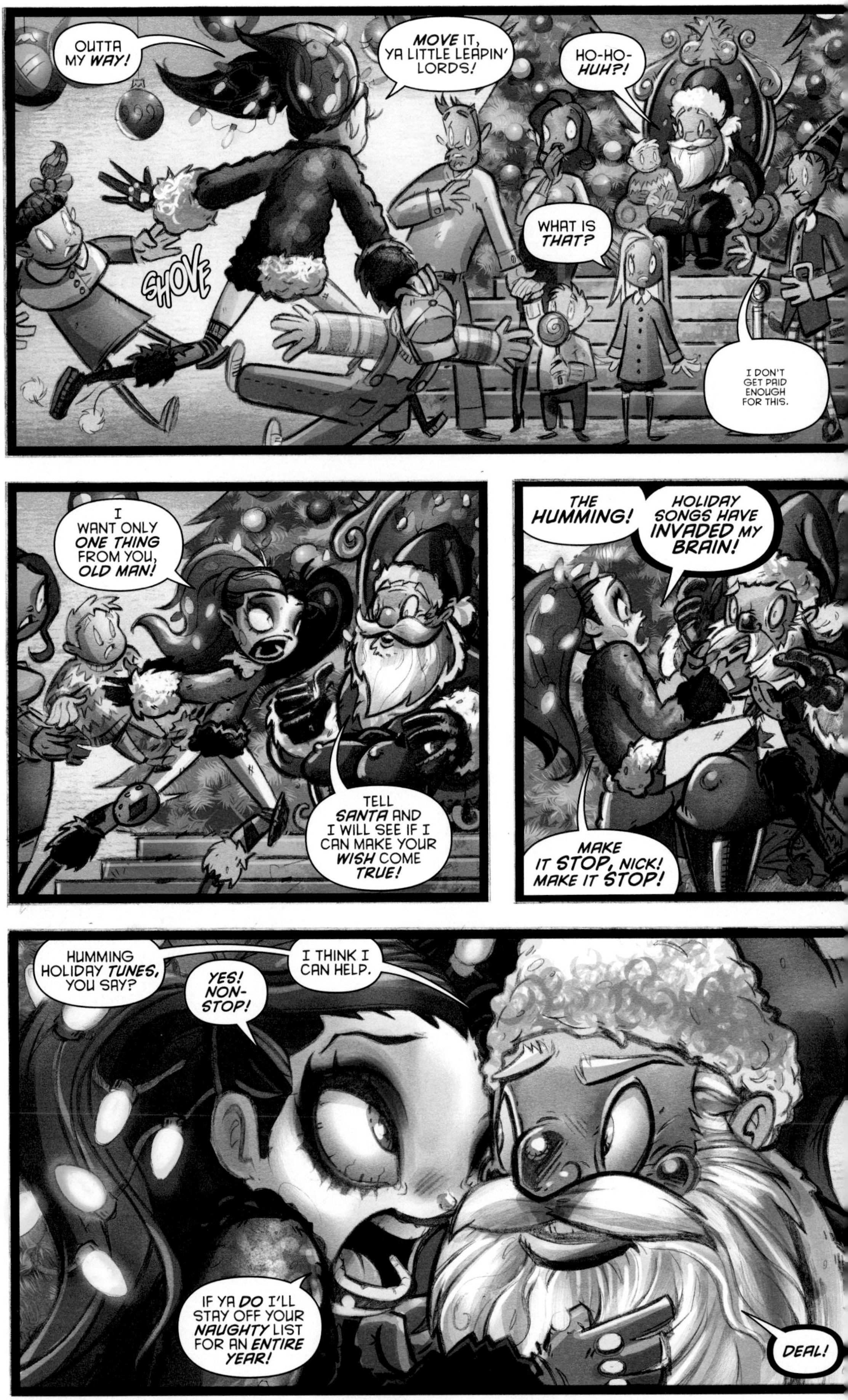

OUTTA MY WAY!
MOVE IT, YA LITTLE LEAPIN' LORDS!
HO-HO-HUH?!
SHOVE
WHAT IS THAT?
I DON'T GET PAID ENOUGH FOR THIS.
I WANT ONLY ONE THING FROM YOU, OLD MAN!
TELL SANTA AND I WILL SEE IF I CAN MAKE YOUR WISH COME TRUE!
THE HUMMING!
HOLIDAY SONGS HAVE INVADED MY BRAIN!
MAKE IT STOP, NICK! MAKE IT STOP!
HUMMING HOLIDAY TUNES, YOU SAY?
YES! NON-STOP!
I THINK I CAN HELP.
IF YA DO I'LL STAY OFF YOUR NAUGHTY LIST FOR AN ENTIRE YEAR!
DEAL!

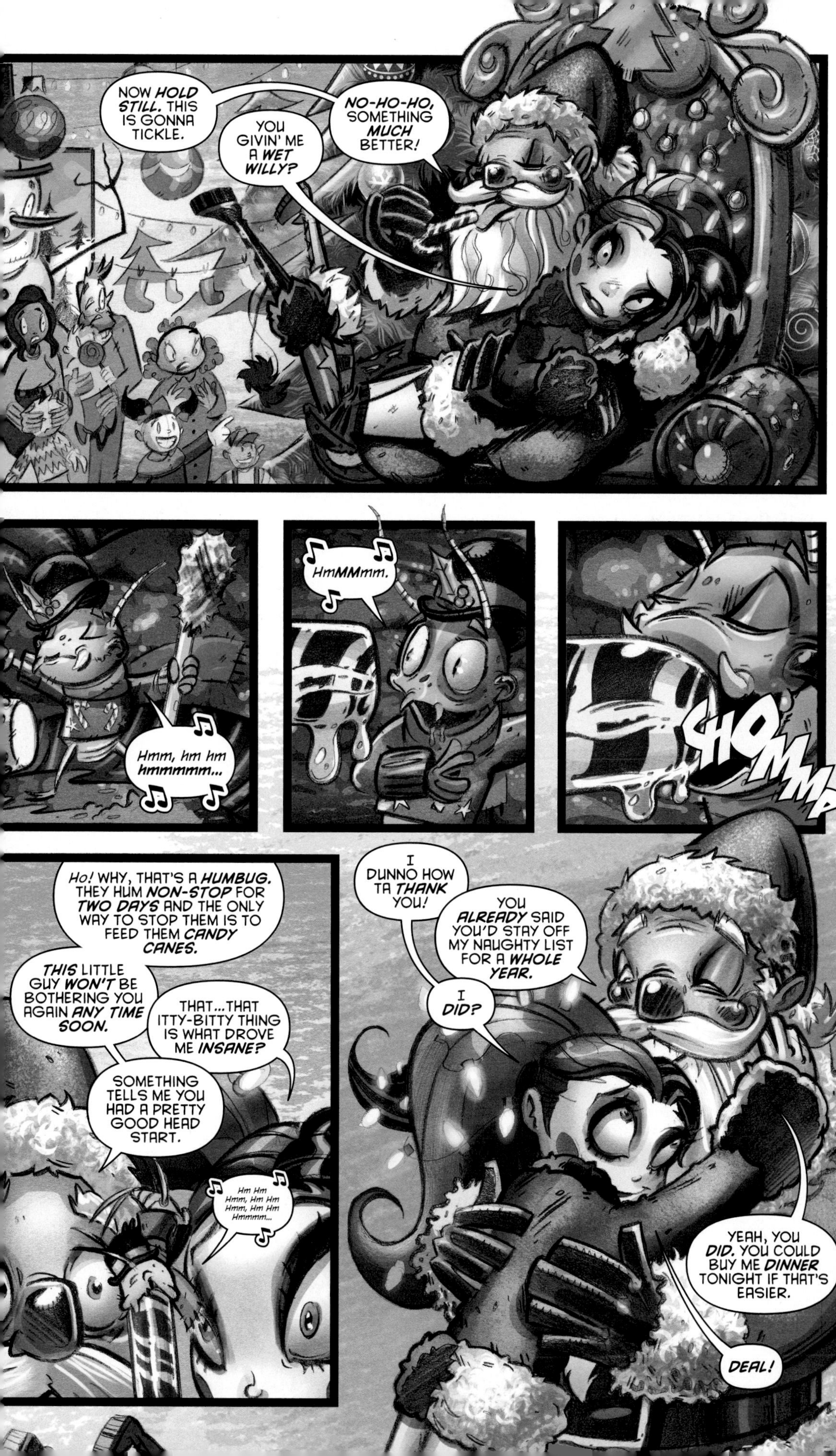
NOW HOLD STILL. THIS IS GONNA TICKLE.
YOU GIVIN' ME A WET WILLY?
NO-HO-HO, SOMETHING MUCH BETTER!
Hmm, hm hm hmmmmm...
HmMMmm.
CHOMMP
Ho! WHY, THAT'S A HUMBUG. THEY HUM NON-STOP FOR TWO DAYS AND THE ONLY WAY TO STOP THEM IS TO FEED THEM CANDY CANES.
THIS LITTLE GUY WON'T BE BOTHERING YOU AGAIN ANY TIME SOON.
THAT...THAT ITTY-BITTY THING IS WHAT DROVE ME INSANE?
SOMETHING TELLS ME YOU HAD A PRETTY GOOD HEAD START.
Hm Hm Hmm, Hm Hm Hmm, Hm Hm Hmmmm...
I DUNNO HOW TA THANK YOU!
YOU ALREADY SAID YOU'D STAY OFF MY NAUGHTY LIST FOR A WHOLE YEAR.
I DID?
YEAH, YOU DID. YOU COULD BUY ME DINNER TONIGHT IF THAT'S EASIER.
DEAL!

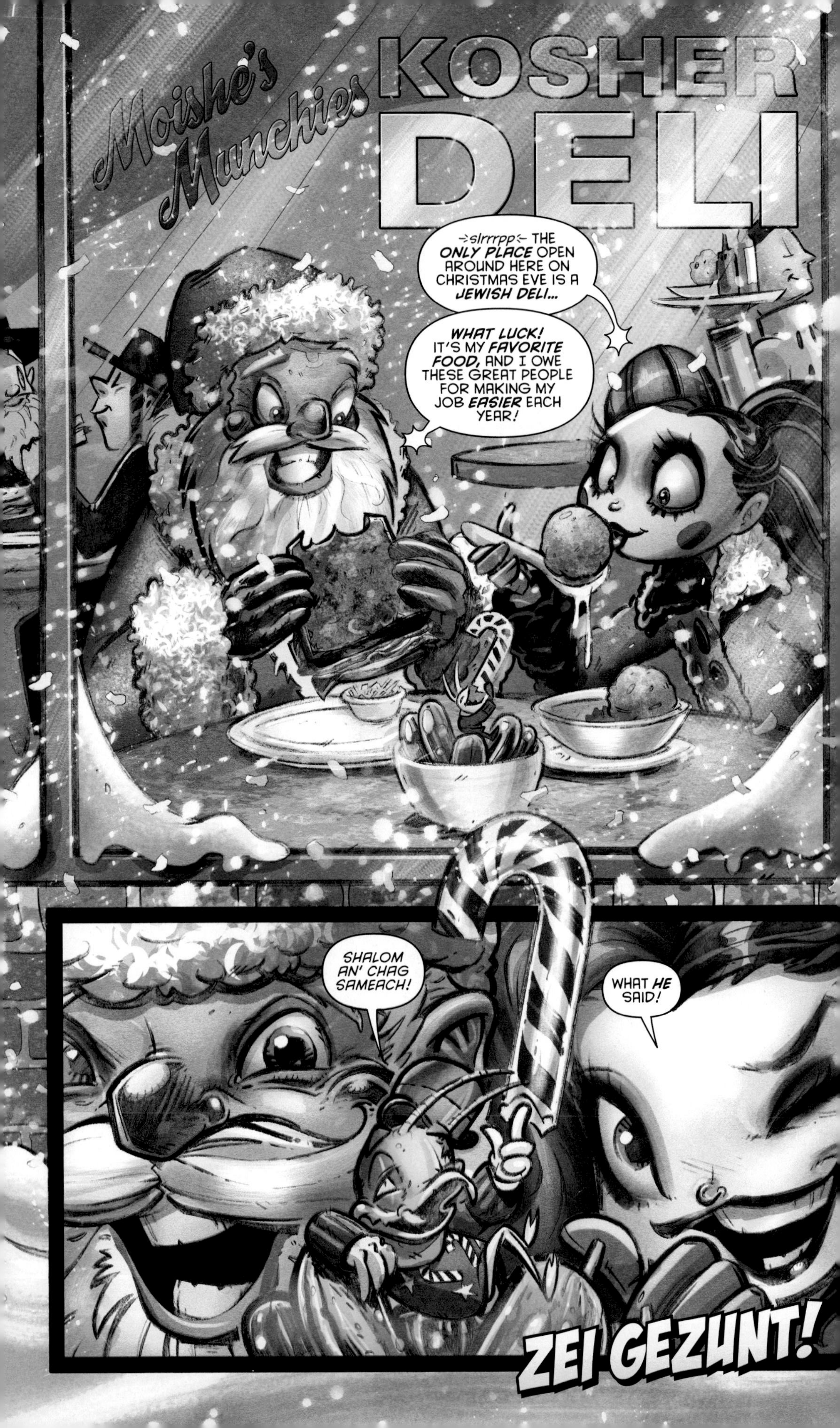
Moishe's Munchies
KOSHER DELI
slrrrpp THE ONLY PLACE OPEN AROUND HERE ON CHRISTMAS EVE IS A JEWISH DELI...
WHAT LUCK! IT'S MY FAVORITE FOOD, AND I OWE THESE GREAT PEOPLE FOR MAKING MY JOB EASIER EACH YEAR!
SHALOM AN' CHAG SAMEACH!
WHAT HE SAID!
ZEI GEZUNT!

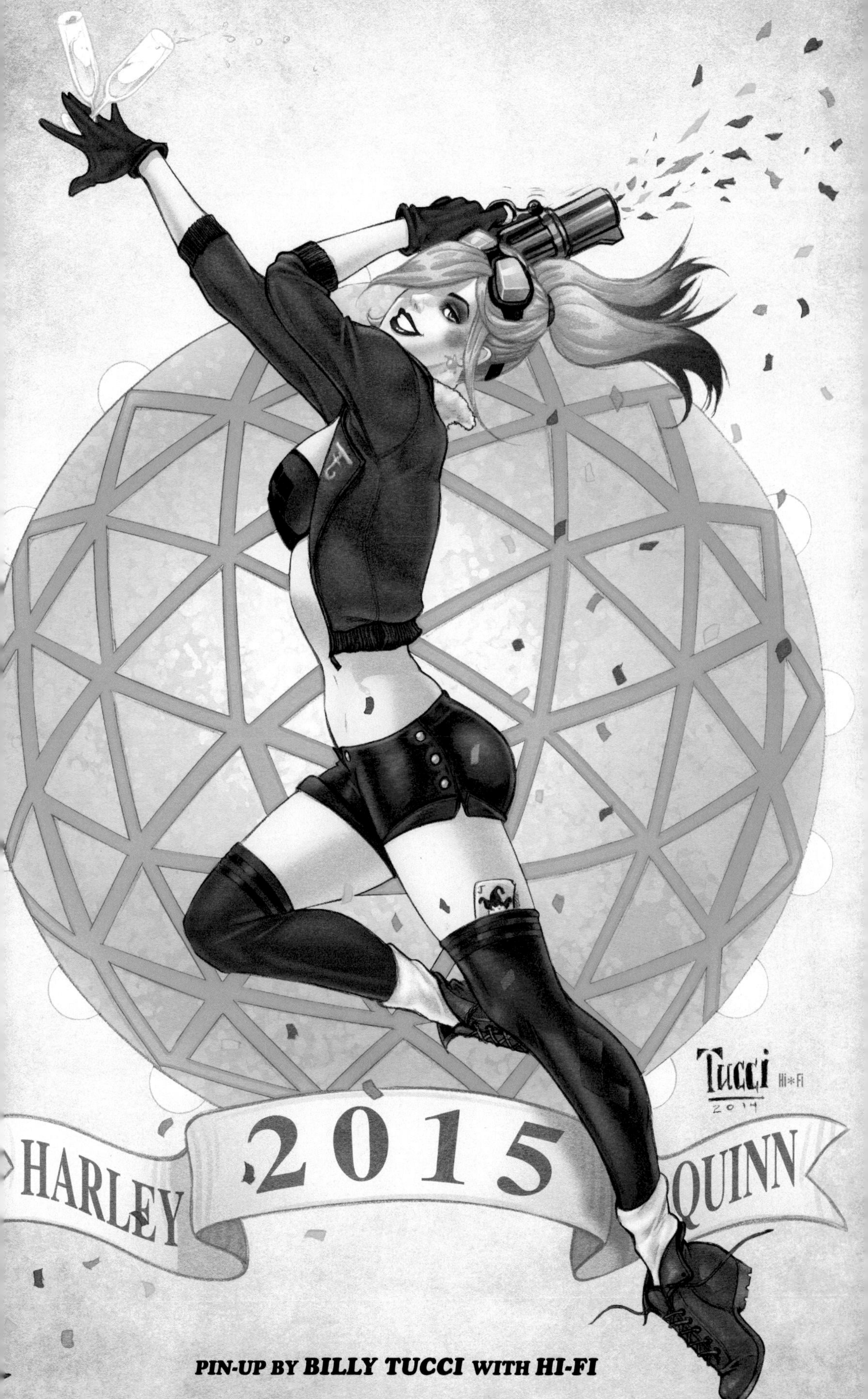
TUCCI
Hi*Fi
2014
HARLEY
2015
QUINN

PIN-UP BY BILLY TUCCI WITH HI-FI

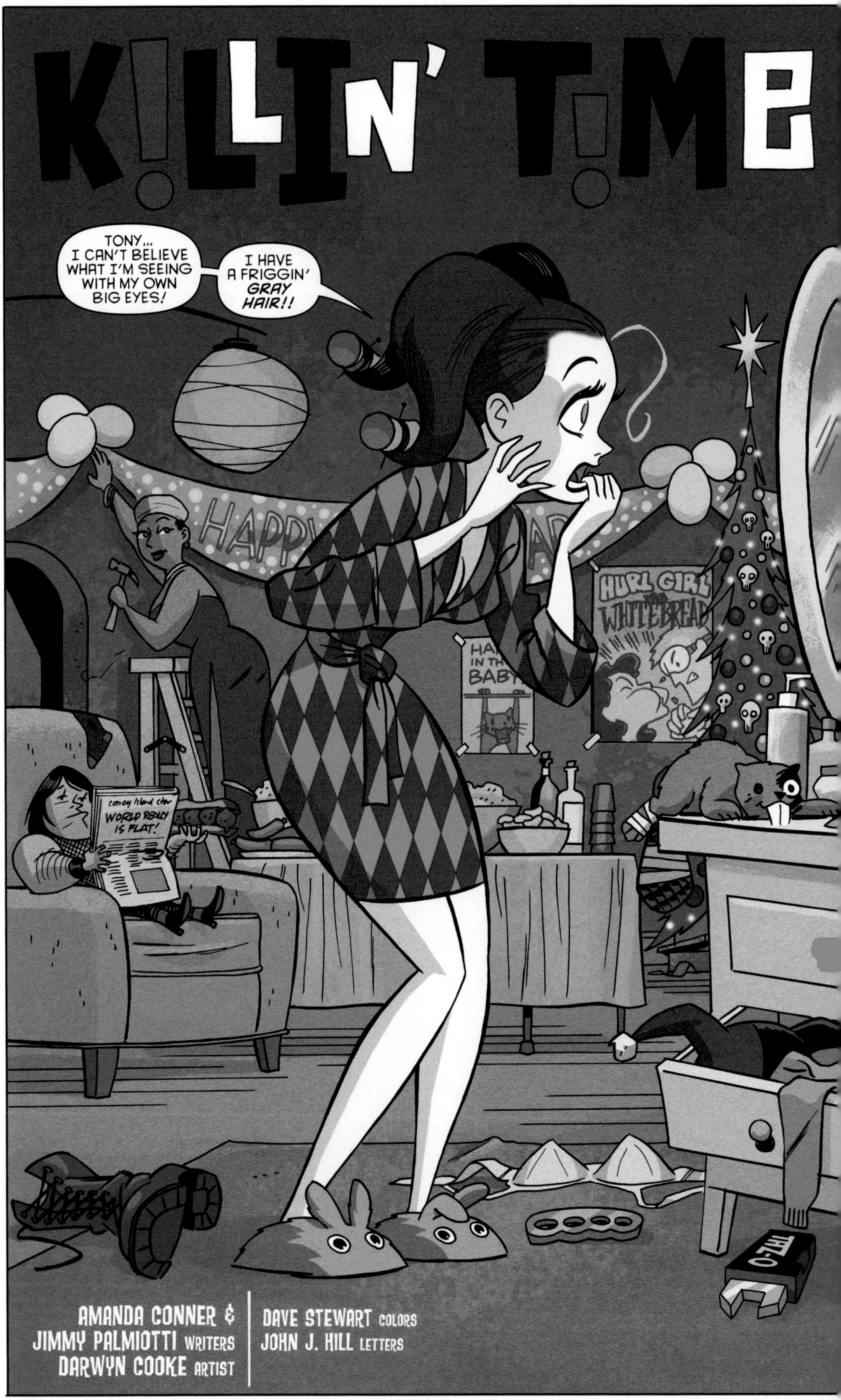
KILLIN' TIME
TONY... I CAN'T BELIEVE WHAT I'M SEEING WITH MY OWN BIG EYES!
I HAVE A FRIGGIN' GRAY HAIR!!
HAPPY
HURL GIRL WHITEBREAD
coney island star WORLD REALLY IS FLAT!
AMANDA CONNER & JIMMY PALMIOTTI WRITERS
DARWYN COOKE ARTIST
DAVE STEWART COLORS
JOHN J. HILL LETTERS

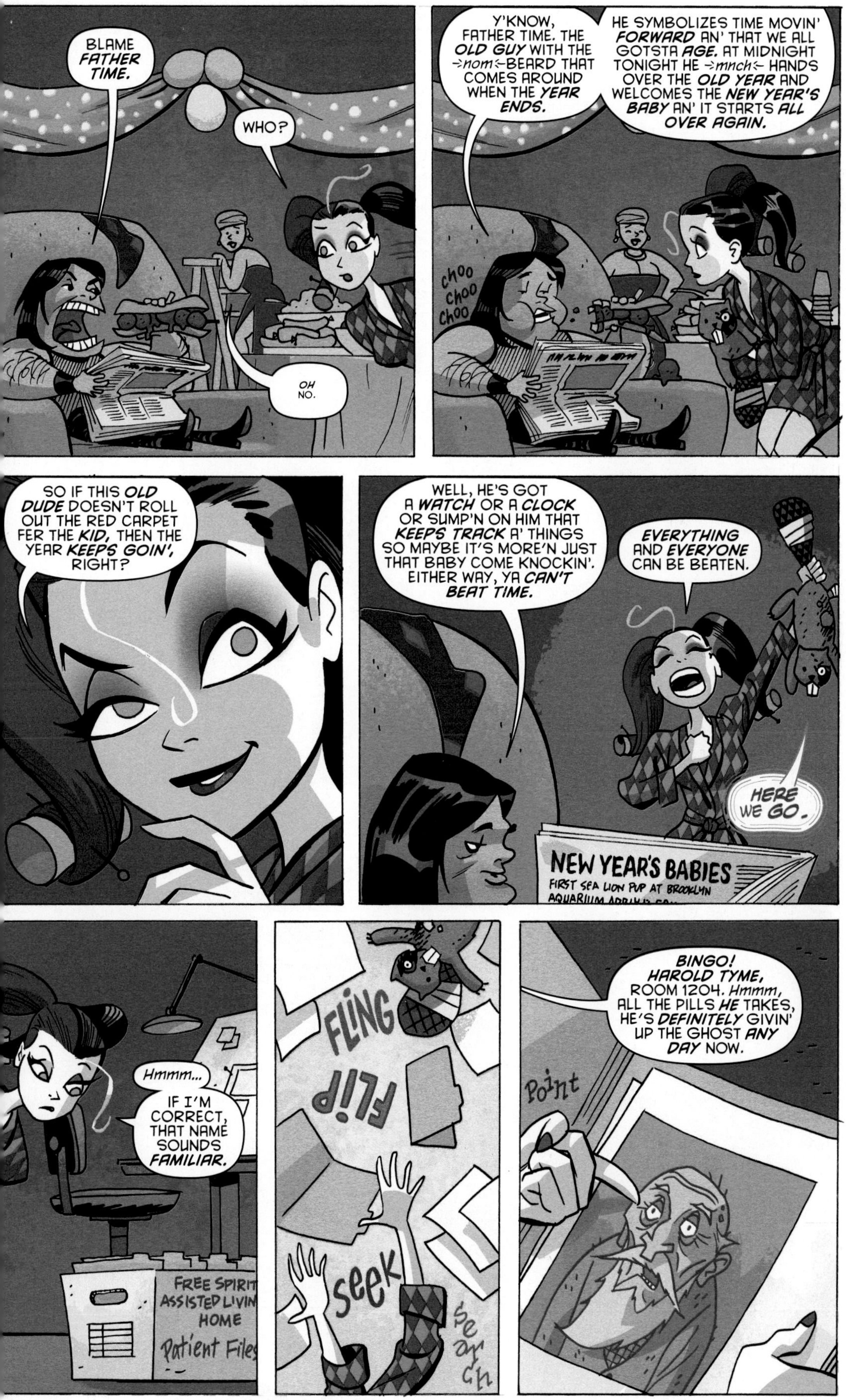

BLAME FATHER TIME.
WHO?
OH NO.
Y'KNOW, FATHER TIME. THE OLD GUY WITH THE ⇒nom⇐ BEARD THAT COMES AROUND WHEN THE YEAR ENDS.
HE SYMBOLIZES TIME MOVIN' FORWARD AN' THAT WE ALL GOTSTA AGE. AT MIDNIGHT TONIGHT HE ⇒mnch⇐ HANDS OVER THE OLD YEAR AND WELCOMES THE NEW YEAR'S BABY AN' IT STARTS ALL OVER AGAIN.
choo choo choo
SO IF THIS OLD DUDE DOESN'T ROLL OUT THE RED CARPET FER THE KID, THEN THE YEAR KEEPS GOIN', RIGHT?
WELL, HE'S GOT A WATCH OR A CLOCK OR SUMP'N ON HIM THAT KEEPS TRACK A' THINGS SO MAYBE IT'S MORE'N JUST THAT BABY COME KNOCKIN'. EITHER WAY, YA CAN'T BEAT TIME.
EVERYTHING AND EVERYONE CAN BE BEATEN.
HERE WE GO.
NEW YEAR'S BABIES
FIRST SEA LION PUP AT BROOKLYN
Hmmm...
IF I'M CORRECT, THAT NAME SOUNDS FAMILIAR.
FREE SPIRIT ASSISTED LIVIN HOME
Patient Files
FLING
FLIP
seek
search
BINGO! HAROLD TYME, ROOM 1204. Hmmm, ALL THE PILLS HE TAKES, HE'S DEFINITELY GIVIN' UP THE GHOST ANY DAY NOW.
Point

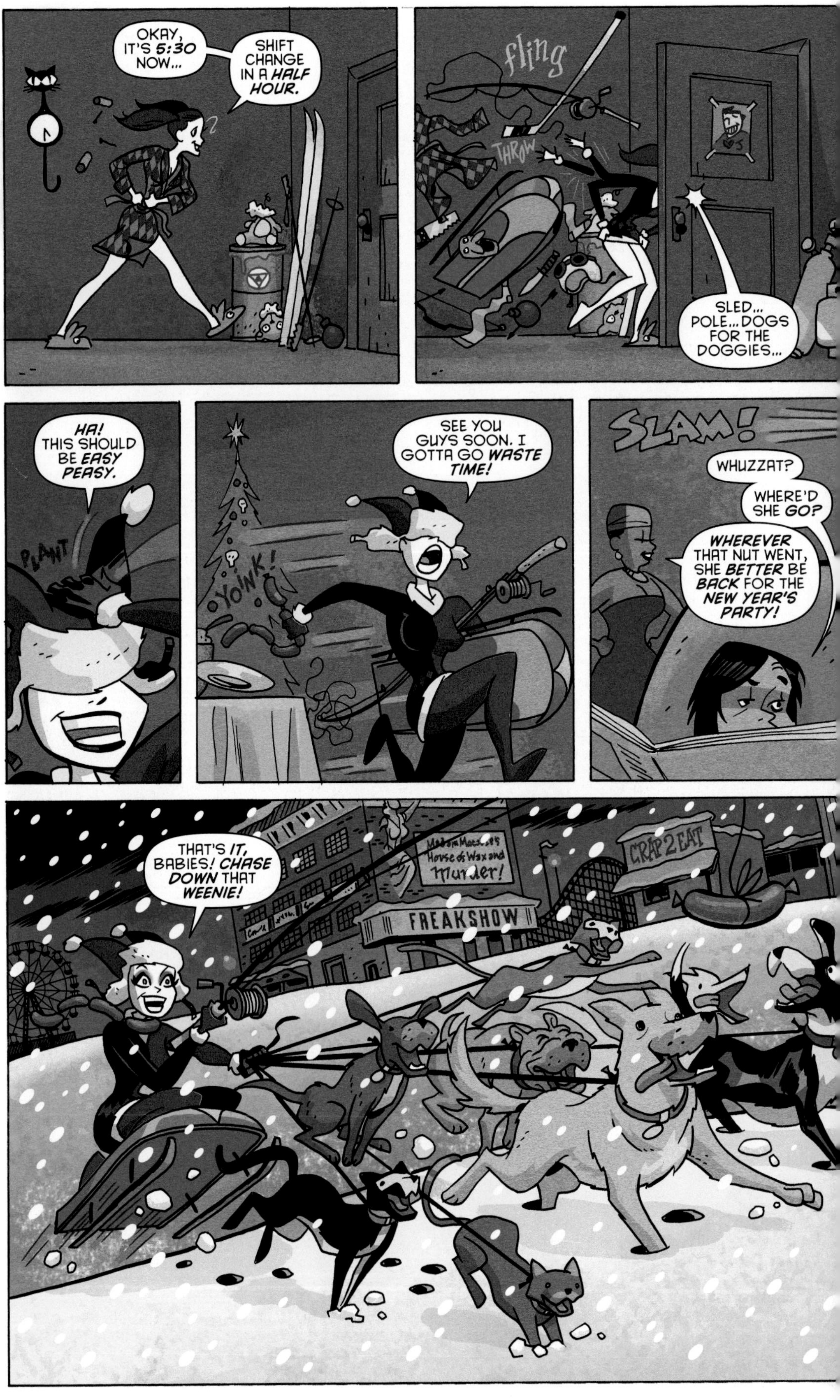
OKAY, IT'S 5:30 NOW...
SHIFT CHANGE IN A HALF HOUR.
fling
THROW
SLED... POLE... DOGS FOR THE DOGGIES...
HA! THIS SHOULD BE EASY PEASY.
PLANT
SEE YOU GUYS SOON. I GOTTA GO WASTE TIME!
YOINK!
SLAM!
WHUZZAT?
WHERE'D SHE GO?
WHEREVER THAT NUT WENT, SHE BETTER BE BACK FOR THE NEW YEAR'S PARTY!
THAT'S IT, BABIES! CHASE DOWN THAT WEENIE!
House of Wax and Murder!
FREAKSHOW
CRAP 2 EAT

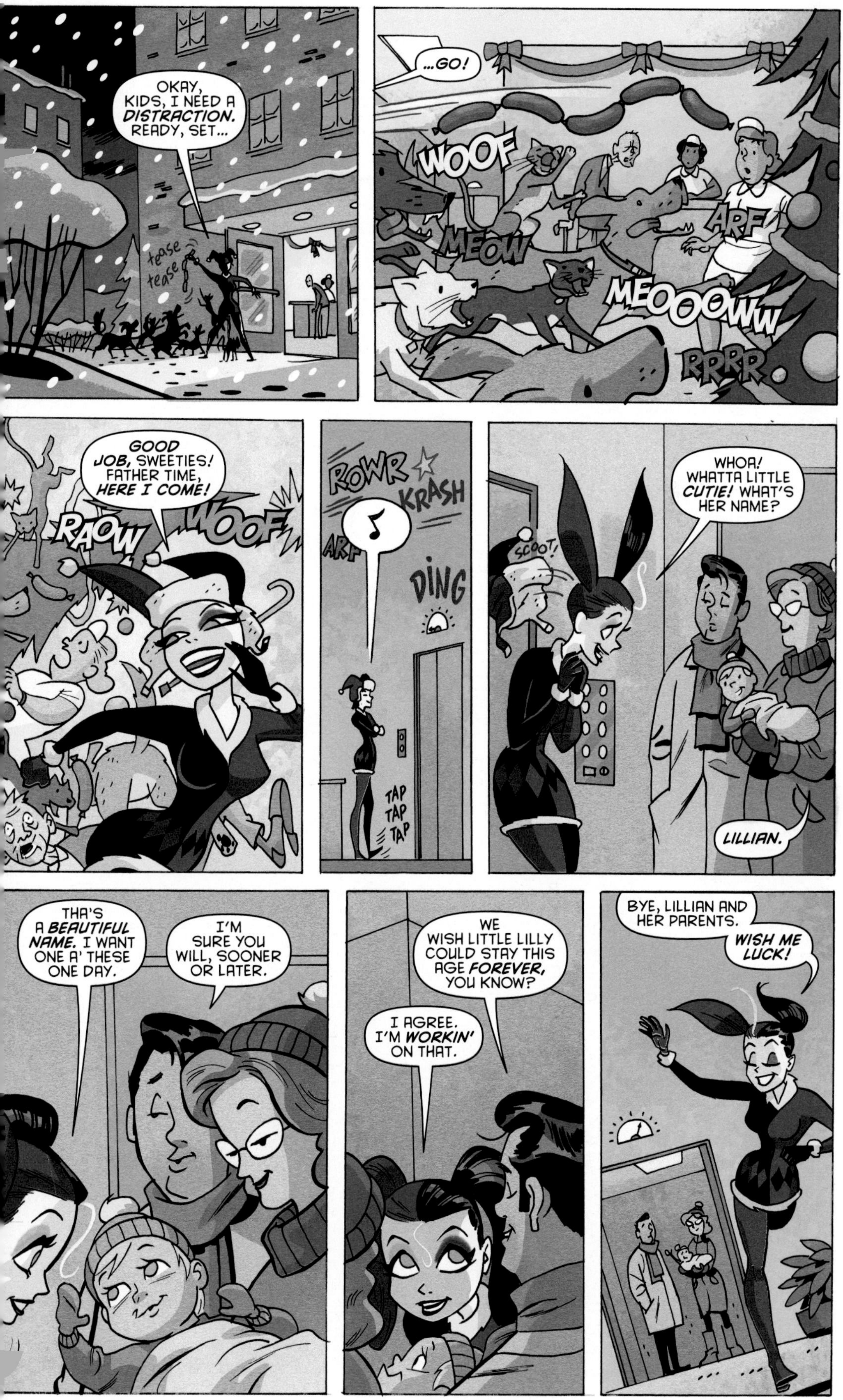
OKAY, KIDS, I NEED A DISTRACTION. READY, SET...
tease tease
...GO!
WOOF
MEOW
ARF
MEOOOWW
RRRR
GOOD JOB, SWEETIES! FATHER TIME, HERE I COME!
RAOW
WOOF
ROWR
KRASH
ARF
DING
TAP TAP TAP
SCOOT!
WHOA! WHATTA LITTLE CUTIE! WHAT'S HER NAME?
LILLIAN.
THA'S A BEAUTIFUL NAME. I WANT ONE A' THESE ONE DAY.
I'M SURE YOU WILL, SOONER OR LATER.
WE WISH LITTLE LILLY COULD STAY THIS AGE FOREVER, YOU KNOW?
I AGREE. I'M WORKIN' ON THAT.
BYE, LILLIAN AND HER PARENTS.
WISH ME LUCK!

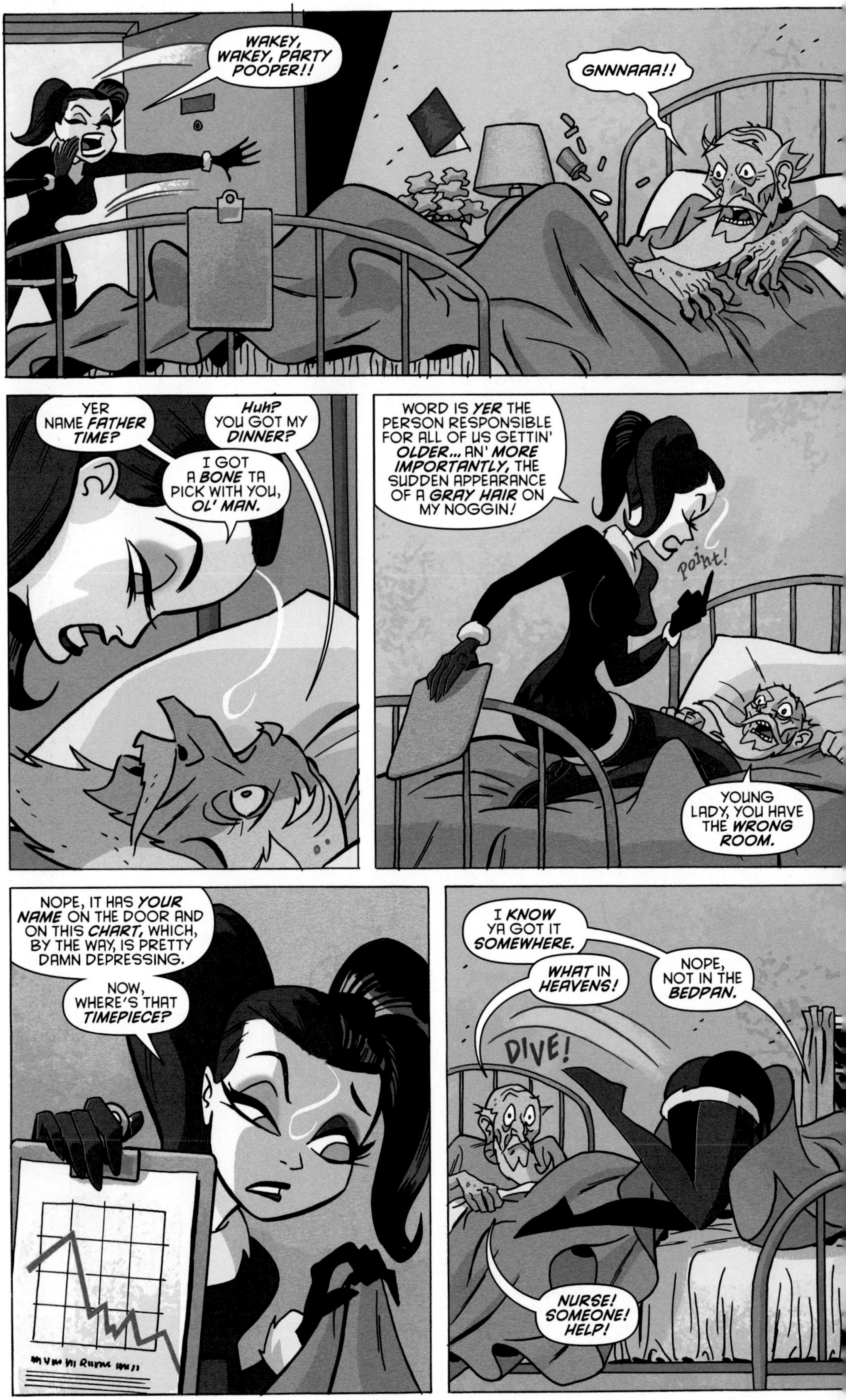
WAKEY, WAKEY, PARTY POOPER!!
GNNAAA!!
YER NAME FATHER TIME?
Huh? YOU GOT MY DINNER?
I GOT A BONE TA PICK WITH YOU, OL' MAN.
WORD IS YER THE PERSON RESPONSIBLE FOR ALL OF US GETTIN' OLDER... AN' MORE IMPORTANTLY, THE SUDDEN APPEARANCE OF A GRAY HAIR ON MY NOGGIN!
Point!
YOUNG LADY, YOU HAVE THE WRONG ROOM.
NOPE, IT HAS YOUR NAME ON THE DOOR AND ON THIS CHART, WHICH, BY THE WAY, IS PRETTY DAMN DEPRESSING.
NOW, WHERE'S THAT TIMEPIECE?
I KNOW YA GOT IT SOMEWHERE.
WHAT IN HEAVENS!
NOPE, NOT IN THE BEDPAN.
DIVE!
NURSE! SOMEONE! HELP!

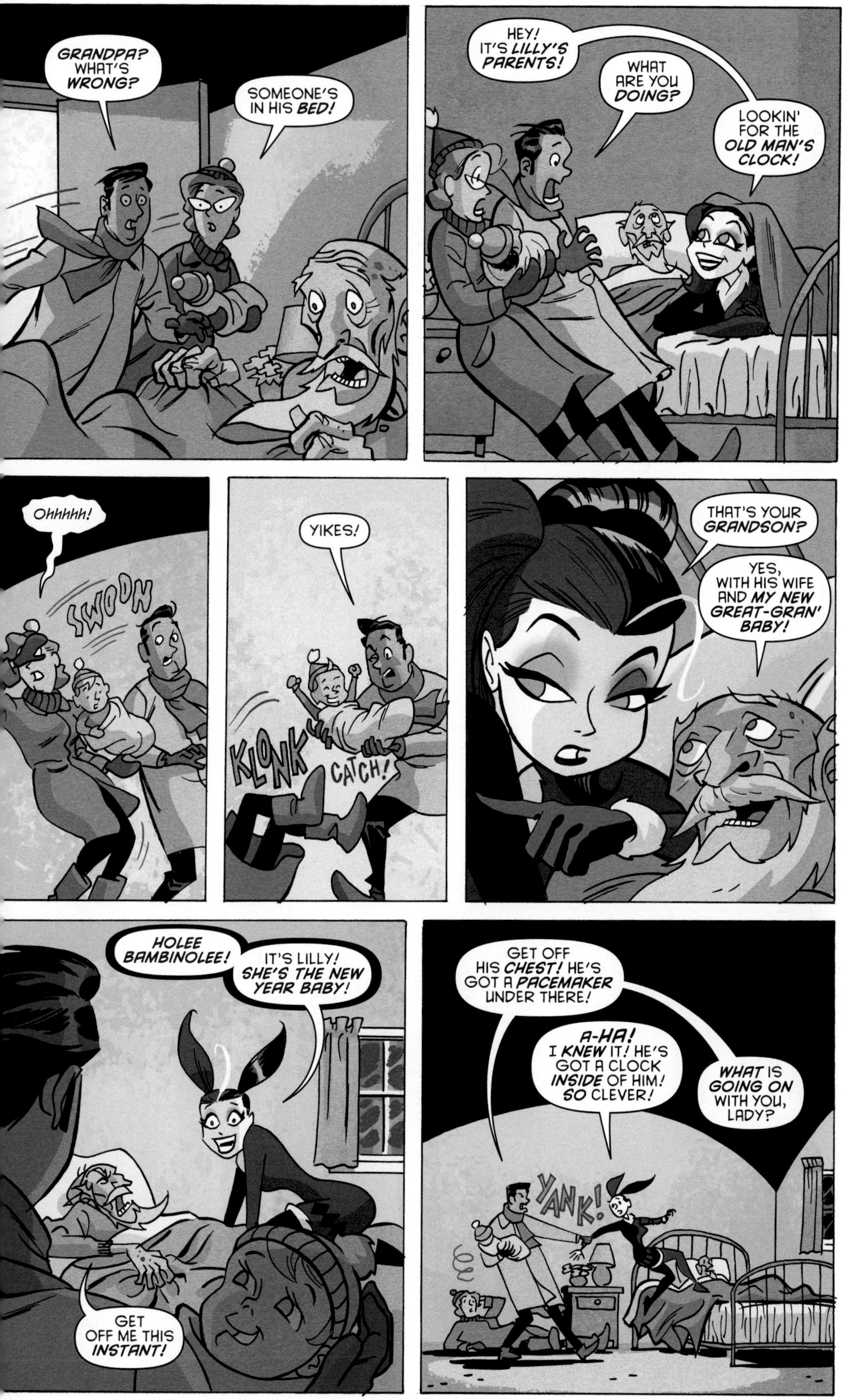
GRANDPA? WHAT'S WRONG?
SOMEONE'S IN HIS BED!
HEY! IT'S LILLY'S PARENTS!
WHAT ARE YOU DOING?
LOOKIN' FOR THE OLD MAN'S CLOCK!
Ohhhhh!
SWOON
YIKES!
KLONK
CATCH!
THAT'S YOUR GRANDSON?
YES, WITH HIS WIFE AND MY NEW GREAT-GRAN' BABY!
HOLEE BAMBINOLEE!
IT'S LILLY! SHE'S THE NEW YEAR BABY!
GET OFF ME THIS INSTANT!
GET OFF HIS CHEST! HE'S GOT A PACEMAKER UNDER THERE!
A-HA! I KNEW IT! HE'S GOT A CLOCK INSIDE OF HIM! SO CLEVER!
WHAT IS GOING ON WITH YOU, LADY?
YANK!

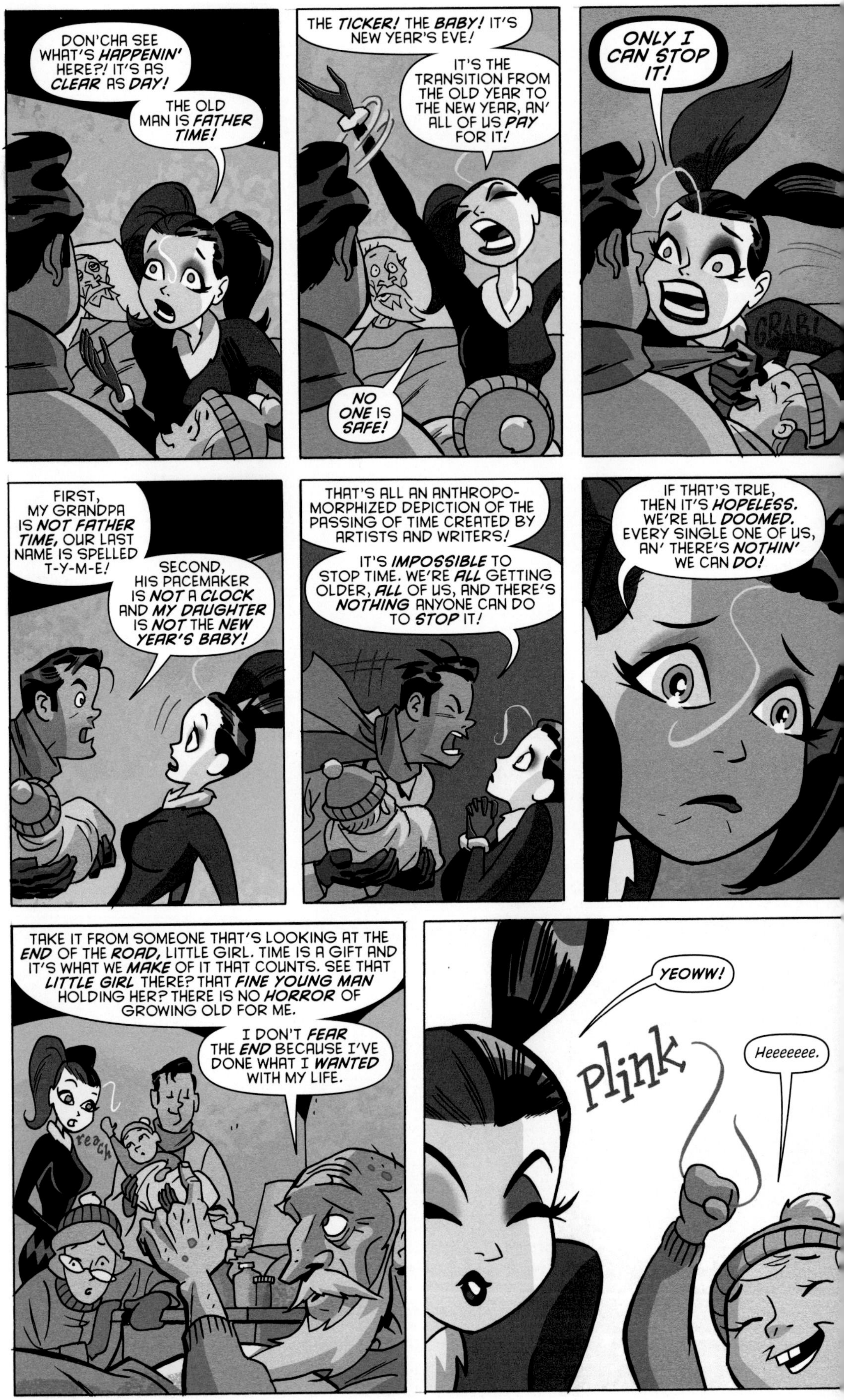
DON'CHA SEE WHAT'S HAPPENIN' HERE?! IT'S AS CLEAR AS DAY!
THE OLD MAN IS FATHER TIME!
THE TICKER! THE BABY! IT'S NEW YEAR'S EVE!
IT'S THE TRANSITION FROM THE OLD YEAR TO THE NEW YEAR, AN' ALL OF US PAY FOR IT!
NO ONE IS SAFE!
ONLY I CAN STOP IT!
GRAB!
FIRST, MY GRANDPA IS NOT FATHER TIME, OUR LAST NAME IS SPELLED T-Y-M-E!
SECOND, HIS PACEMAKER IS NOT A CLOCK AND MY DAUGHTER IS NOT THE NEW YEAR'S BABY!
THAT'S ALL AN ANTHROPOMORPHIZED DEPICTION OF THE PASSING OF TIME CREATED BY ARTISTS AND WRITERS!
IT'S IMPOSSIBLE TO STOP TIME. WE'RE ALL GETTING OLDER, ALL OF US, AND THERE'S NOTHING ANYONE CAN DO TO STOP IT!
IF THAT'S TRUE, THEN IT'S HOPELESS. WE'RE ALL DOOMED. EVERY SINGLE ONE OF US, AN' THERE'S NOTHIN' WE CAN DO!
TAKE IT FROM SOMEONE THAT'S LOOKING AT THE END OF THE ROAD, LITTLE GIRL. TIME IS A GIFT AND IT'S WHAT WE MAKE OF IT THAT COUNTS. SEE THAT LITTLE GIRL THERE? THAT FINE YOUNG MAN HOLDING HER? THERE IS NO HORROR OF GROWING OLD FOR ME.
I DON'T FEAR THE END BECAUSE I'VE DONE WHAT I WANTED WITH MY LIFE.
reach
YEOWW!
Plink
Heeeeeee.

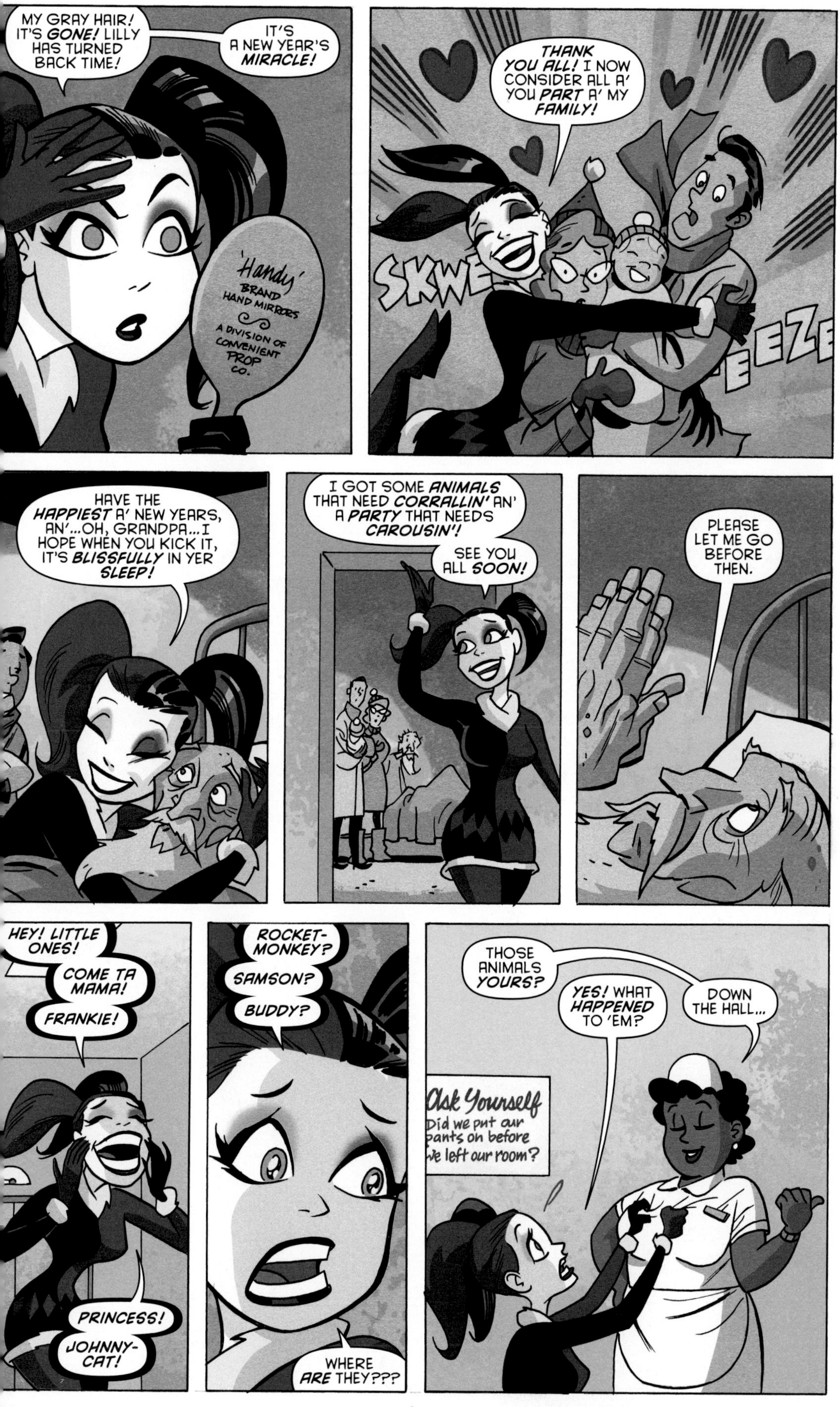
MY GRAY HAIR! IT'S GONE! LILLY HAS TURNED BACK TIME!
IT'S A NEW YEAR'S MIRACLE!
'Handy' BRAND HAND MIRRORS A DIVISION OF CONVENIENT PROP CO.
THANK YOU ALL! I NOW CONSIDER ALL A' YOU PART A' MY FAMILY!
SKWEEEZE
HAVE THE HAPPIEST A' NEW YEARS, AN'...OH, GRANDPA...I HOPE WHEN YOU KICK IT, IT'S BLISSFULLY IN YER SLEEP!
I GOT SOME ANIMALS THAT NEED CORRALLIN' AN' A PARTY THAT NEEDS CAROUSIN'!
SEE YOU ALL SOON!
PLEASE LET ME GO BEFORE THEN.
HEY! LITTLE ONES!
COME TA MAMA!
FRANKIE!
PRINCESS!
JOHNNY-CAT!
ROCKET-MONKEY?
SAMSON?
BUDDY?
WHERE ARE THEY???
THOSE ANIMALS YOURS?
YES! WHAT HAPPENED TO 'EM?
DOWN THE HALL...
Ask Yourself Did we put our pants on before we left our room?

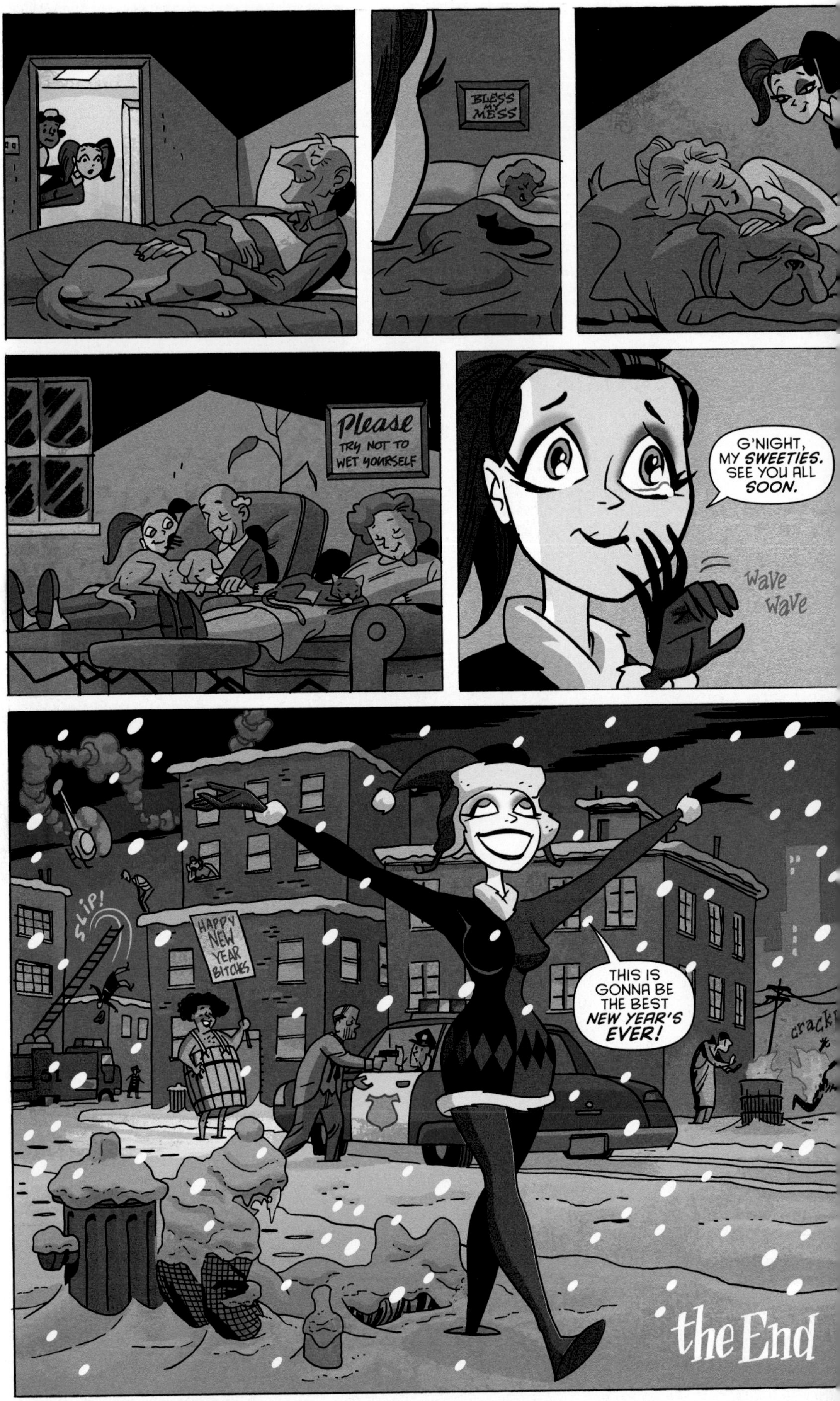
BLESS MY MESS
Please TRY NOT TO WET YOURSELF
G'NIGHT, MY SWEETIES. SEE YOU ALL SOON.
wave wave
SLIP!
HAPPY NEW YEAR BITCHES
THIS IS GONNA BE THE BEST NEW YEAR'S EVER!
the End

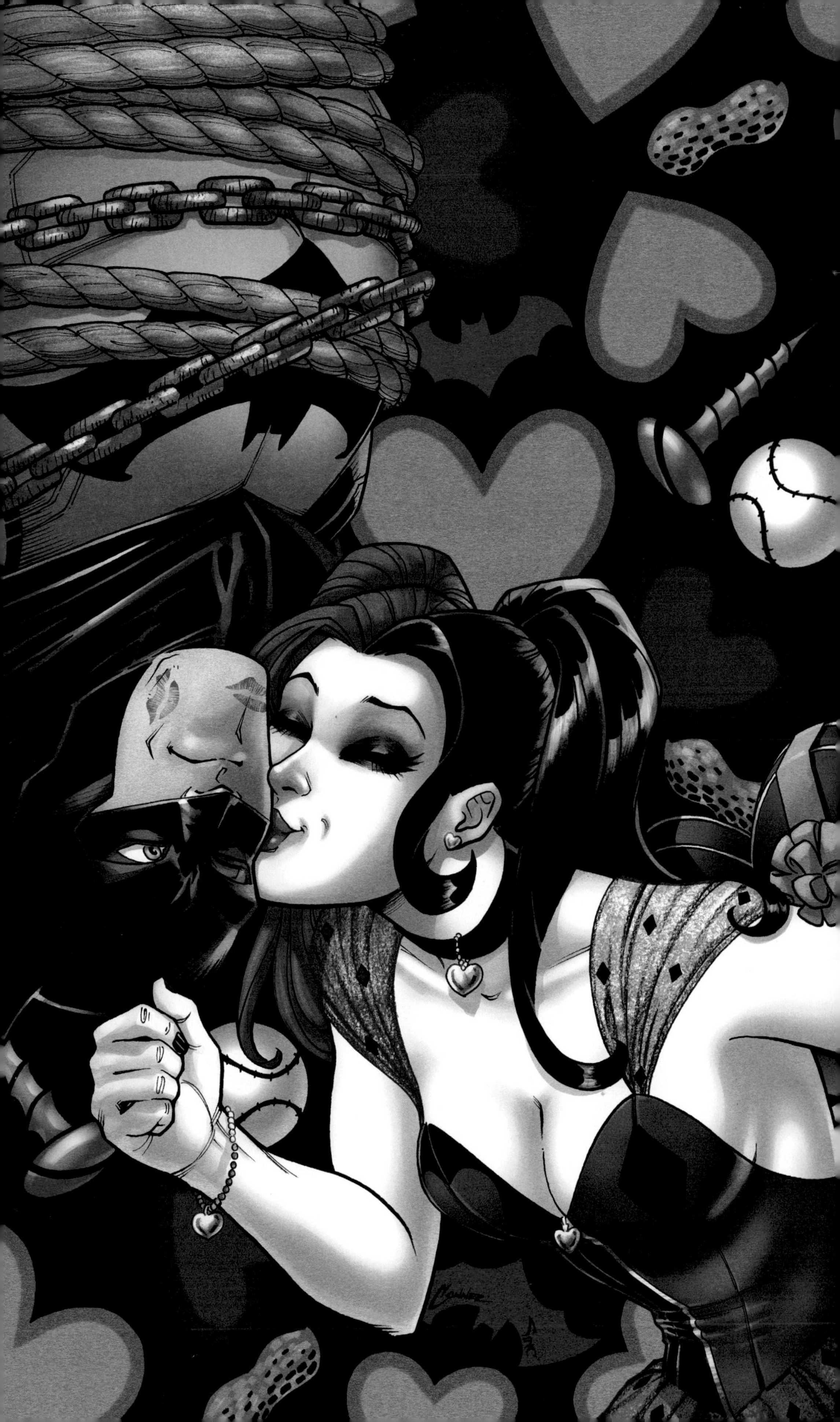

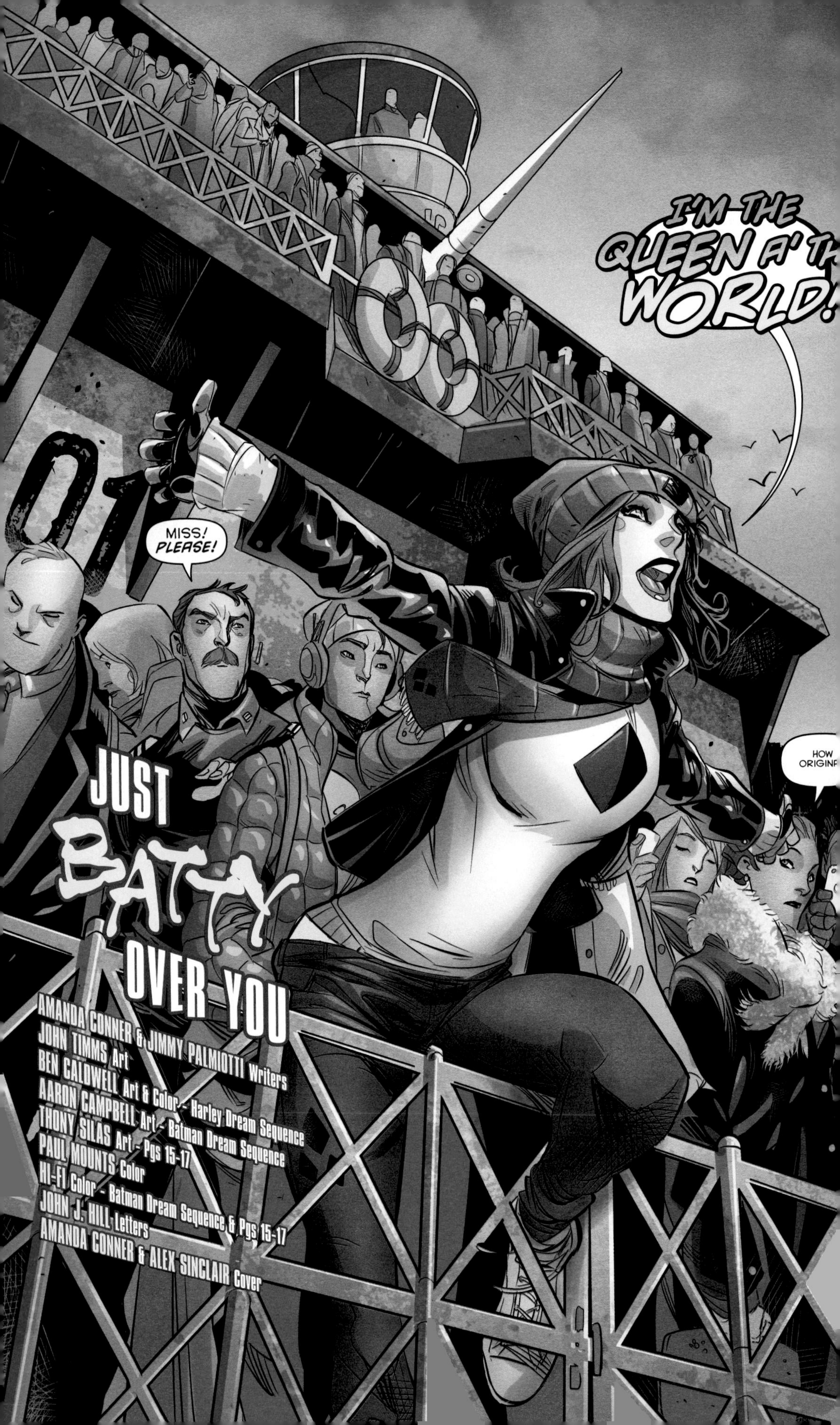

I'M THE QUEEN A' TH WORLD!
MISS! PLEASE!
HOW ORIGINA
01
JUST BATTY OVER YOU
AMANDA CONNER & JIMMY PALMIOTTI Writers
JOHN TIMMS Art
BEN CALDWELL Art & Color - Harley Dream Sequence
AARON CAMPBELL Art - Batman Dream Sequence
THONY SILAS Art - Pgs 15-17
PAUL MOUNTS Color
HI-FI Color - Batman Dream Sequence & Pgs 15-17
JOHN J. HILL Letters
AMANDA CONNER & ALEX SINCLAIR Cover

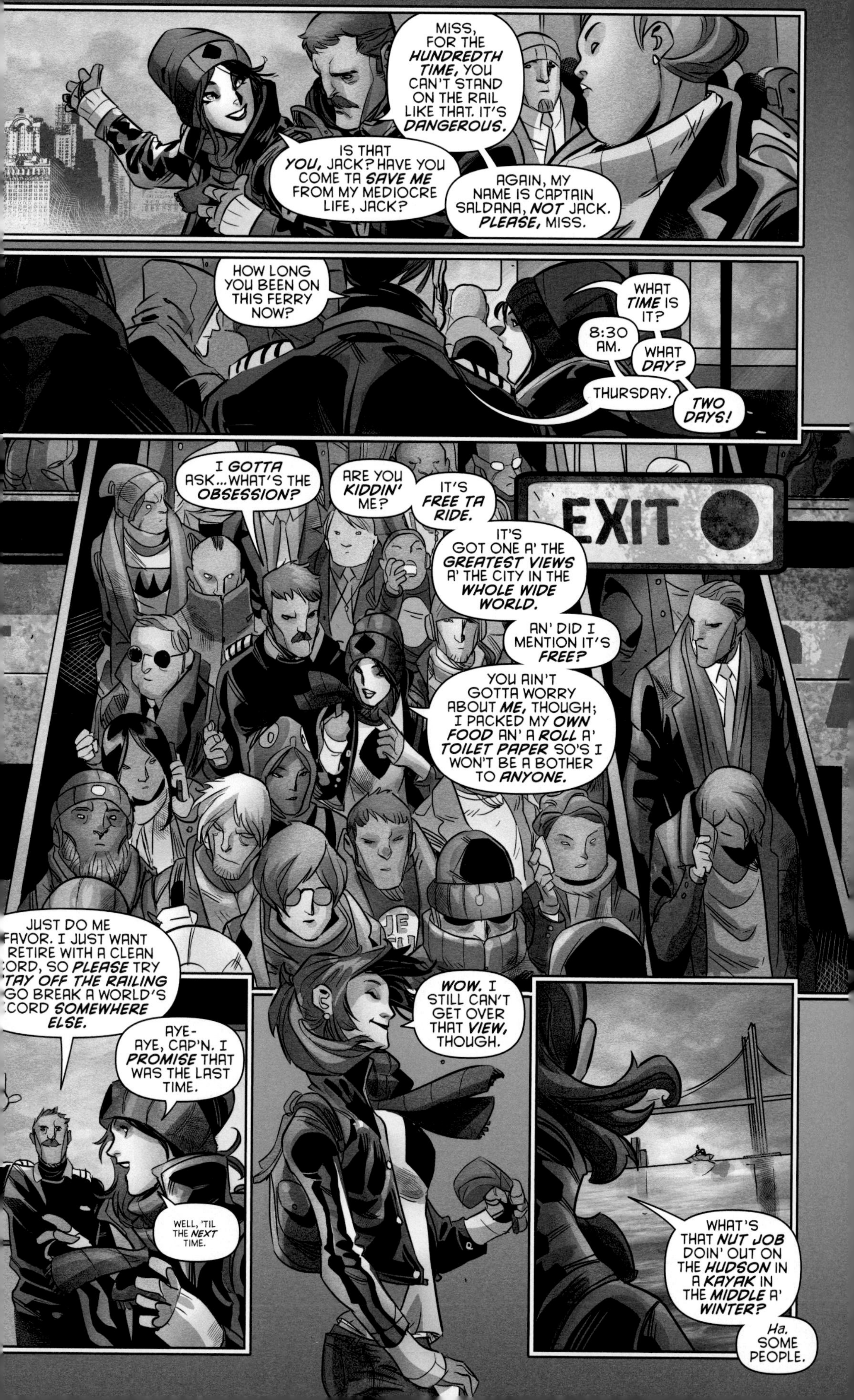
MISS, FOR THE HUNDREDTH TIME, YOU CAN'T STAND ON THE RAIL LIKE THAT. IT'S DANGEROUS.
IS THAT YOU, JACK? HAVE YOU COME TA SAVE ME FROM MY MEDIOCRE LIFE, JACK?
AGAIN, MY NAME IS CAPTAIN SALDANA, NOT JACK. PLEASE, MISS.
HOW LONG YOU BEEN ON THIS FERRY NOW?
WHAT TIME IS IT?
8:30 AM.
WHAT DAY?
THURSDAY.
TWO DAYS!
I GOTTA ASK...WHAT'S THE OBSESSION?
ARE YOU KIDDIN' ME?
IT'S FREE TA RIDE.
IT'S GOT ONE A' THE GREATEST VIEWS A' THE CITY IN THE WHOLE WIDE WORLD.
AN' DID I MENTION IT'S FREE?
YOU AIN'T GOTTA WORRY ABOUT ME, THOUGH; I PACKED MY OWN FOOD AN' A ROLL A' TOILET PAPER SO'S I WON'T BE A BOTHER TO ANYONE.
EXIT
JUST DO ME FAVOR. I JUST WANT RETIRE WITH A CLEAN CORD, SO PLEASE TRY TAY OFF THE RAILING GO BREAK A WORLD'S CORD SOMEWHERE ELSE.
AYE-AYE, CAP'N. I PROMISE THAT WAS THE LAST TIME.
WELL, 'TIL THE NEXT TIME.
WOW. I STILL CAN'T GET OVER THAT VIEW, THOUGH.
WHAT'S THAT NUT JOB DOIN' OUT ON THE HUDSON IN A KAYAK IN THE MIDDLE A' WINTER?
Ha. SOME PEOPLE.

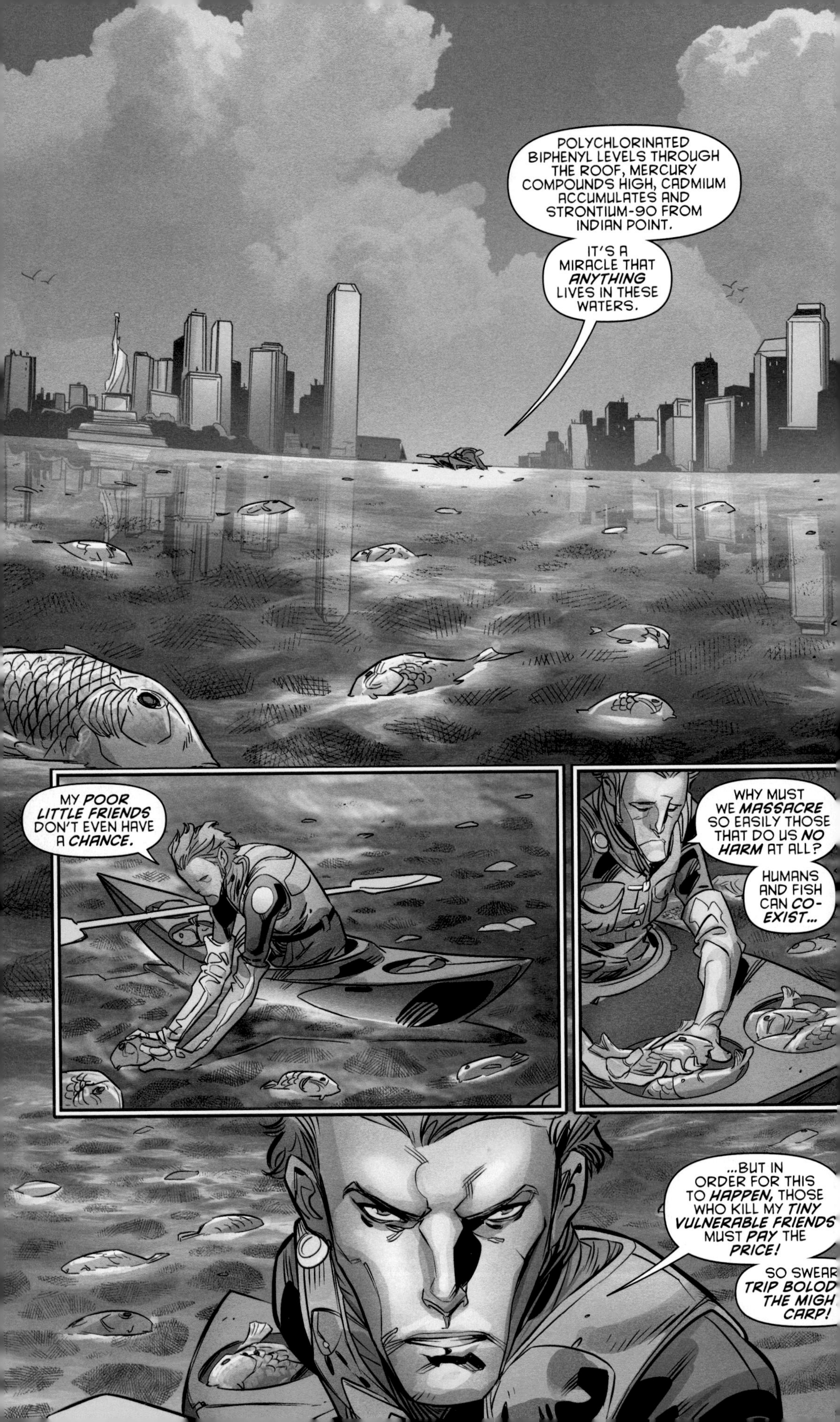
POLYCHLORINATED BIPHENYL LEVELS THROUGH THE ROOF, MERCURY COMPOUNDS HIGH, CADMIUM ACCUMULATES AND STRONTIUM-90 FROM INDIAN POINT.
IT'S A MIRACLE THAT *ANYTHING* LIVES IN THESE WATERS.
MY *POOR LITTLE FRIENDS* DON'T EVEN HAVE A *CHANCE.*
WHY MUST WE *MASSACRE* SO EASILY THOSE THAT DO US *NO HARM* AT ALL?
HUMANS AND FISH CAN *CO-EXIST...*
...BUT IN ORDER FOR THIS TO *HAPPEN,* THOSE WHO KILL MY *TINY VULNERABLE FRIENDS* MUST *PAY* THE *PRICE!*
SO SWEAR *TRIP BOLOD THE MIGH CARP!*

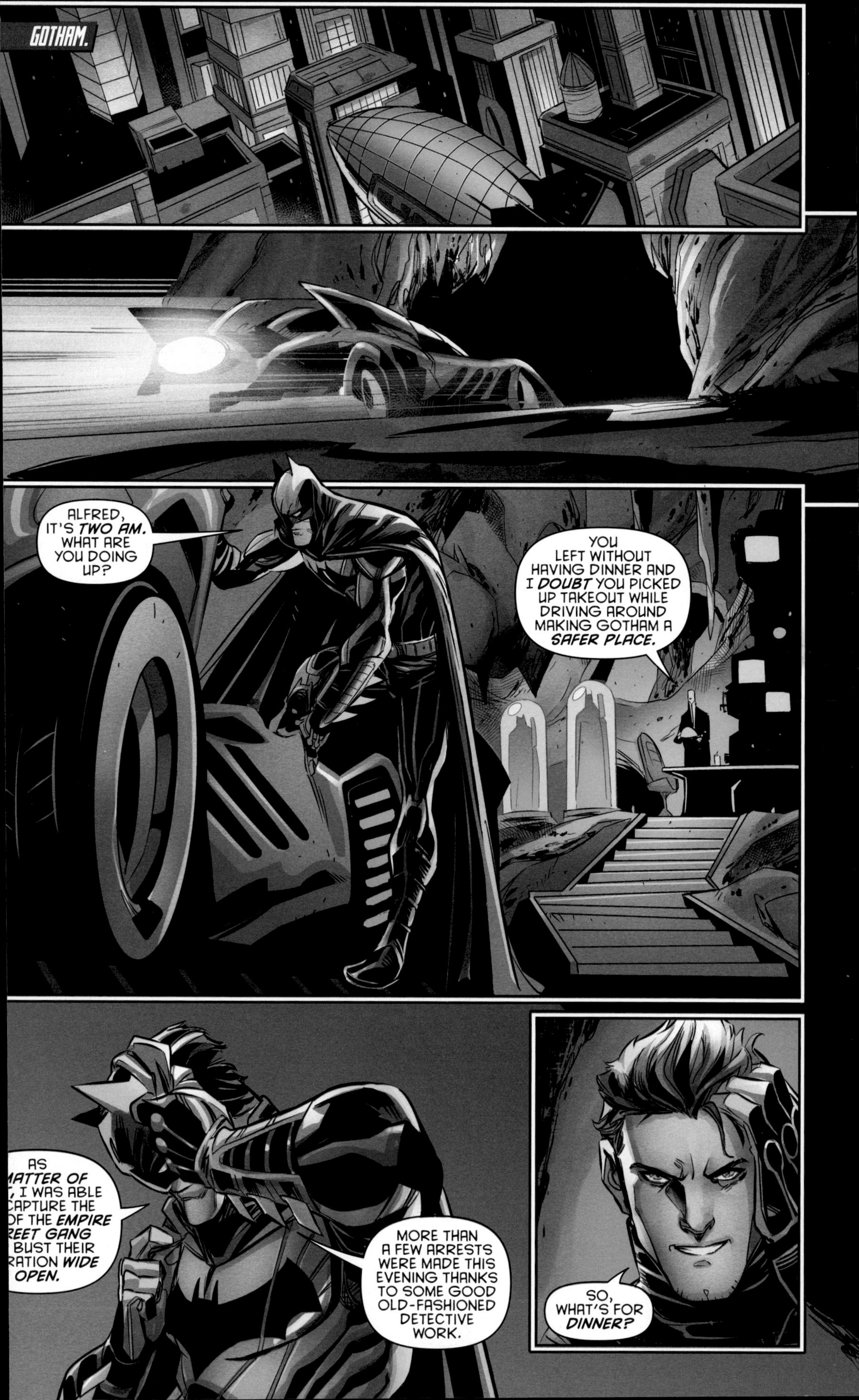
GOTHAM.
ALFRED, IT'S TWO AM. WHAT ARE YOU DOING UP?
YOU LEFT WITHOUT HAVING DINNER AND I DOUBT YOU PICKED UP TAKEOUT WHILE DRIVING AROUND MAKING GOTHAM A SAFER PLACE.
AS MATTER OF T, I WAS ABLE CAPTURE THE OF THE EMPIRE REET GANG BUST THEIR RATION WIDE OPEN.
MORE THAN A FEW ARRESTS WERE MADE THIS EVENING THANKS TO SOME GOOD OLD-FASHIONED DETECTIVE WORK.
SO, WHAT'S FOR DINNER?

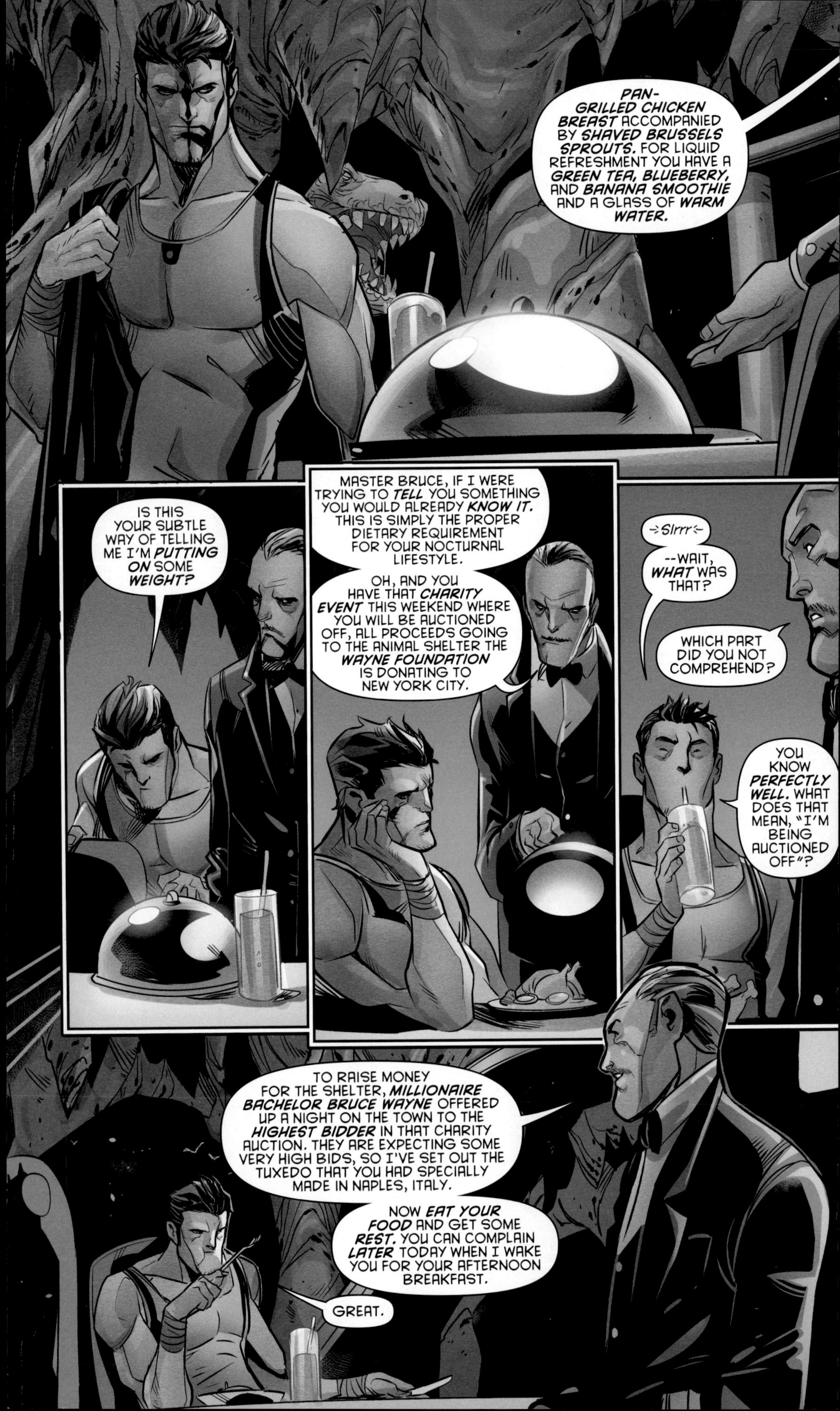
PAN-GRILLED CHICKEN BREAST ACCOMPANIED BY SHAVED BRUSSELS SPROUTS. FOR LIQUID REFRESHMENT YOU HAVE A GREEN TEA, BLUEBERRY, AND BANANA SMOOTHIE AND A GLASS OF WARM WATER.
IS THIS YOUR SUBTLE WAY OF TELLING ME I'M PUTTING ON SOME WEIGHT?
MASTER BRUCE, IF I WERE TRYING TO TELL YOU SOMETHING YOU WOULD ALREADY KNOW IT. THIS IS SIMPLY THE PROPER DIETARY REQUIREMENT FOR YOUR NOCTURNAL LIFESTYLE.
OH, AND YOU HAVE THAT CHARITY EVENT THIS WEEKEND WHERE YOU WILL BE AUCTIONED OFF, ALL PROCEEDS GOING TO THE ANIMAL SHELTER THE WAYNE FOUNDATION IS DONATING TO NEW YORK CITY.
Slrrr
--WAIT, WHAT WAS THAT?
WHICH PART DID YOU NOT COMPREHEND?
YOU KNOW PERFECTLY WELL. WHAT DOES THAT MEAN, "I'M BEING AUCTIONED OFF"?
TO RAISE MONEY FOR THE SHELTER, MILLIONAIRE BACHELOR BRUCE WAYNE OFFERED UP A NIGHT ON THE TOWN TO THE HIGHEST BIDDER IN THAT CHARITY AUCTION. THEY ARE EXPECTING SOME VERY HIGH BIDS, SO I'VE SET OUT THE TUXEDO THAT YOU HAD SPECIALLY MADE IN NAPLES, ITALY.
NOW EAT YOUR FOOD AND GET SOME REST. YOU CAN COMPLAIN LATER TODAY WHEN I WAKE YOU FOR YOUR AFTERNOON BREAKFAST.
GREAT.

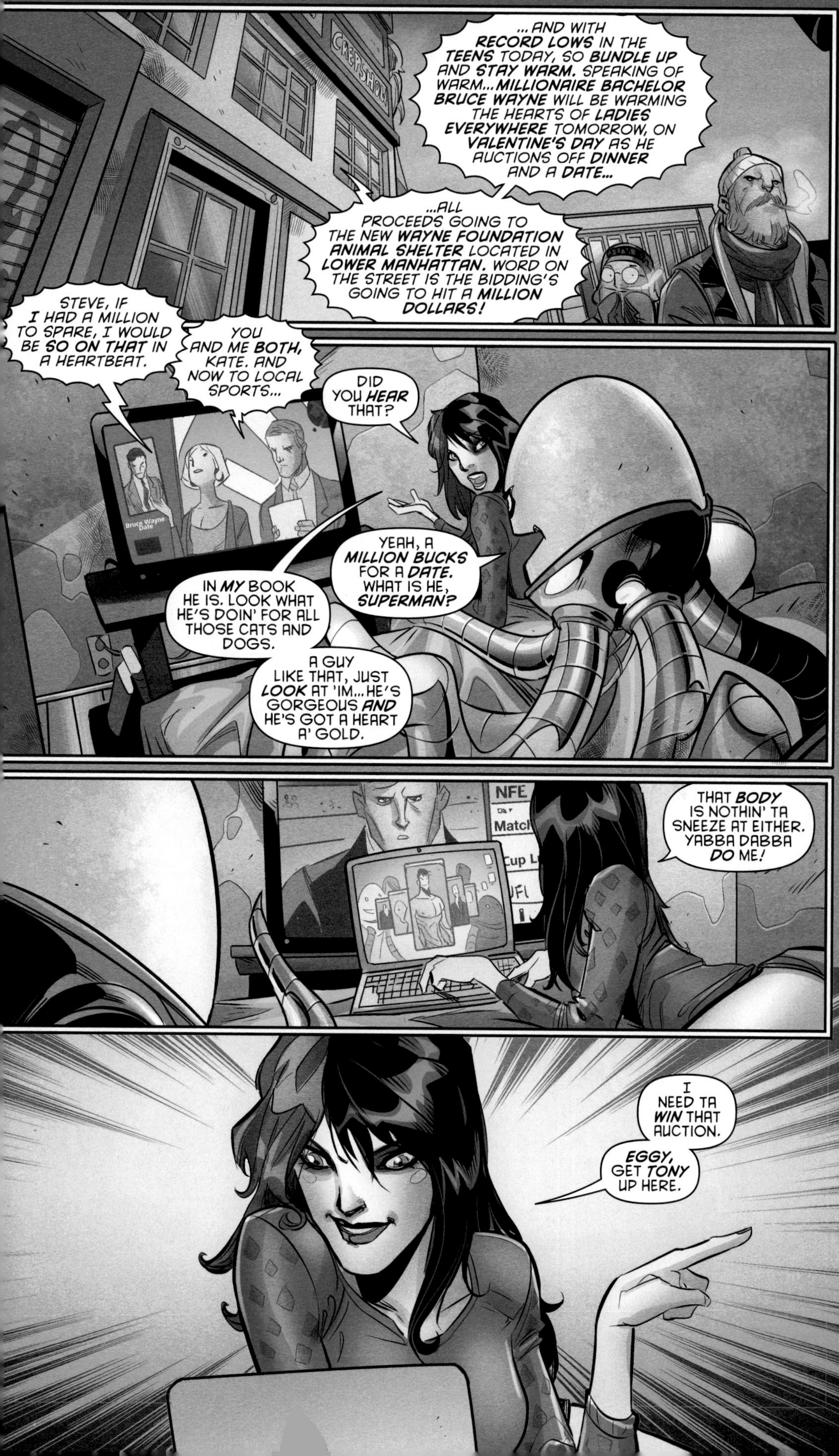
CREPSHOW
...AND WITH RECORD LOWS IN THE TEENS TODAY, SO BUNDLE UP AND STAY WARM. SPEAKING OF WARM... MILLIONAIRE BACHELOR BRUCE WAYNE WILL BE WARMING THE HEARTS OF LADIES EVERYWHERE TOMORROW, ON VALENTINE'S DAY AS HE AUCTIONS OFF DINNER AND A DATE...
...ALL PROCEEDS GOING TO THE NEW WAYNE FOUNDATION ANIMAL SHELTER LOCATED IN LOWER MANHATTAN. WORD ON THE STREET IS THE BIDDING'S GOING TO HIT A MILLION DOLLARS!
STEVE, IF I HAD A MILLION TO SPARE, I WOULD BE SO ON THAT IN A HEARTBEAT.
YOU AND ME BOTH, KATE. AND NOW TO LOCAL SPORTS...
DID YOU HEAR THAT?
Bruce Wayne Date
YEAH, A MILLION BUCKS FOR A DATE. WHAT IS HE, SUPERMAN?
IN MY BOOK HE IS. LOOK WHAT HE'S DOIN' FOR ALL THOSE CATS AND DOGS.
A GUY LIKE THAT, JUST LOOK AT 'IM... HE'S GORGEOUS AND HE'S GOT A HEART A' GOLD.
NFE
THAT BODY IS NOTHIN' TA SNEEZE AT EITHER. YABBA DABBA DO ME!
I NEED TA WIN THAT AUCTION.
EGGY, GET TONY UP HERE.

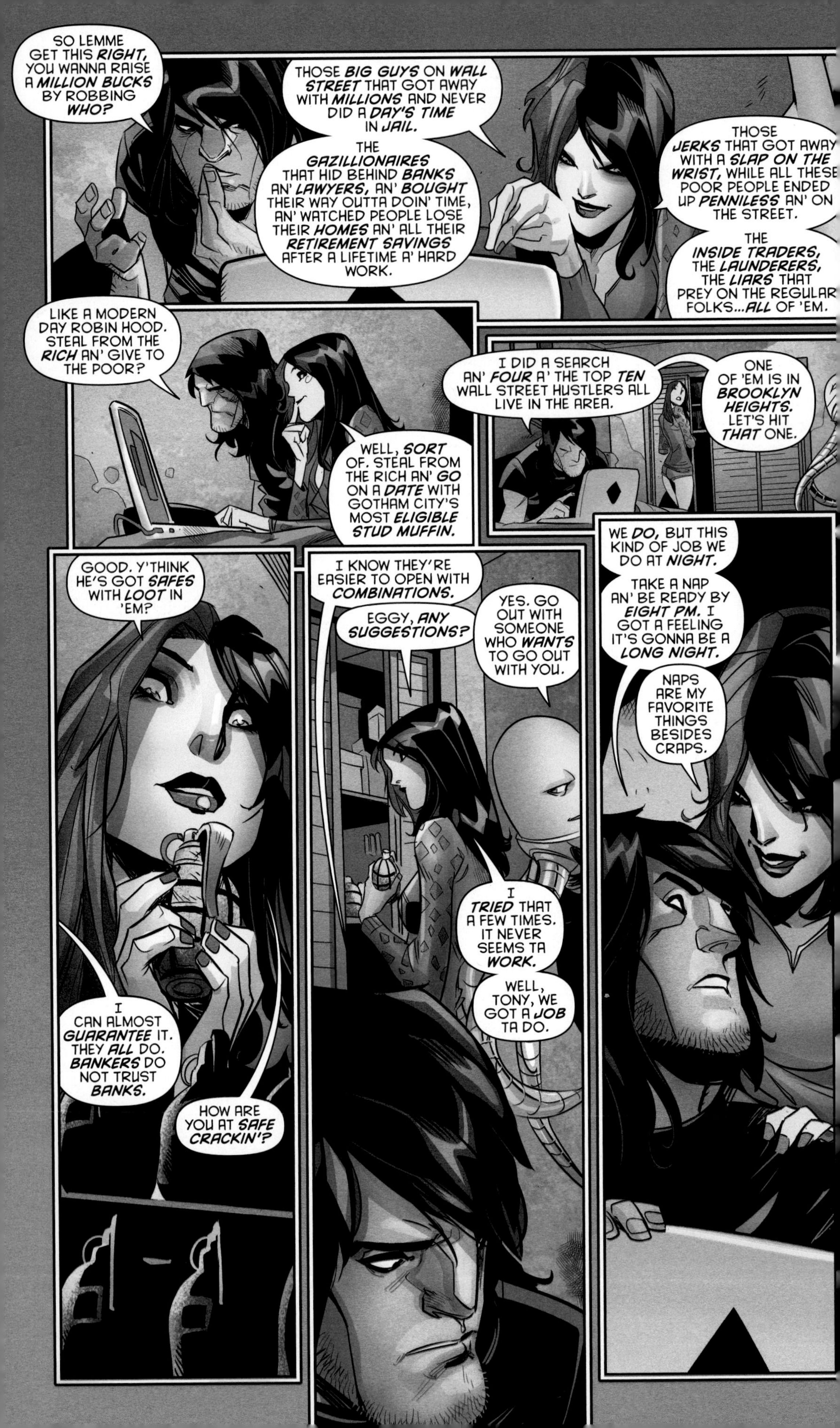
SO LEMME GET THIS RIGHT, YOU WANNA RAISE A MILLION BUCKS BY ROBBING WHO?
THOSE BIG GUYS ON WALL STREET THAT GOT AWAY WITH MILLIONS AND NEVER DID A DAY'S TIME IN JAIL.
THE GAZILLIONAIRES THAT HID BEHIND BANKS AN' LAWYERS, AN' BOUGHT THEIR WAY OUTTA DOIN' TIME, AN' WATCHED PEOPLE LOSE THEIR HOMES AN' ALL THEIR RETIREMENT SAVINGS AFTER A LIFETIME A' HARD WORK.
THOSE JERKS THAT GOT AWAY WITH A SLAP ON THE WRIST, WHILE ALL THESE POOR PEOPLE ENDED UP PENNILESS AN' ON THE STREET.
THE INSIDE TRADERS, THE LAUNDERERS, THE LIARS THAT PREY ON THE REGULAR FOLKS...ALL OF 'EM.
LIKE A MODERN DAY ROBIN HOOD. STEAL FROM THE RICH AN' GIVE TO THE POOR?
WELL, SORT OF. STEAL FROM THE RICH AN' GO ON A DATE WITH GOTHAM CITY'S MOST ELIGIBLE STUD MUFFIN.
I DID A SEARCH AN' FOUR A' THE TOP TEN WALL STREET HUSTLERS ALL LIVE IN THE AREA.
ONE OF 'EM IS IN BROOKLYN HEIGHTS. LET'S HIT THAT ONE.
GOOD. Y'THINK HE'S GOT SAFES WITH LOOT IN 'EM?
I CAN ALMOST GUARANTEE IT. THEY ALL DO. BANKERS DO NOT TRUST BANKS.
HOW ARE YOU AT SAFE CRACKIN'?
I KNOW THEY'RE EASIER TO OPEN WITH COMBINATIONS.
EGGY, ANY SUGGESTIONS?
YES. GO OUT WITH SOMEONE WHO WANTS TO GO OUT WITH YOU.
I TRIED THAT A FEW TIMES. IT NEVER SEEMS TA WORK.
WELL, TONY, WE GOT A JOB TA DO.
WE DO, BUT THIS KIND OF JOB WE DO AT NIGHT.
TAKE A NAP AN' BE READY BY EIGHT PM. I GOT A FEELING IT'S GONNA BE A LONG NIGHT.
NAPS ARE MY FAVORITE THINGS BESIDES CRAPS.

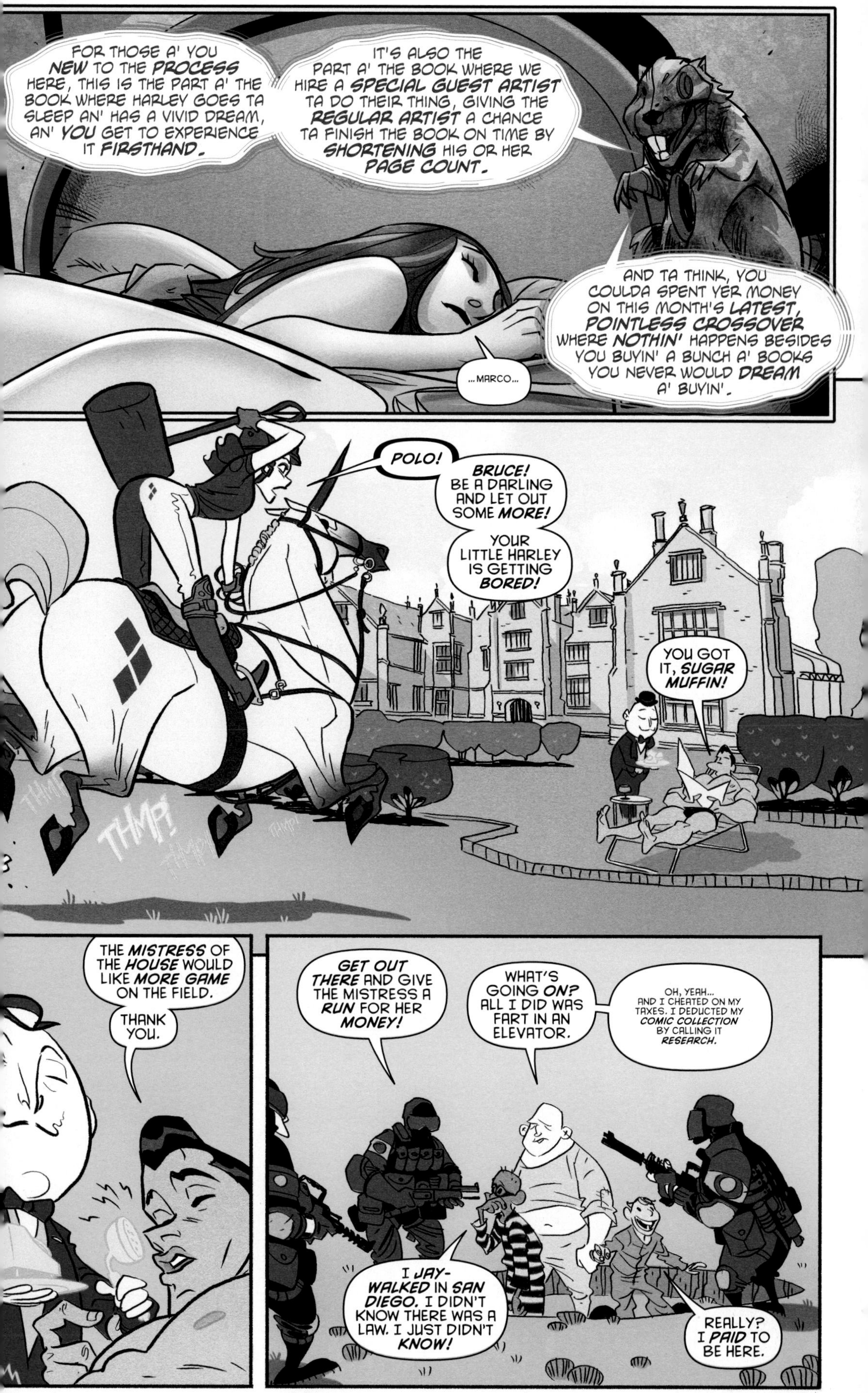
FOR THOSE A' YOU NEW TO THE PROCESS HERE, THIS IS THE PART A' THE BOOK WHERE HARLEY GOES TA SLEEP AN' HAS A VIVID DREAM, AN' YOU GET TO EXPERIENCE IT FIRSTHAND.
IT'S ALSO THE PART A' THE BOOK WHERE WE HIRE A SPECIAL GUEST ARTIST TA DO THEIR THING, GIVING THE REGULAR ARTIST A CHANCE TA FINISH THE BOOK ON TIME BY SHORTENING HIS OR HER PAGE COUNT.
AND TA THINK, YOU COULDA SPENT YER MONEY ON THIS MONTH'S LATEST, POINTLESS CROSSOVER WHERE NOTHIN' HAPPENS BESIDES YOU BUYIN' A BUNCH A' BOOKS YOU NEVER WOULD DREAM A' BUYIN'.
...MARCO...
POLO!
BRUCE! BE A DARLING AND LET OUT SOME MORE!
YOUR LITTLE HARLEY IS GETTING BORED!
YOU GOT IT, SUGAR MUFFIN!
THMP!
THMP!
THMP!
THMP!
THE MISTRESS OF THE HOUSE WOULD LIKE MORE GAME ON THE FIELD.
THANK YOU.
GET OUT THERE AND GIVE THE MISTRESS A RUN FOR HER MONEY!
WHAT'S GOING ON? ALL I DID WAS FART IN AN ELEVATOR.
OH, YEAH... AND I CHEATED ON MY TAXES. I DEDUCTED MY COMIC COLLECTION BY CALLING IT RESEARCH.
I JAY-WALKED IN SAN DIEGO. I DIDN'T KNOW THERE WAS A LAW. I JUST DIDN'T KNOW!
REALLY? I PAID TO BE HERE.

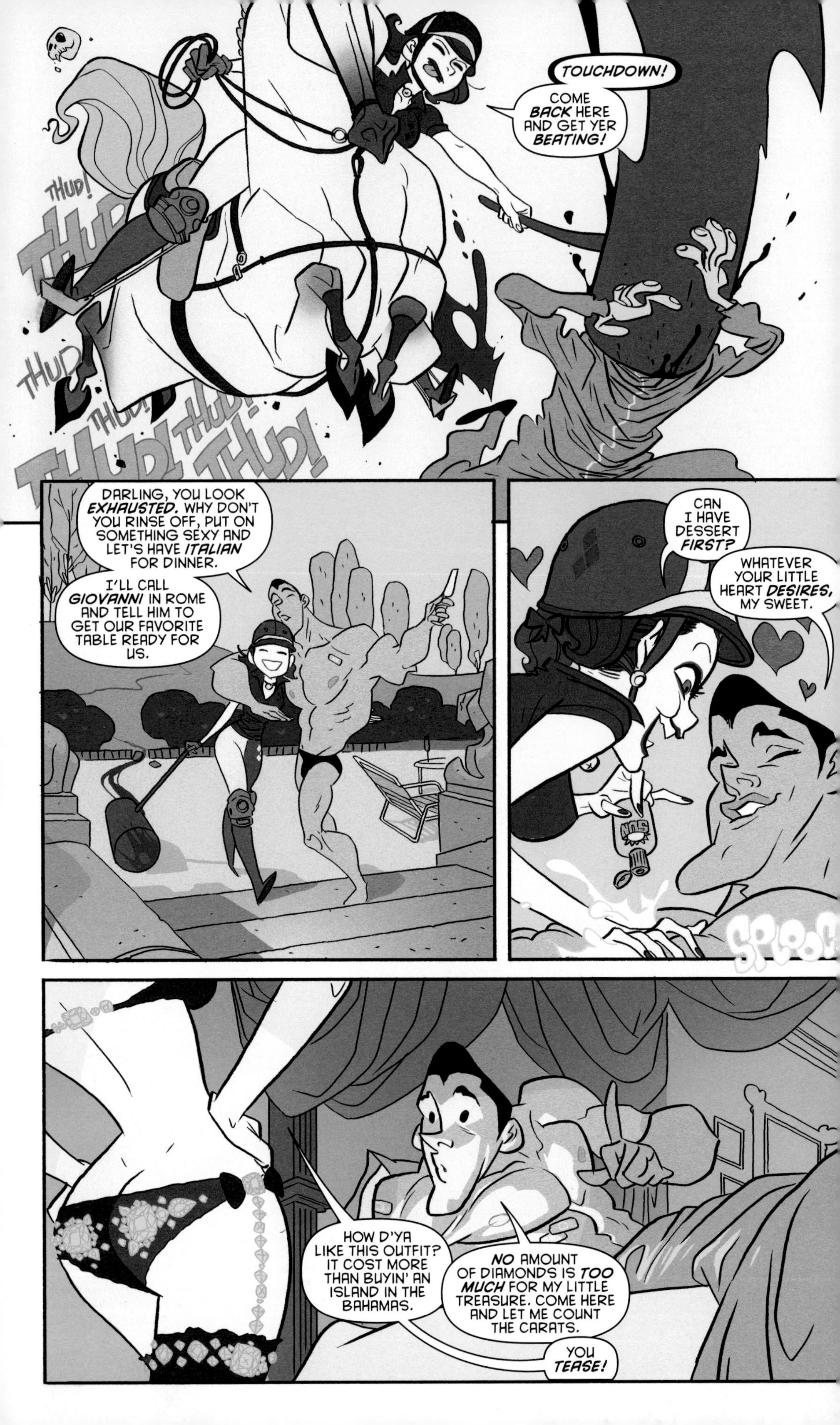
THUD!
THUD!
THUD!
THUD!
THUD!
THUD!
THUD!
TOUCHDOWN!
COME BACK HERE AND GET YER BEATING!
DARLING, YOU LOOK EXHAUSTED. WHY DON'T YOU RINSE OFF, PUT ON SOMETHING SEXY AND LET'S HAVE ITALIAN FOR DINNER.
I'LL CALL GIOVANNI IN ROME AND TELL HIM TO GET OUR FAVORITE TABLE READY FOR US.
CAN I HAVE DESSERT FIRST?
WHATEVER YOUR LITTLE HEART DESIRES, MY SWEET.
SPLOO
HOW D'YA LIKE THIS OUTFIT? IT COST MORE THAN BUYIN' AN ISLAND IN THE BAHAMAS.
NO AMOUNT OF DIAMONDS IS TOO MUCH FOR MY LITTLE TREASURE. COME HERE AND LET ME COUNT THE CARATS.
YOU TEASE!

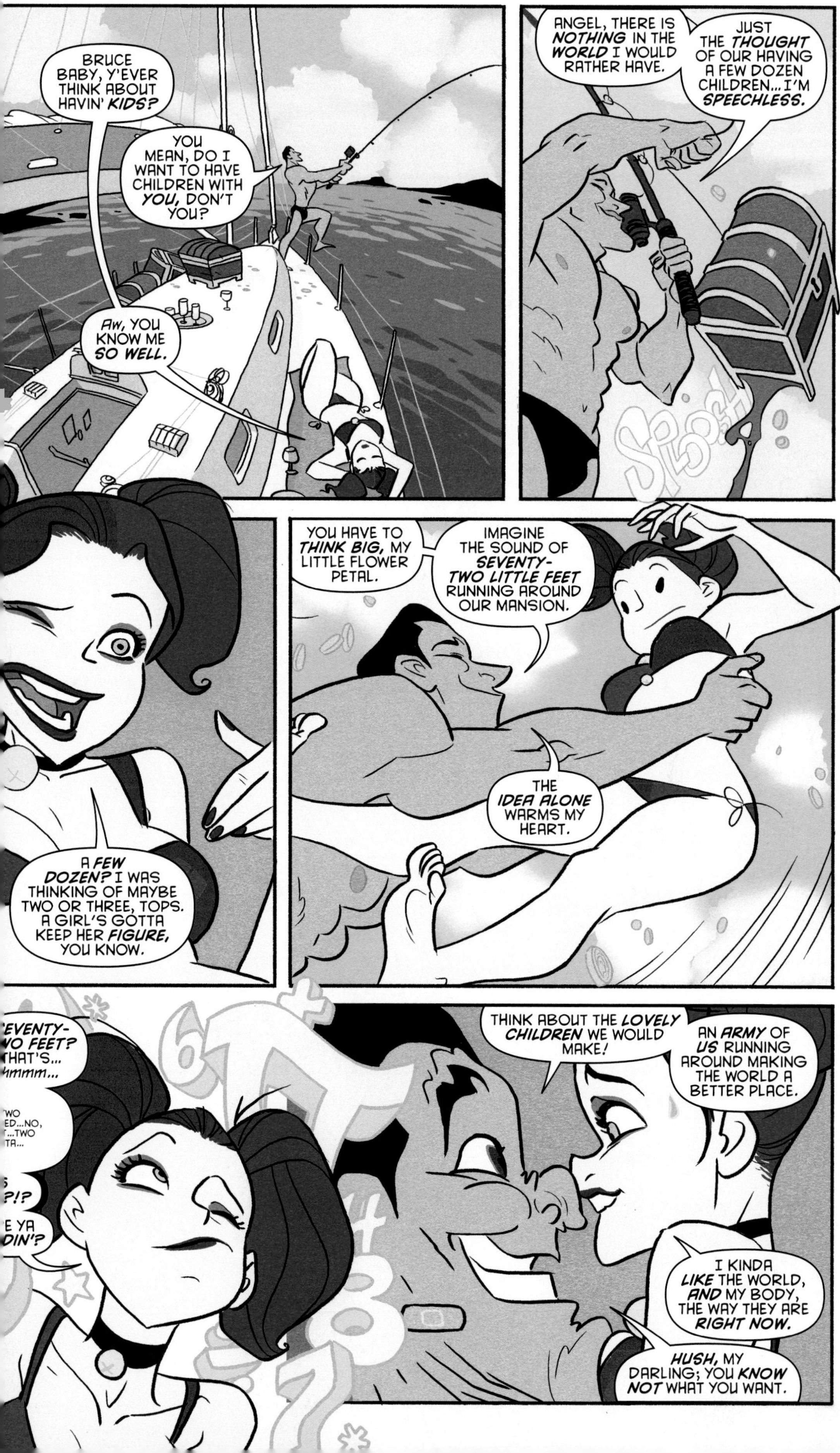

BRUCE BABY, Y'EVER THINK ABOUT HAVIN' KIDS?
YOU MEAN, DO I WANT TO HAVE CHILDREN WITH YOU, DON'T YOU?
AW, YOU KNOW ME SO WELL.
ANGEL, THERE IS NOTHING IN THE WORLD I WOULD RATHER HAVE.
JUST THE THOUGHT OF OUR HAVING A FEW DOZEN CHILDREN... I'M SPEECHLESS.
SPLOOSH
A FEW DOZEN? I WAS THINKING OF MAYBE TWO OR THREE, TOPS. A GIRL'S GOTTA KEEP HER FIGURE, YOU KNOW.
YOU HAVE TO THINK BIG, MY LITTLE FLOWER PETAL.
IMAGINE THE SOUND OF SEVENTY-TWO LITTLE FEET RUNNING AROUND OUR MANSION.
THE IDEA ALONE WARMS MY HEART.
EVENTY- O FEET? THAT'S... hmmm...
WO ED...NO, ...TWO TA...
?!?
E YA DIN'?
THINK ABOUT THE LOVELY CHILDREN WE WOULD MAKE!
AN ARMY OF US RUNNING AROUND MAKING THE WORLD A BETTER PLACE.
I KINDA LIKE THE WORLD, AND MY BODY, THE WAY THEY ARE RIGHT NOW.
HUSH, MY DARLING; YOU KNOW NOT WHAT YOU WANT.

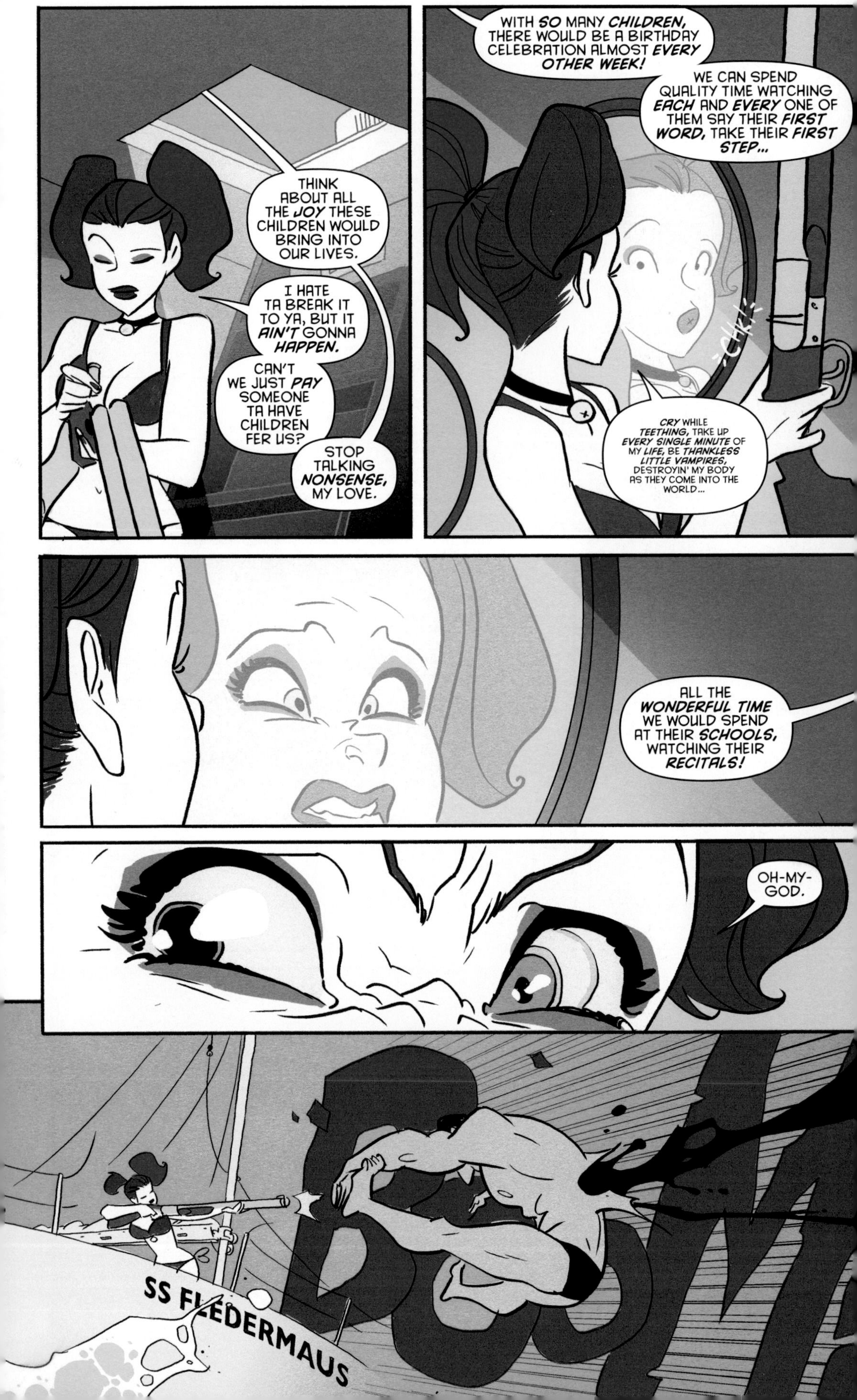
THINK ABOUT ALL THE JOY THESE CHILDREN WOULD BRING INTO OUR LIVES.
I HATE TA BREAK IT TO YA, BUT IT AIN'T GONNA HAPPEN.
CAN'T WE JUST PAY SOMEONE TA HAVE CHILDREN FER US?
STOP TALKING NONSENSE, MY LOVE.
WITH SO MANY CHILDREN, THERE WOULD BE A BIRTHDAY CELEBRATION ALMOST EVERY OTHER WEEK!
WE CAN SPEND QUALITY TIME WATCHING EACH AND EVERY ONE OF THEM SAY THEIR FIRST WORD, TAKE THEIR FIRST STEP...
CHK!
CRY WHILE TEETHING, TAKE UP EVERY SINGLE MINUTE OF MY LIFE, BE THANKLESS LITTLE VAMPIRES, DESTROYIN' MY BODY AS THEY COME INTO THE WORLD...
ALL THE WONDERFUL TIME WE WOULD SPEND AT THEIR SCHOOLS, WATCHING THEIR RECITALS!
OH-MY-GOD.
SS FLEDERMAUS

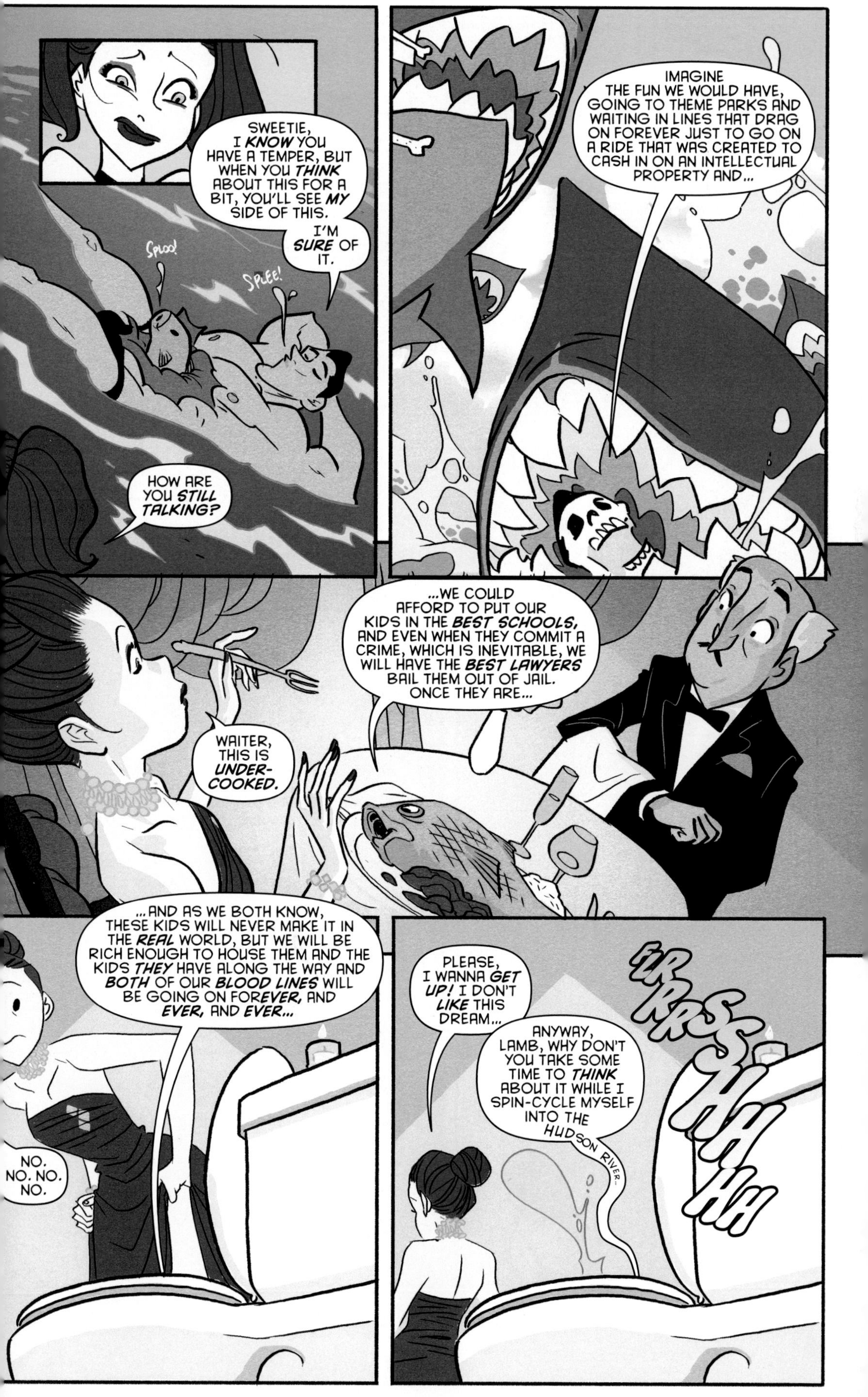

SWEETIE, I KNOW YOU HAVE A TEMPER, BUT WHEN YOU THINK ABOUT THIS FOR A BIT, YOU'LL SEE MY SIDE OF THIS.
I'M SURE OF IT.
SPLOO!
SPLEE!
HOW ARE YOU STILL TALKING?
IMAGINE THE FUN WE WOULD HAVE, GOING TO THEME PARKS AND WAITING IN LINES THAT DRAG ON FOREVER JUST TO GO ON A RIDE THAT WAS CREATED TO CASH IN ON AN INTELLECTUAL PROPERTY AND...
...WE COULD AFFORD TO PUT OUR KIDS IN THE BEST SCHOOLS, AND EVEN WHEN THEY COMMIT A CRIME, WHICH IS INEVITABLE, WE WILL HAVE THE BEST LAWYERS BAIL THEM OUT OF JAIL. ONCE THEY ARE...
WAITER, THIS IS UNDER-COOKED.
...AND AS WE BOTH KNOW, THESE KIDS WILL NEVER MAKE IT IN THE REAL WORLD, BUT WE WILL BE RICH ENOUGH TO HOUSE THEM AND THE KIDS THEY HAVE ALONG THE WAY AND BOTH OF OUR BLOOD LINES WILL BE GOING ON FOREVER, AND EVER, AND EVER...
NO. NO. NO. NO.
PLEASE, I WANNA GET UP! I DON'T LIKE THIS DREAM...
ANYWAY, LAMB, WHY DON'T YOU TAKE SOME TIME TO THINK ABOUT IT WHILE I SPIN-CYCLE MYSELF INTO THE HUDSON RIVER...
FLRRRSSSHHHHHH

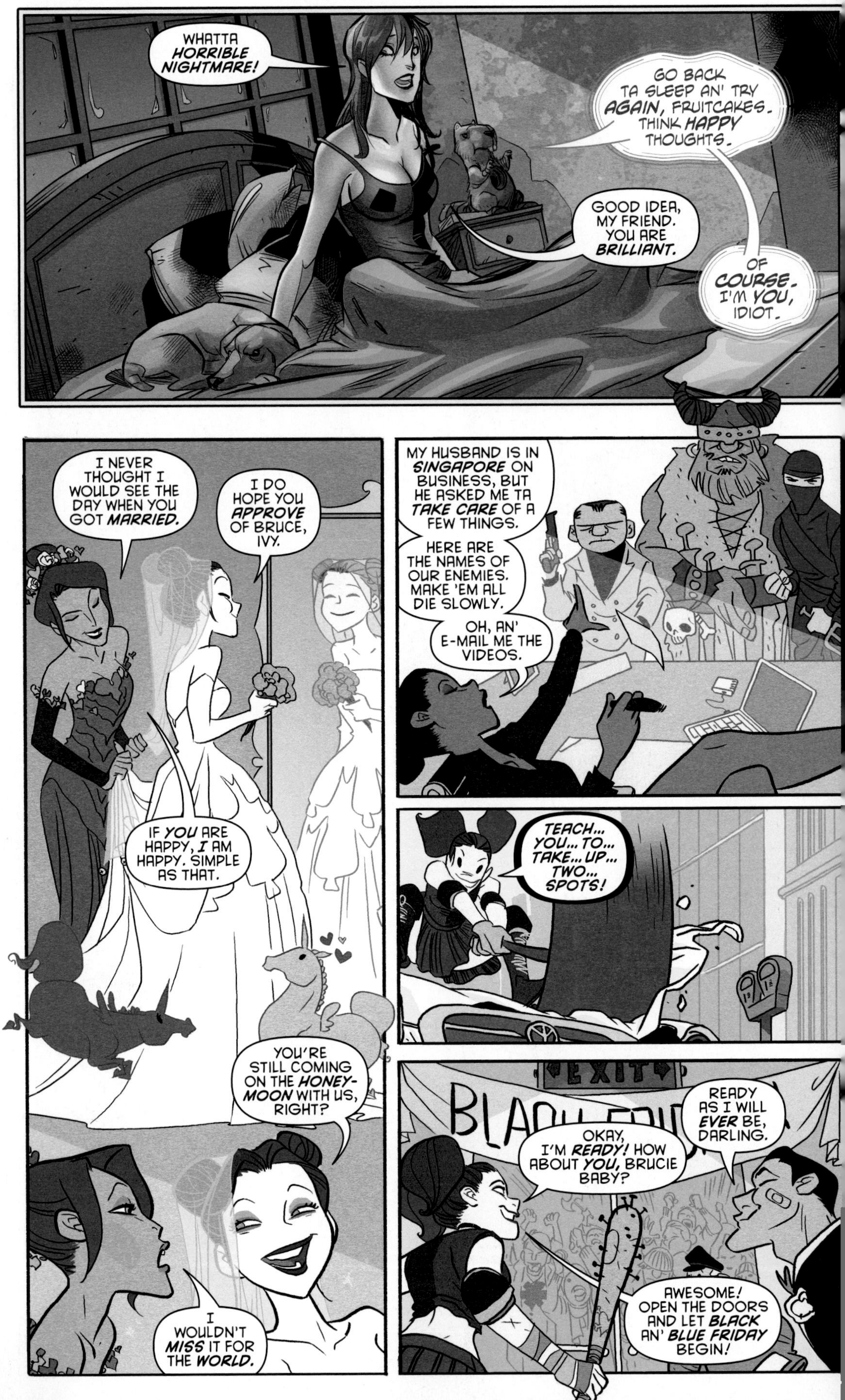
WHATTA HORRIBLE NIGHTMARE!
GO BACK TA SLEEP AN' TRY AGAIN, FRUITCAKES. THINK HAPPY THOUGHTS.
GOOD IDEA, MY FRIEND. YOU ARE BRILLIANT.
OF COURSE. I'M YOU, IDIOT.
I NEVER THOUGHT I WOULD SEE THE DAY WHEN YOU GOT MARRIED.
I DO HOPE YOU APPROVE OF BRUCE, IVY.
IF YOU ARE HAPPY, I AM HAPPY. SIMPLE AS THAT.
YOU'RE STILL COMING ON THE HONEY-MOON WITH US, RIGHT?
I WOULDN'T MISS IT FOR THE WORLD.
MY HUSBAND IS IN SINGAPORE ON BUSINESS, BUT HE ASKED ME TA TAKE CARE OF A FEW THINGS.
HERE ARE THE NAMES OF OUR ENEMIES. MAKE 'EM ALL DIE SLOWLY.
OH, AN' E-MAIL ME THE VIDEOS.
TEACH... YOU... TO... TAKE... UP... TWO... SPOTS!
EXIT
OKAY, I'M READY! HOW ABOUT YOU, BRUCIE BABY?
READY AS I WILL EVER BE, DARLING.
AWESOME! OPEN THE DOORS AND LET BLACK AN' BLUE FRIDAY BEGIN!

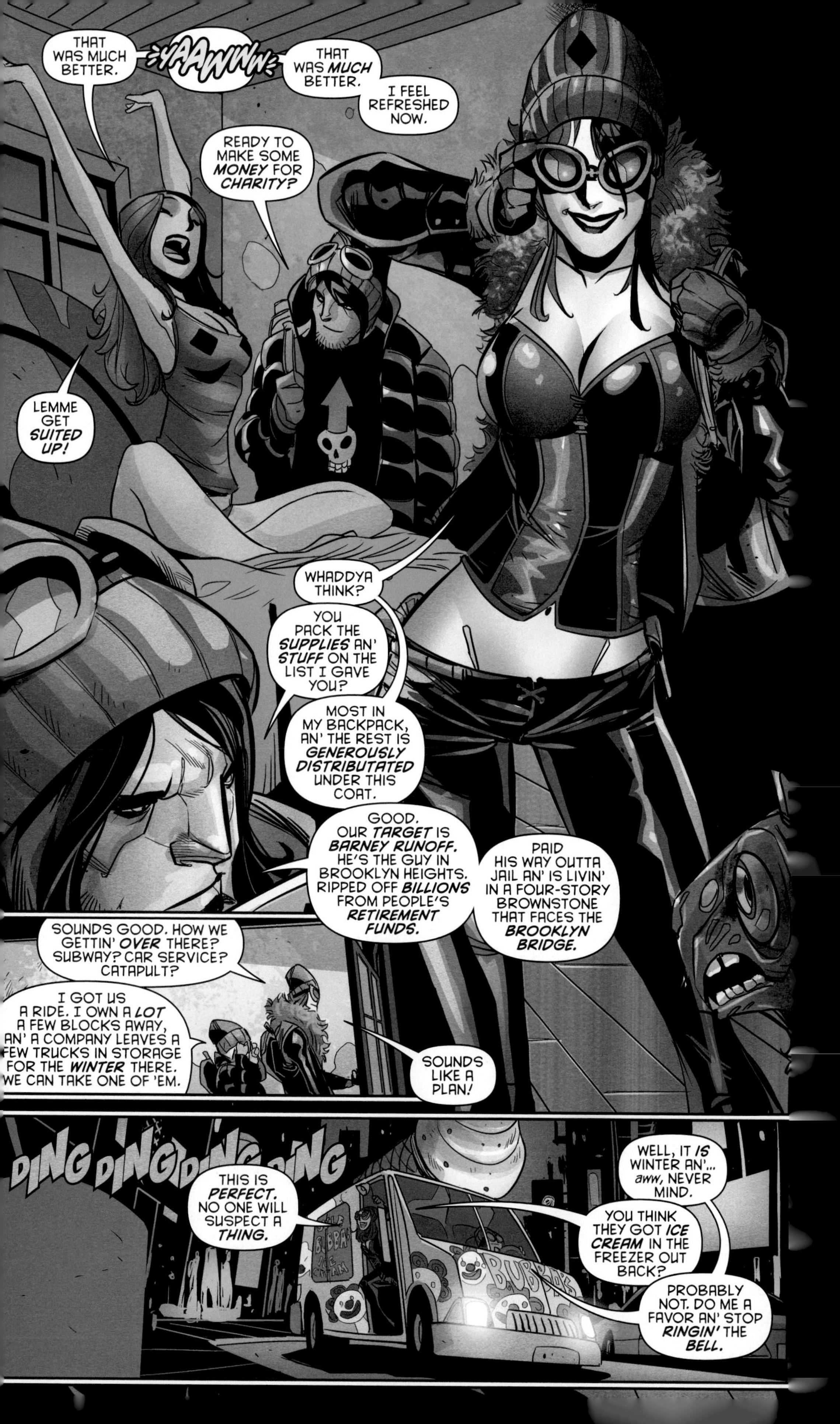

THAT WAS MUCH BETTER.
YAAWWW
THAT WAS MUCH BETTER.
I FEEL REFRESHED NOW.
READY TO MAKE SOME MONEY FOR CHARITY?
LEMME GET SUITED UP!
WHADDYA THINK?
YOU PACK THE SUPPLIES AN' STUFF ON THE LIST I GAVE YOU?
MOST IN MY BACKPACK, AN' THE REST IS GENEROUSLY DISTRIBUTATED UNDER THIS COAT.
GOOD. OUR TARGET IS BARNEY RUNOFF. HE'S THE GUY IN BROOKLYN HEIGHTS. RIPPED OFF BILLIONS FROM PEOPLE'S RETIREMENT FUNDS.
PAID HIS WAY OUTTA JAIL AN' IS LIVIN' IN A FOUR-STORY BROWNSTONE THAT FACES THE BROOKLYN BRIDGE.
SOUNDS GOOD. HOW WE GETTIN' OVER THERE? SUBWAY? CAR SERVICE? CATAPULT?
I GOT US A RIDE. I OWN A LOT A FEW BLOCKS AWAY, AN' A COMPANY LEAVES A FEW TRUCKS IN STORAGE FOR THE WINTER THERE. WE CAN TAKE ONE OF 'EM.
SOUNDS LIKE A PLAN!
DING DING DING DING DING
THIS IS PERFECT. NO ONE WILL SUSPECT A THING.
WELL, IT IS WINTER AN'... aww, NEVER MIND.
YOU THINK THEY GOT ICE CREAM IN THE FREEZER OUT BACK?
PROBABLY NOT. DO ME A FAVOR AN' STOP RINGIN' THE BELL.
BUBBA'S

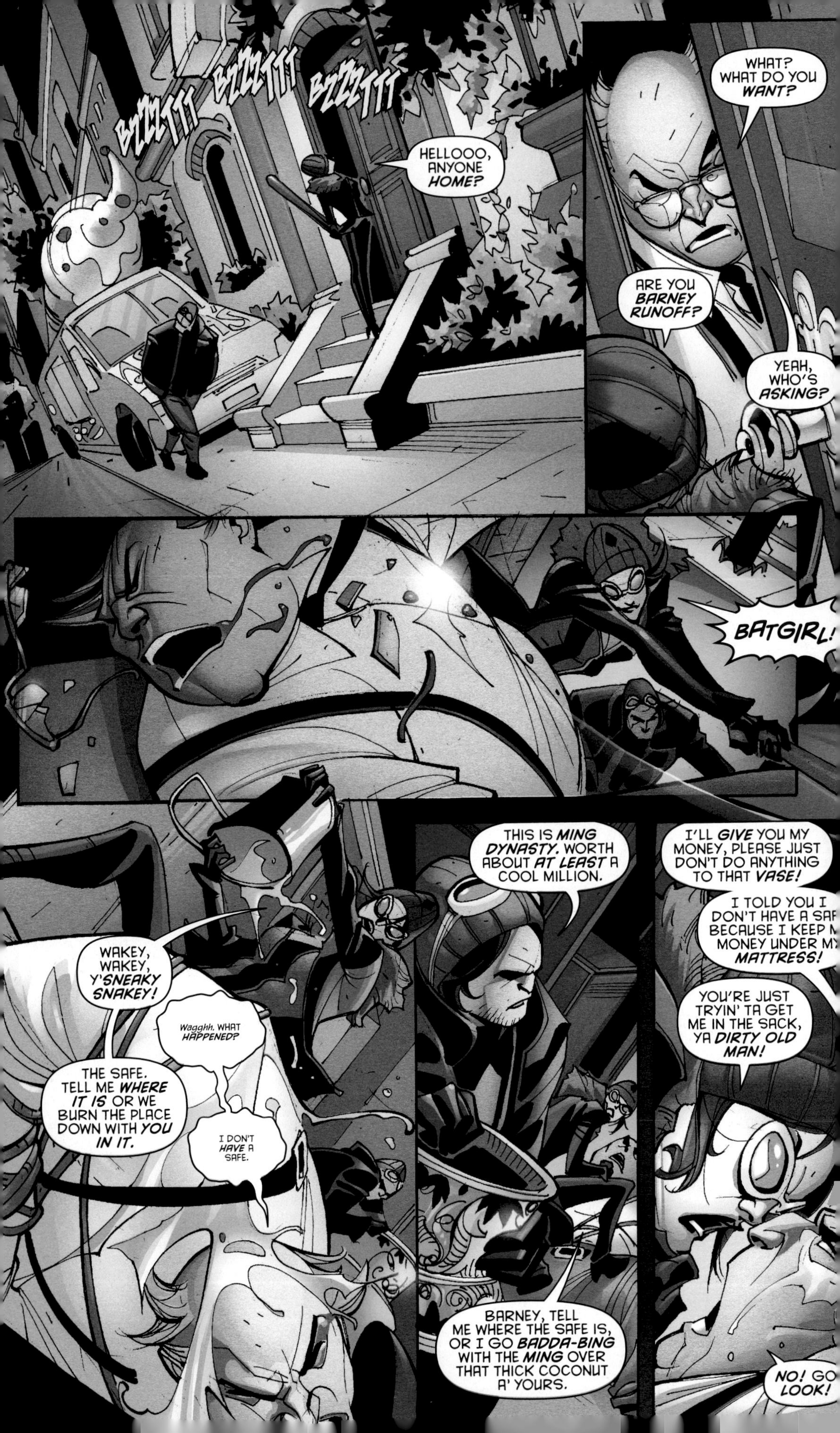
BZZZTTT BZZZTTT BZZZTTT
HELLOOO, ANYONE HOME?
WHAT? WHAT DO YOU WANT?
ARE YOU BARNEY RUNOFF?
YEAH, WHO'S ASKING?
BATGIRL!
WAKEY, WAKEY, Y'SNEAKY SNAKEY!
Wagghh. WHAT HAPPENED?
THE SAFE. TELL ME WHERE IT IS OR WE BURN THE PLACE DOWN WITH YOU IN IT.
I DON'T HAVE A SAFE.
THIS IS MING DYNASTY. WORTH ABOUT AT LEAST A COOL MILLION.
BARNEY, TELL ME WHERE THE SAFE IS, OR I GO BADDA-BING WITH THE MING OVER THAT THICK COCONUT A' YOURS.
I'LL GIVE YOU MY MONEY, PLEASE JUST DON'T DO ANYTHING TO THAT VASE!
YOU'RE JUST TRYIN' TA GET ME IN THE SACK, YA DIRTY OLD MAN!
NO! GO LOOK!

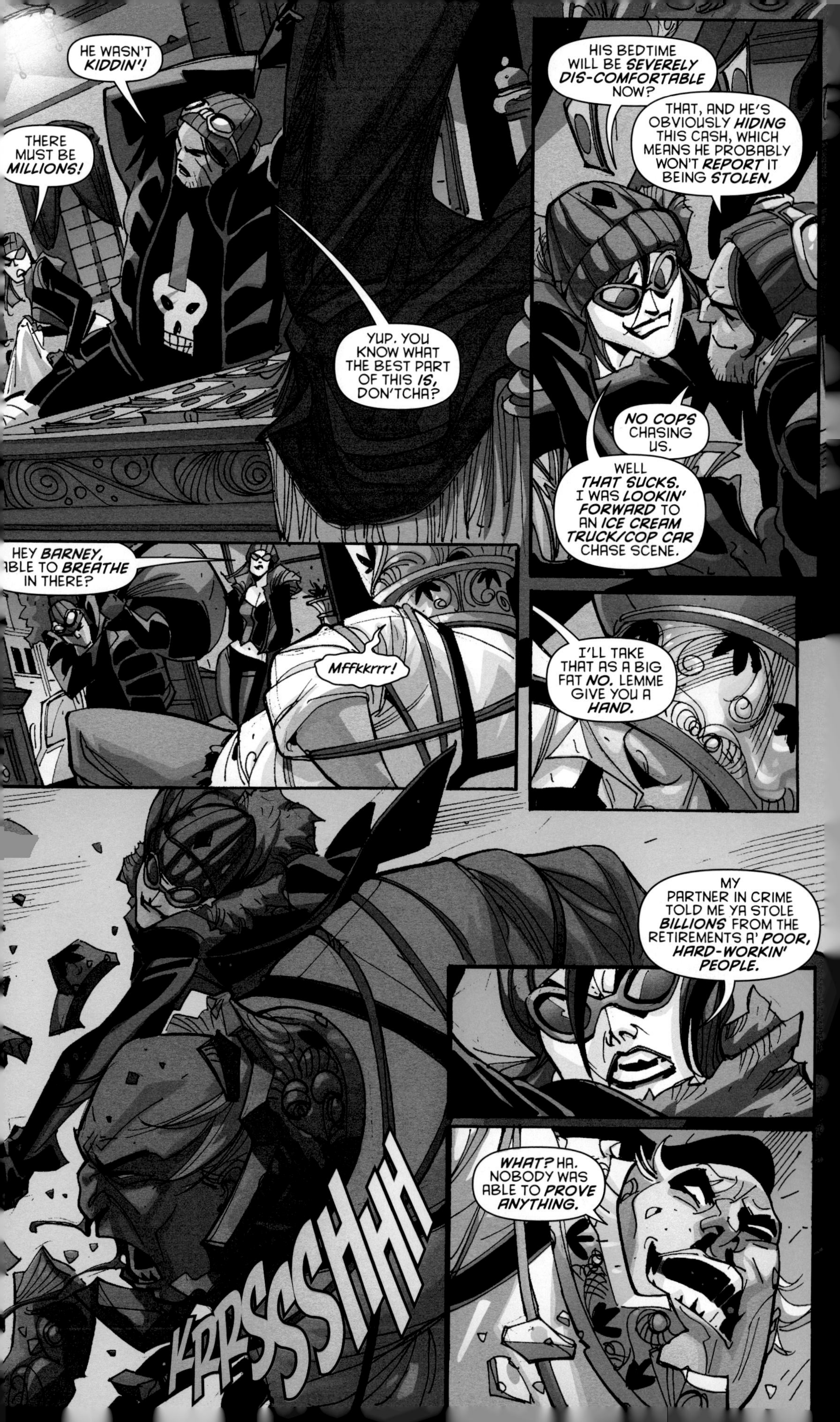

HE WASN'T KIDDIN'!
THERE MUST BE MILLIONS!
YUP. YOU KNOW WHAT THE BEST PART OF THIS IS, DON'TCHA?
HIS BEDTIME WILL BE SEVERELY DIS-COMFORTABLE NOW?
THAT, AND HE'S OBVIOUSLY HIDING THIS CASH, WHICH MEANS HE PROBABLY WON'T REPORT IT BEING STOLEN.
NO COPS CHASING US.
WELL THAT SUCKS. I WAS LOOKIN' FORWARD TO AN ICE CREAM TRUCK/COP CAR CHASE SCENE.
HEY BARNEY, ABLE TO BREATHE IN THERE?
Mffkkrrr!
I'LL TAKE THAT AS A BIG FAT NO. LEMME GIVE YOU A HAND.
KRRSSSHHH
MY PARTNER IN CRIME TOLD ME YA STOLE BILLIONS FROM THE RETIREMENTS A' POOR, HARD-WORKIN' PEOPLE.
WHAT? HA. NOBODY WAS ABLE TO PROVE ANYTHING.

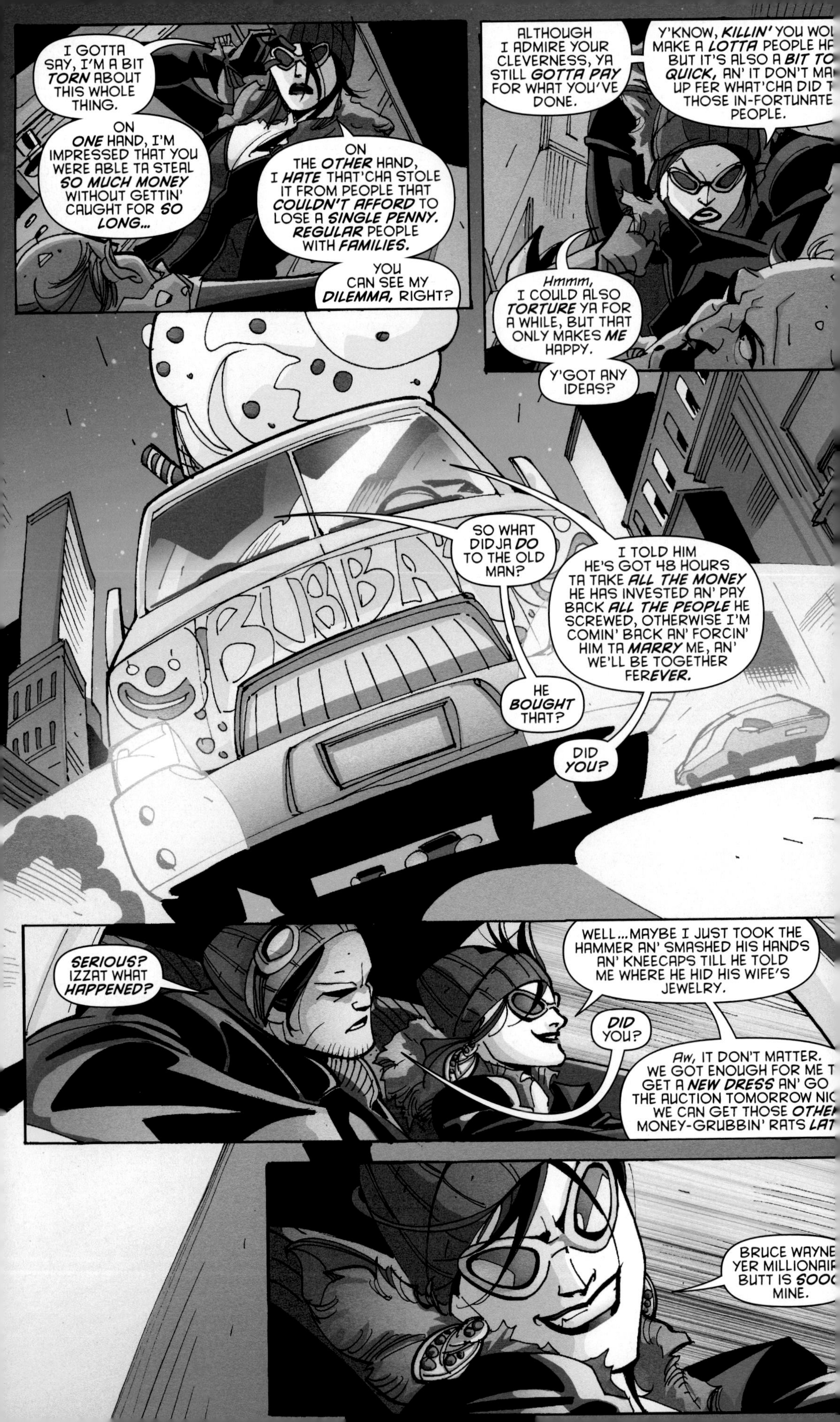

I GOTTA SAY, I'M A BIT TORN ABOUT THIS WHOLE THING.
ON ONE HAND, I'M IMPRESSED THAT YOU WERE ABLE TA STEAL SO MUCH MONEY WITHOUT GETTIN' CAUGHT FOR SO LONG...
ON THE OTHER HAND, I HATE THAT'CHA STOLE IT FROM PEOPLE THAT COULDN'T AFFORD TO LOSE A SINGLE PENNY. REGULAR PEOPLE WITH FAMILIES.
YOU CAN SEE MY DILEMMA, RIGHT?
ALTHOUGH I ADMIRE YOUR CLEVERNESS, YA STILL GOTTA PAY FOR WHAT YOU'VE DONE.
Hmmm, I COULD ALSO TORTURE YA FOR A WHILE, BUT THAT ONLY MAKES ME HAPPY.
Y'GOT ANY IDEAS?
BUBBA
SO WHAT DIDJA DO TO THE OLD MAN?
I TOLD HIM HE'S GOT 48 HOURS TA TAKE ALL THE MONEY HE HAS INVESTED AN' PAY BACK ALL THE PEOPLE HE SCREWED, OTHERWISE I'M COMIN' BACK AN' FORCIN' HIM TA MARRY ME, AN' WE'LL BE TOGETHER FEREVER.
HE BOUGHT THAT?
DID YOU?
SERIOUS? IZZAT WHAT HAPPENED?
WELL...MAYBE I JUST TOOK THE HAMMER AN' SMASHED HIS HANDS AN' KNEECAPS TILL HE TOLD ME WHERE HE HID HIS WIFE'S JEWELRY.
DID YOU?

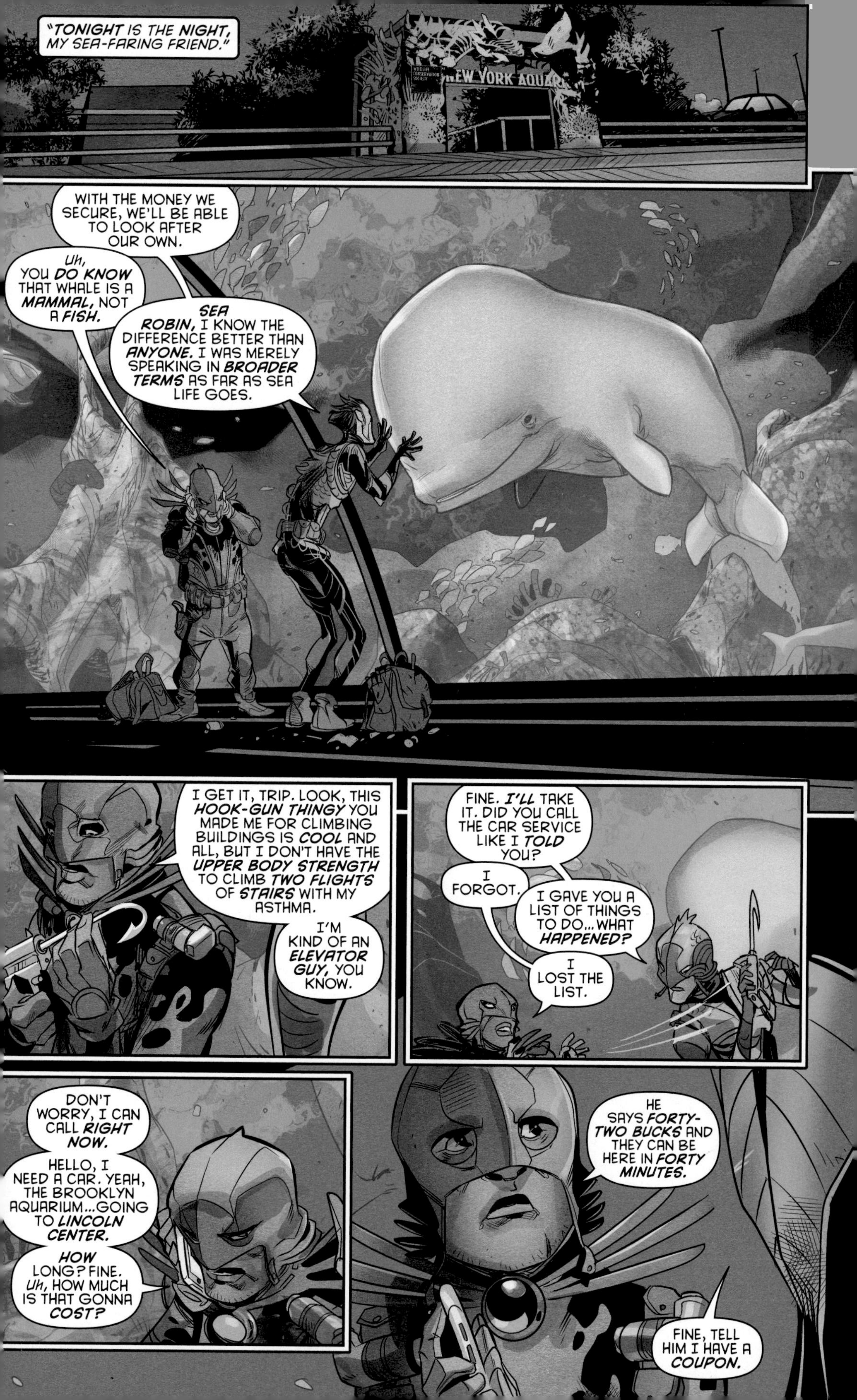
"TONIGHT IS THE NIGHT, MY SEA-FARING FRIEND."
WILDLIFE CONSERVATION SOCIETY
NEW YORK AQUA
WITH THE MONEY WE SECURE, WE'LL BE ABLE TO LOOK AFTER OUR OWN.
UH, YOU DO KNOW THAT WHALE IS A MAMMAL, NOT A FISH.
SEA ROBIN, I KNOW THE DIFFERENCE BETTER THAN ANYONE. I WAS MERELY SPEAKING IN BROADER TERMS AS FAR AS SEA LIFE GOES.
I GET IT, TRIP. LOOK, THIS HOOK-GUN THINGY YOU MADE ME FOR CLIMBING BUILDINGS IS COOL AND ALL, BUT I DON'T HAVE THE UPPER BODY STRENGTH TO CLIMB TWO FLIGHTS OF STAIRS WITH MY ASTHMA.
I'M KIND OF AN ELEVATOR GUY, YOU KNOW.
FINE. I'LL TAKE IT. DID YOU CALL THE CAR SERVICE LIKE I TOLD YOU?
I FORGOT.
I GAVE YOU A LIST OF THINGS TO DO... WHAT HAPPENED?
I LOST THE LIST.
DON'T WORRY, I CAN CALL RIGHT NOW.
HELLO, I NEED A CAR. YEAH, THE BROOKLYN AQUARIUM...GOING TO LINCOLN CENTER.
HOW LONG? FINE. UH, HOW MUCH IS THAT GONNA COST?
HE SAYS FORTY-TWO BUCKS AND THEY CAN BE HERE IN FORTY MINUTES.
FINE, TELL HIM I HAVE A COUPON.

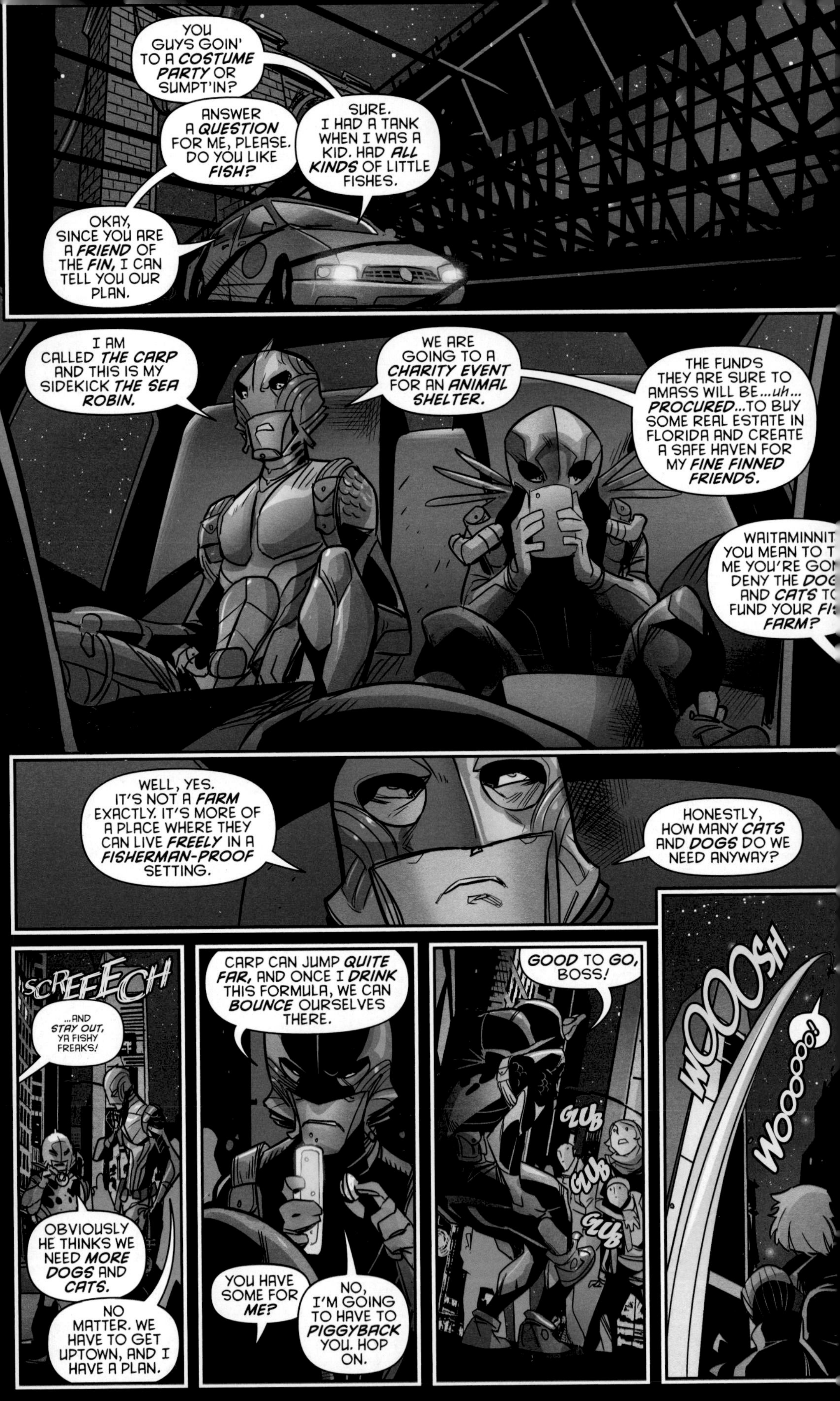
YOU GUYS GOIN' TO A *COSTUME PARTY* OR SUMPT'IN?
ANSWER A *QUESTION* FOR ME, PLEASE. DO YOU LIKE *FISH?*
SURE. I HAD A TANK WHEN I WAS A KID. HAD *ALL KINDS* OF LITTLE FISHES.
OKAY, SINCE YOU ARE A *FRIEND* OF THE *FIN,* I CAN TELL YOU OUR PLAN.
I AM CALLED *THE CARP* AND THIS IS MY SIDEKICK *THE SEA ROBIN.*
WE ARE GOING TO A *CHARITY EVENT* FOR AN *ANIMAL SHELTER.*
THE FUNDS THEY ARE SURE TO AMASS WILL BE...*uh*... *PROCURED*...TO BUY SOME REAL ESTATE IN FLORIDA AND CREATE A SAFE HAVEN FOR MY *FINE FINNED FRIENDS.*
WAITAMINNIT YOU MEAN TO T ME YOU'RE GO DENY THE *DOG* AND *CATS* T FUND YOUR *FI FARM?*
WELL, YES. IT'S NOT A *FARM* EXACTLY. IT'S MORE OF A PLACE WHERE THEY CAN LIVE *FREELY* IN A *FISHERMAN-PROOF* SETTING.
HONESTLY, HOW MANY *CATS* AND *DOGS* DO WE NEED ANYWAY?
SCREEECH
...AND *STAY OUT,* YA FISHY FREAKS!
OBVIOUSLY HE THINKS WE NEED *MORE DOGS* AND *CATS.*
NO MATTER. WE HAVE TO GET UPTOWN, AND I HAVE A PLAN.
CARP CAN JUMP *QUITE FAR,* AND ONCE I *DRINK* THIS FORMULA, WE CAN *BOUNCE* OURSELVES THERE.
YOU HAVE SOME FOR *ME?*
NO, I'M GOING TO HAVE TO *PIGGYBACK* YOU. HOP ON.
GOOD TO GO, BOSS!
GLUB
GLUB
GLUB
WOOOOSH
WOOOOOO!
WOOOOOO!

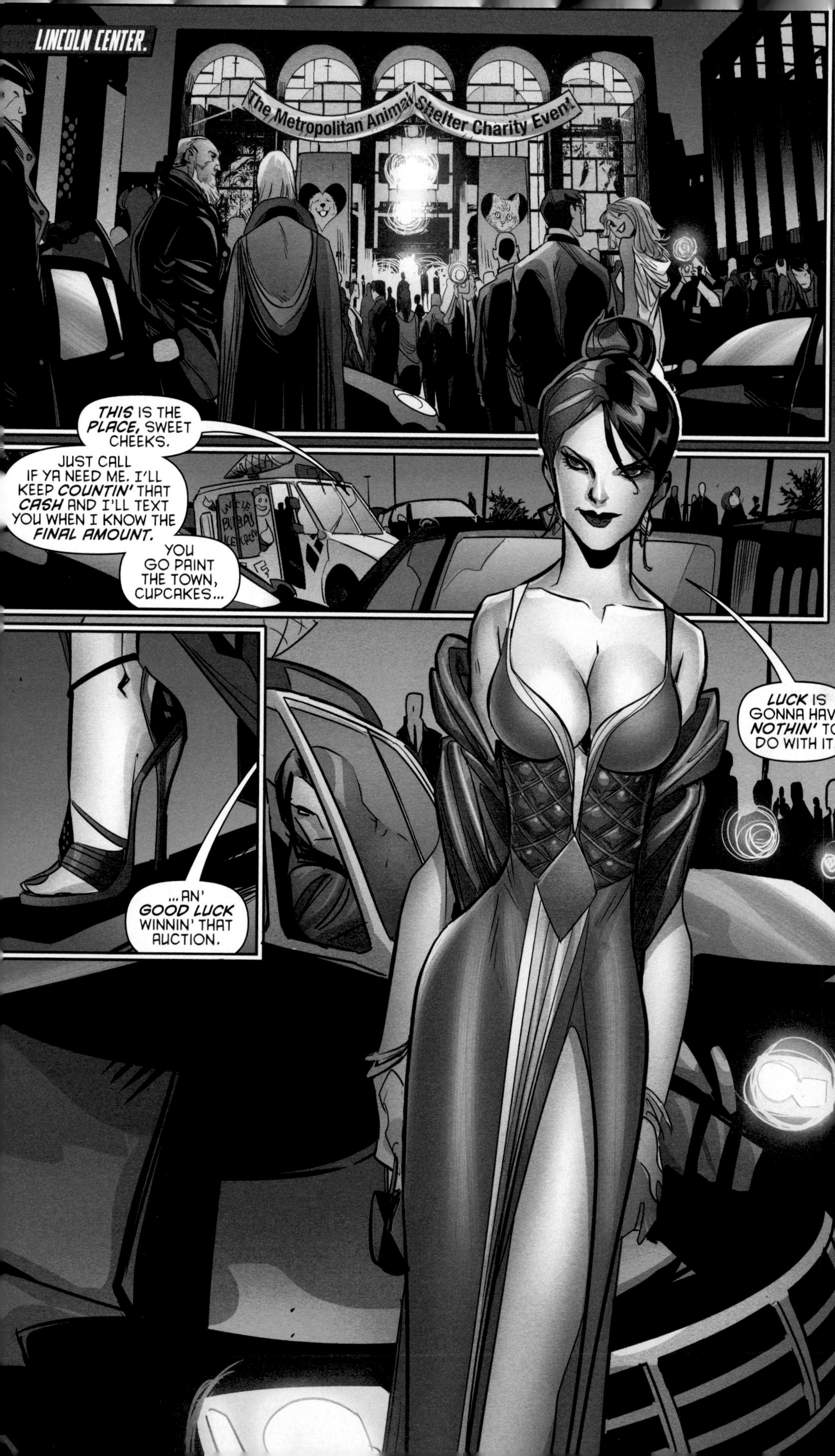
LINCOLN CENTER.
The Metropolitan Animal Shelter Charity Event
THIS IS THE PLACE, SWEET CHEEKS.
JUST CALL IF YA NEED ME. I'LL KEEP COUNTIN' THAT CASH AND I'LL TEXT YOU WHEN I KNOW THE FINAL AMOUNT.
YOU GO PAINT THE TOWN, CUPCAKES...
...AN' GOOD LUCK WINNIN' THAT AUCTION.
LUCK IS GONNA HAVE NOTHIN' TO DO WITH IT.

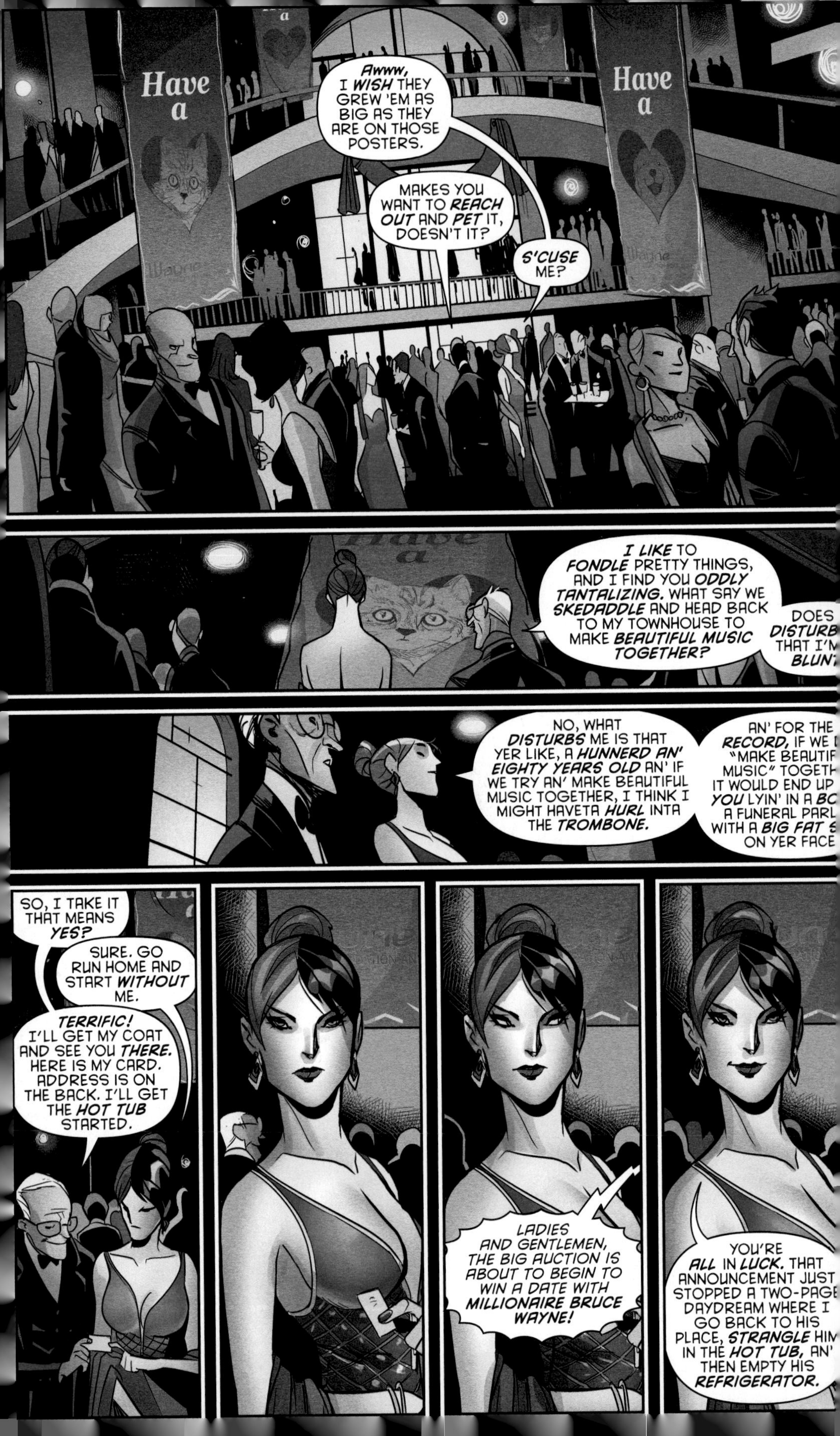

Have a
Have a
Awww, I WISH THEY GREW 'EM AS BIG AS THEY ARE ON THOSE POSTERS.
MAKES YOU WANT TO REACH OUT AND PET IT, DOESN'T IT?
S'CUSE ME?
I LIKE TO FONDLE PRETTY THINGS, AND I FIND YOU ODDLY TANTALIZING. WHAT SAY WE SKEDADDLE AND HEAD BACK TO MY TOWNHOUSE TO MAKE BEAUTIFUL MUSIC TOGETHER?
DOES DISTURB THAT I'M BLUN
NO, WHAT DISTURBS ME IS THAT YER LIKE, A HUNNERD AN' EIGHTY YEARS OLD AN' IF WE TRY AN' MAKE BEAUTIFUL MUSIC TOGETHER, I THINK I MIGHT HAVETA HURL INTA THE TROMBONE.
AN' FOR THE RECORD, IF WE "MAKE BEAUTIF MUSIC" TOGETH IT WOULD END UP YOU LYIN' IN A BO A FUNERAL PARL WITH A BIG FAT ON YER FACE
SO, I TAKE IT THAT MEANS YES?
SURE. GO RUN HOME AND START WITHOUT ME.
TERRIFIC! I'LL GET MY COAT AND SEE YOU THERE. HERE IS MY CARD. ADDRESS IS ON THE BACK. I'LL GET THE HOT TUB STARTED.
LADIES AND GENTLEMEN, THE BIG AUCTION IS ABOUT TO BEGIN TO WIN A DATE WITH MILLIONAIRE BRUCE WAYNE!
YOU'RE ALL IN LUCK. THAT ANNOUNCEMENT JUST STOPPED A TWO-PAGE DAYDREAM WHERE I GO BACK TO HIS PLACE, STRANGLE HIM IN THE HOT TUB, AN' THEN EMPTY HIS REFRIGERATOR.

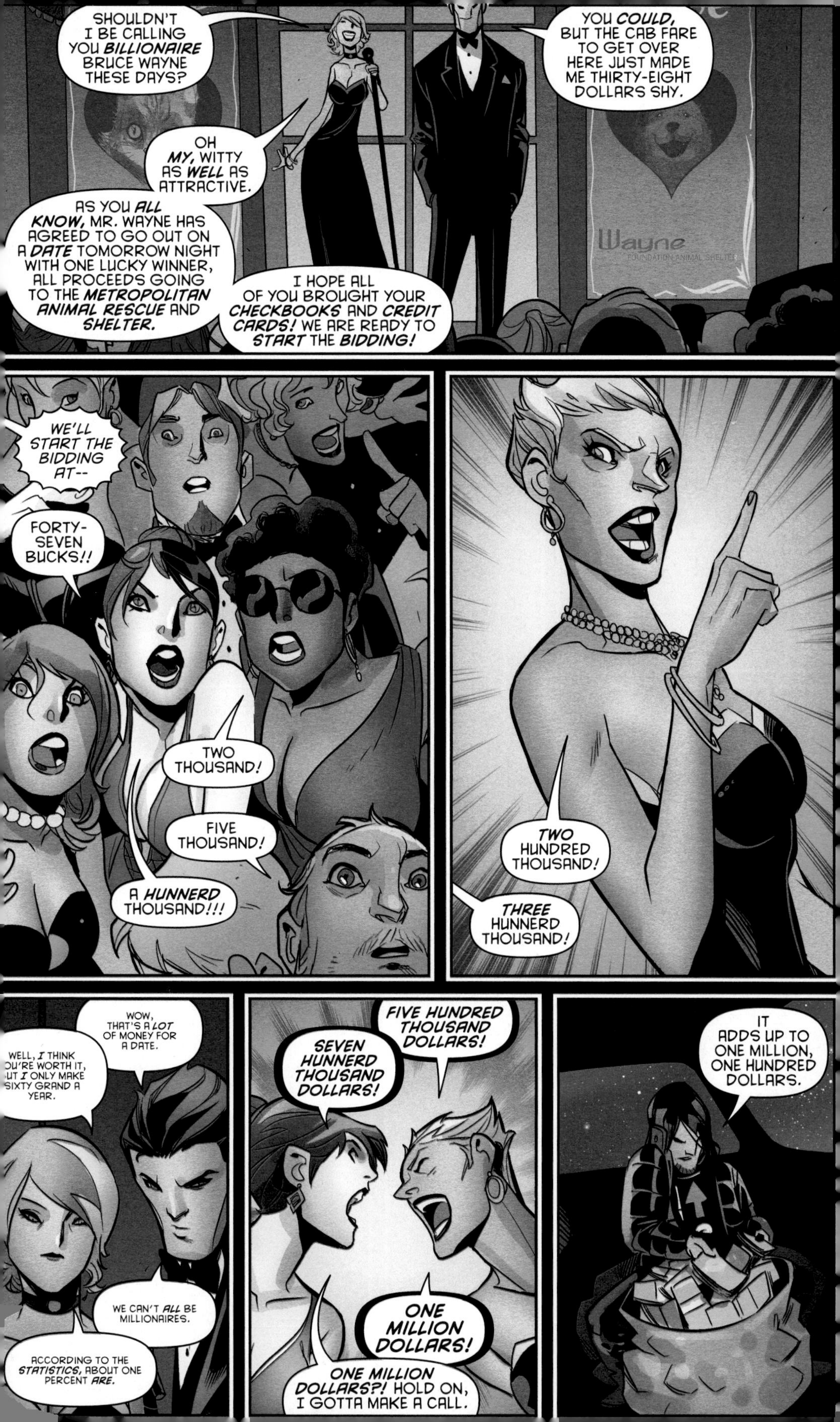
SHOULDN'T I BE CALLING YOU BILLIONAIRE BRUCE WAYNE THESE DAYS?
YOU COULD, BUT THE CAB FARE TO GET OVER HERE JUST MADE ME THIRTY-EIGHT DOLLARS SHY.
OH MY, WITTY AS WELL AS ATTRACTIVE.
AS YOU ALL KNOW, MR. WAYNE HAS AGREED TO GO OUT ON A DATE TOMORROW NIGHT WITH ONE LUCKY WINNER, ALL PROCEEDS GOING TO THE METROPOLITAN ANIMAL RESCUE AND SHELTER.
I HOPE ALL OF YOU BROUGHT YOUR CHECKBOOKS AND CREDIT CARDS! WE ARE READY TO START THE BIDDING!
Wayne
FOUNDATION ANIMAL SHELTER
WE'LL START THE BIDDING AT--
FORTY-SEVEN BUCKS!!
TWO THOUSAND!
FIVE THOUSAND!
A HUNNERD THOUSAND!!!
TWO HUNDRED THOUSAND!
THREE HUNNERD THOUSAND!
WOW, THAT'S A LOT OF MONEY FOR A DATE.
WELL, I THINK YOU'RE WORTH IT, BUT I ONLY MAKE SIXTY GRAND A YEAR.
WE CAN'T ALL BE MILLIONAIRES.
ACCORDING TO THE STATISTICS, ABOUT ONE PERCENT ARE.
FIVE HUNDRED THOUSAND DOLLARS!
SEVEN HUNNERD THOUSAND DOLLARS!
ONE MILLION DOLLARS!
ONE MILLION DOLLARS?! HOLD ON, I GOTTA MAKE A CALL.
IT ADDS UP TO ONE MILLION, ONE HUNDRED DOLLARS.

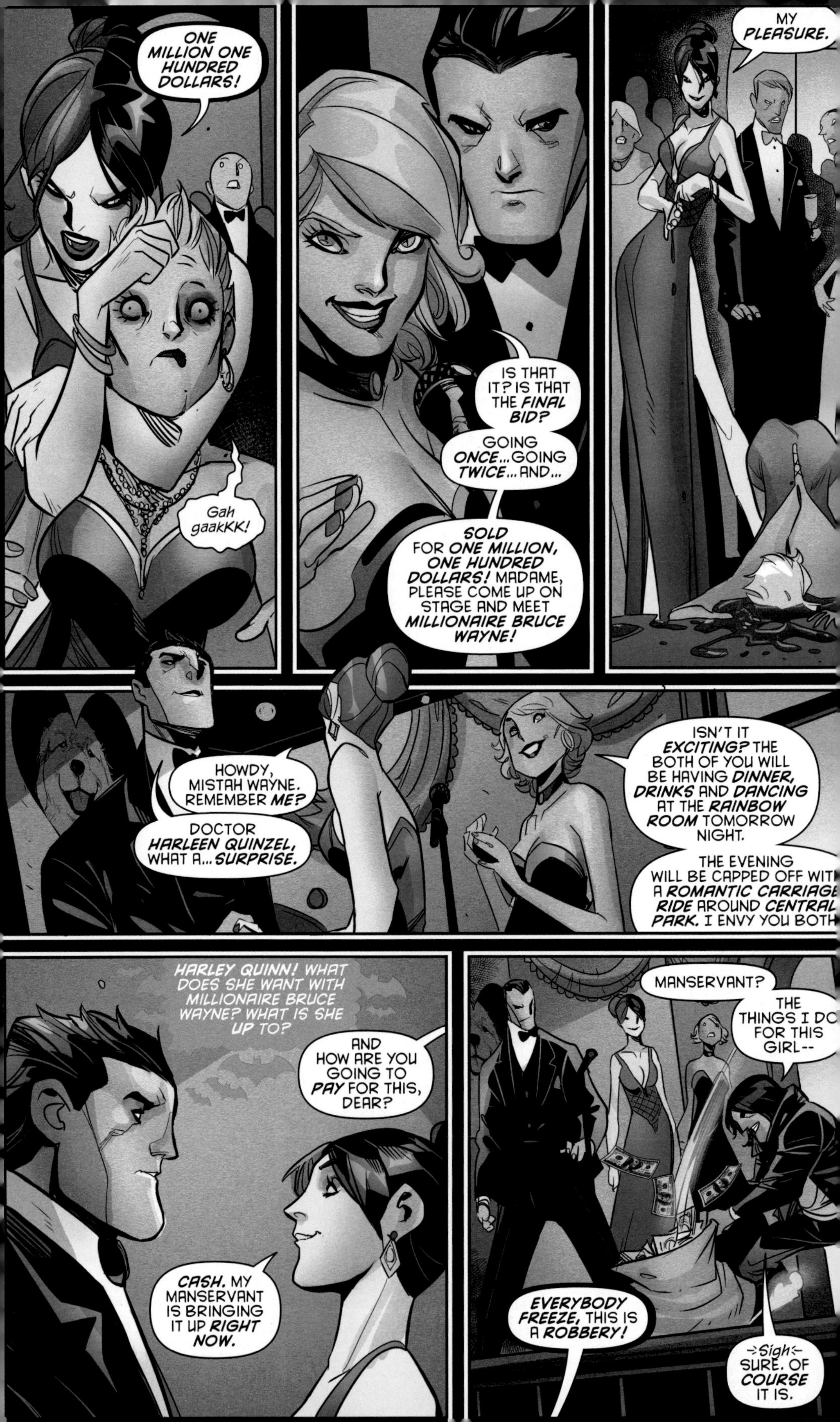

ONE MILLION ONE HUNDRED DOLLARS!
Gah gaakKK!
IS THAT IT? IS THAT THE FINAL BID?
GOING ONCE... GOING TWICE... AND...
SOLD FOR ONE MILLION, ONE HUNDRED DOLLARS! MADAME, PLEASE COME UP ON STAGE AND MEET MILLIONAIRE BRUCE WAYNE!
MY PLEASURE.
HOWDY, MISTAH WAYNE. REMEMBER ME?
DOCTOR HARLEEN QUINZEL, WHAT A... SURPRISE.
ISN'T IT EXCITING? THE BOTH OF YOU WILL BE HAVING DINNER, DRINKS AND DANCING AT THE RAINBOW ROOM TOMORROW NIGHT.
THE EVENING WILL BE CAPPED OFF WITH A ROMANTIC CARRIAGE RIDE AROUND CENTRAL PARK. I ENVY YOU BOTH
HARLEY QUINN! WHAT DOES SHE WANT WITH MILLIONAIRE BRUCE WAYNE? WHAT IS SHE UP TO?
AND HOW ARE YOU GOING TO PAY FOR THIS, DEAR?
CASH. MY MANSERVANT IS BRINGING IT UP RIGHT NOW.
MANSERVANT?
THE THINGS I DO FOR THIS GIRL--
EVERYBODY FREEZE, THIS IS A ROBBERY!
Sigh
SURE. OF COURSE IT IS.

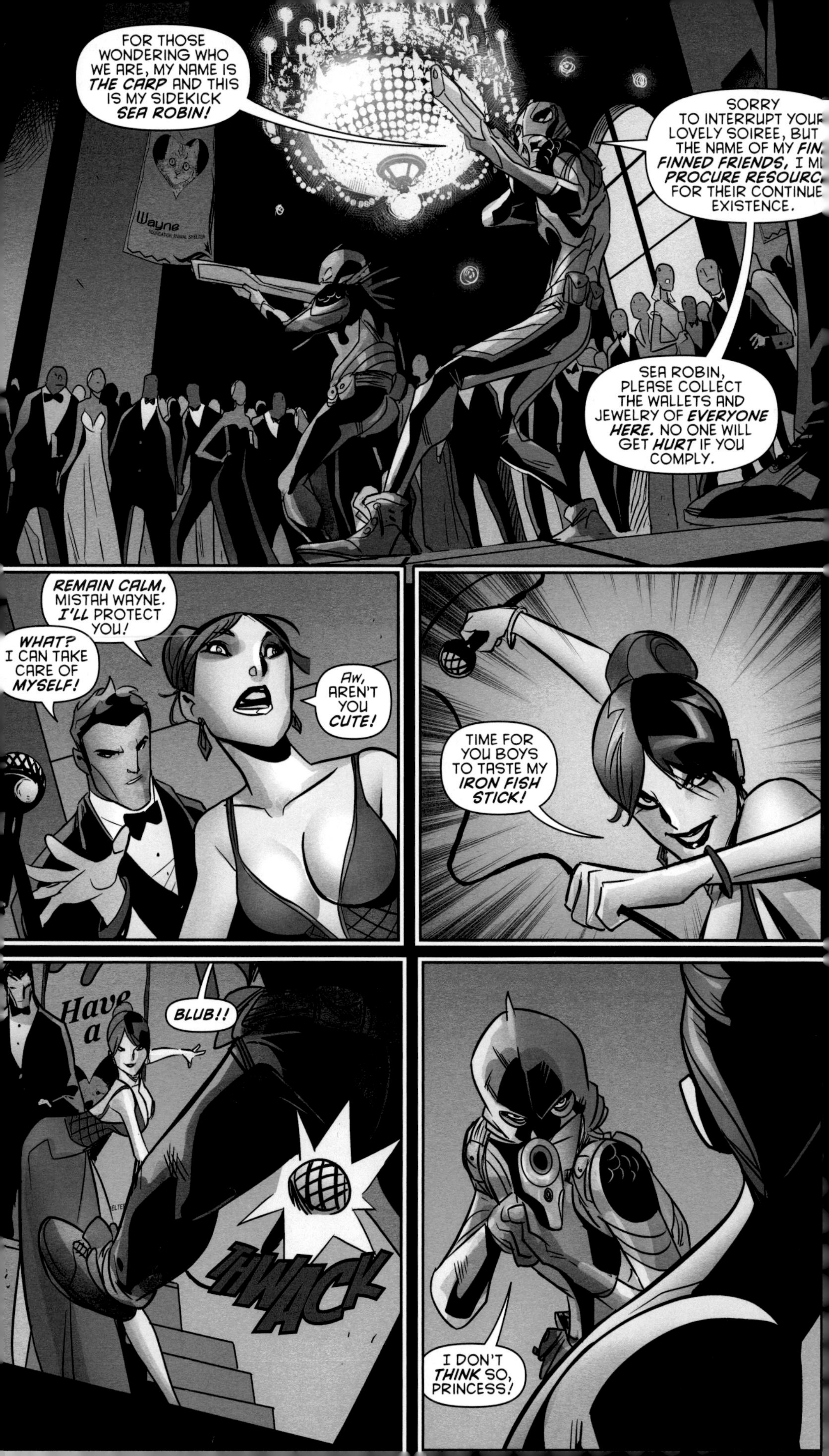

Wayne
FOUNDATION ANIMAL SHELTER
FOR THOSE WONDERING WHO WE ARE, MY NAME IS *THE CARP* AND THIS IS MY SIDEKICK *SEA ROBIN!*
SORRY TO INTERRUPT YOUR LOVELY SOIREE, BUT THE NAME OF MY *FIN FINNED FRIENDS,* I M *PROCURE RESOURC* FOR THEIR CONTINUE EXISTENCE.
SEA ROBIN, PLEASE COLLECT THE WALLETS AND JEWELRY OF *EVERYONE HERE.* NO ONE WILL GET *HURT* IF YOU COMPLY.
REMAIN CALM, MISTAH WAYNE. *I'LL* PROTECT YOU!
WHAT? I CAN TAKE CARE OF *MYSELF!*
AW, AREN'T YOU *CUTE!*
TIME FOR YOU BOYS TO TASTE MY *IRON FISH STICK!*
Have a
BLUB!!
THWACK
I DON'T *THINK* SO, PRINCESS!

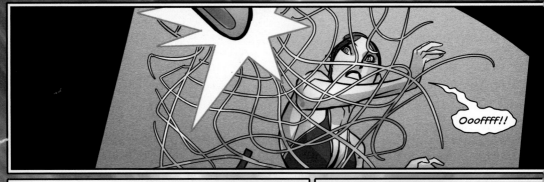

Ooooffff!!

A LADY *ALWAYS* COMES PREPARED. MISTAH CARP, TODAY IS *NOT* YOUR *LUCKY DAY.* WHEN I GET OUTTA HERE, I'M GONNA *SCALE* YOUR ASS *RAW!*

THAT NET ISN'T *JUST A NET,* YOUNG LADY; IT'S A *TASER* AS WELL GOODNIGHT.

TASER SCHMASERrrrrrrr...

WHUMP

HEY! THAT'S MY *FRIEND!*

STAND *BACK,* MR. WAYNE.

HARLEY HAS A *FRIEND?*

NO YOU *DON'T,* LITTLE MAN! THIS SPECIAL *SEA SLIME* SHOULD DO THE TRICK!

IT HAS *TETRODOTOXIN* FROM A *PUFFER FISH.*

DON'T WORRY, YOU WON'T *DIE,* BUT YOU'LL BE *PARALYZED* AND *HALLUCINATE* YOURSELF INTO *SLUMBER LAND!*

MAN... I'M GETTIN' SO... SLEEPY...

CAN'T STAY *AWAKE*... MUST... CHANGE INTO...

WAIT, HOW DID I *GET* HERE?

MORNIN', *LOVER.*

HAVE A *BAD DREAM?* COME LET ME MAKE IT *BETTER.*

HARLEY?!?

YES, IT'S *ME!* I HAVE TO ASK YOU A *SERIOUS QUESTION.*

UH, SURE.

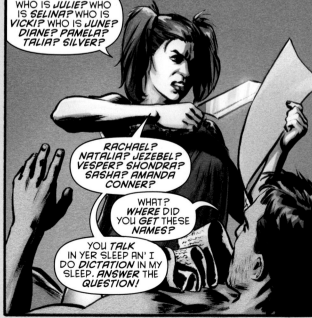

WHO IS *JULIE?* WHO IS *SELINA?* WHO IS *VICKI?* WHO IS *JUNE? DIANE? PAMELA? TALIA? SILVER?*

RACHAEL? NATALIA? JEZEBEL? VESPER? SHONDRA? SASHA? AMANDA CONNER?

WHAT? *WHERE DID* YOU GET THESE *NAMES?*

YOU *TALK* IN YER SLEEP AN' I DO *DICTATION* IN MY SLEEP. *ANSWER THE* QUESTION!

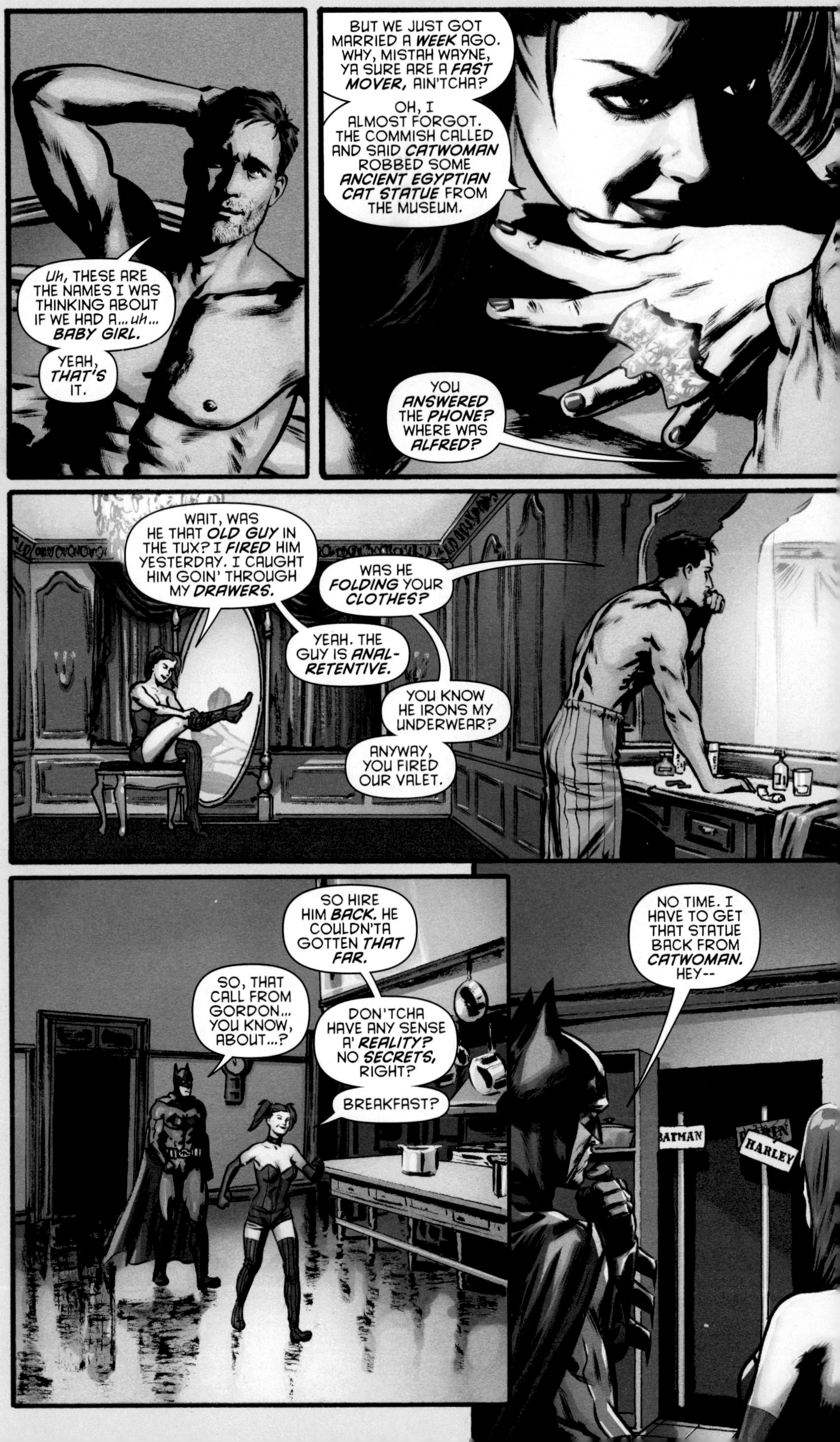
Uh, THESE ARE THE NAMES I WAS THINKING ABOUT IF WE HAD A...uh... BABY GIRL.
YEAH, THAT'S IT.
BUT WE JUST GOT MARRIED A WEEK AGO. WHY, MISTAH WAYNE, YA SURE ARE A FAST MOVER, AIN'TCHA?
OH, I ALMOST FORGOT. THE COMMISH CALLED AND SAID CATWOMAN ROBBED SOME ANCIENT EGYPTIAN CAT STATUE FROM THE MUSEUM.
YOU ANSWERED THE PHONE? WHERE WAS ALFRED?
WAIT, WAS HE THAT OLD GUY IN THE TUX? I FIRED HIM YESTERDAY. I CAUGHT HIM GOIN' THROUGH MY DRAWERS.
WAS HE FOLDING YOUR CLOTHES?
YEAH. THE GUY IS ANAL-RETENTIVE.
YOU KNOW HE IRONS MY UNDERWEAR?
ANYWAY, YOU FIRED OUR VALET.
SO, THAT CALL FROM GORDON... YOU KNOW, ABOUT...?
SO HIRE HIM BACK. HE COULDN'TA GOTTEN THAT FAR.
DON'TCHA HAVE ANY SENSE A' REALITY? NO SECRETS, RIGHT?
BREAKFAST?
NO TIME. I HAVE TO GET THAT STATUE BACK FROM CATWOMAN. HEY--
BATMAN
HARLEY

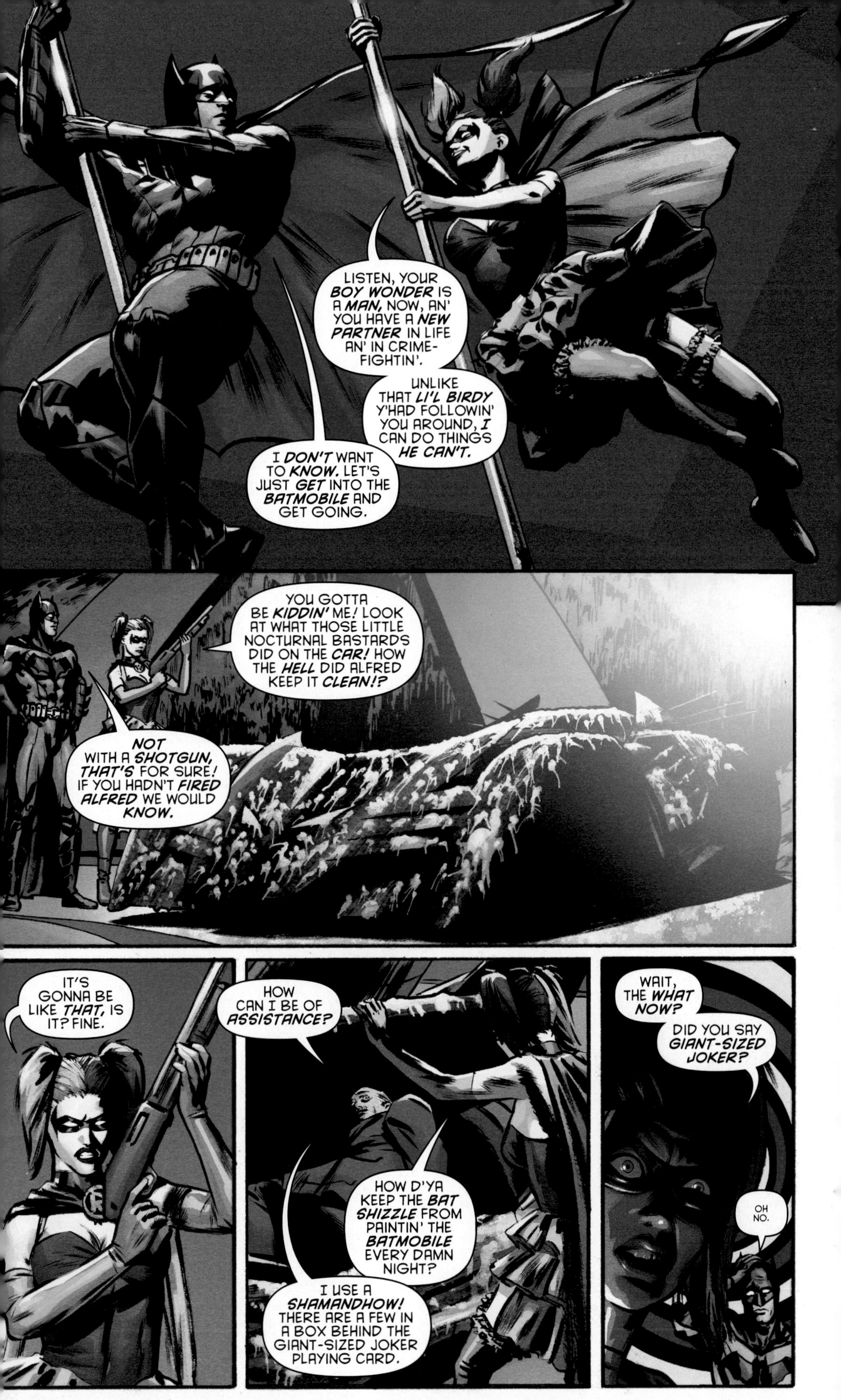
LISTEN, YOUR BOY WONDER IS A MAN, NOW, AN' YOU HAVE A NEW PARTNER IN LIFE AN' IN CRIME-FIGHTIN'.
UNLIKE THAT LI'L BIRDY Y'HAD FOLLOWIN' YOU AROUND, I CAN DO THINGS HE CAN'T.
I DON'T WANT TO KNOW. LET'S JUST GET INTO THE BATMOBILE AND GET GOING.
YOU GOTTA BE KIDDIN' ME! LOOK AT WHAT THOSE LITTLE NOCTURNAL BASTARDS DID ON THE CAR! HOW THE HELL DID ALFRED KEEP IT CLEAN!?
NOT WITH A SHOTGUN, THAT'S FOR SURE! IF YOU HADN'T FIRED ALFRED WE WOULD KNOW.
IT'S GONNA BE LIKE THAT, IS IT? FINE.
HOW CAN I BE OF ASSISTANCE?
HOW D'YA KEEP THE BAT SHIZZLE FROM PAINTIN' THE BATMOBILE EVERY DAMN NIGHT?
I USE A SHAMANDHOW! THERE ARE A FEW IN A BOX BEHIND THE GIANT-SIZED JOKER PLAYING CARD.
WAIT, THE WHAT NOW?
DID YOU SAY GIANT-SIZED JOKER?
OH NO.

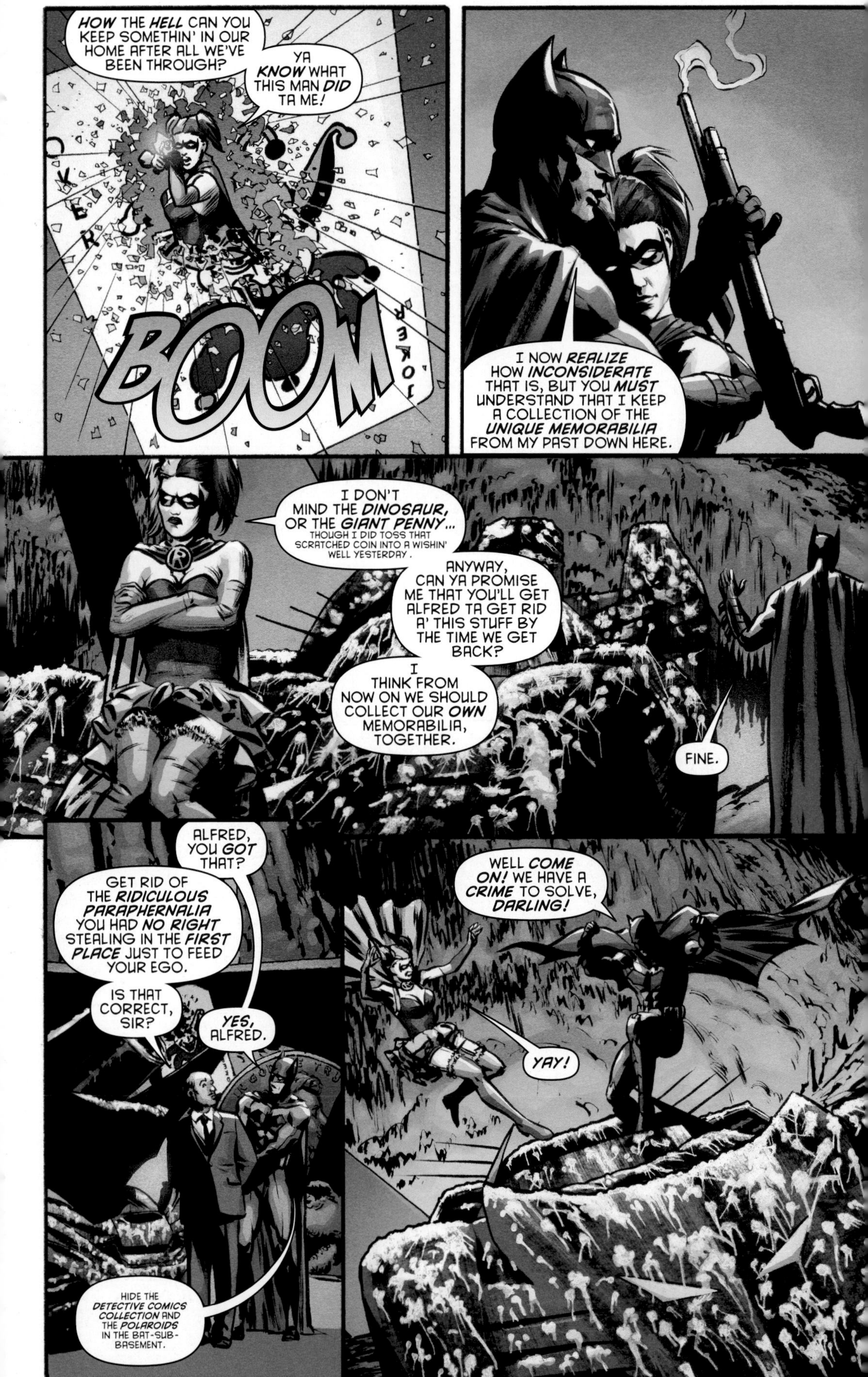

HOW THE HELL CAN YOU KEEP SOMETHIN' IN OUR HOME AFTER ALL WE'VE BEEN THROUGH?
YA KNOW WHAT THIS MAN DID TA ME!
KRRK
BOOM
JOKER
I NOW REALIZE HOW INCONSIDERATE THAT IS, BUT YOU MUST UNDERSTAND THAT I KEEP A COLLECTION OF THE UNIQUE MEMORABILIA FROM MY PAST DOWN HERE.
I DON'T MIND THE DINOSAUR, OR THE GIANT PENNY... THOUGH I DID TOSS THAT SCRATCHED COIN INTO A WISHIN' WELL YESTERDAY.
ANYWAY, CAN YA PROMISE ME THAT YOU'LL GET ALFRED TA GET RID A' THIS STUFF BY THE TIME WE GET BACK?
I THINK FROM NOW ON WE SHOULD COLLECT OUR OWN MEMORABILIA, TOGETHER.
FINE.
ALFRED, YOU GOT THAT?
GET RID OF THE RIDICULOUS PARAPHERNALIA YOU HAD NO RIGHT STEALING IN THE FIRST PLACE JUST TO FEED YOUR EGO.
IS THAT CORRECT, SIR?
YES, ALFRED.
HIDE THE DETECTIVE COMICS COLLECTION AND THE POLAROIDS IN THE BAT-SUB-BASEMENT.
WELL COME ON! WE HAVE A CRIME TO SOLVE, DARLING!
YAY!

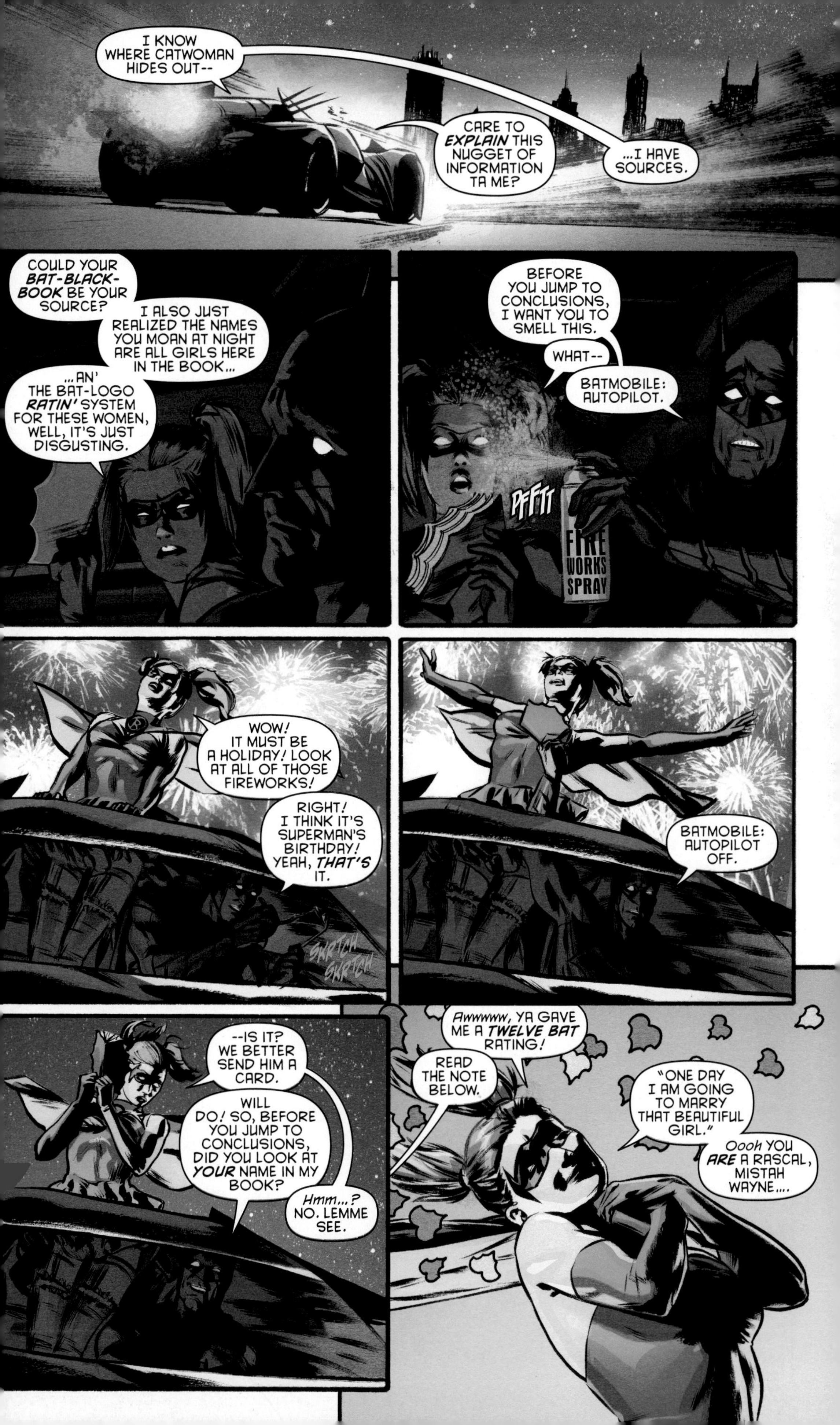
I KNOW WHERE CATWOMAN HIDES OUT--
CARE TO *EXPLAIN* THIS NUGGET OF INFORMATION TA ME?
...I HAVE SOURCES.
COULD YOUR *BAT-BLACK-BOOK* BE YOUR SOURCE?
I ALSO JUST REALIZED THE NAMES YOU MOAN AT NIGHT ARE ALL GIRLS HERE IN THE BOOK...
...AN' THE BAT-LOGO *RATIN'* SYSTEM FOR THESE WOMEN, WELL, IT'S JUST DISGUSTING.
BEFORE YOU JUMP TO CONCLUSIONS, I WANT YOU TO SMELL THIS.
WHAT--
BATMOBILE: AUTOPILOT.
PFFTT
FIRE WORKS SPRAY
WOW! IT MUST BE A HOLIDAY! LOOK AT ALL OF THOSE FIREWORKS!
RIGHT! I THINK IT'S SUPERMAN'S BIRTHDAY! YEAH, *THAT'S* IT.
SKRTCH SKRTCH
BATMOBILE: AUTOPILOT OFF.
--IS IT? WE BETTER SEND HIM A CARD.
WILL DO! SO, BEFORE YOU JUMP TO CONCLUSIONS, DID YOU LOOK AT *YOUR* NAME IN MY BOOK?
Hmm...? NO. LEMME SEE.
Awwwww, YA GAVE ME A *TWELVE BAT* RATING!
READ THE NOTE BELOW.
"ONE DAY I AM GOING TO MARRY THAT BEAUTIFUL GIRL."
Oooh YOU *ARE* A RASCAL, MISTAH WAYNE....

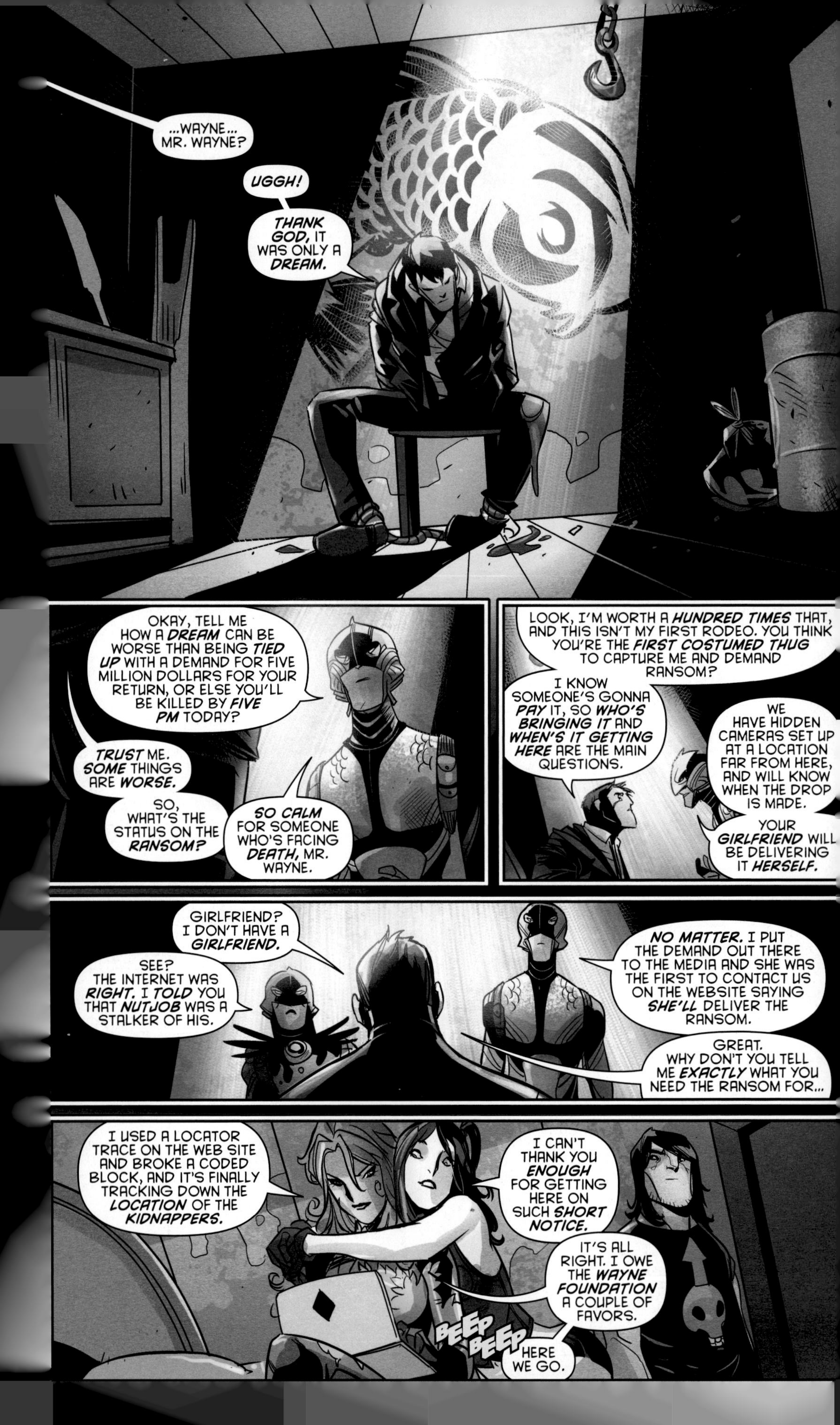

...WAYNE... MR. WAYNE?
UGGH!
THANK GOD, IT WAS ONLY A DREAM.
OKAY, TELL ME HOW A DREAM CAN BE WORSE THAN BEING TIED UP WITH A DEMAND FOR FIVE MILLION DOLLARS FOR YOUR RETURN, OR ELSE YOU'LL BE KILLED BY FIVE PM TODAY?
TRUST ME. SOME THINGS ARE WORSE.
SO, WHAT'S THE STATUS ON THE RANSOM?
SO CALM FOR SOMEONE WHO'S FACING DEATH, MR. WAYNE.
LOOK, I'M WORTH A HUNDRED TIMES THAT, AND THIS ISN'T MY FIRST RODEO. YOU THINK YOU'RE THE FIRST COSTUMED THUG TO CAPTURE ME AND DEMAND RANSOM?
I KNOW SOMEONE'S GONNA PAY IT, SO WHO'S BRINGING IT AND WHEN'S IT GETTING HERE ARE THE MAIN QUESTIONS.
WE HAVE HIDDEN CAMERAS SET UP AT A LOCATION FAR FROM HERE, AND WILL KNOW WHEN THE DROP IS MADE.
YOUR GIRLFRIEND WILL BE DELIVERING IT HERSELF.
GIRLFRIEND? I DON'T HAVE A GIRLFRIEND.
SEE? THE INTERNET WAS RIGHT. I TOLD YOU THAT NUTJOB WAS A STALKER OF HIS.
NO MATTER. I PUT THE DEMAND OUT THERE TO THE MEDIA AND SHE WAS THE FIRST TO CONTACT US ON THE WEBSITE SAYING SHE'LL DELIVER THE RANSOM.
GREAT. WHY DON'T YOU TELL ME EXACTLY WHAT YOU NEED THE RANSOM FOR...
I USED A LOCATOR TRACE ON THE WEB SITE AND BROKE A CODED BLOCK, AND IT'S FINALLY TRACKING DOWN THE LOCATION OF THE KIDNAPPERS.
I CAN'T THANK YOU ENOUGH FOR GETTING HERE ON SUCH SHORT NOTICE.
IT'S ALL RIGHT. I OWE THE WAYNE FOUNDATION A COUPLE OF FAVORS.
BEEP BEEP
HERE WE GO.

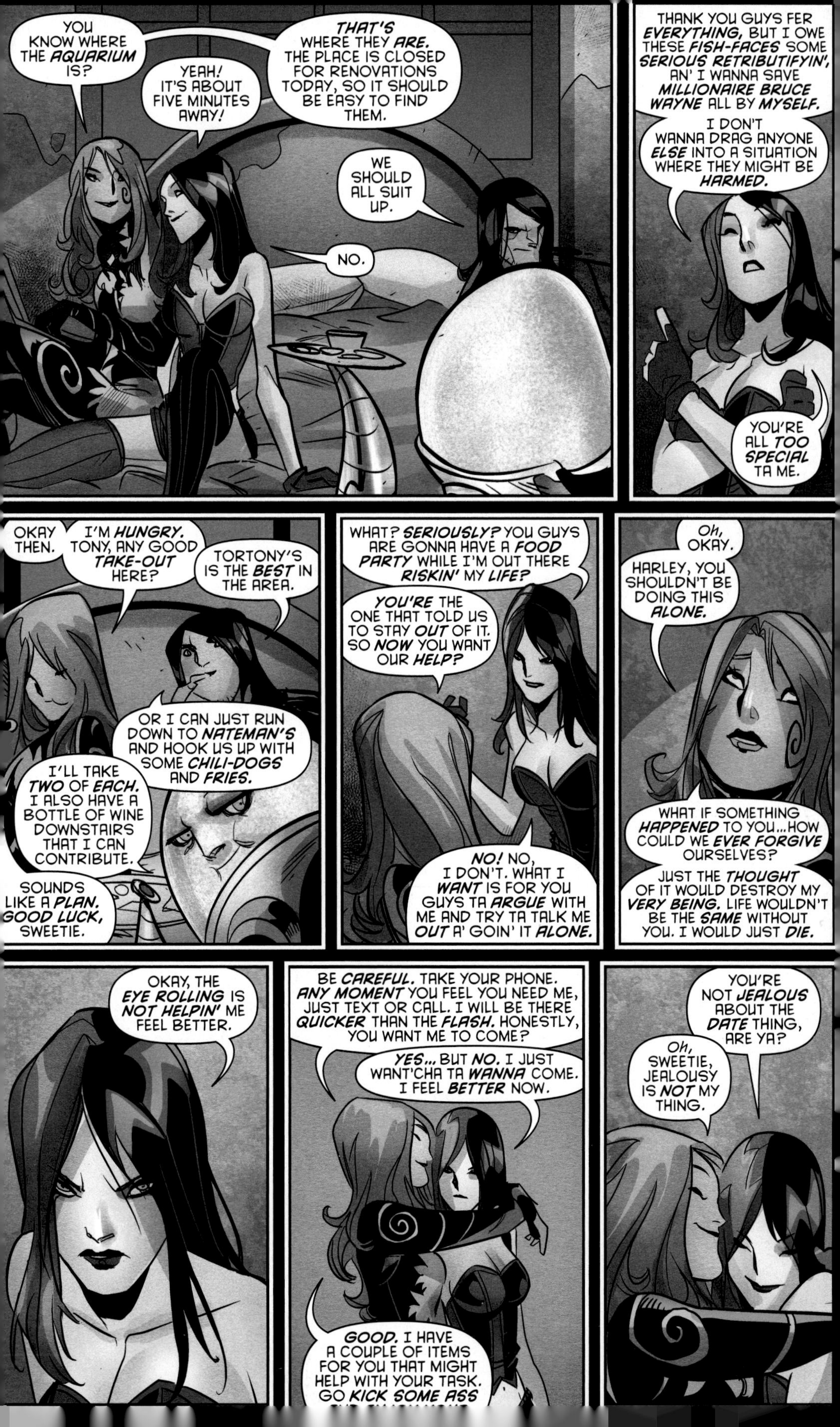
YOU KNOW WHERE THE AQUARIUM IS?
YEAH! IT'S ABOUT FIVE MINUTES AWAY!
THAT'S WHERE THEY ARE. THE PLACE IS CLOSED FOR RENOVATIONS TODAY, SO IT SHOULD BE EASY TO FIND THEM.
WE SHOULD ALL SUIT UP.
NO.
THANK YOU GUYS FER EVERYTHING, BUT I OWE THESE FISH-FACES SOME SERIOUS RETRIBUTIFYIN', AN' I WANNA SAVE MILLIONAIRE BRUCE WAYNE ALL BY MYSELF.
I DON'T WANNA DRAG ANYONE ELSE INTO A SITUATION WHERE THEY MIGHT BE HARMED.
YOU'RE ALL TOO SPECIAL TA ME.
OKAY THEN.
I'M HUNGRY. TONY, ANY GOOD TAKE-OUT HERE?
TORTONY'S IS THE BEST IN THE AREA.
OR I CAN JUST RUN DOWN TO NATEMAN'S AND HOOK US UP WITH SOME CHILI-DOGS AND FRIES.
I'LL TAKE TWO OF EACH. I ALSO HAVE A BOTTLE OF WINE DOWNSTAIRS THAT I CAN CONTRIBUTE.
SOUNDS LIKE A PLAN. GOOD LUCK, SWEETIE.
WHAT? SERIOUSLY? YOU GUYS ARE GONNA HAVE A FOOD PARTY WHILE I'M OUT THERE RISKIN' MY LIFE?
YOU'RE THE ONE THAT TOLD US TO STAY OUT OF IT. SO NOW YOU WANT OUR HELP?
NO! NO, I DON'T. WHAT I WANT IS FOR YOU GUYS TA ARGUE WITH ME AND TRY TA TALK ME OUT A' GOIN' IT ALONE.
Oh, OKAY.
HARLEY, YOU SHOULDN'T BE DOING THIS ALONE.
WHAT IF SOMETHING HAPPENED TO YOU...HOW COULD WE EVER FORGIVE OURSELVES?
JUST THE THOUGHT OF IT WOULD DESTROY MY VERY BEING. LIFE WOULDN'T BE THE SAME WITHOUT YOU. I WOULD JUST DIE.
OKAY, THE EYE ROLLING IS NOT HELPIN' ME FEEL BETTER.
BE CAREFUL. TAKE YOUR PHONE. ANY MOMENT YOU FEEL YOU NEED ME, JUST TEXT OR CALL. I WILL BE THERE QUICKER THAN THE FLASH. HONESTLY, YOU WANT ME TO COME?
YES... BUT NO. I JUST WANT'CHA TA WANNA COME. I FEEL BETTER NOW.
GOOD. I HAVE A COUPLE OF ITEMS FOR YOU THAT MIGHT HELP WITH YOUR TASK. GO KICK SOME ASS
YOU'RE NOT JEALOUS ABOUT THE DATE THING, ARE YA?
Oh, SWEETIE, JEALOUSY IS NOT MY THING.

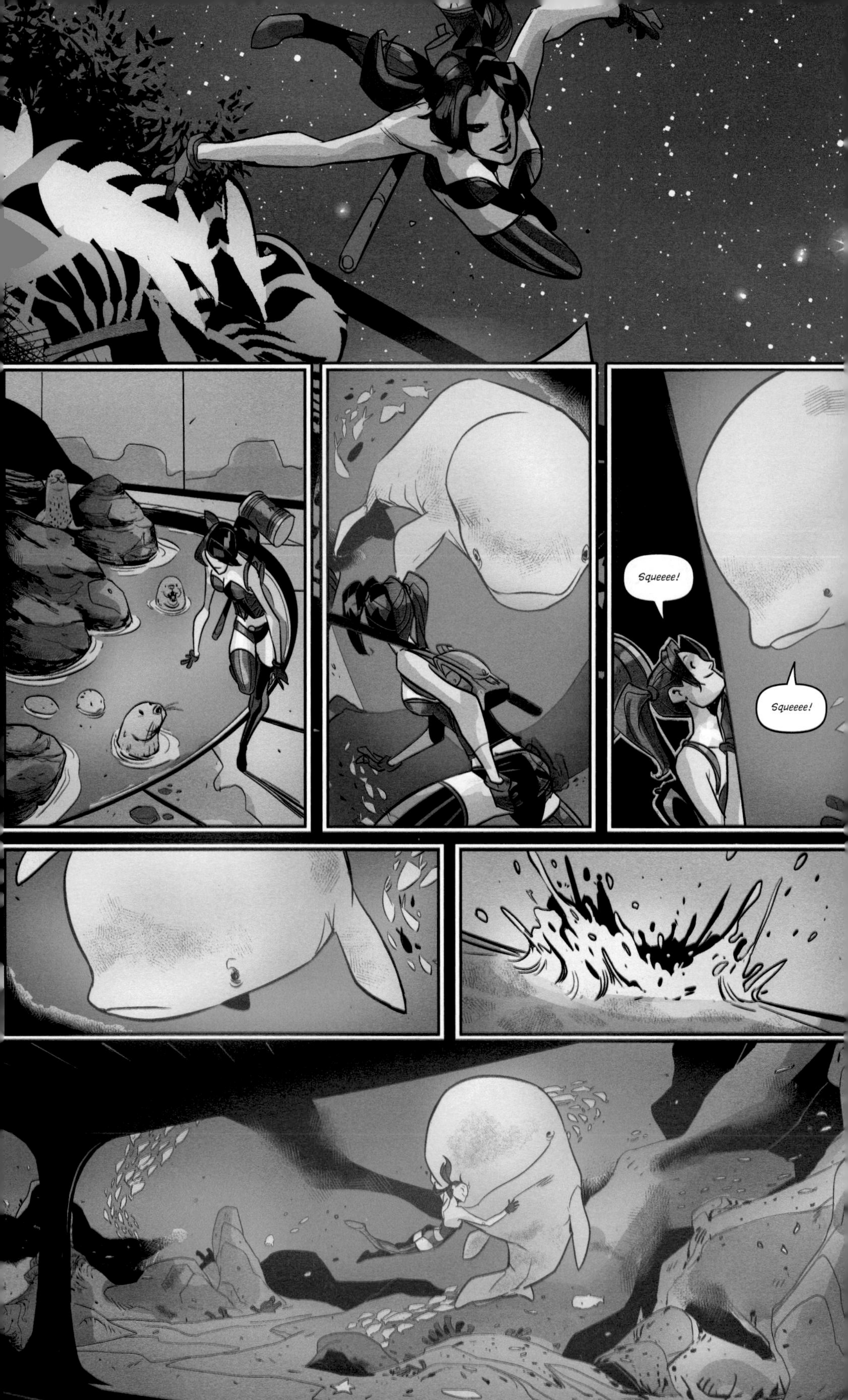
Squeeee!
Squeeee!

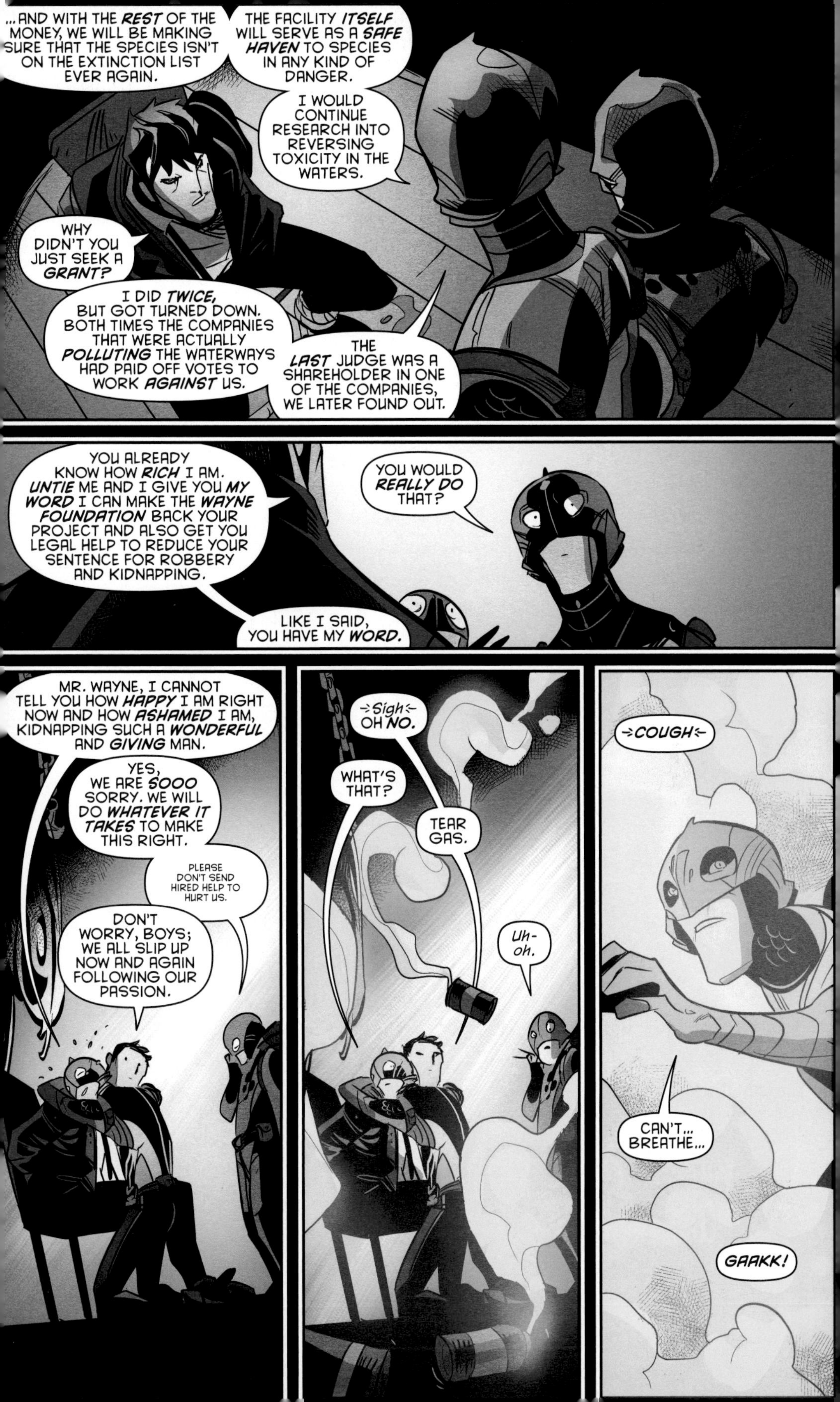

...AND WITH THE REST OF THE MONEY, WE WILL BE MAKING SURE THAT THE SPECIES ISN'T ON THE EXTINCTION LIST EVER AGAIN.
THE FACILITY ITSELF WILL SERVE AS A SAFE HAVEN TO SPECIES IN ANY KIND OF DANGER.
I WOULD CONTINUE RESEARCH INTO REVERSING TOXICITY IN THE WATERS.
WHY DIDN'T YOU JUST SEEK A GRANT?
I DID TWICE, BUT GOT TURNED DOWN. BOTH TIMES THE COMPANIES THAT WERE ACTUALLY POLLUTING THE WATERWAYS HAD PAID OFF VOTES TO WORK AGAINST US.
THE LAST JUDGE WAS A SHAREHOLDER IN ONE OF THE COMPANIES, WE LATER FOUND OUT.
YOU ALREADY KNOW HOW RICH I AM. UNTIE ME AND I GIVE YOU MY WORD I CAN MAKE THE WAYNE FOUNDATION BACK YOUR PROJECT AND ALSO GET YOU LEGAL HELP TO REDUCE YOUR SENTENCE FOR ROBBERY AND KIDNAPPING.
YOU WOULD REALLY DO THAT?
LIKE I SAID, YOU HAVE MY WORD.
MR. WAYNE, I CANNOT TELL YOU HOW HAPPY I AM RIGHT NOW AND HOW ASHAMED I AM, KIDNAPPING SUCH A WONDERFUL AND GIVING MAN.
YES, WE ARE SOOO SORRY. WE WILL DO WHATEVER IT TAKES TO MAKE THIS RIGHT.
PLEASE DON'T SEND HIRED HELP TO HURT US.
DON'T WORRY, BOYS; WE ALL SLIP UP NOW AND AGAIN FOLLOWING OUR PASSION.
Sigh OH NO.
WHAT'S THAT?
TEAR GAS.
Uh-oh.
COUGH
CAN'T... BREATHE...
GAAKK!

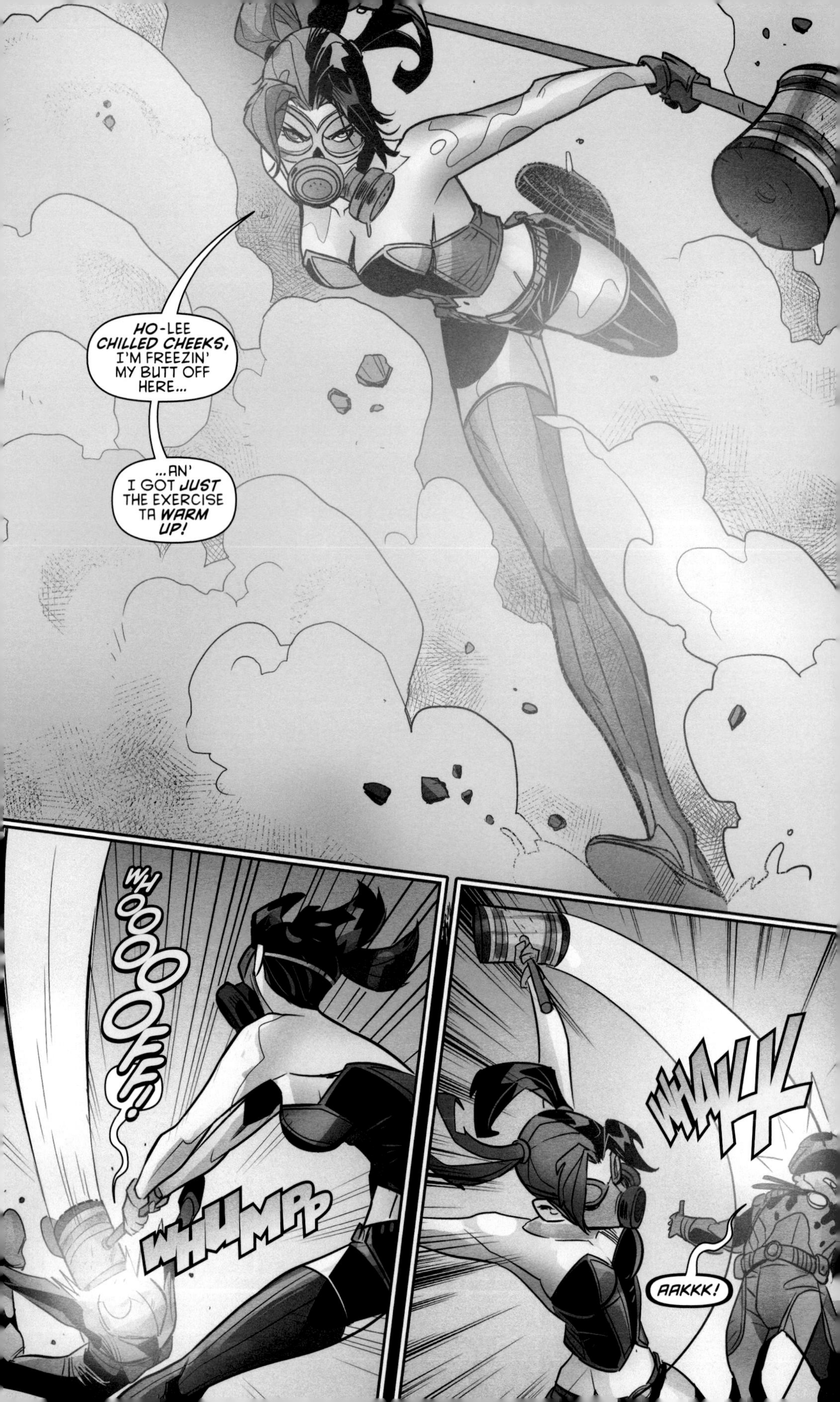
HO-LEE CHILLED CHEEKS, I'M FREEZIN' MY BUTT OFF HERE...
...AN' I GOT JUST THE EXERCISE TA WARM UP!
WHOOOOOOFF!
WHUMPP
WHAKK
AAKKK!

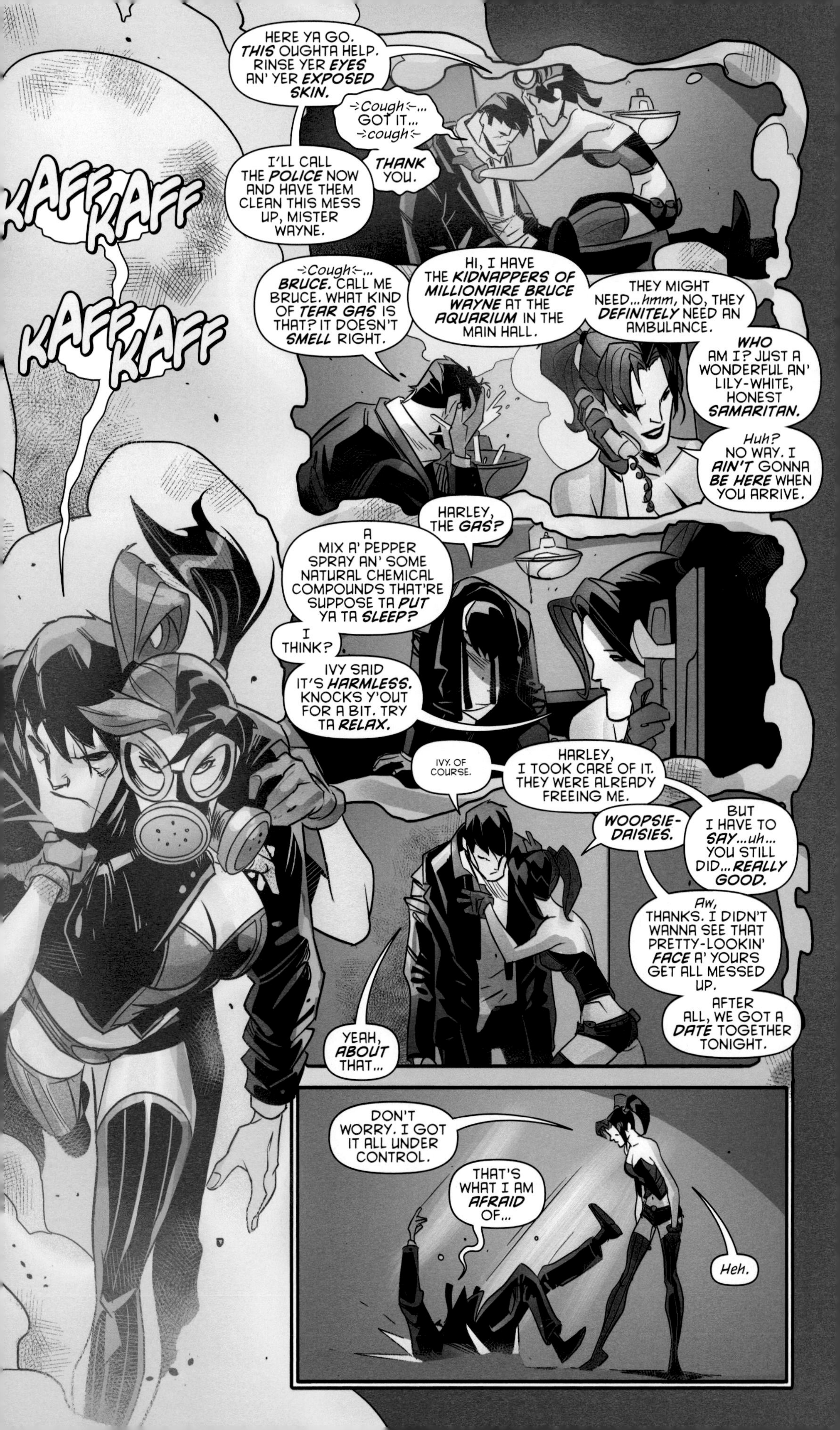
HERE YA GO. THIS OUGHTA HELP. RINSE YER EYES AN' YER EXPOSED SKIN.
>Cough<... GOT IT... >cough<
I'LL CALL THE POLICE NOW AND HAVE THEM CLEAN THIS MESS UP, MISTER WAYNE.
THANK YOU.
KAFF KAFF
KAFF KAFF
>Cough<... BRUCE. CALL ME BRUCE. WHAT KIND OF TEAR GAS IS THAT? IT DOESN'T SMELL RIGHT.
HI, I HAVE THE KIDNAPPERS OF MILLIONAIRE BRUCE WAYNE AT THE AQUARIUM IN THE MAIN HALL.
THEY MIGHT NEED...hmm, NO, THEY DEFINITELY NEED AN AMBULANCE.
WHO AM I? JUST A WONDERFUL AN' LILY-WHITE, HONEST SAMARITAN.
Huh? NO WAY. I AIN'T GONNA BE HERE WHEN YOU ARRIVE.
HARLEY, THE GAS?
A MIX A' PEPPER SPRAY AN' SOME NATURAL CHEMICAL COMPOUNDS THAT'RE SUPPOSE TA PUT YA TA SLEEP?
I THINK?
IVY SAID IT'S HARMLESS. KNOCKS Y'OUT FOR A BIT. TRY TA RELAX.
IVY. OF COURSE.
HARLEY, I TOOK CARE OF IT. THEY WERE ALREADY FREEING ME.
WOOPSIE-DAISIES.
BUT I HAVE TO SAY...uh... YOU STILL DID...REALLY GOOD.
Aw, THANKS. I DIDN'T WANNA SEE THAT PRETTY-LOOKIN' FACE A' YOURS GET ALL MESSED UP.
AFTER ALL, WE GOT A DATE TOGETHER TONIGHT.
YEAH, ABOUT THAT...
DON'T WORRY. I GOT IT ALL UNDER CONTROL.
THAT'S WHAT I AM AFRAID OF...
Heh.

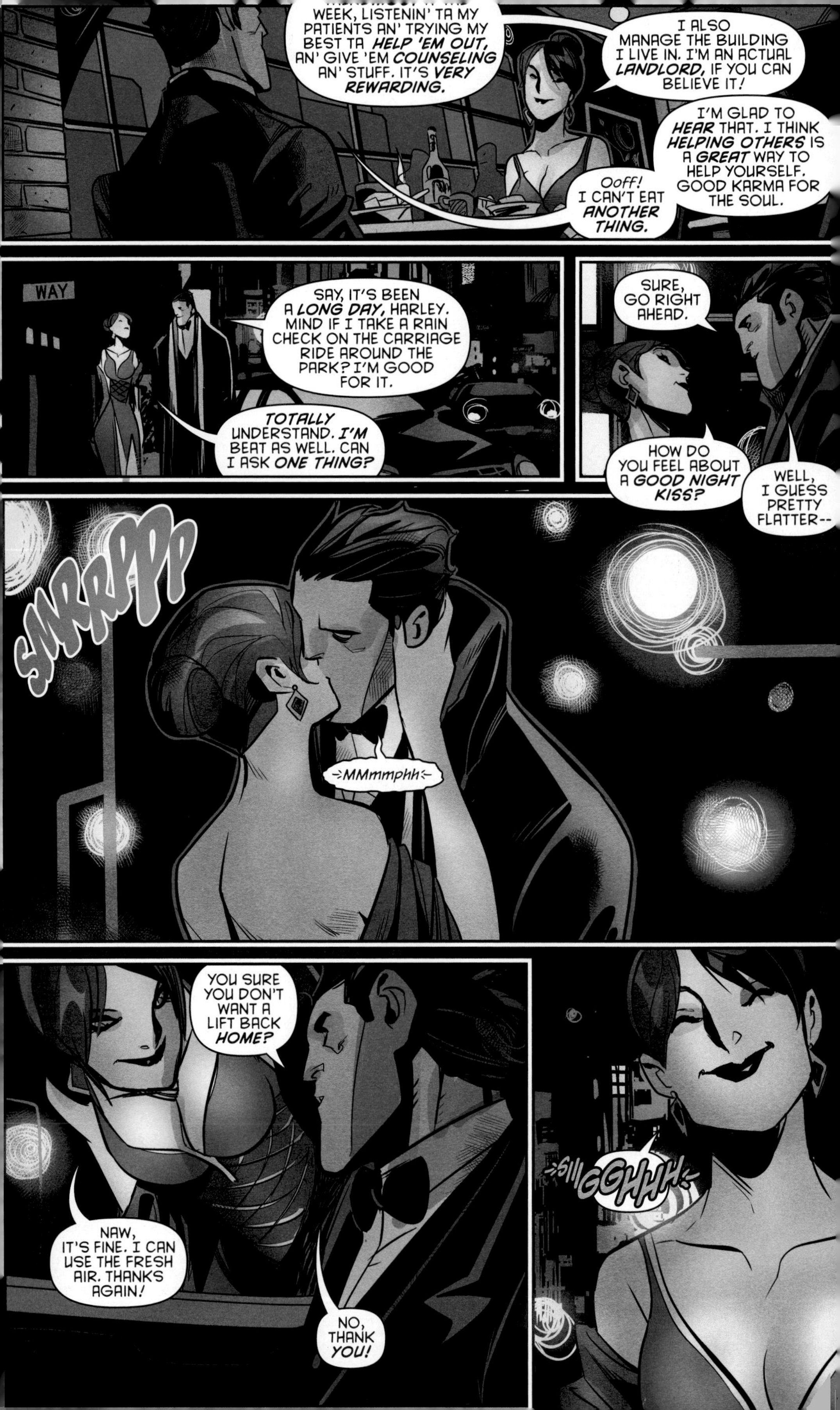
WEEK, LISTENIN' TA MY PATIENTS AN' TRYING MY BEST TA HELP 'EM OUT, AN' GIVE 'EM COUNSELING AN' STUFF. IT'S VERY REWARDING.
I ALSO MANAGE THE BUILDING I LIVE IN. I'M AN ACTUAL LANDLORD, IF YOU CAN BELIEVE IT!
I'M GLAD TO HEAR THAT. I THINK HELPING OTHERS IS A GREAT WAY TO HELP YOURSELF. GOOD KARMA FOR THE SOUL.
Ooff! I CAN'T EAT ANOTHER THING.
WAY
SAY, IT'S BEEN A LONG DAY, HARLEY. MIND IF I TAKE A RAIN CHECK ON THE CARRIAGE RIDE AROUND THE PARK? I'M GOOD FOR IT.
TOTALLY UNDERSTAND. I'M BEAT AS WELL. CAN I ASK ONE THING?
SURE, GO RIGHT AHEAD.
HOW DO YOU FEEL ABOUT A GOOD NIGHT KISS?
WELL, I GUESS PRETTY FLATTER--
SMRPPP
MMmmphh
YOU SURE YOU DON'T WANT A LIFT BACK HOME?
NAW, IT'S FINE. I CAN USE THE FRESH AIR. THANKS AGAIN!
NO, THANK YOU!
SIIIGGHHHH

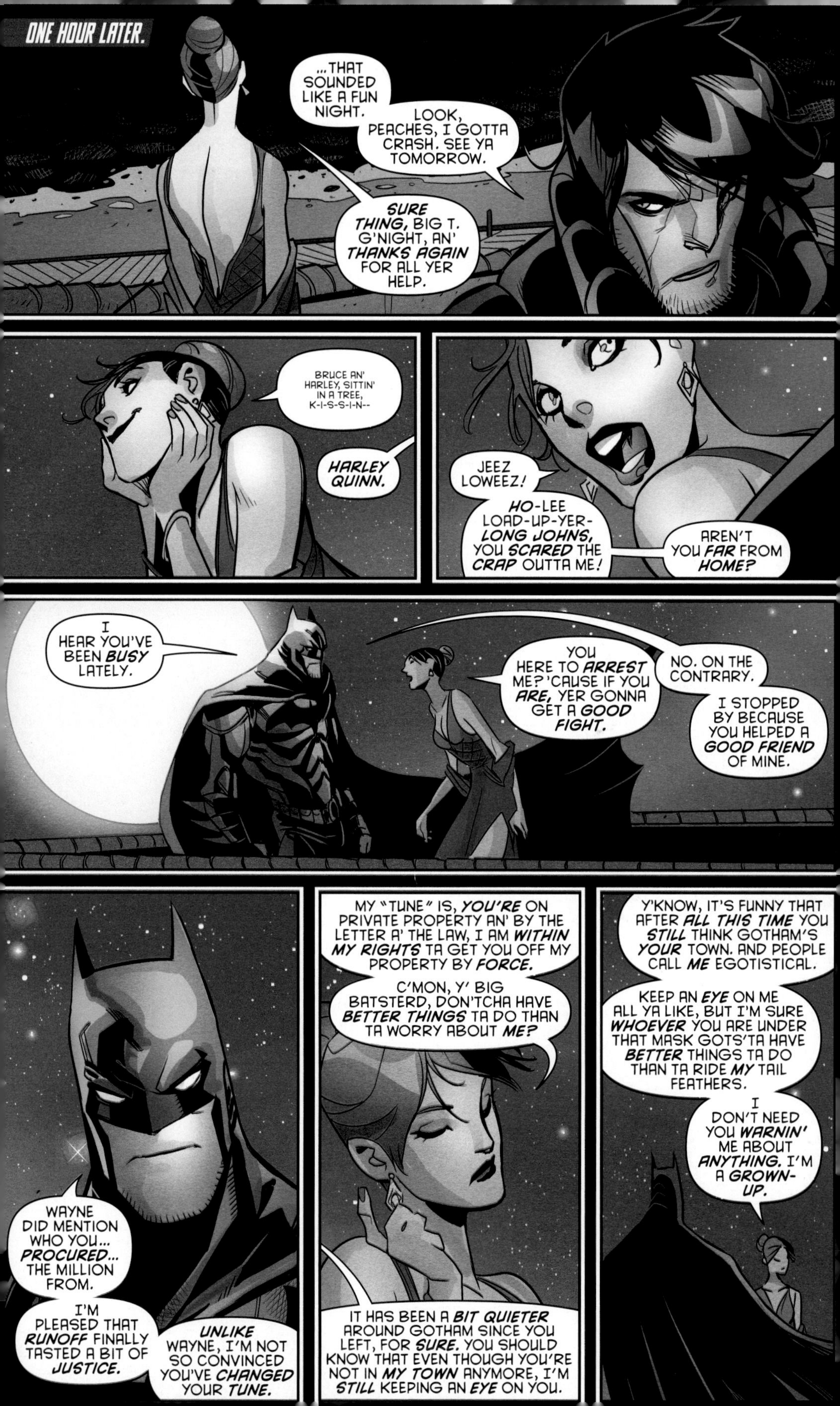
ONE HOUR LATER.
...THAT SOUNDED LIKE A FUN NIGHT.
LOOK, PEACHES, I GOTTA CRASH. SEE YA TOMORROW.
SURE THING, BIG T. G'NIGHT, AN' THANKS AGAIN FOR ALL YER HELP.
BRUCE AN' HARLEY, SITTIN' IN A TREE, K-I-S-S-I-N--
HARLEY QUINN.
JEEZ LOWEEZ!
HO-LEE LOAD-UP-YER-LONG JOHNS, YOU SCARED THE CRAP OUTTA ME!
AREN'T YOU FAR FROM HOME?
I HEAR YOU'VE BEEN BUSY LATELY.
YOU HERE TO ARREST ME? 'CAUSE IF YOU ARE, YER GONNA GET A GOOD FIGHT.
NO. ON THE CONTRARY.
I STOPPED BY BECAUSE YOU HELPED A GOOD FRIEND OF MINE.
WAYNE DID MENTION WHO YOU... PROCURED... THE MILLION FROM.
I'M PLEASED THAT RUNOFF FINALLY TASTED A BIT OF JUSTICE.
UNLIKE WAYNE, I'M NOT SO CONVINCED YOU'VE CHANGED YOUR TUNE.
MY "TUNE" IS, YOU'RE ON PRIVATE PROPERTY AN' BY THE LETTER A' THE LAW, I AM WITHIN MY RIGHTS TA GET YOU OFF MY PROPERTY BY FORCE.
C'MON, Y' BIG BATSTERD, DON'TCHA HAVE BETTER THINGS TA DO THAN TA WORRY ABOUT ME?
IT HAS BEEN A BIT QUIETER AROUND GOTHAM SINCE YOU LEFT, FOR SURE. YOU SHOULD KNOW THAT EVEN THOUGH YOU'RE NOT IN MY TOWN ANYMORE, I'M STILL KEEPING AN EYE ON YOU.
Y'KNOW, IT'S FUNNY THAT AFTER ALL THIS TIME YOU STILL THINK GOTHAM'S YOUR TOWN. AND PEOPLE CALL ME EGOTISTICAL.
KEEP AN EYE ON ME ALL YA LIKE, BUT I'M SURE WHOEVER YOU ARE UNDER THAT MASK GOTS'TA HAVE BETTER THINGS TA DO THAN TA RIDE MY TAIL FEATHERS.
I DON'T NEED YOU WARNIN' ME ABOUT ANYTHING. I'M A GROWN-UP.

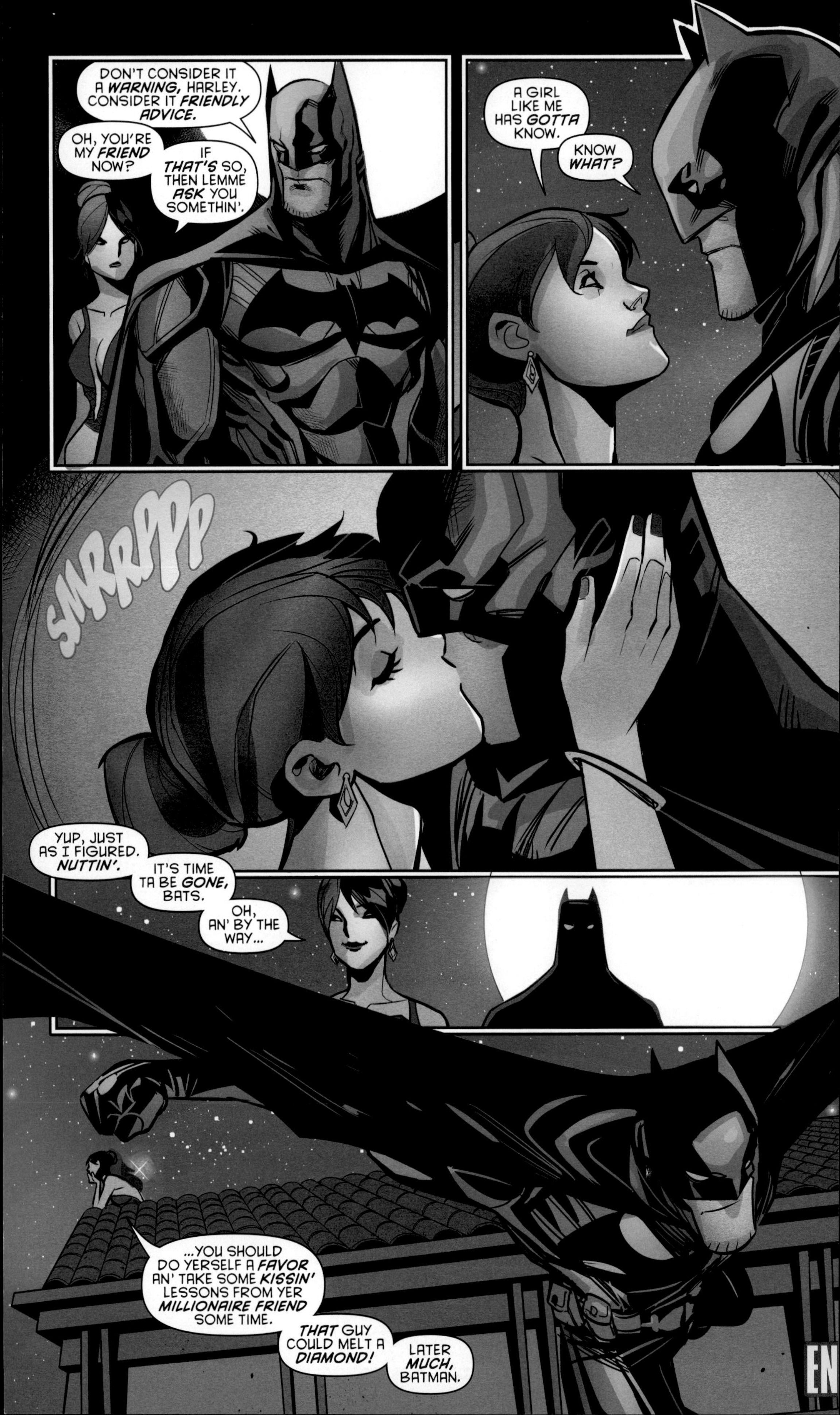

DON'T CONSIDER IT A WARNING, HARLEY. CONSIDER IT FRIENDLY ADVICE.
OH, YOU'RE MY FRIEND NOW?
IF THAT'S SO, THEN LEMME ASK YOU SOMETHIN'.
A GIRL LIKE ME HAS GOTTA KNOW.
KNOW WHAT?
SMRPPP
YUP, JUST AS I FIGURED. NUTTIN'.
IT'S TIME TA BE GONE, BATS.
OH, AN' BY THE WAY...
...YOU SHOULD DO YERSELF A FAVOR AN' TAKE SOME KISSIN' LESSONS FROM YER MILLIONAIRE FRIEND SOME TIME.
THAT GUY COULD MELT A DIAMOND!
LATER MUCH, BATMAN.

HARLEY QUINN ANNUAL #1
Bombshells variant cover by **ANT LUCIA**

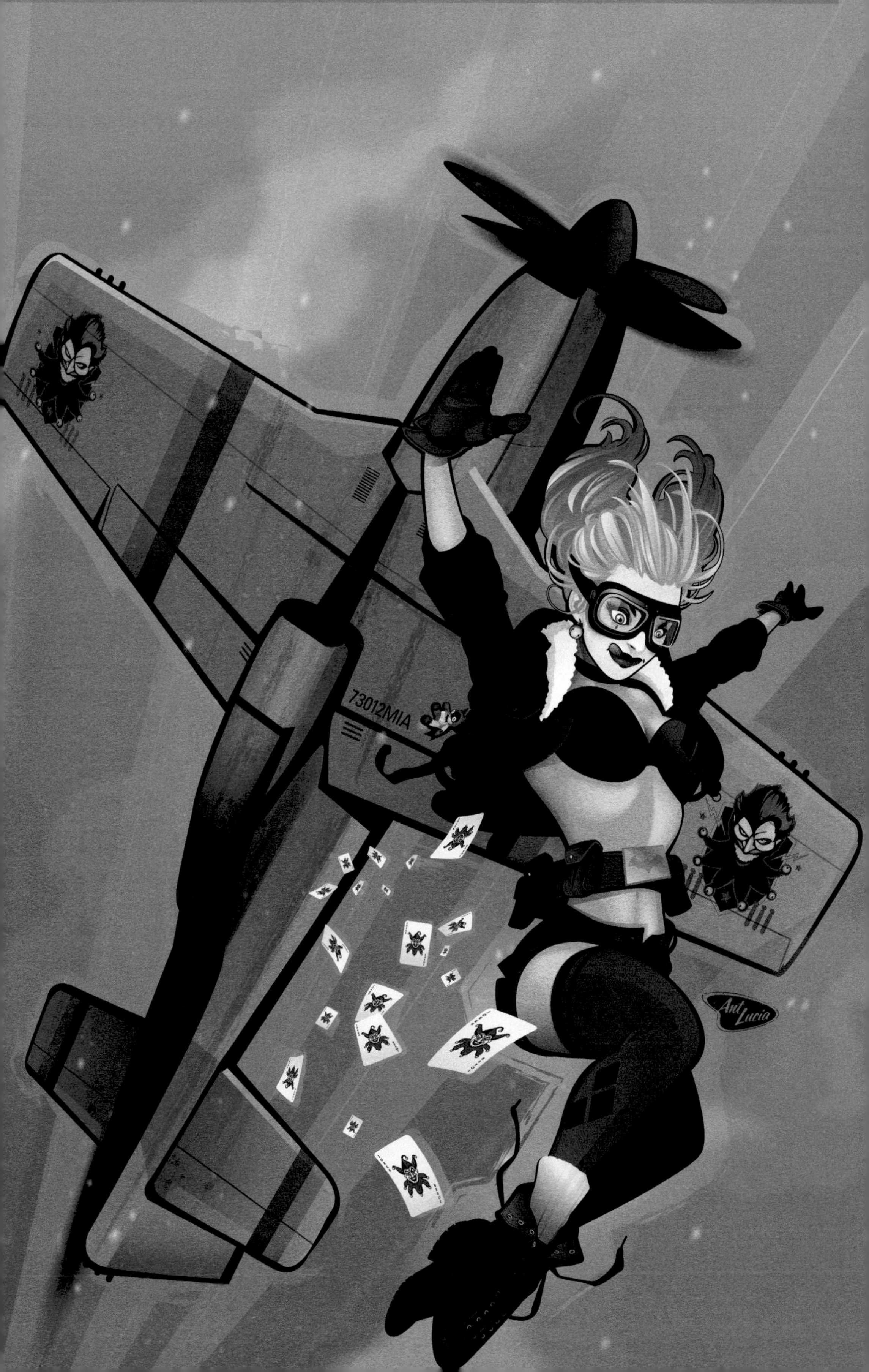
73012MIA
Ant Lucia

HARLEY QUINN HOLIDAY SPECIAL #1
Variant cover by **AMANDA CONNER & ALEX SINCLAIR**

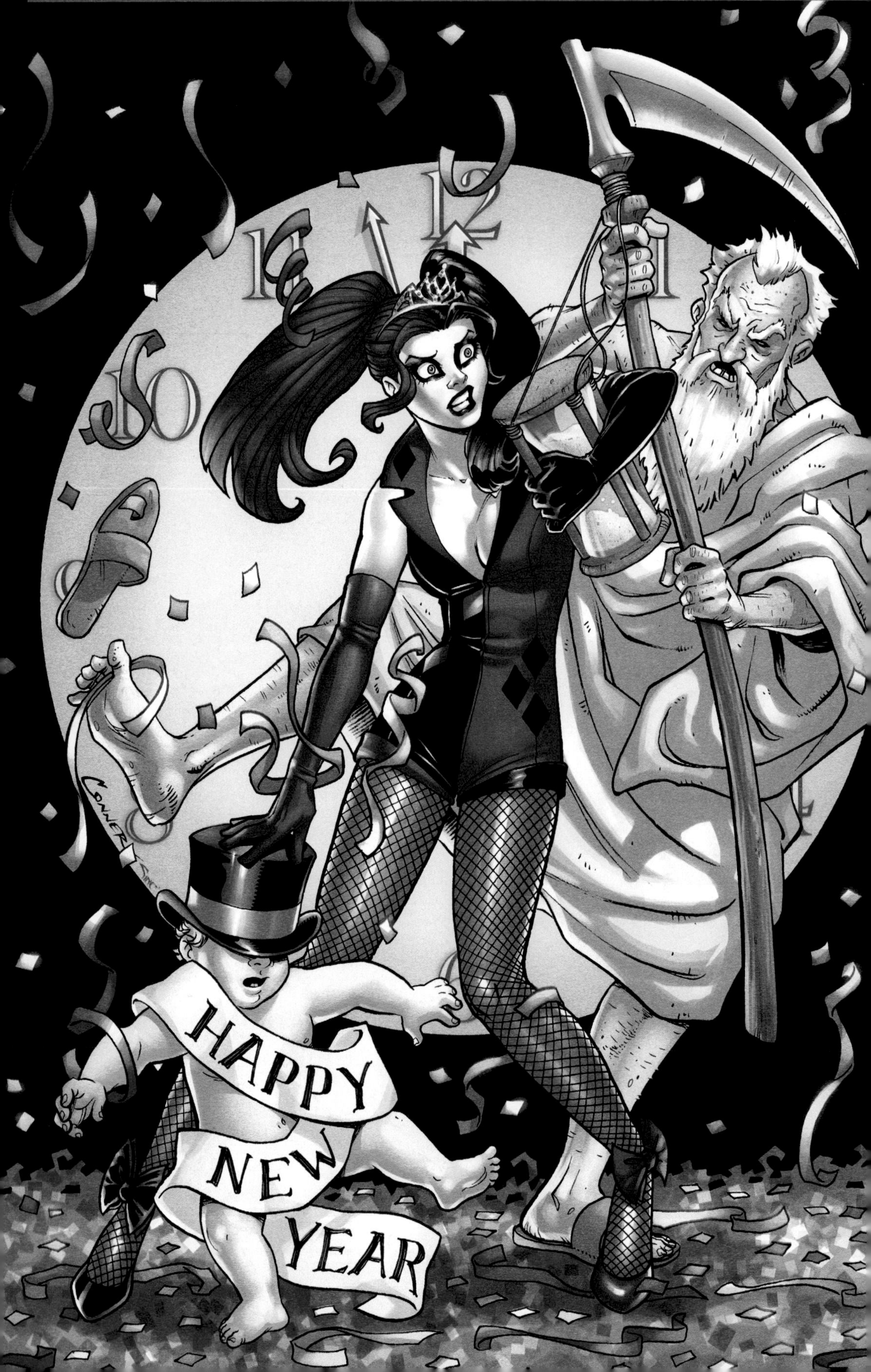
HAPPY
NEW
YEAR
CONNER

HARLEY QUINN VALENTINE'S DAY SPECIAL #1
Variant cover by **AMANDA CONNER , DAVE JOHNSON & ALEX SINCLAIR**

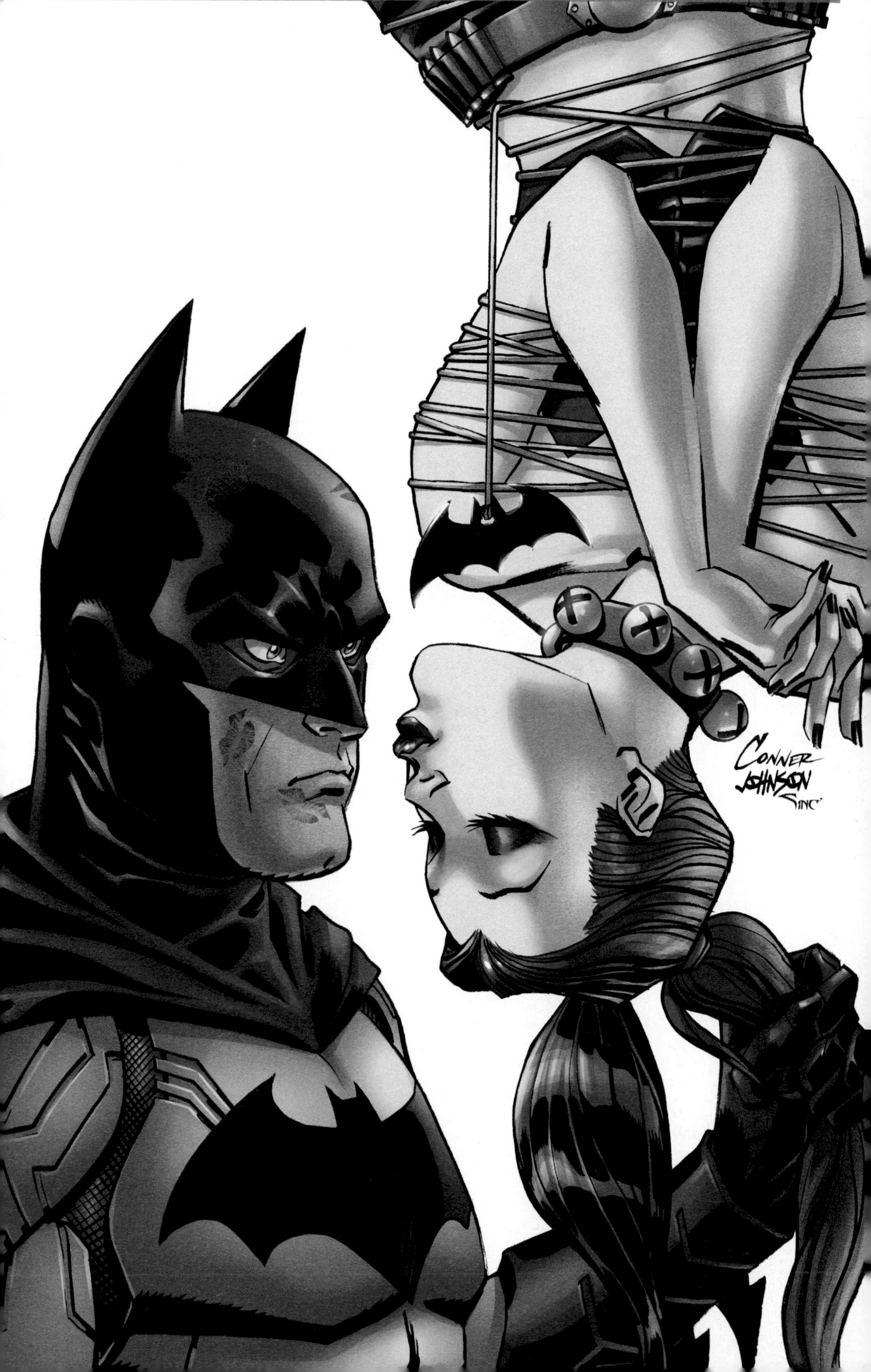

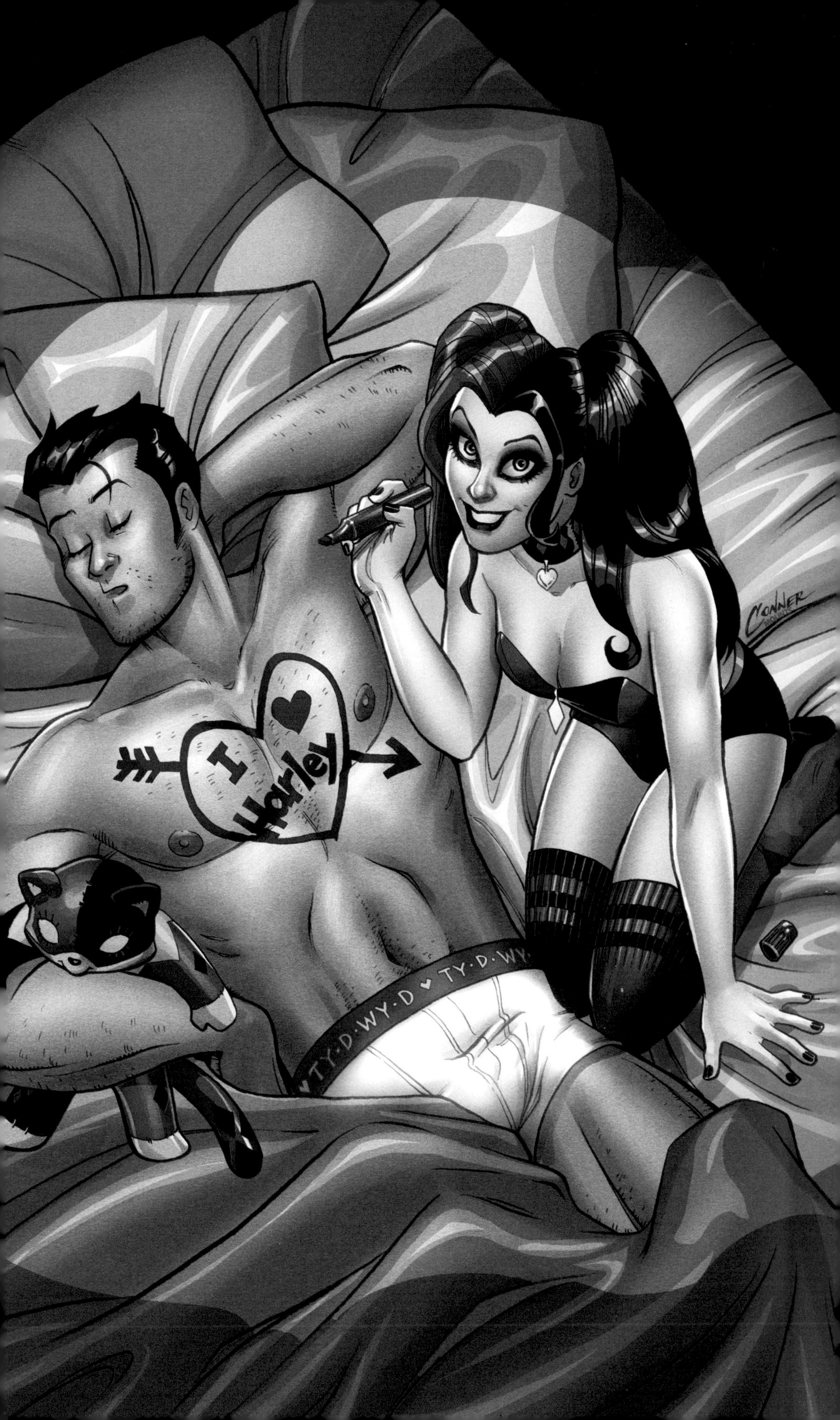
I ♥ Harley
CONNER

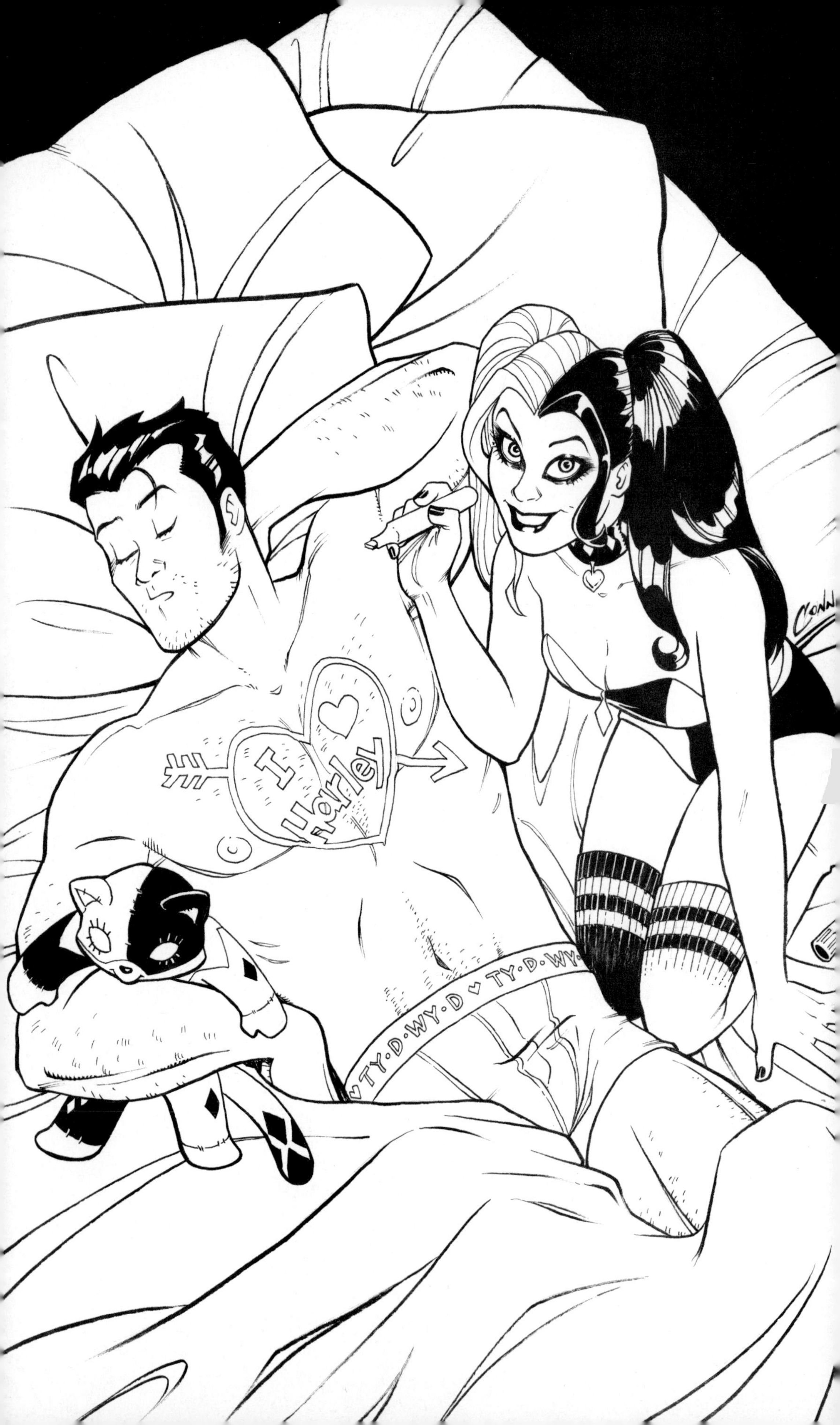
I ♥ Harley
TY·D·WY·D ♥ TY·D·WY·

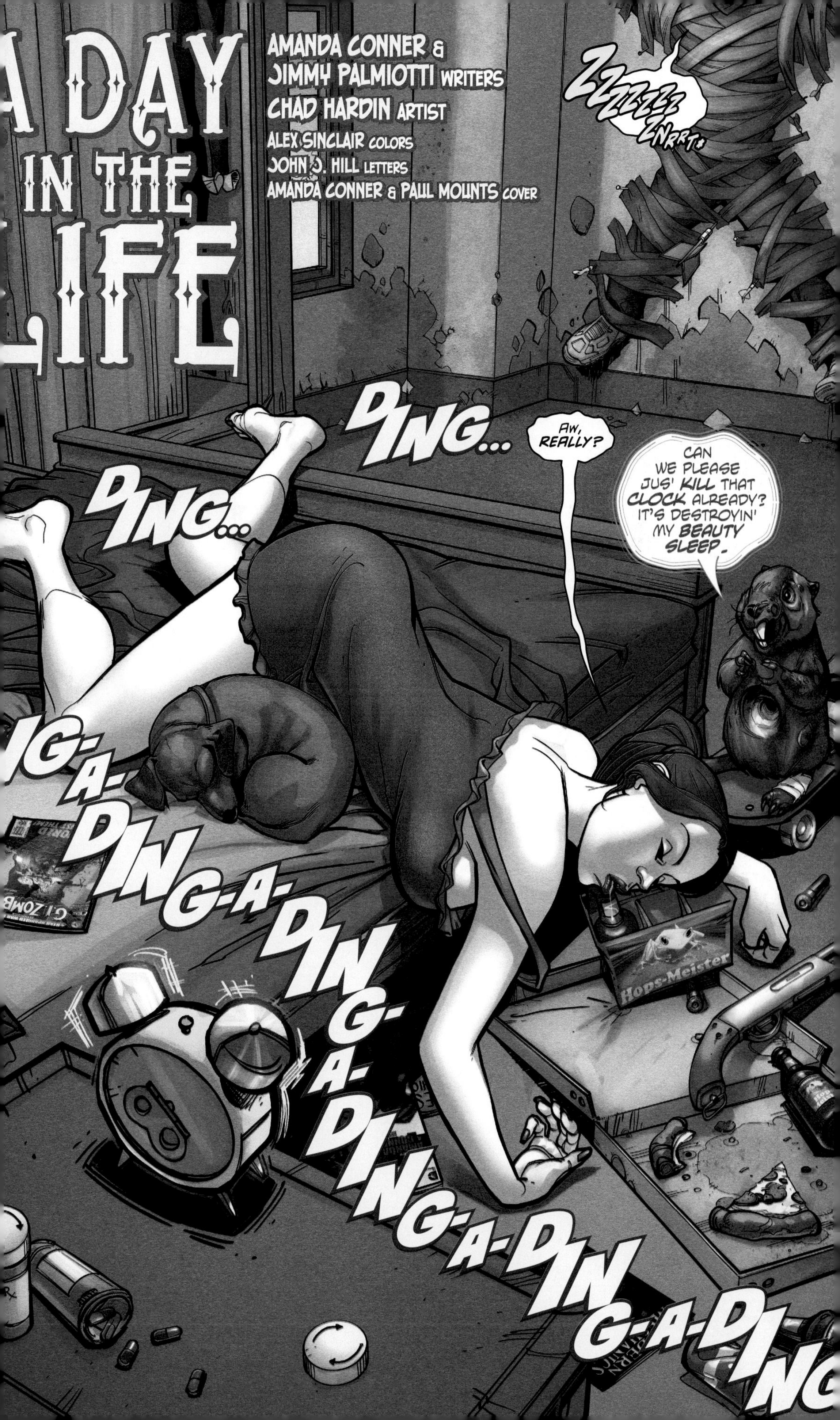

A DAY IN THE LIFE
AMANDA CONNER & JIMMY PALMIOTTI WRITERS
CHAD HARDIN ARTIST
ALEX SINCLAIR COLORS
JOHN J. HILL LETTERS
AMANDA CONNER & PAUL MOUNTS COVER
ZZZZZZZ ZNRRT*
DING...
DING...
AW, REALLY?
CAN WE PLEASE JUS' KILL THAT CLOCK ALREADY? IT'S DESTROYIN' MY BEAUTY SLEEP.
NG-A-DING-A-DING-A-DING-A-DING-A-DING-A-DING
Hops-Meister

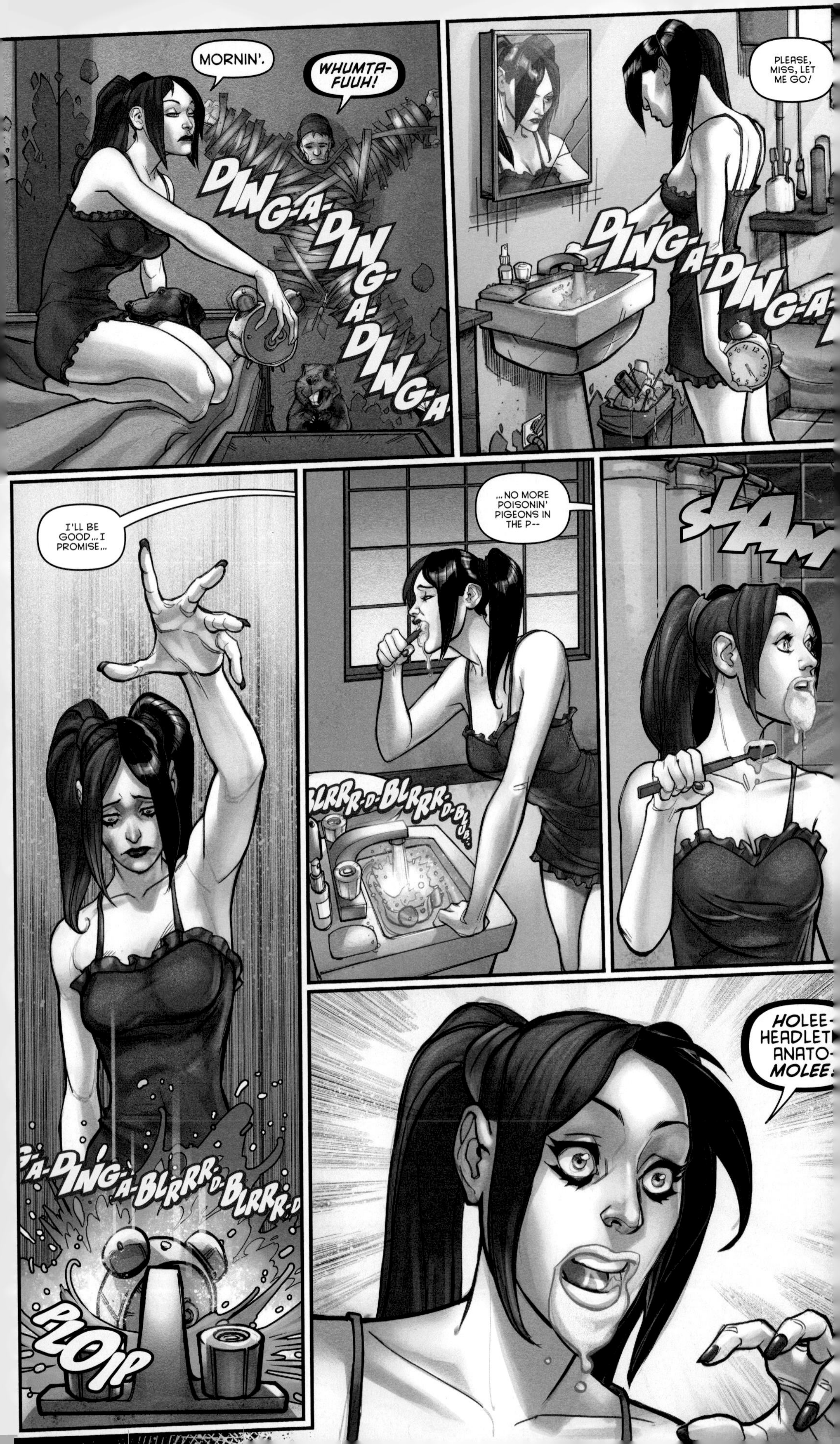
MORNIN'.
WHUMTA-FUUH!
DING-A-DING-A-DING-A-DING-A
PLEASE, MISS, LET ME GO!
DING-A-DING-A-DING-A
I'LL BE GOOD... I PROMISE...
G-A-DING-A-BLRRR-D-BLRRR-D
PLOIP
...NO MORE POISONIN' PIGEONS IN THE P--
BLRRR-D-BLRRR-D-BLB...
SLAM
HOLEE-HEADLET ANATO-MOLEE!

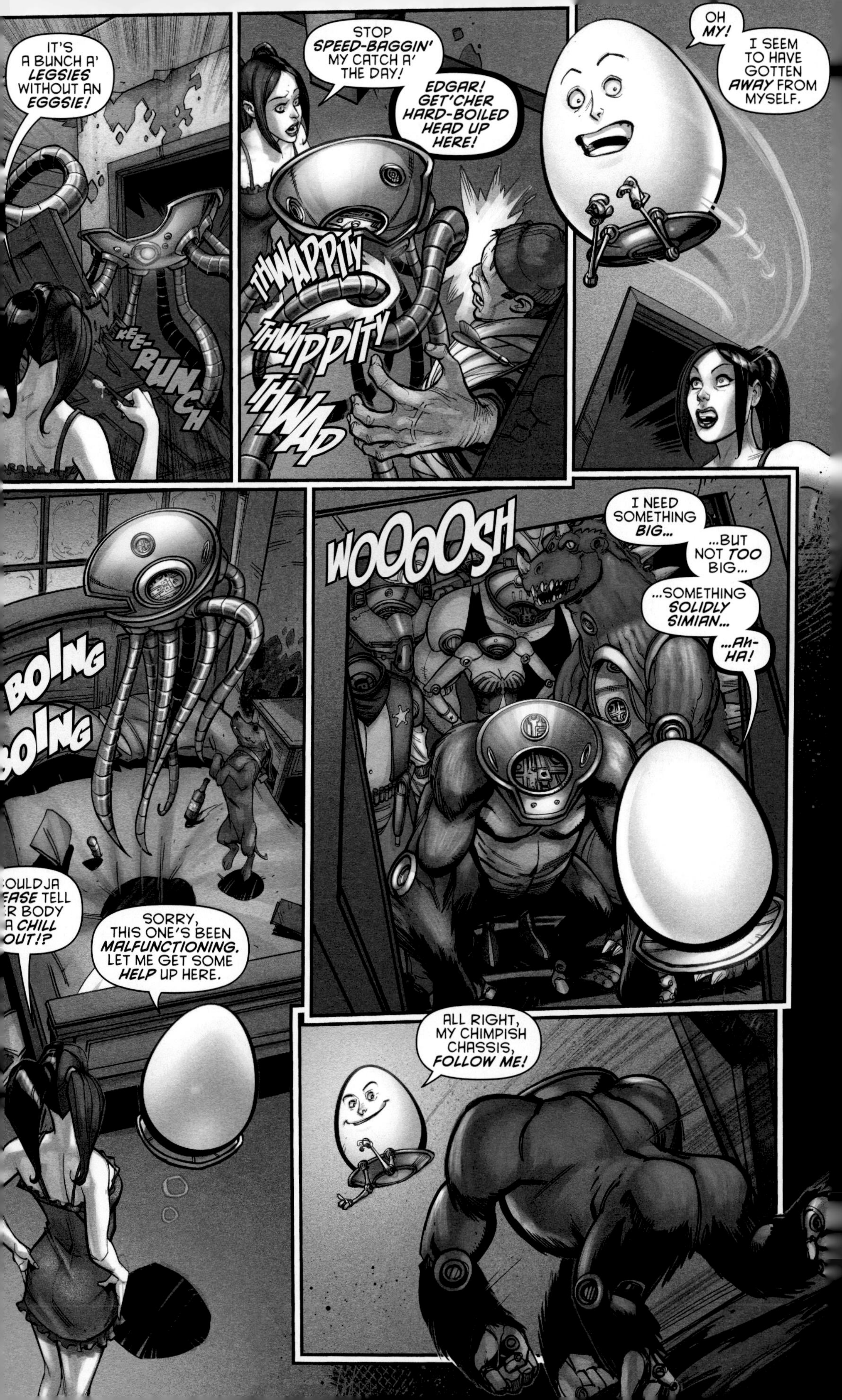
IT'S A BUNCH A' LEGSIES WITHOUT AN EGGSIE!
KEE-RUNCH
STOP SPEED-BAGGIN' MY CATCH A' THE DAY!
EDGAR! GET'CHER HARD-BOILED HEAD UP HERE!
THWAPPITY
THWIPPITY
THWAP
OH MY!
I SEEM TO HAVE GOTTEN AWAY FROM MYSELF.
BOING
BOING
OULDJA
EASE TELL
R BODY
A CHILL
OUT!?
SORRY, THIS ONE'S BEEN MALFUNCTIONING. LET ME GET SOME HELP UP HERE.
WOOOOOSH
I NEED SOMETHING BIG...
...BUT NOT TOO BIG...
...SOMETHING SOLIDLY SIMIAN...
...AH-HA!
ALL RIGHT, MY CHIMPISH CHASSIS, FOLLOW ME!

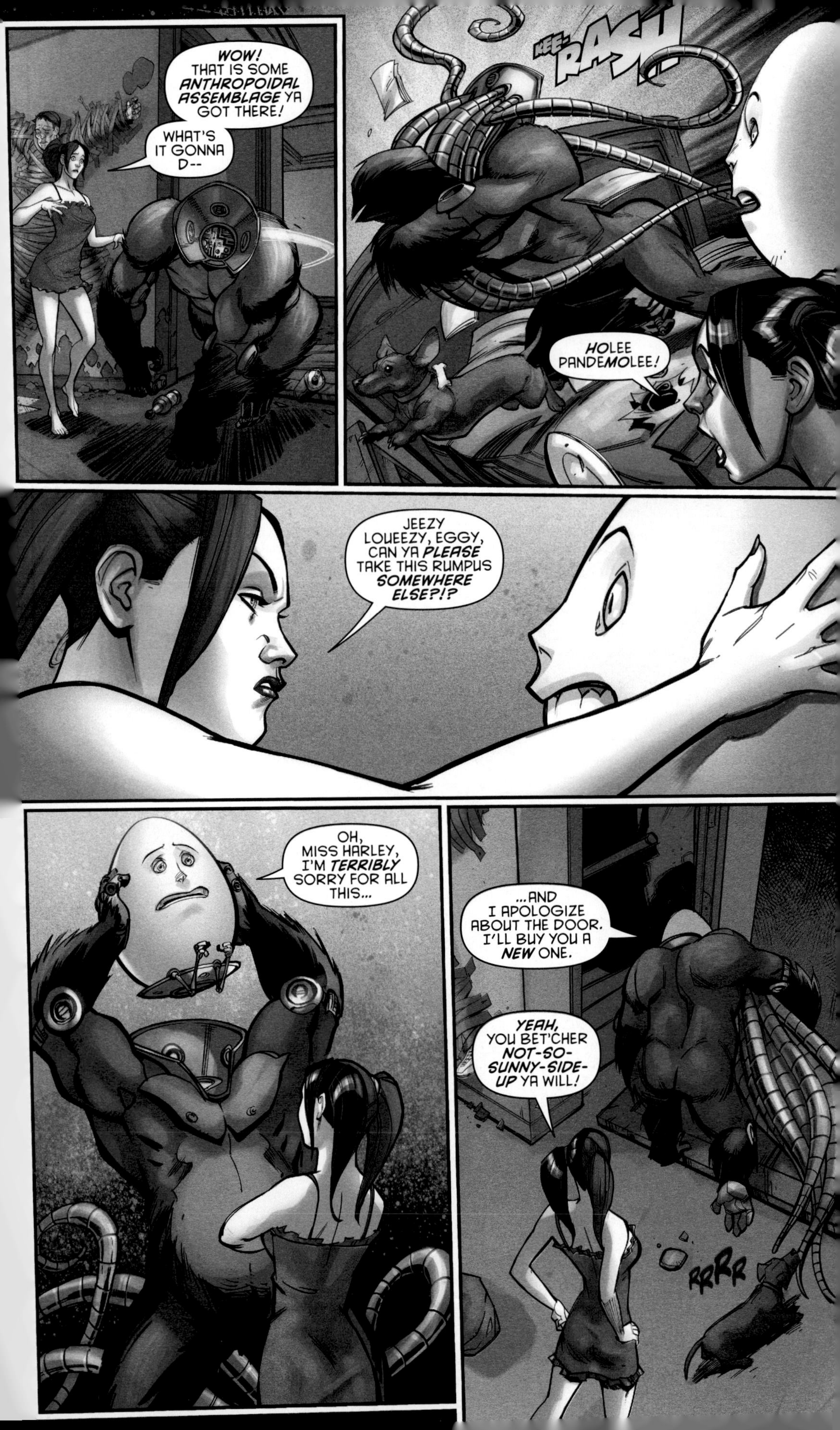
WOW! THAT IS SOME ANTHROPOIDAL ASSEMBLAGE YA GOT THERE!
WHAT'S IT GONNA D--
KEE-RASH!
HOLEE PANDEMOLEE!
JEEZY LOUEEZY, EGGY, CAN YA PLEASE TAKE THIS RUMPUS SOMEWHERE ELSE?!?
OH, MISS HARLEY, I'M TERRIBLY SORRY FOR ALL THIS...
...AND I APOLOGIZE ABOUT THE DOOR. I'LL BUY YOU A NEW ONE.
YEAH, YOU BET'CHER NOT-SO-SUNNY-SIDE-UP YA WILL!
RRRR

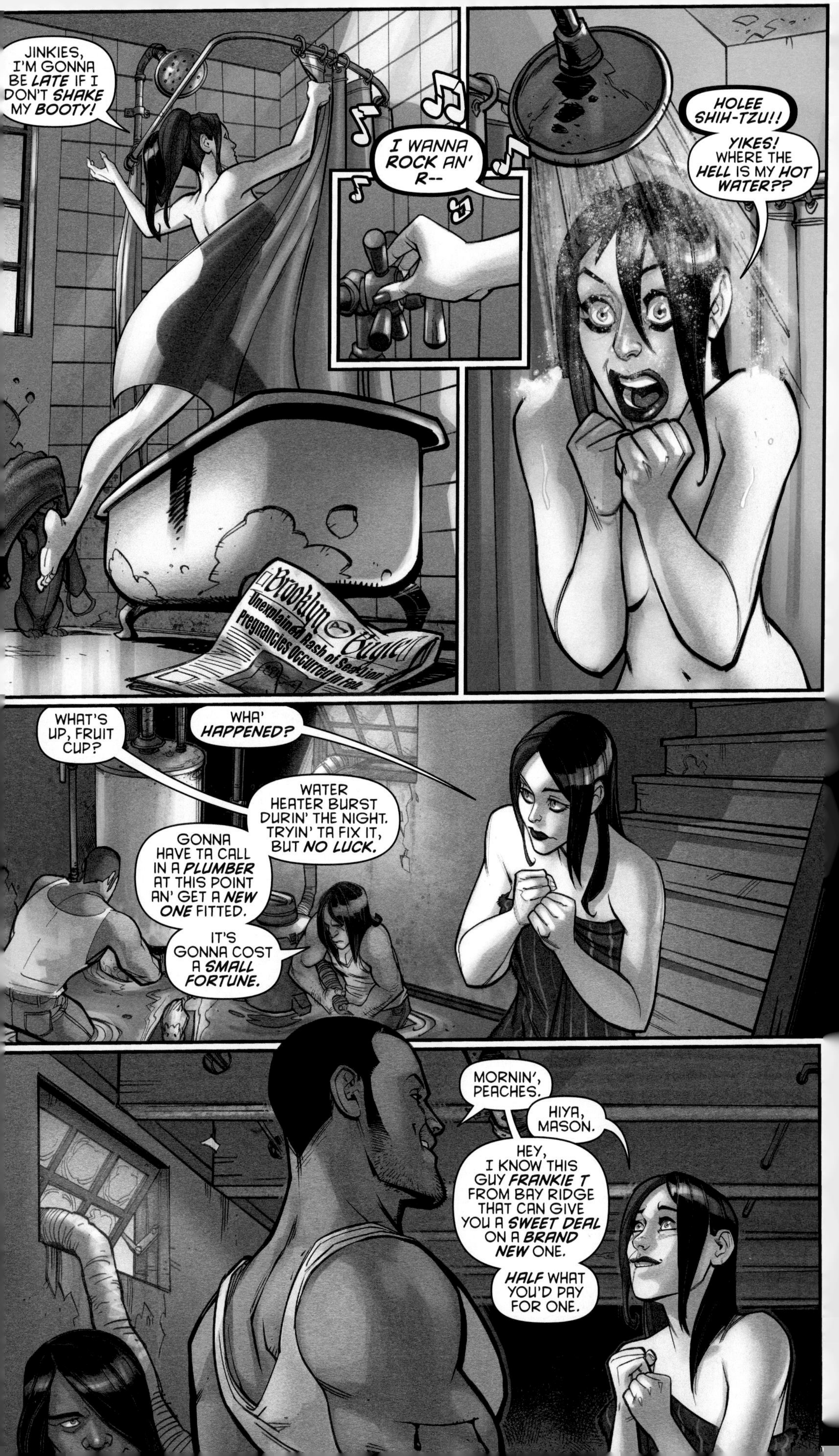

JINKIES, I'M GONNA BE *LATE* IF I DON'T *SHAKE* MY *BOOTY!*
Brooklyn Bugle
Unexplained Rash of Sea Lion Pregnancies Occurred in Feb.
I WANNA *ROCK* AN' R--
HOLEE SHIH-TZU!!
YIKES! WHERE THE *HELL* IS MY *HOT WATER??*
WHAT'S UP, FRUIT CUP?
WHA' *HAPPENED?*
WATER HEATER BURST DURIN' THE NIGHT. TRYIN' TA FIX IT, BUT *NO LUCK.*
GONNA HAVE TA CALL IN A *PLUMBER* AT THIS POINT AN' GET A *NEW ONE* FITTED.
IT'S GONNA COST A *SMALL FORTUNE.*
MORNIN', PEACHES.
HIYA, MASON.
HEY, I KNOW THIS GUY *FRANKIE T* FROM BAY RIDGE THAT CAN GIVE YOU A *SWEET DEAL* ON A *BRAND NEW* ONE.
HALF WHAT YOU'D PAY FOR ONE.

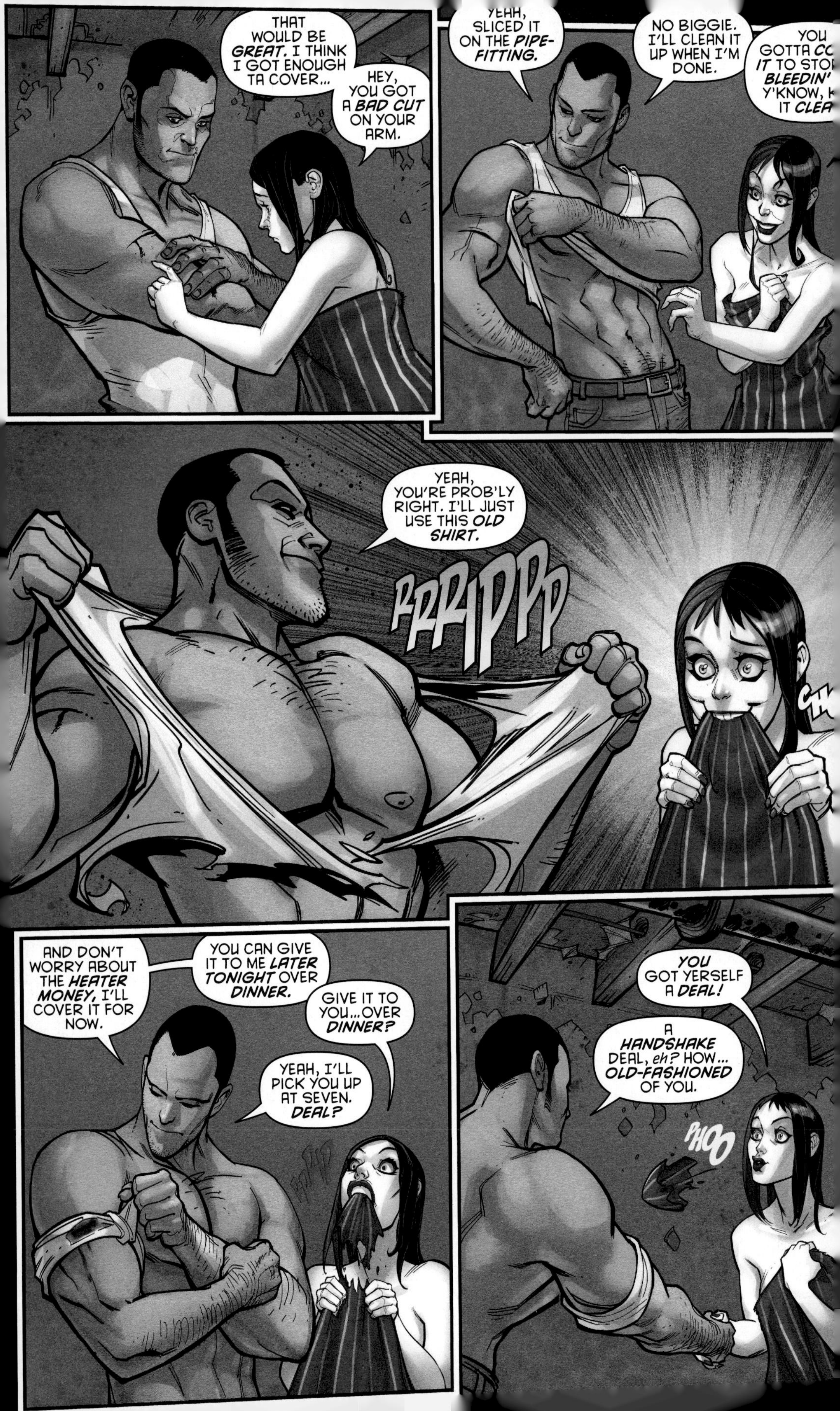

THAT WOULD BE GREAT. I THINK I GOT ENOUGH TA COVER...
HEY, YOU GOT A BAD CUT ON YOUR ARM.
YEAH, SLICED IT ON THE PIPE-FITTING.
NO BIGGIE. I'LL CLEAN IT UP WHEN I'M DONE.
YOU GOTTA CO
IT TO STO
BLEEDIN'
Y'KNOW,
IT CLEA
YEAH, YOU'RE PROB'LY RIGHT. I'LL JUST USE THIS OLD SHIRT.
RRRIPPP
AND DON'T WORRY ABOUT THE HEATER MONEY, I'LL COVER IT FOR NOW.
YOU CAN GIVE IT TO ME LATER TONIGHT OVER DINNER.
GIVE IT TO YOU...OVER DINNER?
YEAH, I'LL PICK YOU UP AT SEVEN. DEAL?
YOU GOT YERSELF A DEAL!
A HANDSHAKE DEAL, eh? HOW... OLD-FASHIONED OF YOU.
PHOO

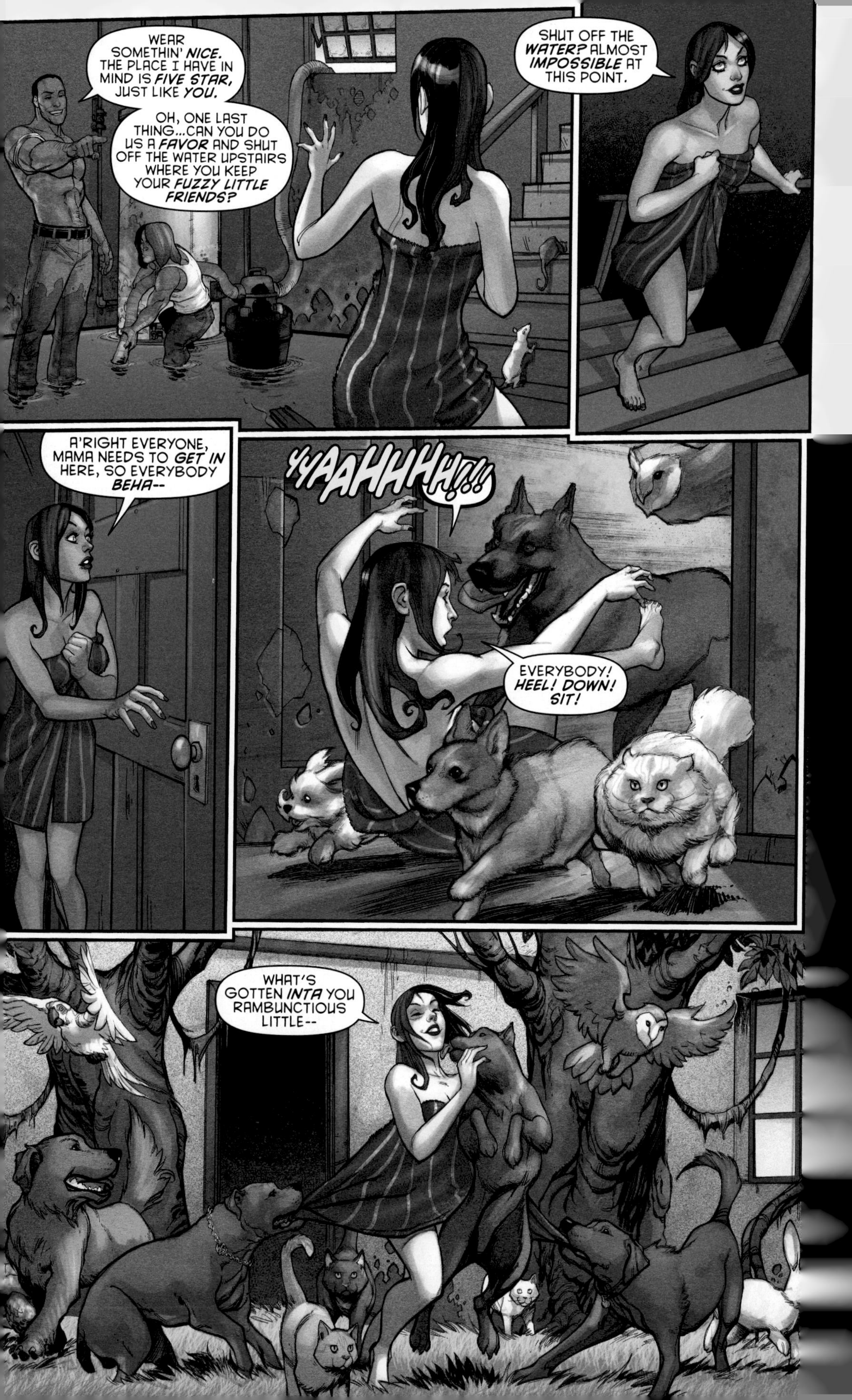
WEAR SOMETHIN' *NICE.* THE PLACE I HAVE IN MIND IS *FIVE STAR,* JUST LIKE *YOU.*
OH, ONE LAST THING...CAN YOU DO US A *FAVOR* AND SHUT OFF THE WATER UPSTAIRS WHERE YOU KEEP YOUR *FUZZY LITTLE FRIENDS?*
SHUT OFF THE *WATER?* ALMOST *IMPOSSIBLE* AT THIS POINT.
A'RIGHT EVERYONE, MAMA NEEDS TO *GET IN* HERE, SO EVERYBODY *BEHA--*
YYAAHHHH!?!!
EVERYBODY! *HEEL! DOWN! SIT!*
WHAT'S GOTTEN *INTA* YOU RAMBUNCTIOUS LITTLE--

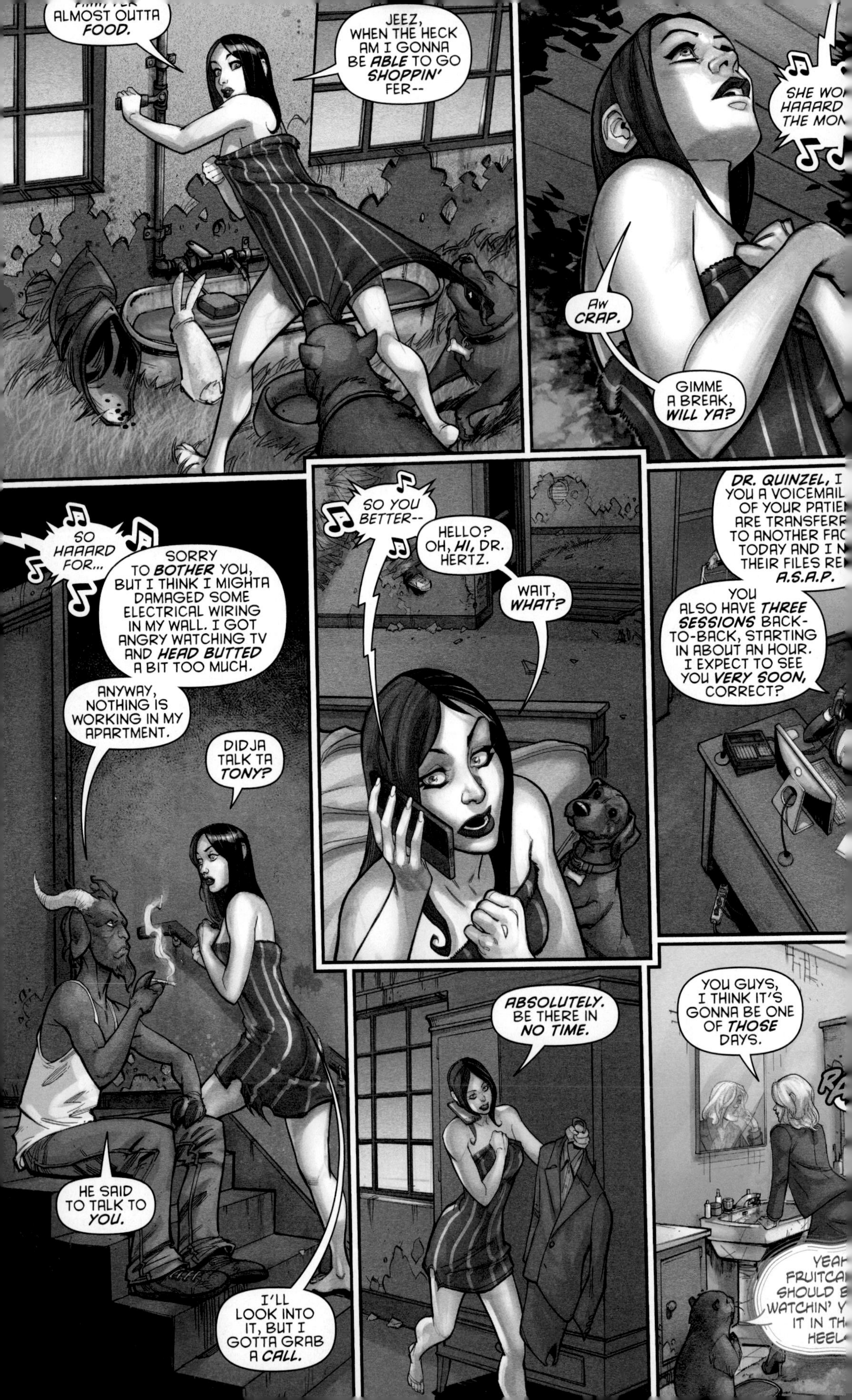
ALMOST OUTTA FOOD.
JEEZ, WHEN THE HECK AM I GONNA BE ABLE TO GO SHOPPIN' FER--
AW CRAP.
GIMME A BREAK, WILL YA?
SO HAAARD FOR...
SORRY TO BOTHER YOU, BUT I THINK I MIGHTA DAMAGED SOME ELECTRICAL WIRING IN MY WALL. I GOT ANGRY WATCHING TV AND HEAD BUTTED A BIT TOO MUCH.
ANYWAY, NOTHING IS WORKING IN MY APARTMENT.
DIDJA TALK TA TONY?
HE SAID TO TALK TO YOU.
I'LL LOOK INTO IT, BUT I GOTTA GRAB A CALL.
SO YOU BETTER--
HELLO? OH, HI, DR. HERTZ.
WAIT, WHAT?
YOU ALSO HAVE THREE SESSIONS BACK-TO-BACK, STARTING IN ABOUT AN HOUR. I EXPECT TO SEE YOU VERY SOON, CORRECT?
ABSOLUTELY. BE THERE IN NO TIME.
YOU GUYS, I THINK IT'S GONNA BE ONE OF THOSE DAYS.

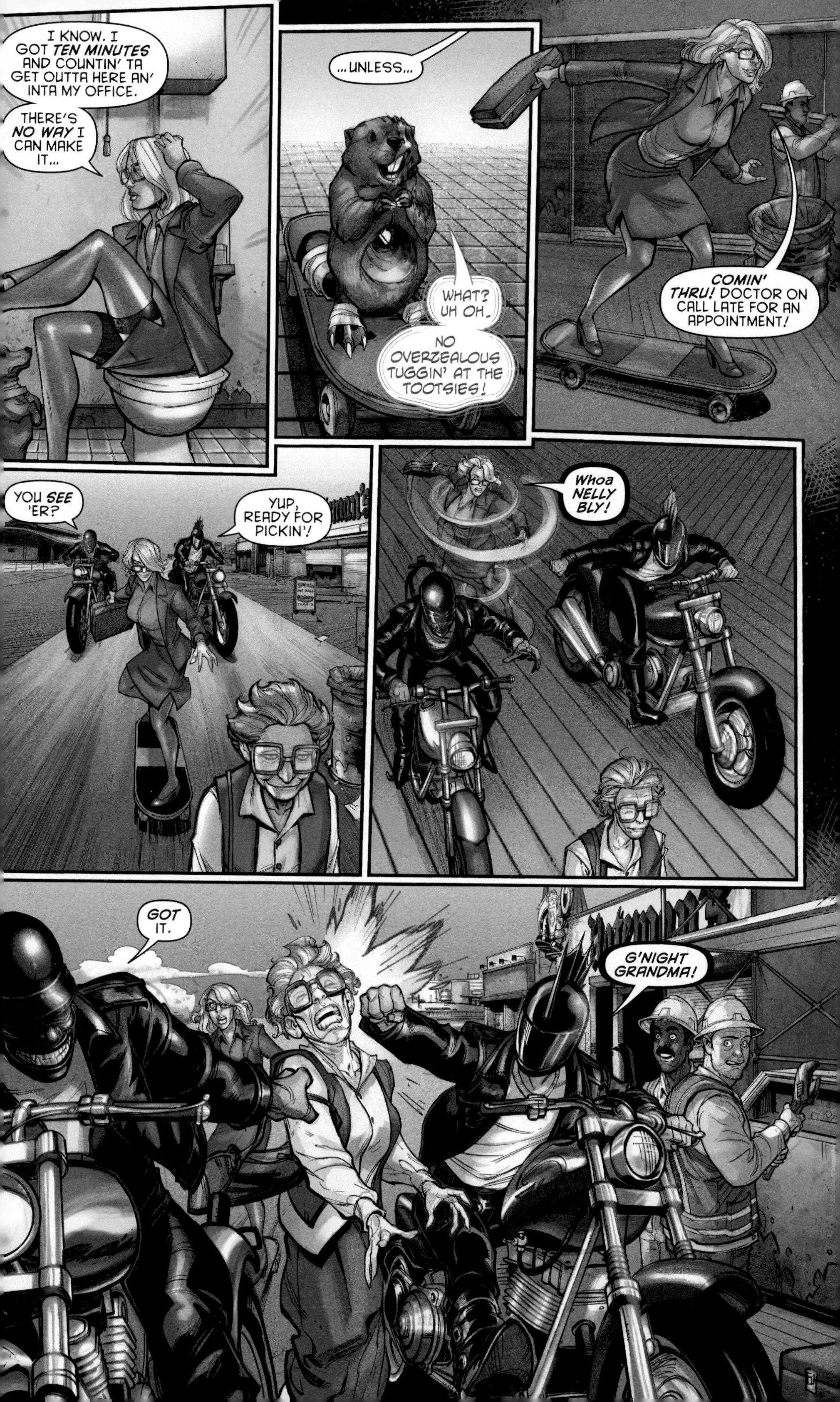
I KNOW. I GOT TEN MINUTES AND COUNTIN' TA GET OUTTA HERE AN' INTA MY OFFICE.
THERE'S NO WAY I CAN MAKE IT...
...UNLESS...
WHAT? UH OH.
NO OVERZEALOUS TUGGIN' AT THE TOOTSIES!
COMIN' THRU! DOCTOR ON CALL LATE FOR AN APPOINTMENT!
YOU SEE 'ER?
YUP, READY FOR PICKIN'!
Whoa NELLY BLY!
GOT IT.
G'NIGHT GRANDMA!

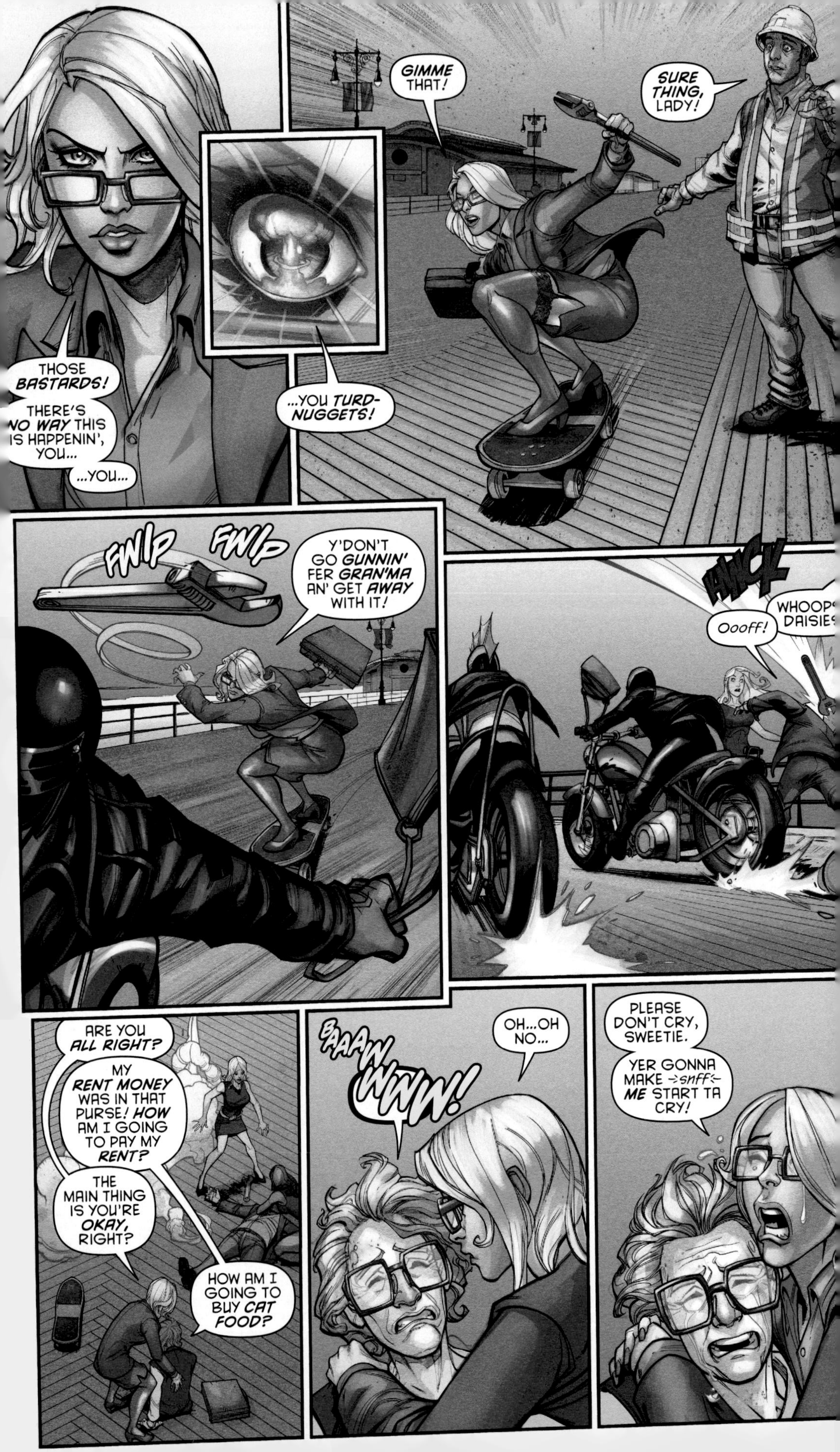

THOSE BASTARDS!
THERE'S NO WAY THIS IS HAPPENIN', YOU...
...YOU...
...YOU TURD-NUGGETS!
GIMME THAT!
SURE THING, LADY!
FWIP FWIP
Y'DON'T GO GUNNIN' FER GRAN'MA AN' GET AWAY WITH IT!
WHOOPS DAISIES
Oooff!
ARE YOU ALL RIGHT?
MY RENT MONEY WAS IN THAT PURSE! HOW AM I GOING TO PAY MY RENT?
THE MAIN THING IS YOU'RE OKAY, RIGHT?
HOW AM I GOING TO BUY CAT FOOD?
BAAAWWWW!
OH...OH NO...
PLEASE DON'T CRY, SWEETIE.
YER GONNA MAKE -snff- ME START TA CRY!

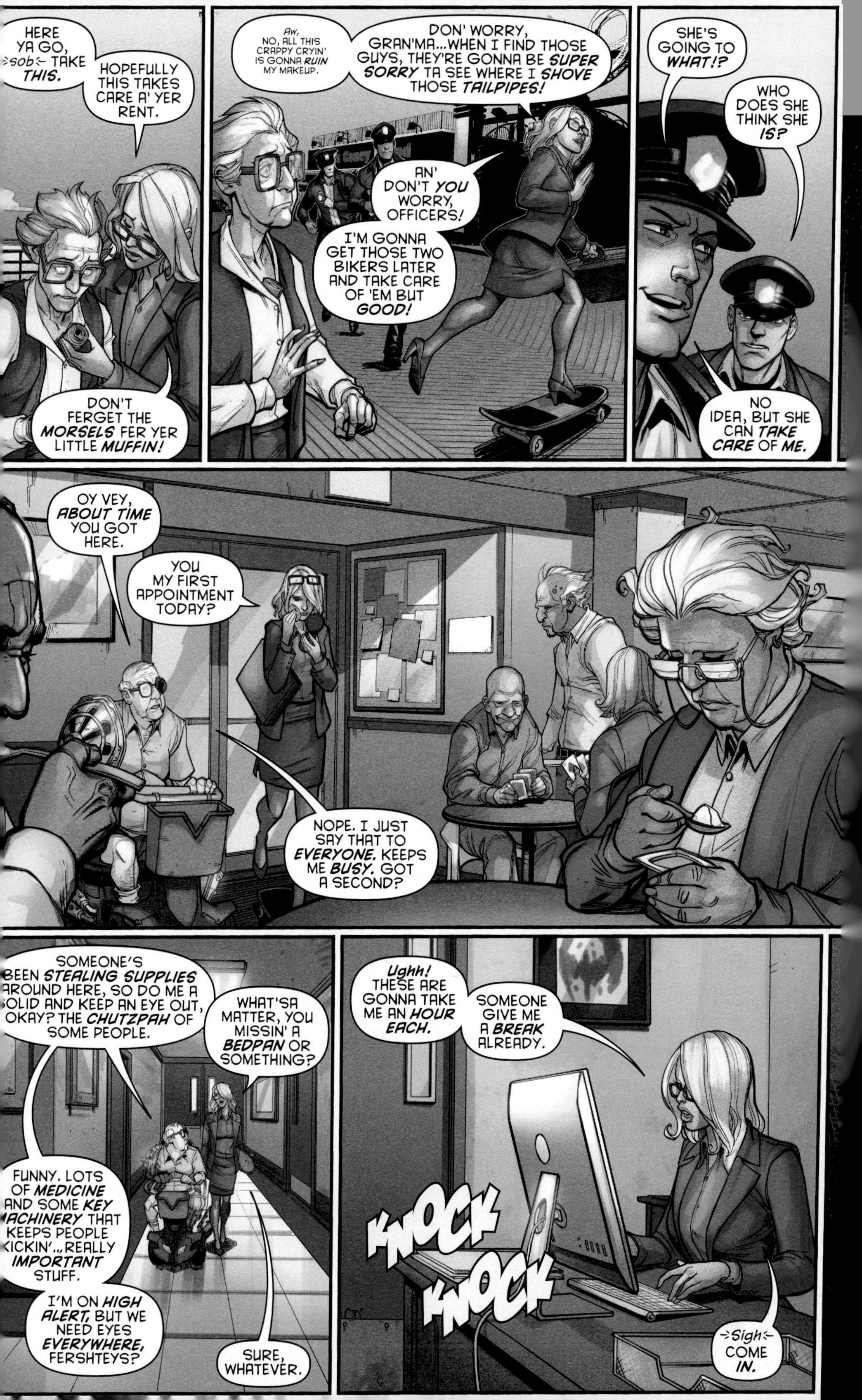
HERE YA GO, >sob< TAKE THIS.
HOPEFULLY THIS TAKES CARE A' YER RENT.
DON'T FERGET THE MORSELS FER YER LITTLE MUFFIN!
AW, NO, ALL THIS CRAPPY CRYIN' IS GONNA RUIN MY MAKEUP.
DON' WORRY, GRAN'MA...WHEN I FIND THOSE GUYS, THEY'RE GONNA BE SUPER SORRY TA SEE WHERE I SHOVE THOSE TAILPIPES!
AN' DON'T YOU WORRY, OFFICERS!
I'M GONNA GET THOSE TWO BIKERS LATER AND TAKE CARE OF 'EM BUT GOOD!
SHE'S GOING TO WHAT!?
WHO DOES SHE THINK SHE IS?
NO IDEA, BUT SHE CAN TAKE CARE OF ME.
OY VEY, ABOUT TIME YOU GOT HERE.
YOU MY FIRST APPOINTMENT TODAY?
NOPE. I JUST SAY THAT TO EVERYONE. KEEPS ME BUSY. GOT A SECOND?
SOMEONE'S BEEN STEALING SUPPLIES AROUND HERE, SO DO ME A SOLID AND KEEP AN EYE OUT, OKAY? THE CHUTZPAH OF SOME PEOPLE.
WHAT'SA MATTER, YOU MISSIN' A BEDPAN OR SOMETHING?
FUNNY. LOTS OF MEDICINE AND SOME KEY MACHINERY THAT KEEPS PEOPLE KICKIN'...REALLY IMPORTANT STUFF.
I'M ON HIGH ALERT, BUT WE NEED EYES EVERYWHERE, FERSHTEYS?
SURE, WHATEVER.
UGHH! THESE ARE GONNA TAKE ME AN HOUR EACH.
SOMEONE GIVE ME A BREAK ALREADY.
KNOCK KNOCK
>SIGH< COME IN.

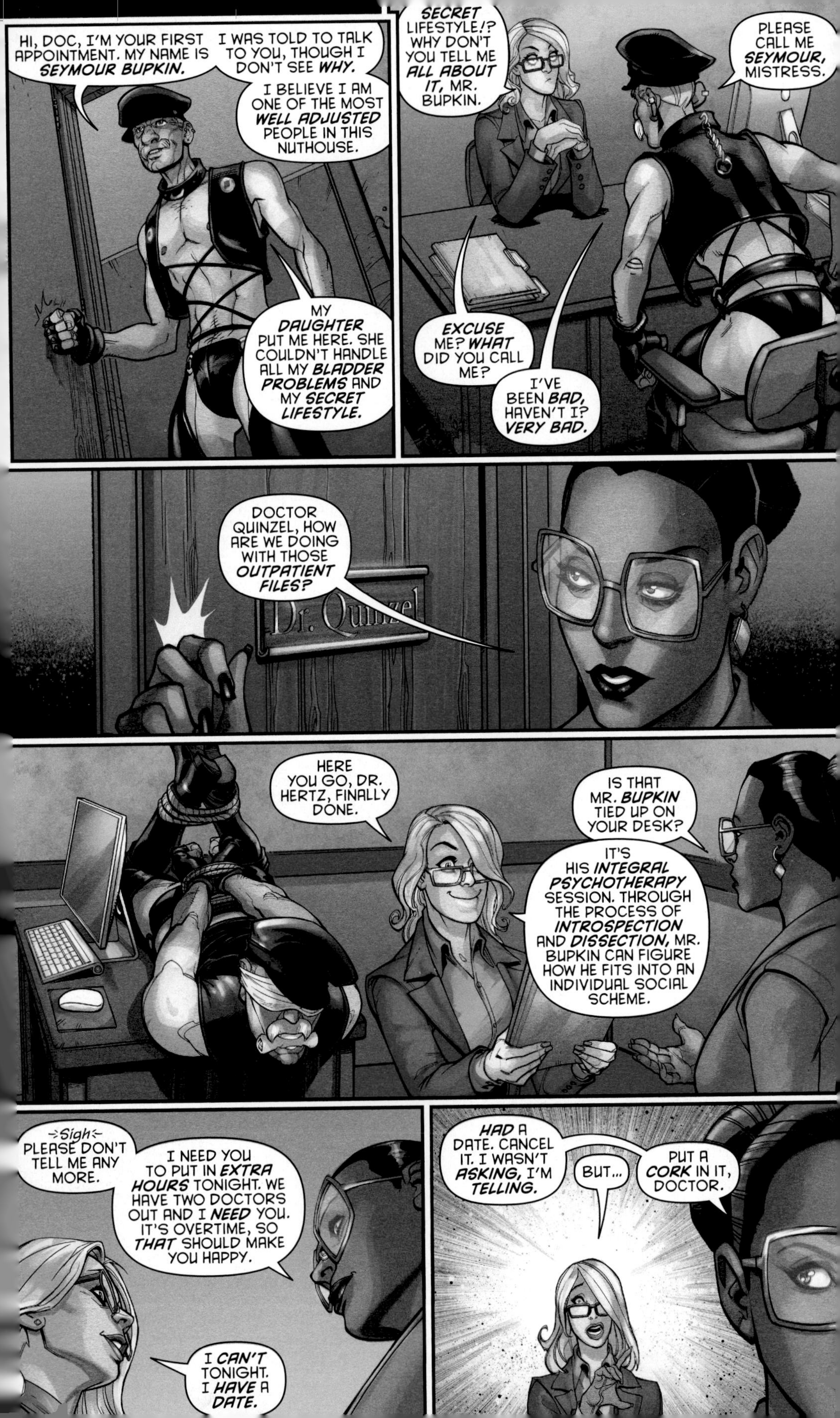
HI, DOC, I'M YOUR FIRST APPOINTMENT. MY NAME IS SEYMOUR BUPKIN.
I WAS TOLD TO TALK TO YOU, THOUGH I DON'T SEE WHY.
I BELIEVE I AM ONE OF THE MOST WELL ADJUSTED PEOPLE IN THIS NUTHOUSE.
MY DAUGHTER PUT ME HERE. SHE COULDN'T HANDLE ALL MY BLADDER PROBLEMS AND MY SECRET LIFESTYLE.
SECRET LIFESTYLE!? WHY DON'T YOU TELL ME ALL ABOUT IT, MR. BUPKIN.
PLEASE CALL ME SEYMOUR, MISTRESS.
EXCUSE ME? WHAT DID YOU CALL ME?
I'VE BEEN BAD, HAVEN'T I? VERY BAD.
DOCTOR QUINZEL, HOW ARE WE DOING WITH THOSE OUTPATIENT FILES?
Dr. Quinzel
HERE YOU GO, DR. HERTZ, FINALLY DONE.
IS THAT MR. BUPKIN TIED UP ON YOUR DESK?
IT'S HIS INTEGRAL PSYCHOTHERAPY SESSION. THROUGH THE PROCESS OF INTROSPECTION AND DISSECTION, MR. BUPKIN CAN FIGURE HOW HE FITS INTO AN INDIVIDUAL SOCIAL SCHEME.
-Sigh- PLEASE DON'T TELL ME ANY MORE.
I NEED YOU TO PUT IN EXTRA HOURS TONIGHT. WE HAVE TWO DOCTORS OUT AND I NEED YOU. IT'S OVERTIME, SO THAT SHOULD MAKE YOU HAPPY.
I CAN'T TONIGHT. I HAVE A DATE.
HAD A DATE. CANCEL IT. I WASN'T ASKING, I'M TELLING.
BUT...
PUT A CORK IN IT, DOCTOR.

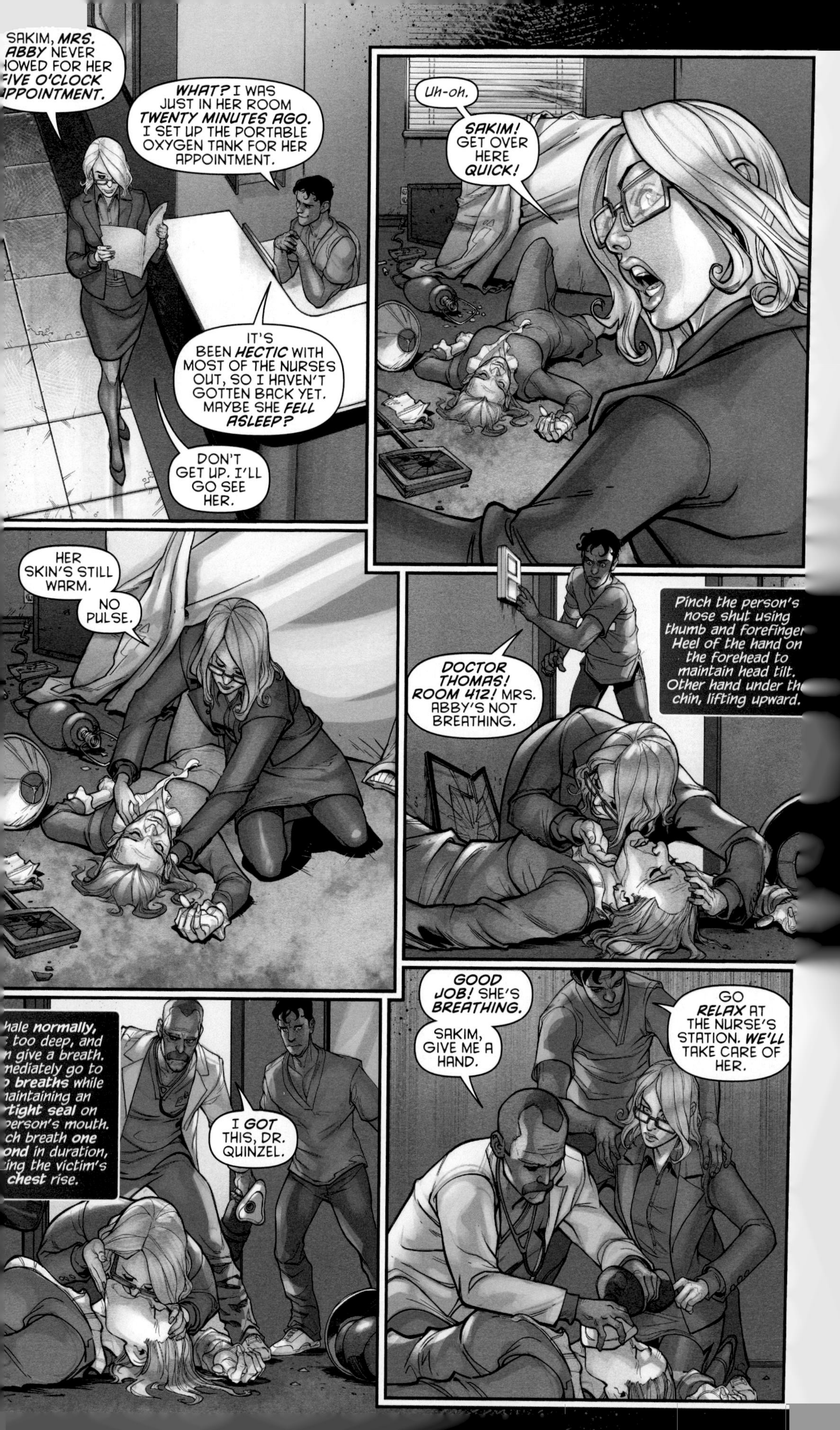

SAKIM, MRS. ABBY NEVER HOWED FOR HER FIVE O'CLOCK APPOINTMENT.
WHAT? I WAS JUST IN HER ROOM TWENTY MINUTES AGO. I SET UP THE PORTABLE OXYGEN TANK FOR HER APPOINTMENT.
IT'S BEEN HECTIC WITH MOST OF THE NURSES OUT, SO I HAVEN'T GOTTEN BACK YET. MAYBE SHE FELL ASLEEP?
DON'T GET UP. I'LL GO SEE HER.
Uh-oh.
SAKIM! GET OVER HERE QUICK!
HER SKIN'S STILL WARM.
NO PULSE.
DOCTOR THOMAS! ROOM 412! MRS. ABBY'S NOT BREATHING.
Pinch the person's nose shut using thumb and forefinger. Heel of the hand on the forehead to maintain head tilt. Other hand under the chin, lifting upward.
hale normally, too deep, and n give a breath. mediately go to breaths while maintaining an rtight seal on person's mouth. ch breath one ond in duration, ing the victim's chest rise.
I GOT THIS, DR. QUINZEL.
GOOD JOB! SHE'S BREATHING.
SAKIM, GIVE ME A HAND.
GO RELAX AT THE NURSE'S STATION. WE'LL TAKE CARE OF HER.

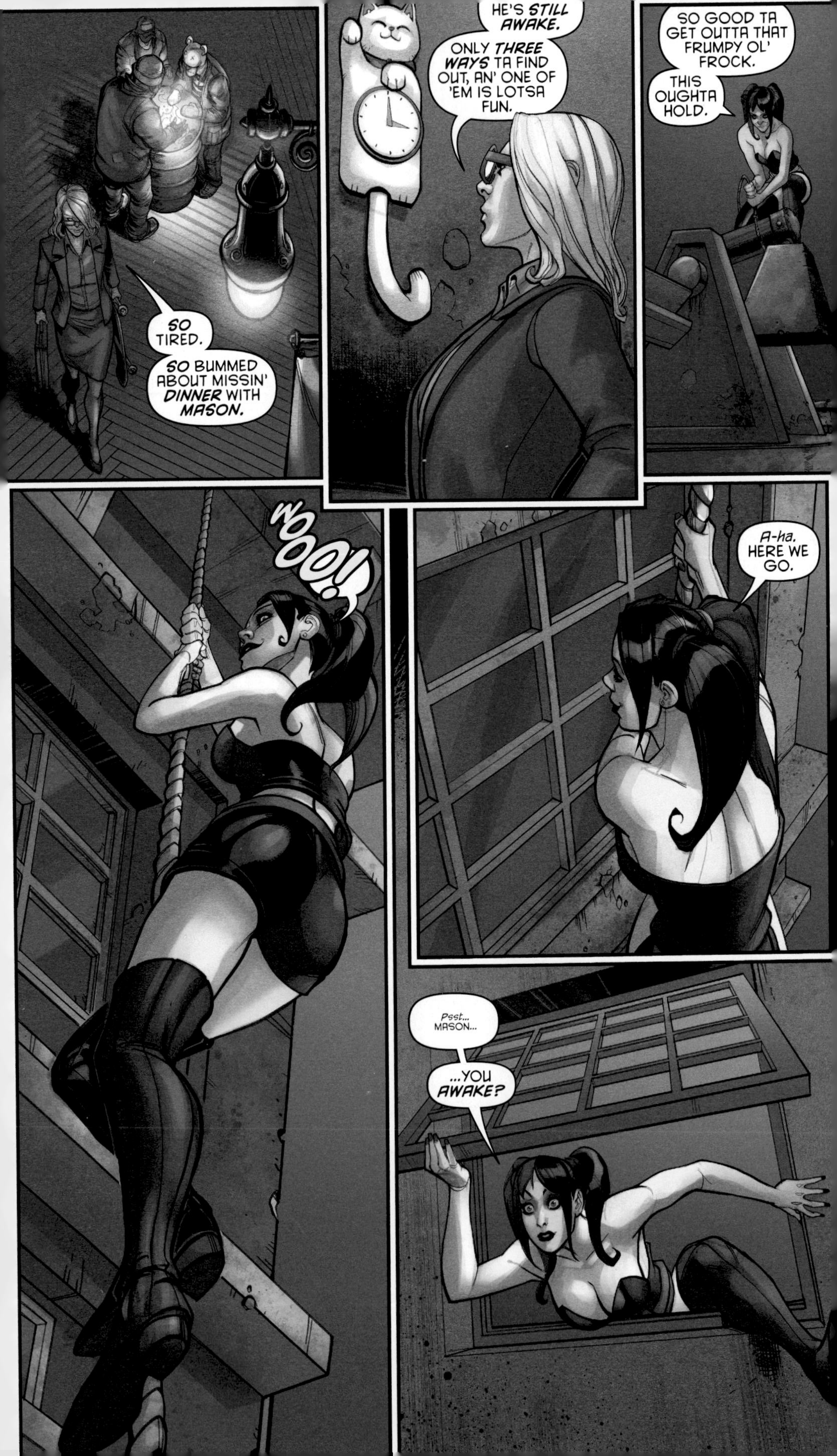
SO TIRED.
SO BUMMED ABOUT MISSIN' DINNER WITH MASON.
HE'S STILL AWAKE.
ONLY THREE WAYS TA FIND OUT, AN' ONE OF 'EM IS LOTSA FUN.
SO GOOD TA GET OUTTA THAT FRUMPY OL' FROCK.
THIS OUGHTA HOLD.
WOO!
A-ha. HERE WE GO.
Psst... MASON...
...YOU AWAKE?

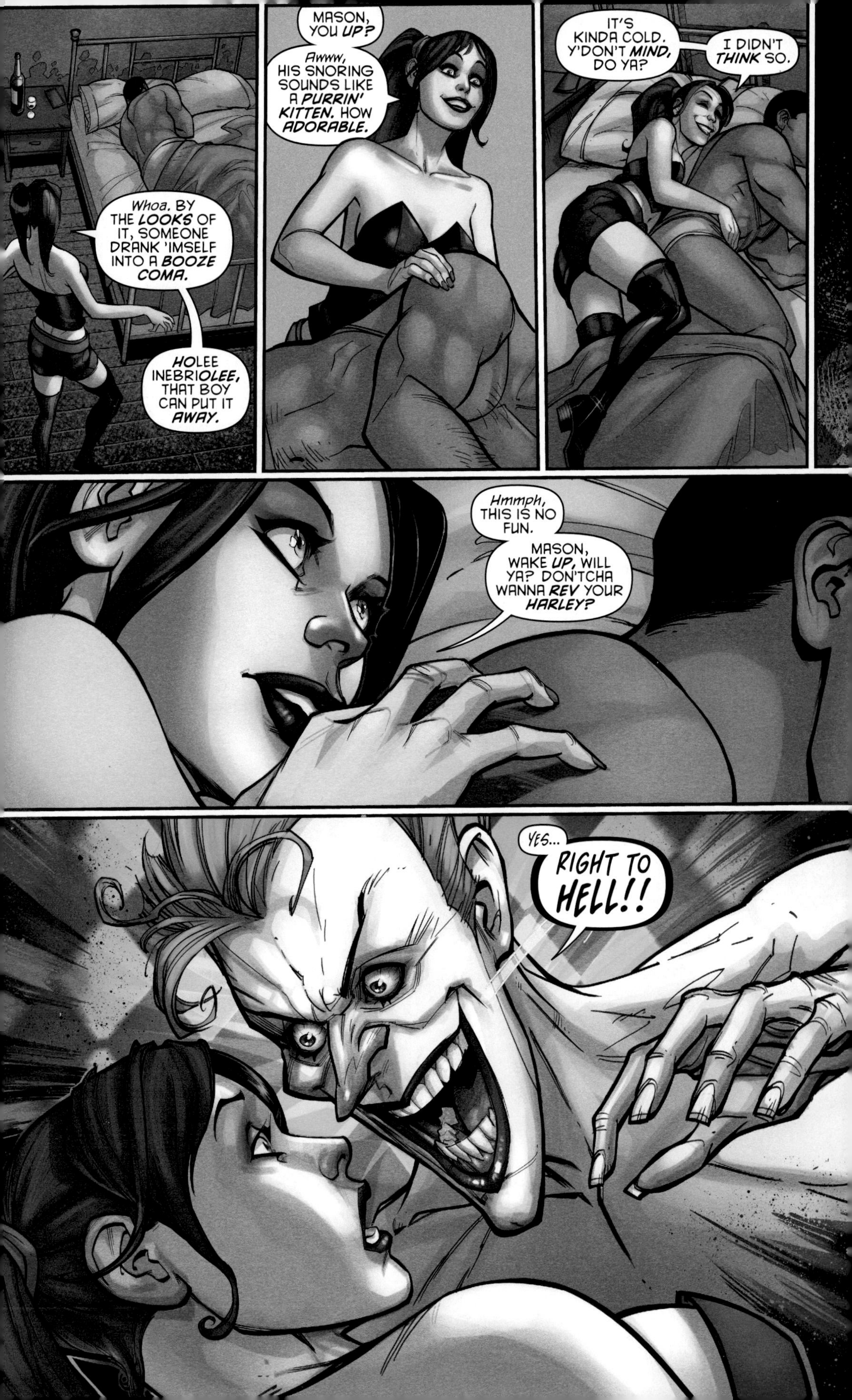

Whoa. BY THE LOOKS OF IT, SOMEONE DRANK 'IMSELF INTO A BOOZE COMA.
HOLEE INEBRIOLEE, THAT BOY CAN PUT IT AWAY.
MASON, YOU UP?
Awww, HIS SNORING SOUNDS LIKE A PURRIN' KITTEN. HOW ADORABLE.
IT'S KINDA COLD. Y'DON'T MIND, DO YA?
I DIDN'T THINK SO.
Hmmph, THIS IS NO FUN.
MASON, WAKE UP, WILL YA? DON'TCHA WANNA REV YOUR HARLEY?
YES...
RIGHT TO HELL!!

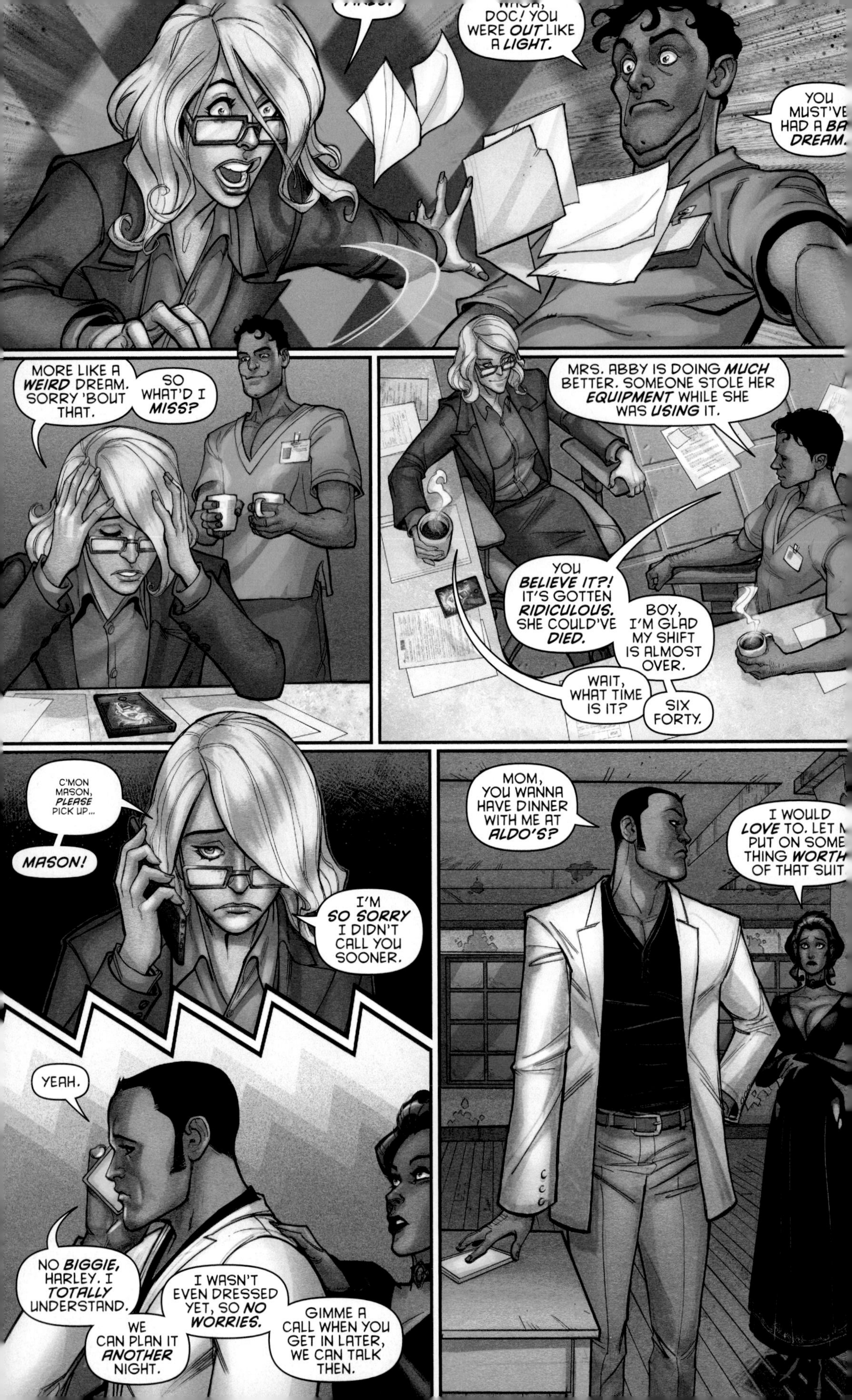
DOC! YOU WERE OUT LIKE A LIGHT.
YOU MUST'VE HAD A BA DREAM.
MORE LIKE A WEIRD DREAM. SORRY 'BOUT THAT.
SO WHAT'D I MISS?
MRS. ABBY IS DOING MUCH BETTER. SOMEONE STOLE HER EQUIPMENT WHILE SHE WAS USING IT.
YOU BELIEVE IT?! IT'S GOTTEN RIDICULOUS. SHE COULD'VE DIED.
BOY, I'M GLAD MY SHIFT IS ALMOST OVER.
WAIT, WHAT TIME IS IT?
SIX FORTY.
C'MON MASON, PLEASE PICK UP...
MASON!
I'M SO SORRY I DIDN'T CALL YOU SOONER.
YEAH.
NO BIGGIE, HARLEY. I TOTALLY UNDERSTAND.
WE CAN PLAN IT ANOTHER NIGHT.
I WASN'T EVEN DRESSED YET, SO NO WORRIES.
GIMME A CALL WHEN YOU GET IN LATER, WE CAN TALK THEN.
MOM, YOU WANNA HAVE DINNER WITH ME AT ALDO'S?
I WOULD LOVE TO. LET M PUT ON SOME THING WORTH OF THAT SUIT

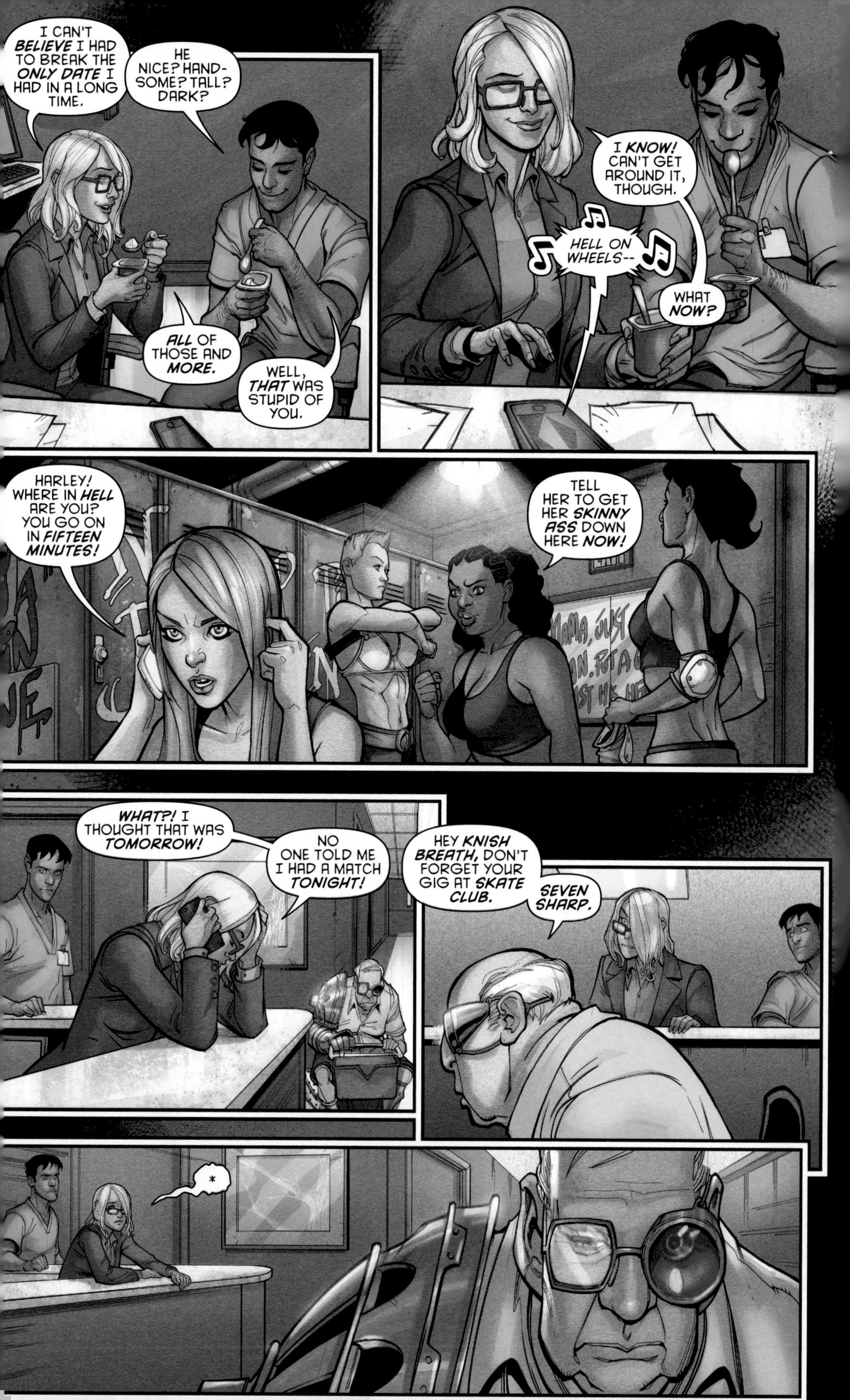
I CAN'T BELIEVE I HAD TO BREAK THE ONLY DATE I HAD IN A LONG TIME.
HE NICE? HAND-SOME? TALL? DARK?
ALL OF THOSE AND MORE.
WELL, THAT WAS STUPID OF YOU.
I KNOW! CAN'T GET AROUND IT, THOUGH.
HELL ON WHEELS--
WHAT NOW?
HARLEY! WHERE IN HELL ARE YOU? YOU GO ON IN FIFTEEN MINUTES!
TELL HER TO GET HER SKINNY ASS DOWN HERE NOW!
WHAT?! I THOUGHT THAT WAS TOMORROW!
NO ONE TOLD ME I HAD A MATCH TONIGHT!
HEY KNISH BREATH, DON'T FORGET YOUR GIG AT SKATE CLUB.
SEVEN SHARP.
*

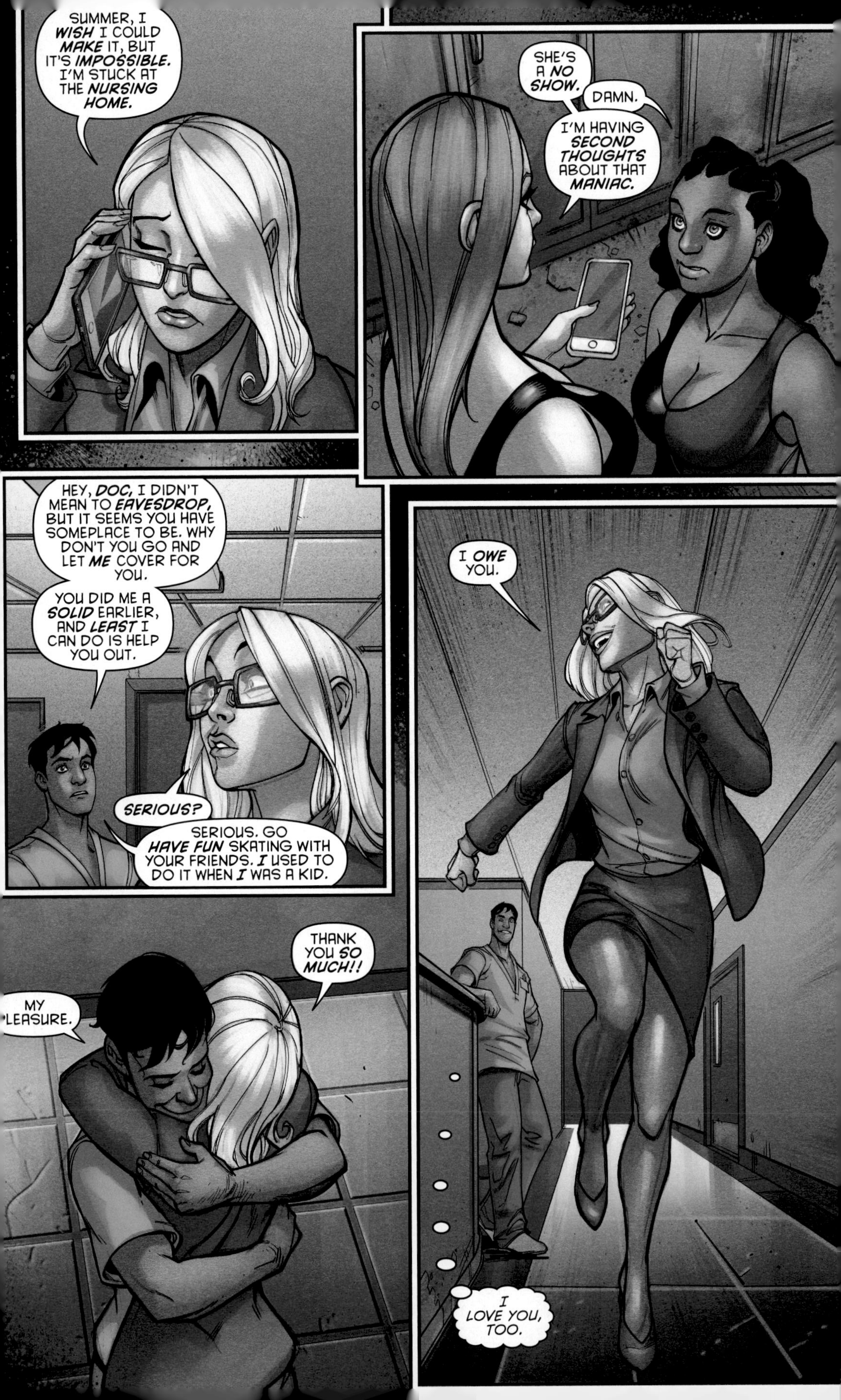

SUMMER, I *WISH* I COULD *MAKE* IT, BUT IT'S *IMPOSSIBLE.* I'M STUCK AT THE *NURSING HOME.*
SHE'S A *NO SHOW.*
DAMN.
I'M HAVING *SECOND THOUGHTS* ABOUT THAT *MANIAC.*
HEY, *DOC,* I DIDN'T MEAN TO *EAVESDROP,* BUT IT SEEMS YOU HAVE SOMEPLACE TO BE. WHY DON'T YOU GO AND LET *ME* COVER FOR YOU.
YOU DID ME A *SOLID* EARLIER, AND *LEAST* I CAN DO IS HELP YOU OUT.
SERIOUS?
SERIOUS. GO *HAVE FUN* SKATING WITH YOUR FRIENDS. *I* USED TO DO IT WHEN *I* WAS A KID.
THANK YOU *SO MUCH!!*
MY PLEASURE.
I *OWE* YOU.
I LOVE YOU, TOO.

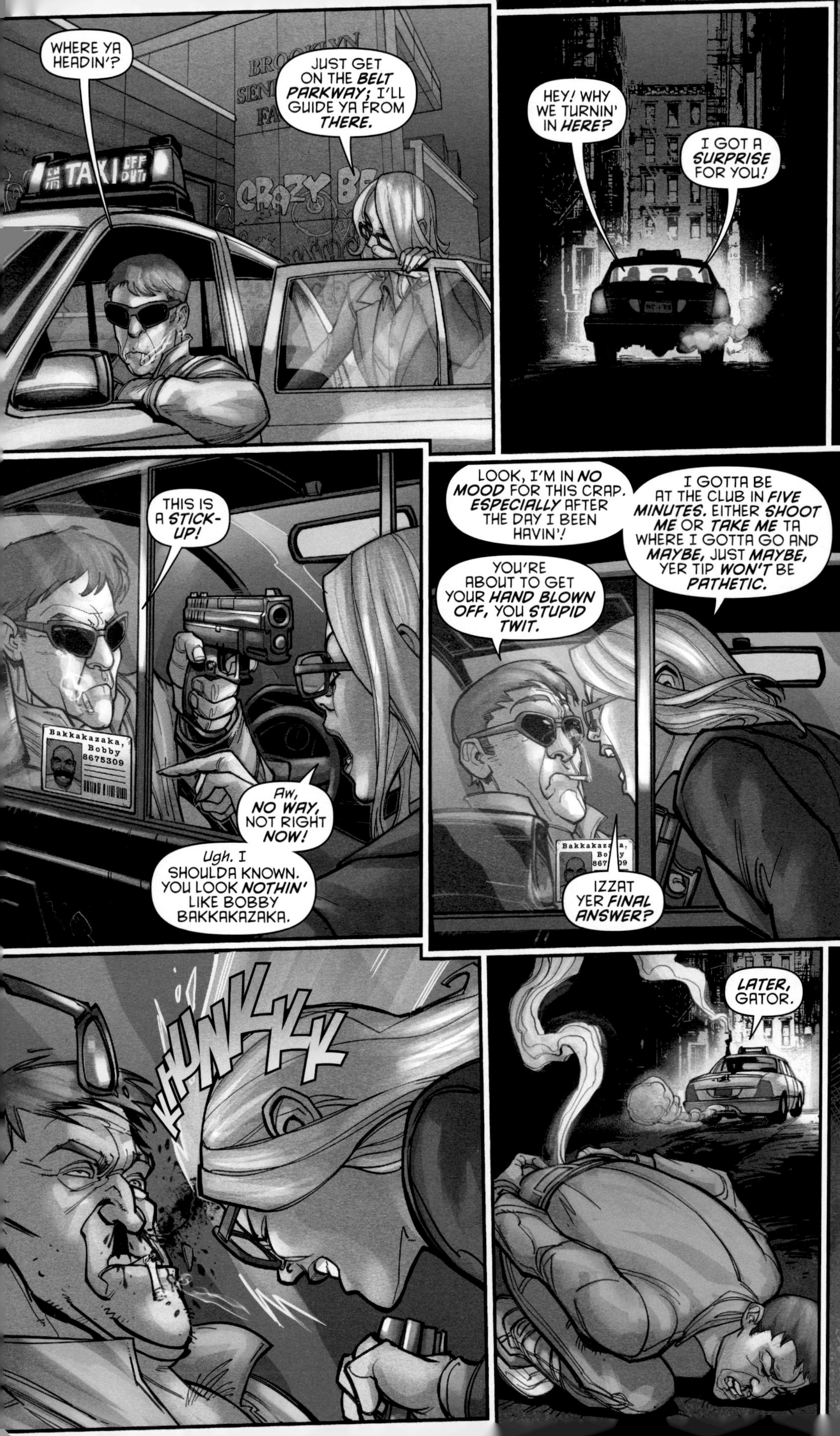
WHERE YA HEADIN'?
JUST GET ON THE BELT PARKWAY; I'LL GUIDE YA FROM THERE.
HEY! WHY WE TURNIN' IN HERE?
I GOT A SURPRISE FOR YOU!
THIS IS A STICK-UP!
Aw, NO WAY, NOT RIGHT NOW!
Ugh. I SHOULDA KNOWN. YOU LOOK NOTHIN' LIKE BOBBY BAKKAKAZAKA.
Bakkakazaka, Bobby 8675309
LOOK, I'M IN NO MOOD FOR THIS CRAP. ESPECIALLY AFTER THE DAY I BEEN HAVIN'!
I GOTTA BE AT THE CLUB IN FIVE MINUTES. EITHER SHOOT ME OR TAKE ME TA WHERE I GOTTA GO AND MAYBE, JUST MAYBE, YER TIP WON'T BE PATHETIC.
YOU'RE ABOUT TO GET YOUR HAND BLOWN OFF, YOU STUPID TWIT.
IZZAT YER FINAL ANSWER?
KHUNKKK
LATER, GATOR.

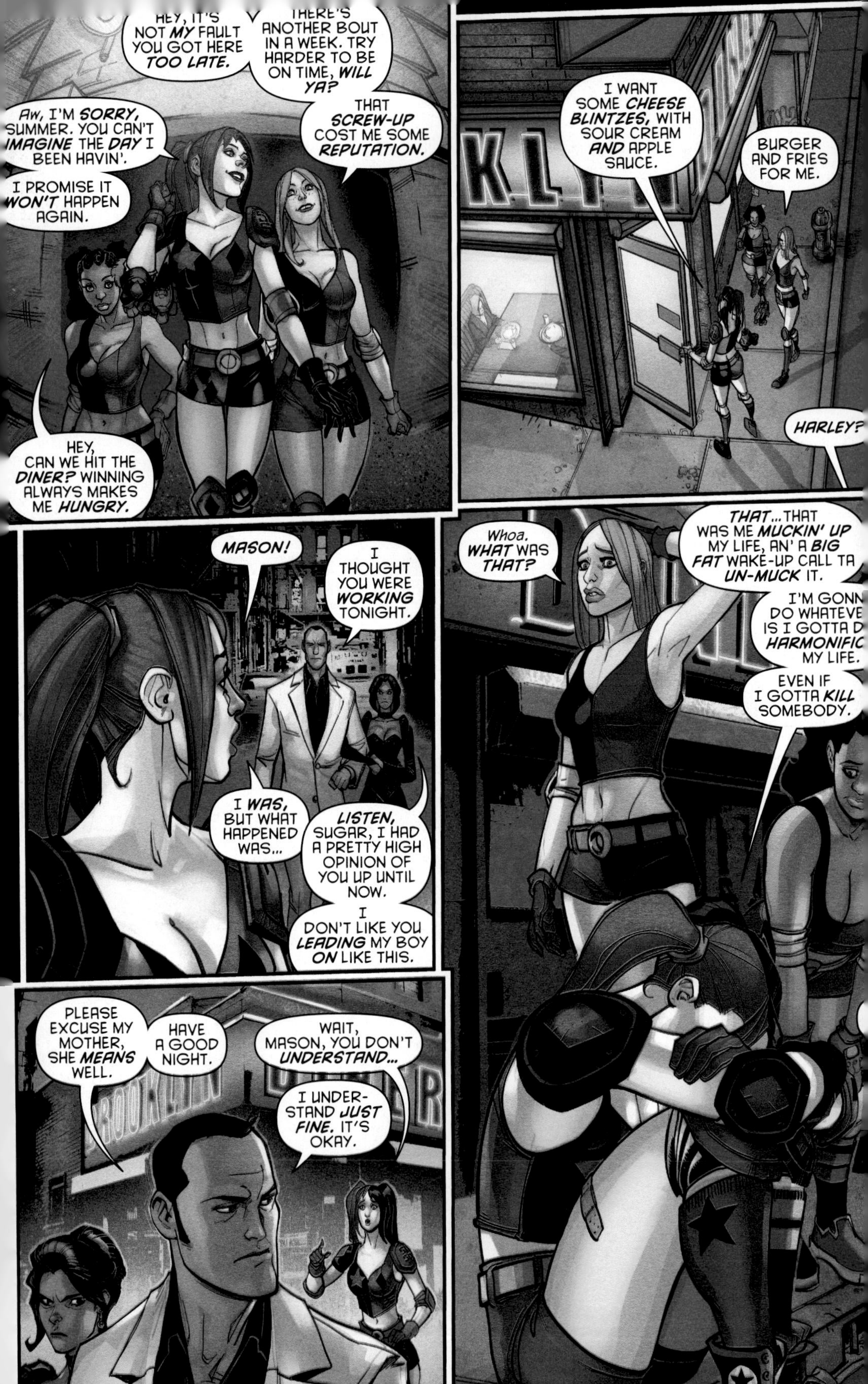
HEY, IT'S NOT MY FAULT YOU GOT HERE TOO LATE.
THERE'S ANOTHER BOUT IN A WEEK. TRY HARDER TO BE ON TIME, WILL YA?
THAT SCREW-UP COST ME SOME REPUTATION.
Aw, I'M SORRY, SUMMER. YOU CAN'T IMAGINE THE DAY I BEEN HAVIN'.
I PROMISE IT WON'T HAPPEN AGAIN.
HEY, CAN WE HIT THE DINER? WINNING ALWAYS MAKES ME HUNGRY.
I WANT SOME CHEESE BLINTZES, WITH SOUR CREAM AND APPLE SAUCE.
BURGER AND FRIES FOR ME.
HARLEY?
MASON!
I THOUGHT YOU WERE WORKING TONIGHT.
I WAS, BUT WHAT HAPPENED WAS...
LISTEN, SUGAR, I HAD A PRETTY HIGH OPINION OF YOU UP UNTIL NOW.
I DON'T LIKE YOU LEADING MY BOY ON LIKE THIS.
PLEASE EXCUSE MY MOTHER, SHE MEANS WELL.
HAVE A GOOD NIGHT.
WAIT, MASON, YOU DON'T UNDERSTAND...
I UNDERSTAND JUST FINE. IT'S OKAY.
Whoa. WHAT WAS THAT?
THAT... THAT WAS ME MUCKIN' UP MY LIFE, AN' A BIG FAT WAKE-UP CALL TA UN-MUCK IT.
I'M GONN DO WHATEVE IS I GOTTA D HARMONIFIC MY LIFE.
EVEN IF I GOTTA KILL SOMEBODY.

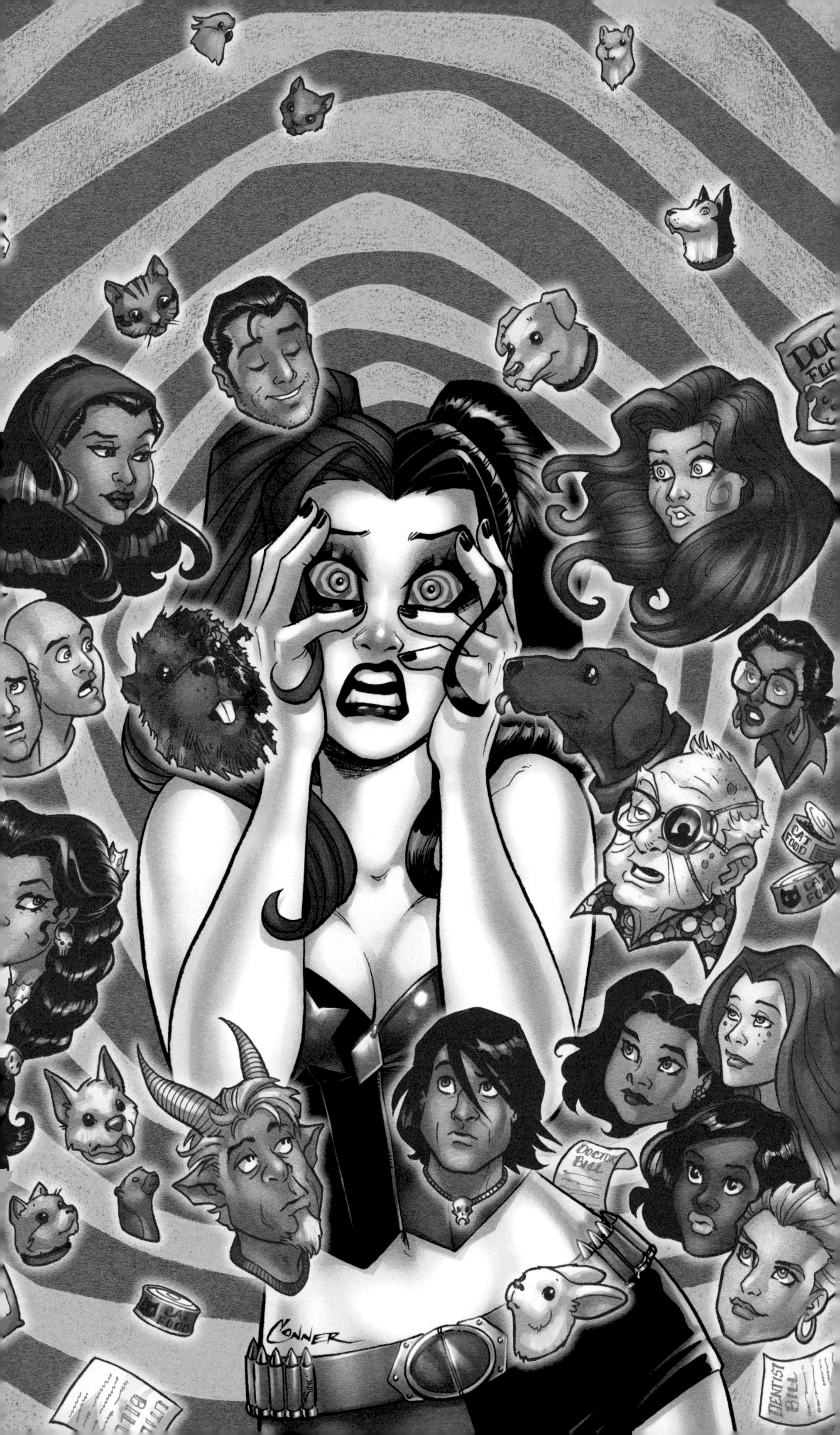
CAT FOOD
CAT FOOD
DOCTOR BILL
CAT FOOD
CONNER
DENTIST BILL

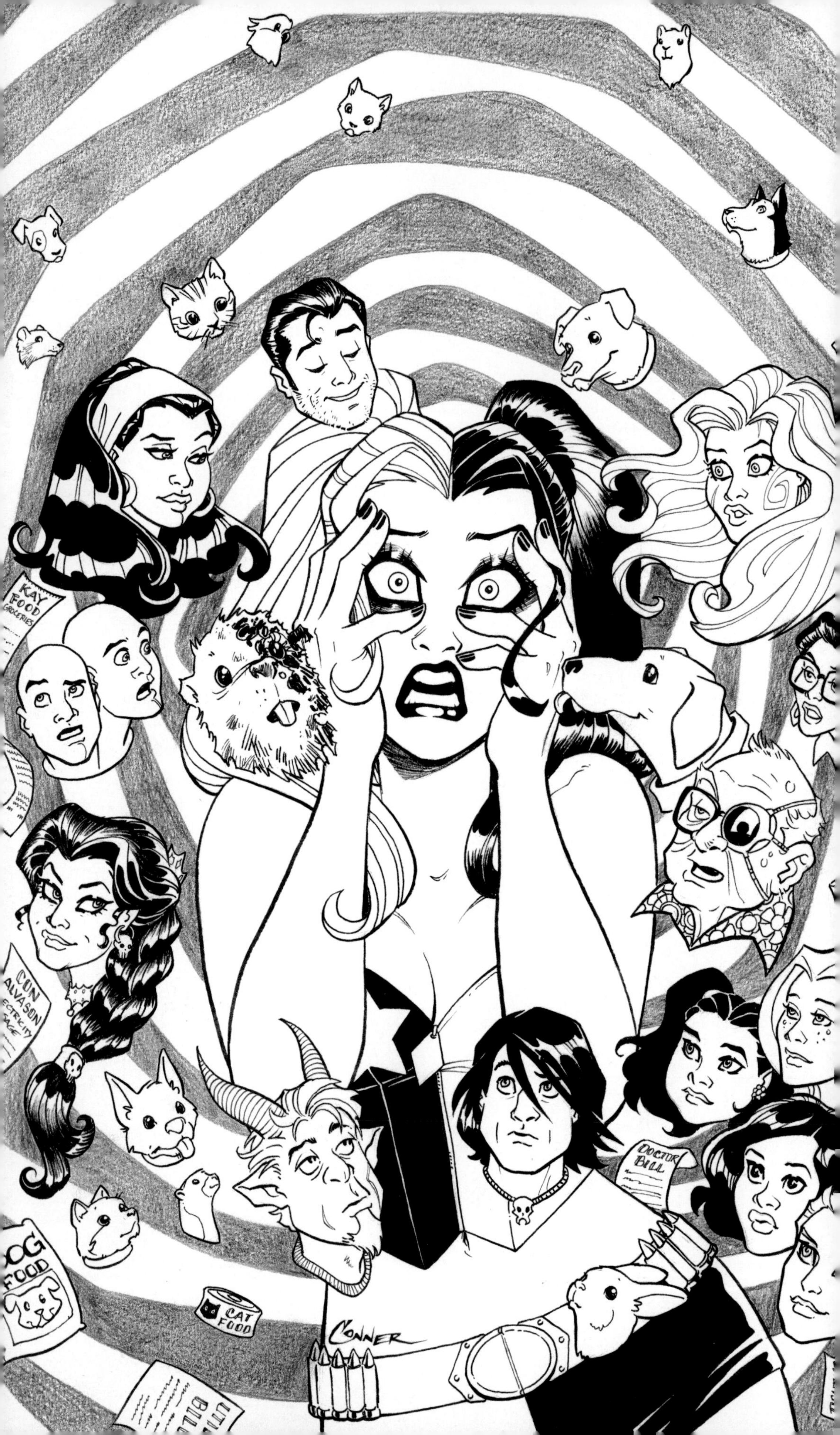
KAY
FOOD
GROCERIES
CON
ALVASON
DOCTOR
BILL
CAT
FOOD
CONNER

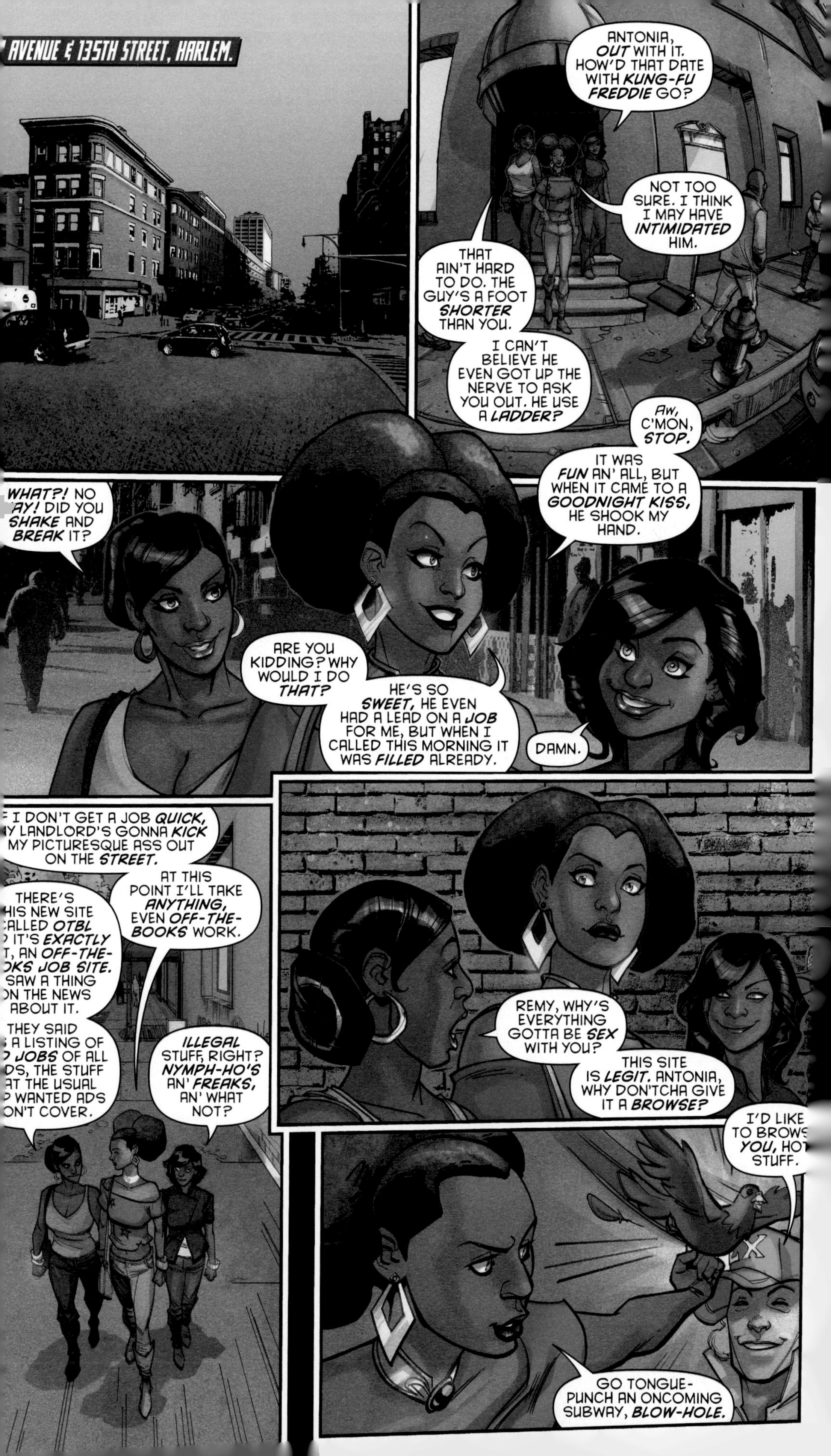
AVENUE & 135TH STREET, HARLEM.
ANTONIA, OUT WITH IT. HOW'D THAT DATE WITH KUNG-FU FREDDIE GO?
NOT TOO SURE. I THINK I MAY HAVE INTIMIDATED HIM.
THAT AIN'T HARD TO DO. THE GUY'S A FOOT SHORTER THAN YOU.
I CAN'T BELIEVE HE EVEN GOT UP THE NERVE TO ASK YOU OUT. HE USE A LADDER?
AW, C'MON, STOP.
IT WAS FUN AN' ALL, BUT WHEN IT CAME TO A GOODNIGHT KISS, HE SHOOK MY HAND.
WHAT?! NO AY! DID YOU SHAKE AND BREAK IT?
ARE YOU KIDDING? WHY WOULD I DO THAT?
HE'S SO SWEET, HE EVEN HAD A LEAD ON A JOB FOR ME, BUT WHEN I CALLED THIS MORNING IT WAS FILLED ALREADY.
DAMN.
I DON'T GET A JOB QUICK, Y LANDLORD'S GONNA KICK MY PICTURESQUE ASS OUT ON THE STREET.
AT THIS POINT I'LL TAKE ANYTHING, EVEN OFF-THE-BOOKS WORK.
THERE'S HIS NEW SITE ALLED OTBL IT'S EXACTLY T, AN OFF-THE- OKS JOB SITE. SAW A THING ON THE NEWS ABOUT IT.
THEY SAID A LISTING OF JOBS OF ALL DS, THE STUFF AT THE USUAL WANTED ADS ON'T COVER.
ILLEGAL STUFF, RIGHT? NYMPH-HO'S AN' FREAKS, AN' WHAT NOT?
REMY, WHY'S EVERYTHING GOTTA BE SEX WITH YOU?
THIS SITE IS LEGIT. ANTONIA, WHY DON'TCHA GIVE IT A BROWSE?
I'D LIKE TO BROWS YOU, HOT STUFF.
GO TONGUE-PUNCH AN ONCOMING SUBWAY, BLOW-HOLE.

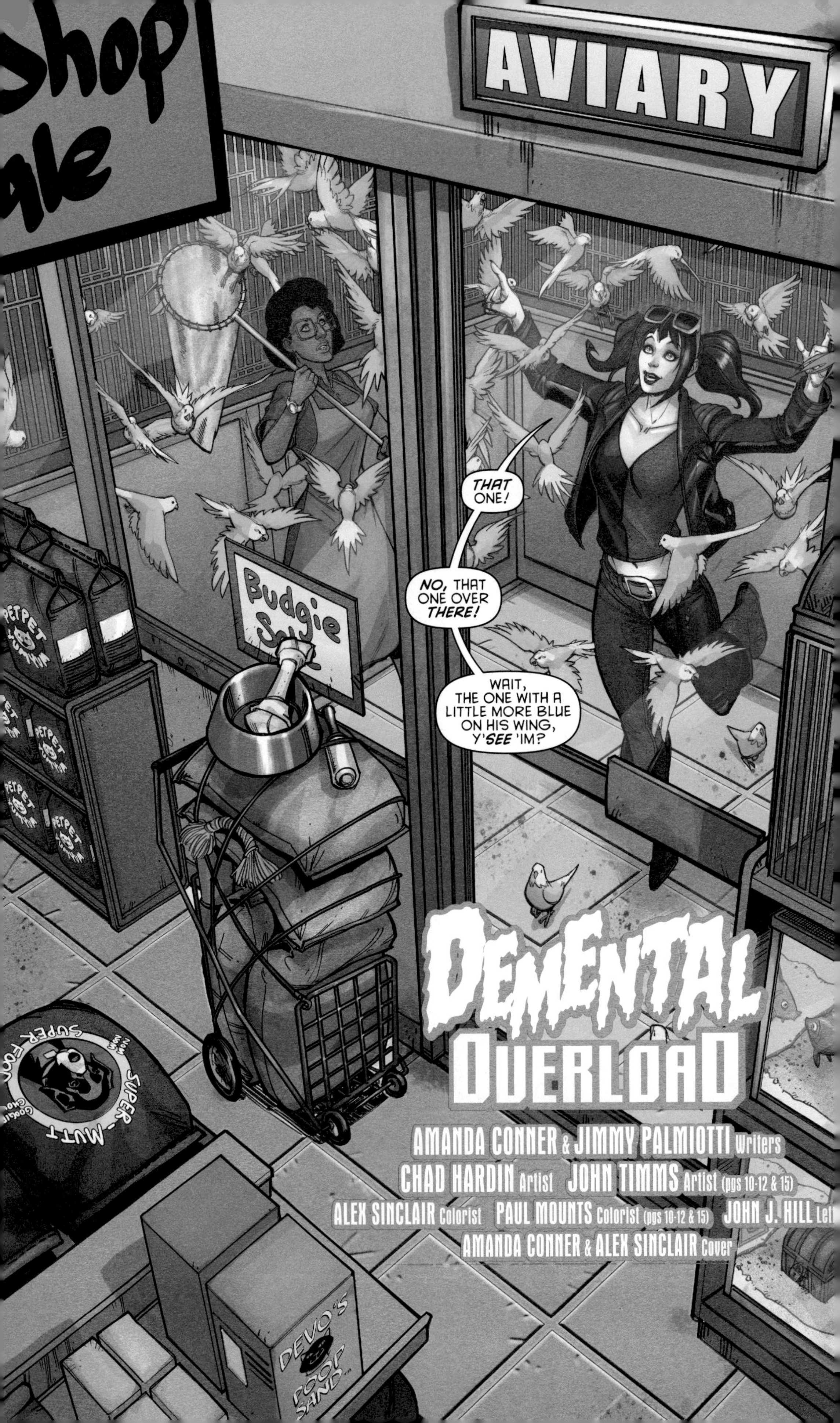

Shop
ale
AVIARY
THAT ONE!
NO, THAT ONE OVER THERE!
WAIT, THE ONE WITH A LITTLE MORE BLUE ON HIS WING, Y'SEE 'IM?
Budgie Sale
PETPET
SUPER-MUTT
DEVO'S POOP SAND
DEMENTAL OVERLOAD
AMANDA CONNER & JIMMY PALMIOTTI Writers
CHAD HARDIN Artist JOHN TIMMS Artist (pgs 10-12 & 15)
ALEX SINCLAIR Colorist PAUL MOUNTS Colorist (pgs 10-12 & 15) JOHN J. HILL Let
AMANDA CONNER & ALEX SINCLAIR Cover

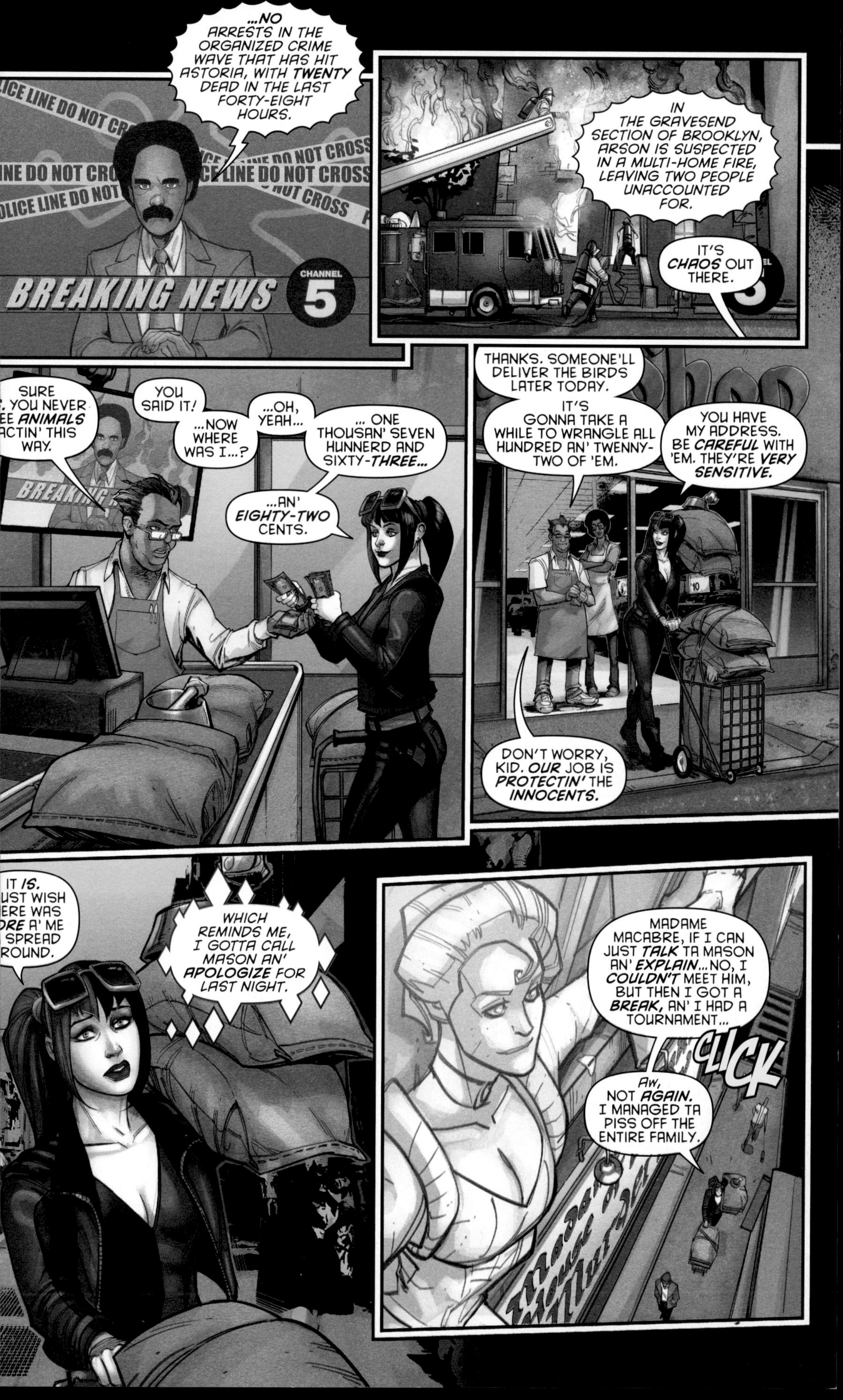
...NO ARRESTS IN THE ORGANIZED CRIME WAVE THAT HAS HIT ASTORIA, WITH TWENTY DEAD IN THE LAST FORTY-EIGHT HOURS.
POLICE LINE DO NOT CROSS
BREAKING NEWS
CHANNEL 5
IN THE GRAVESEND SECTION OF BROOKLYN, ARSON IS SUSPECTED IN A MULTI-HOME FIRE, LEAVING TWO PEOPLE UNACCOUNTED FOR.
IT'S CHAOS OUT THERE.
SURE . YOU NEVER EE ANIMALS ACTIN' THIS WAY.
YOU SAID IT!
...NOW WHERE WAS I...?
...OH, YEAH...
... ONE THOUSAN' SEVEN HUNNERD AND SIXTY-THREE...
...AN' EIGHTY-TWO CENTS.
THANKS. SOMEONE'LL DELIVER THE BIRDS LATER TODAY.
IT'S GONNA TAKE A WHILE TO WRANGLE ALL HUNDRED AN' TWENNY-TWO OF 'EM.
YOU HAVE MY ADDRESS. BE CAREFUL WITH 'EM. THEY'RE VERY SENSITIVE.
DON'T WORRY, KID. OUR JOB IS PROTECTIN' THE INNOCENTS.
IT IS. UST WISH ERE WAS ORE A' ME SPREAD ROUND.
WHICH REMINDS ME, I GOTTA CALL MASON AN' APOLOGIZE FOR LAST NIGHT.
MADAME MACABRE, IF I CAN JUST TALK TA MASON AN' EXPLAIN...NO, I COULDN'T MEET HIM, BUT THEN I GOT A BREAK, AN' I HAD A TOURNAMENT...
CLICK
AW, NOT AGAIN. I MANAGED TA PISS OFF THE ENTIRE FAMILY.

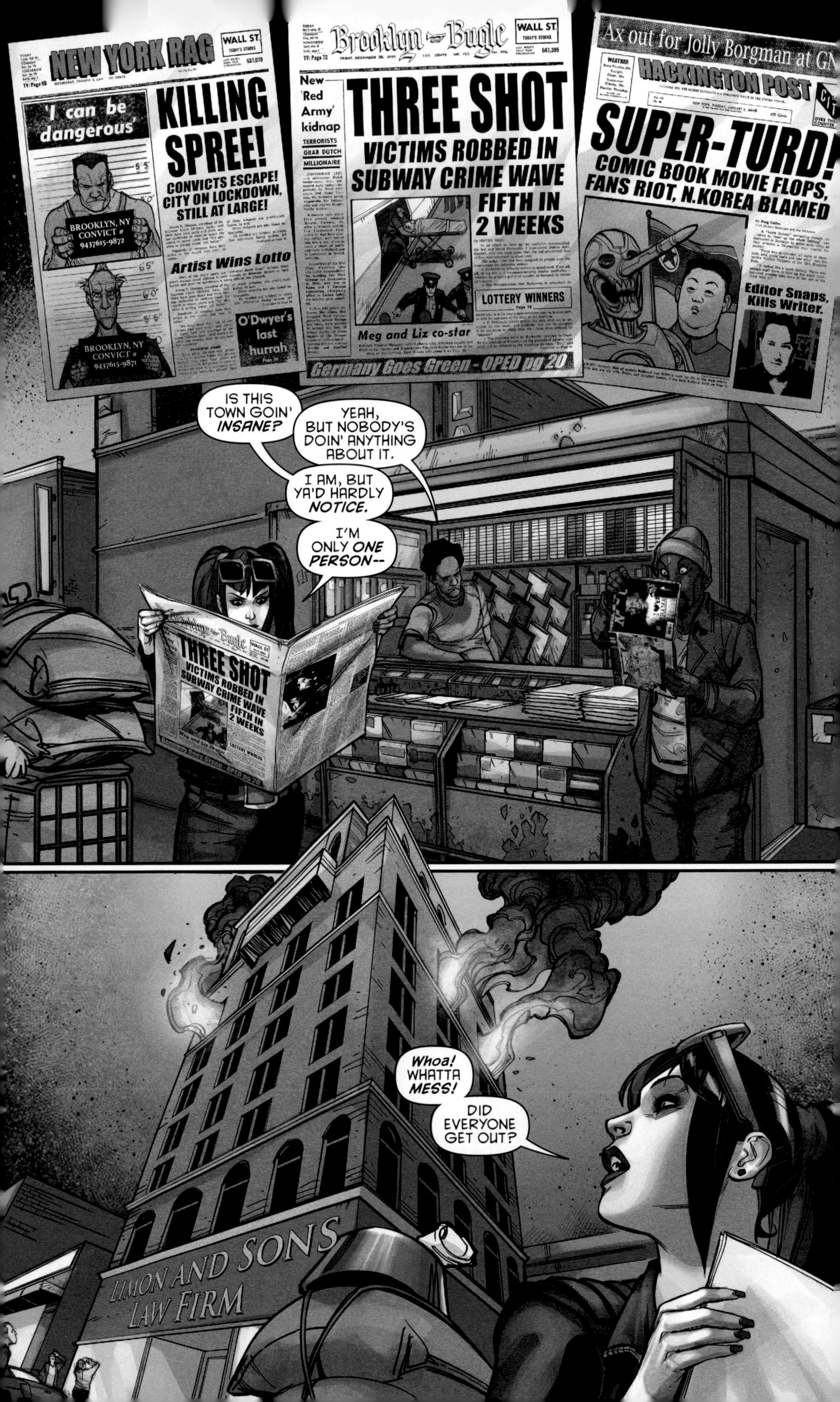
NEW YORK RAG
WALL ST. TODAY'S STOCKS
637,070
TV: Page 50
'I can be dangerous'
KILLING SPREE!
CONVICTS ESCAPE! CITY ON LOCKDOWN, STILL AT LARGE!
BROOKLYN, NY CONVICT # 9437615-9872
BROOKLYN, NY CONVICT # 9437615-9871
Artist Wins Lotto
O'Dwyer's last hurrah
Brooklyn Bugle
WALL ST. TODAY'S STOCKS
647,395
TV: Page 72
New 'Red Army' kidnap
TERRORISTS GRAB DUTCH MILLIONAIRE
THREE SHOT
VICTIMS ROBBED IN SUBWAY CRIME WAVE
FIFTH IN 2 WEEKS
LOTTERY WINNERS
Meg and Liz co-star
Germany Goes Green - OPED pg 20
Ax out for Jolly Borgman at GN
HACKINGTON POST
SUPER-TURD!
COMIC BOOK MOVIE FLOPS, FANS RIOT, N.KOREA BLAMED
Editor Snaps, Kills Writer.
IS THIS TOWN GOIN' *INSANE?*
YEAH, BUT NOBODY'S DOIN' ANYTHING ABOUT IT.
I AM, BUT YA'D HARDLY *NOTICE.*
I'M ONLY *ONE PERSON--*
THREE SHOT
VICTIMS ROBBED IN SUBWAY CRIME WAVE
FIFTH IN 2 WEEKS
Whoa! WHATTA *MESS!*
DID EVERYONE GET OUT?
LIMON AND SONS LAW FIRM

HRRSSSHH

HOLEE SOARING SEATS!

I GUESS THAT ANSWERS MY QUESTION.

HE LOCKED THE ROOF EXIT, AND HE'S COMING AFTER US!

SOMEONE *HELP!*

HELLO... YES...THERE'S A *FIRE* AT SEA VIEW AND FIFTH! PEOPLE ARE TRAPPED ON THE TOP FLOOR!

HOW LONG!?

YER *KIDDIN'* ME, RIGHT? TWO *OTHER* BUILDING FIRES? JEEZ.

MISS! YOU CAN'T GO *IN* THERE!

--?
DY, DA YA N'!?

SOME-BODY'S GOTTA EXTRACTIFY THOSE POOR PEOPLE!

YER *GUARDIAN ANGEL* IS COMIN'!

WOW. THIS PLACE LOOKS LIKE SOMEBODY WRECKED THE HECK OUT OF IT.

≥Koff≤

GONNA D ME A MAN'S XE.

na! OSE GH...

Oof! OH...COME... ON...

THIS LOOKS SO *EASY* IN THE MOVIES.

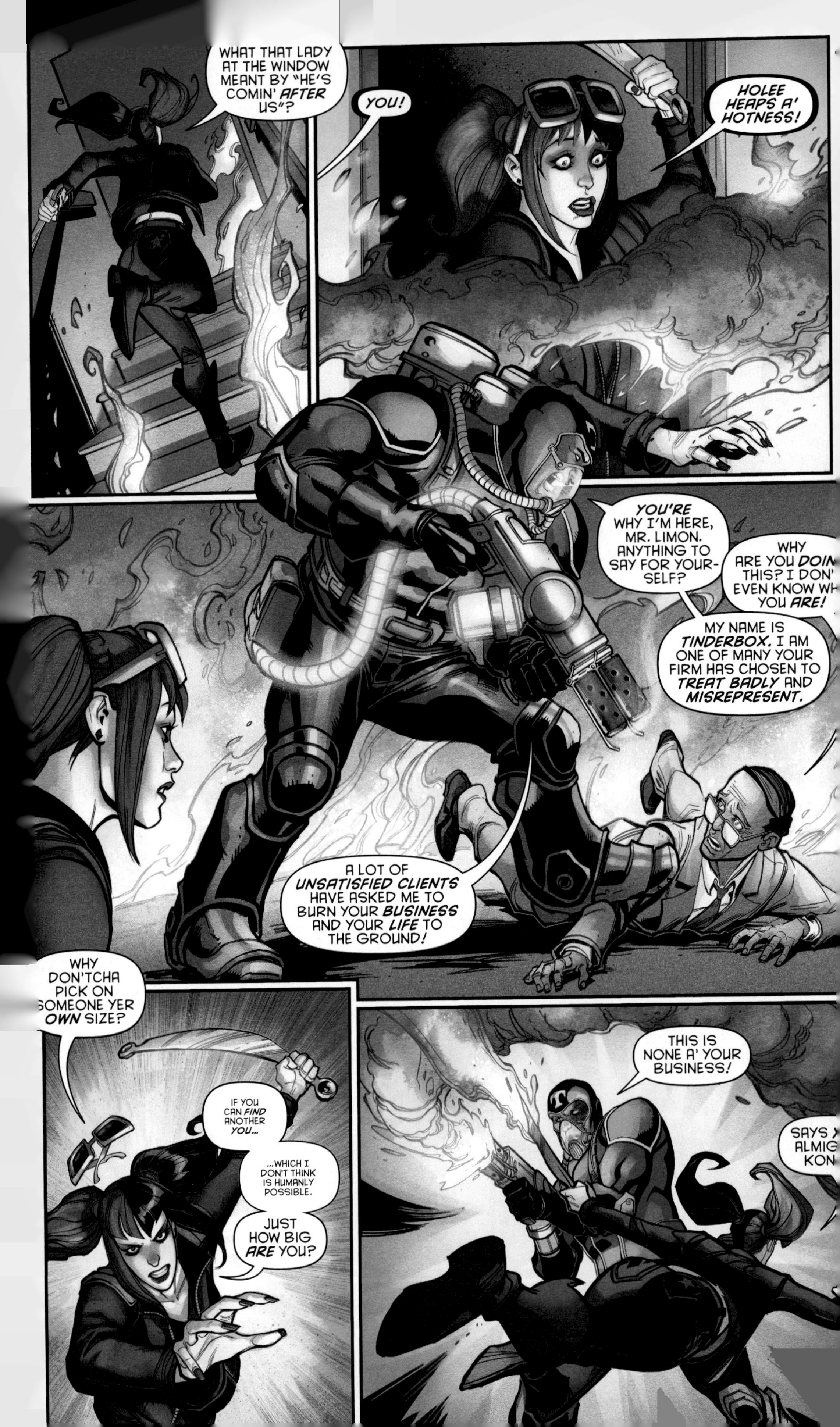
WHAT THAT LADY AT THE WINDOW MEANT BY "HE'S COMIN' AFTER US"?
YOU!
HOLEE HEAPS A' HOTNESS!
YOU'RE WHY I'M HERE, MR. LIMON. ANYTHING TO SAY FOR YOUR-SELF?
WHY ARE YOU DOIN THIS? I DON' EVEN KNOW WH YOU ARE!
MY NAME IS TINDERBOX. I AM ONE OF MANY YOUR FIRM HAS CHOSEN TO TREAT BADLY AND MISREPRESENT.
A LOT OF UNSATISFIED CLIENTS HAVE ASKED ME TO BURN YOUR BUSINESS AND YOUR LIFE TO THE GROUND!
WHY DON'TCHA PICK ON SOMEONE YER OWN SIZE?
IF YOU CAN FIND ANOTHER YOU...
...WHICH I DON'T THINK IS HUMANLY POSSIBLE.
JUST HOW BIG ARE YOU?
THIS IS NONE A' YOUR BUSINESS!
SAYS ALMIG KON

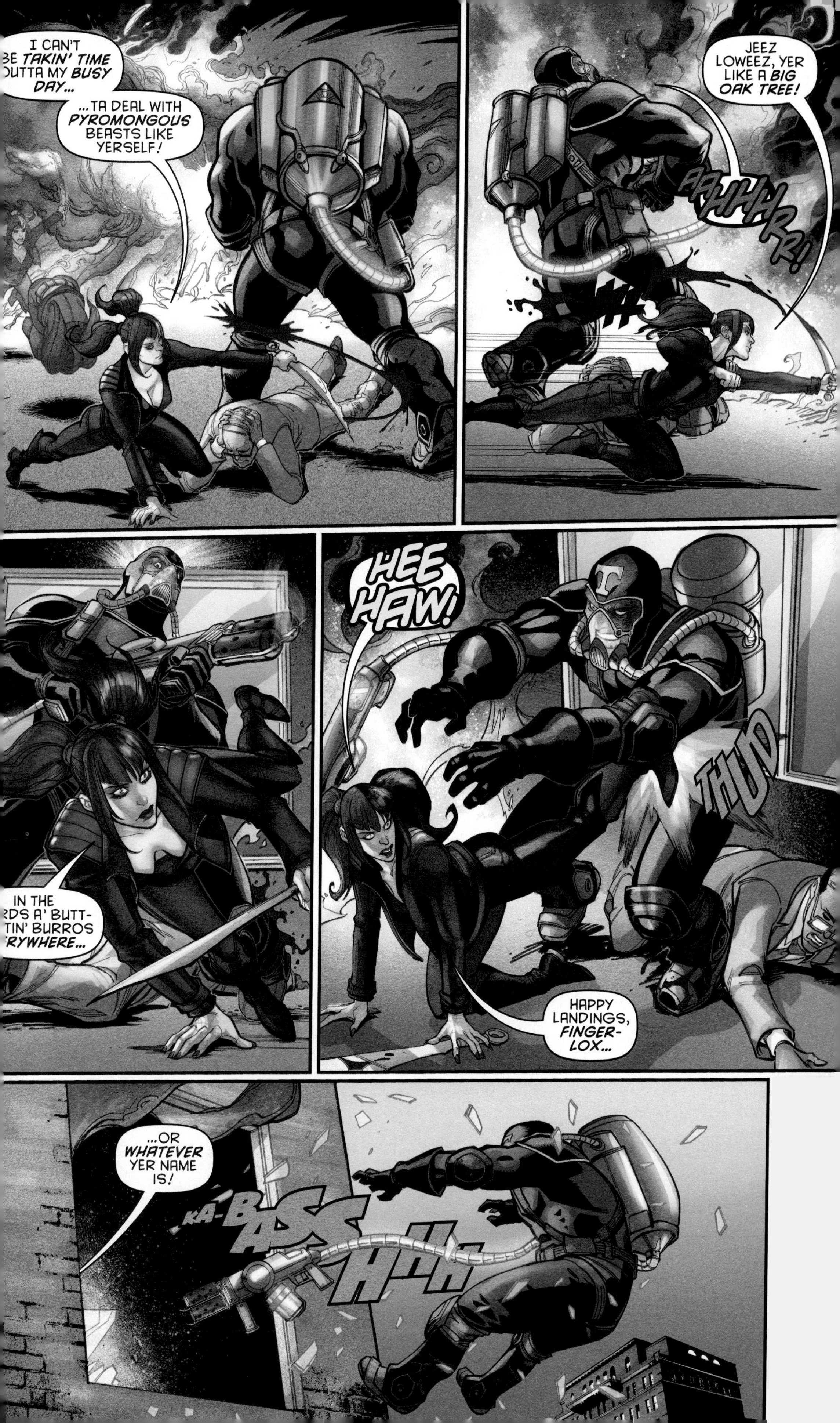

I CAN'T BE TAKIN' TIME OUTTA MY BUSY DAY...
...TA DEAL WITH PYROMONGOUS BEASTS LIKE YERSELF!
JEEZ LOWEEZ, YER LIKE A BIG OAK TREE!
AAHHRR!
IN THE RDS A' BUTT-TIN' BURROS RYWHERE...
HEE HAW!
THUD
HAPPY LANDINGS, FINGER-LOX...
...OR WHATEVER YER NAME IS!
KA-BASSHHH

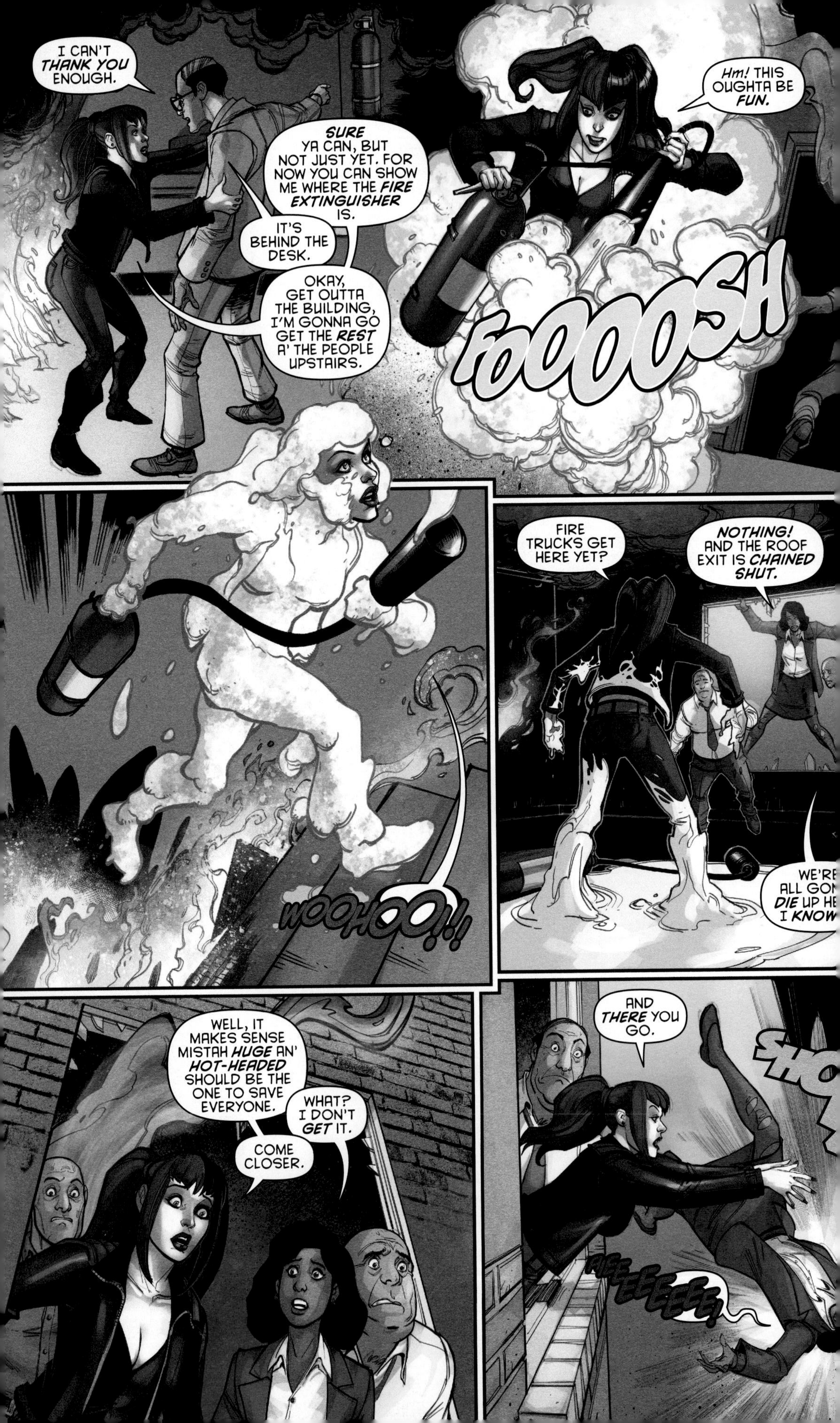
I CAN'T *THANK YOU* ENOUGH.
SURE YA CAN, BUT NOT JUST YET. FOR NOW YOU CAN SHOW ME WHERE THE *FIRE EXTINGUISHER* IS.
IT'S BEHIND THE DESK.
OKAY, GET OUTTA THE BUILDING, I'M GONNA GO GET THE *REST* A' THE PEOPLE UPSTAIRS.
Hm! THIS OUGHTA BE *FUN.*
FOOOOSH
WOOHOO!!
FIRE TRUCKS GET HERE YET?
NOTHING! AND THE ROOF EXIT IS *CHAINED SHUT.*
WELL, IT MAKES SENSE MISTAH *HUGE* AN' *HOT-HEADED* SHOULD BE THE ONE TO SAVE EVERYONE.
WHAT? I DON'T *GET* IT.
COME CLOSER.
AND *THERE* YOU GO.
EEEEEEEE!

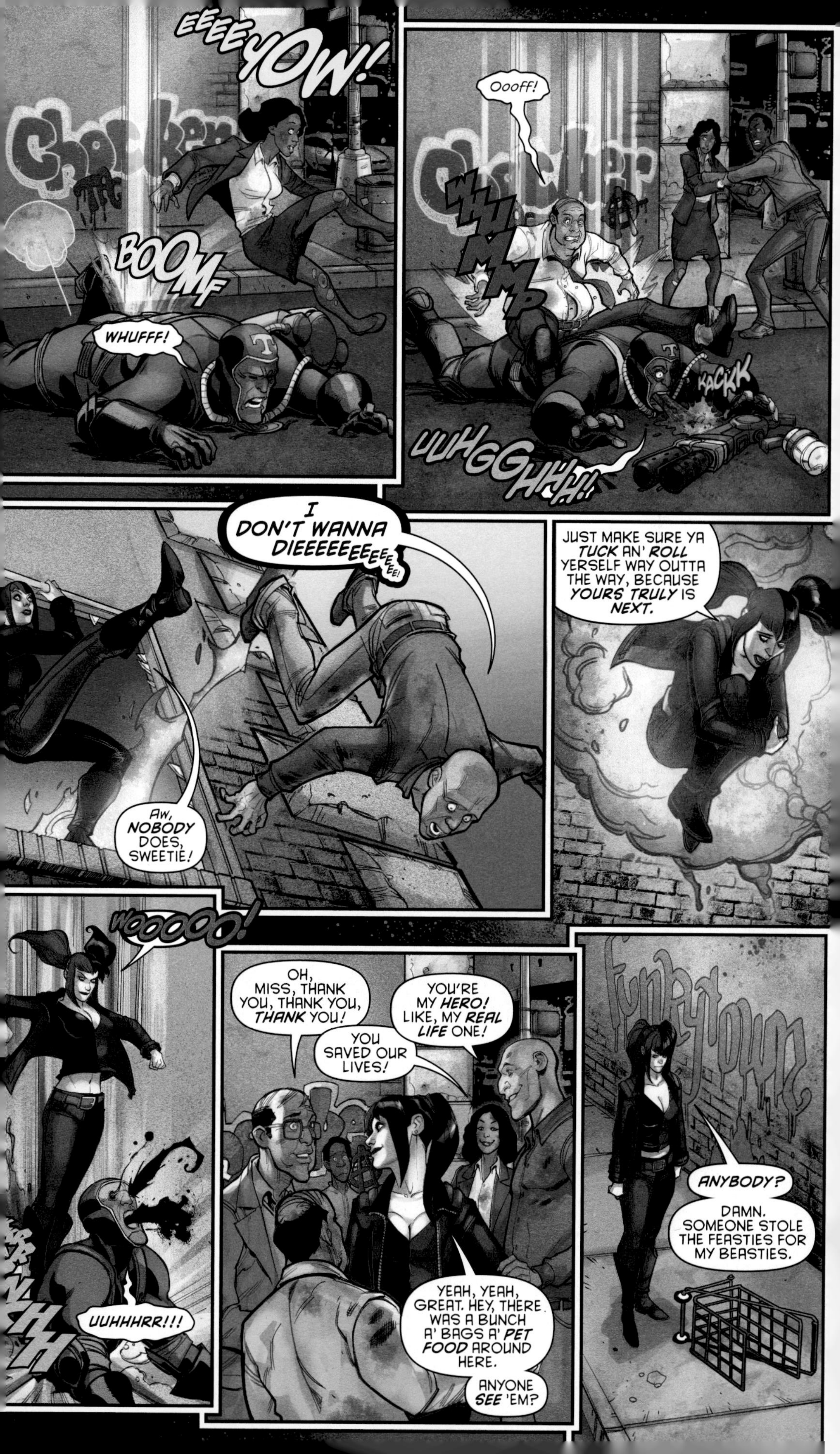
EEEEYOW!
BOOMF
WHUFFF!
Oooff!
WHUMMMP
KACKK
UUHGGHHH!
I DON'T WANNA DIEEEEEEEEEEEE!
AW, NOBODY DOES, SWEETIE!
JUST MAKE SURE YA TUCK AN' ROLL YERSELF WAY OUTTA THE WAY, BECAUSE YOURS TRULY IS NEXT.
WOOOOOO!
UUHHHRR!!!
OH, MISS, THANK YOU, THANK YOU, THANK YOU!
YOU SAVED OUR LIVES!
YOU'RE MY HERO! LIKE, MY REAL LIFE ONE!
YEAH, YEAH, GREAT. HEY, THERE WAS A BUNCH A' BAGS A' PET FOOD AROUND HERE.
ANYONE SEE 'EM?
ANYBODY?
DAMN. SOMEONE STOLE THE FEASTIES FOR MY BEASTIES.

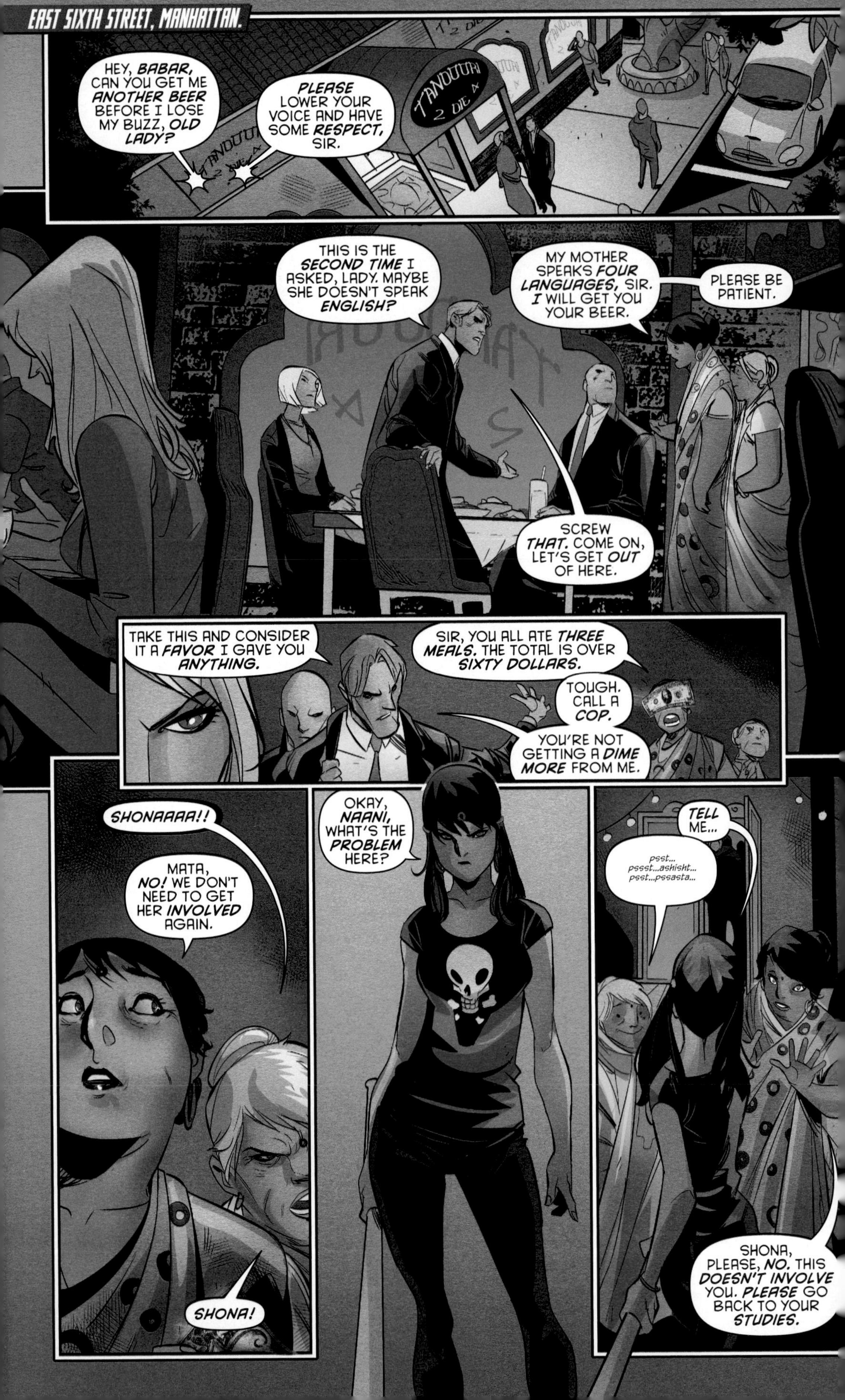
EAST SIXTH STREET, MANHATTAN.
HEY, BABAR, CAN YOU GET ME ANOTHER BEER BEFORE I LOSE MY BUZZ, OLD LADY?
PLEASE LOWER YOUR VOICE AND HAVE SOME RESPECT, SIR.
TANDUURI 2 DIE
THIS IS THE SECOND TIME I ASKED, LADY. MAYBE SHE DOESN'T SPEAK ENGLISH?
MY MOTHER SPEAKS FOUR LANGUAGES, SIR. I WILL GET YOU YOUR BEER.
PLEASE BE PATIENT.
SCREW THAT. COME ON, LET'S GET OUT OF HERE.
TAKE THIS AND CONSIDER IT A FAVOR I GAVE YOU ANYTHING.
SIR, YOU ALL ATE THREE MEALS. THE TOTAL IS OVER SIXTY DOLLARS.
TOUGH. CALL A COP.
YOU'RE NOT GETTING A DIME MORE FROM ME.
SHONAAAA!!
MATA, NO! WE DON'T NEED TO GET HER INVOLVED AGAIN.
SHONA!
OKAY, NAANI, WHAT'S THE PROBLEM HERE?
TELL ME...
psst...
pssst...ashisht...
psst...pssasta...
SHONA, PLEASE, NO. THIS DOESN'T INVOLVE YOU. PLEASE GO BACK TO YOUR STUDIES.

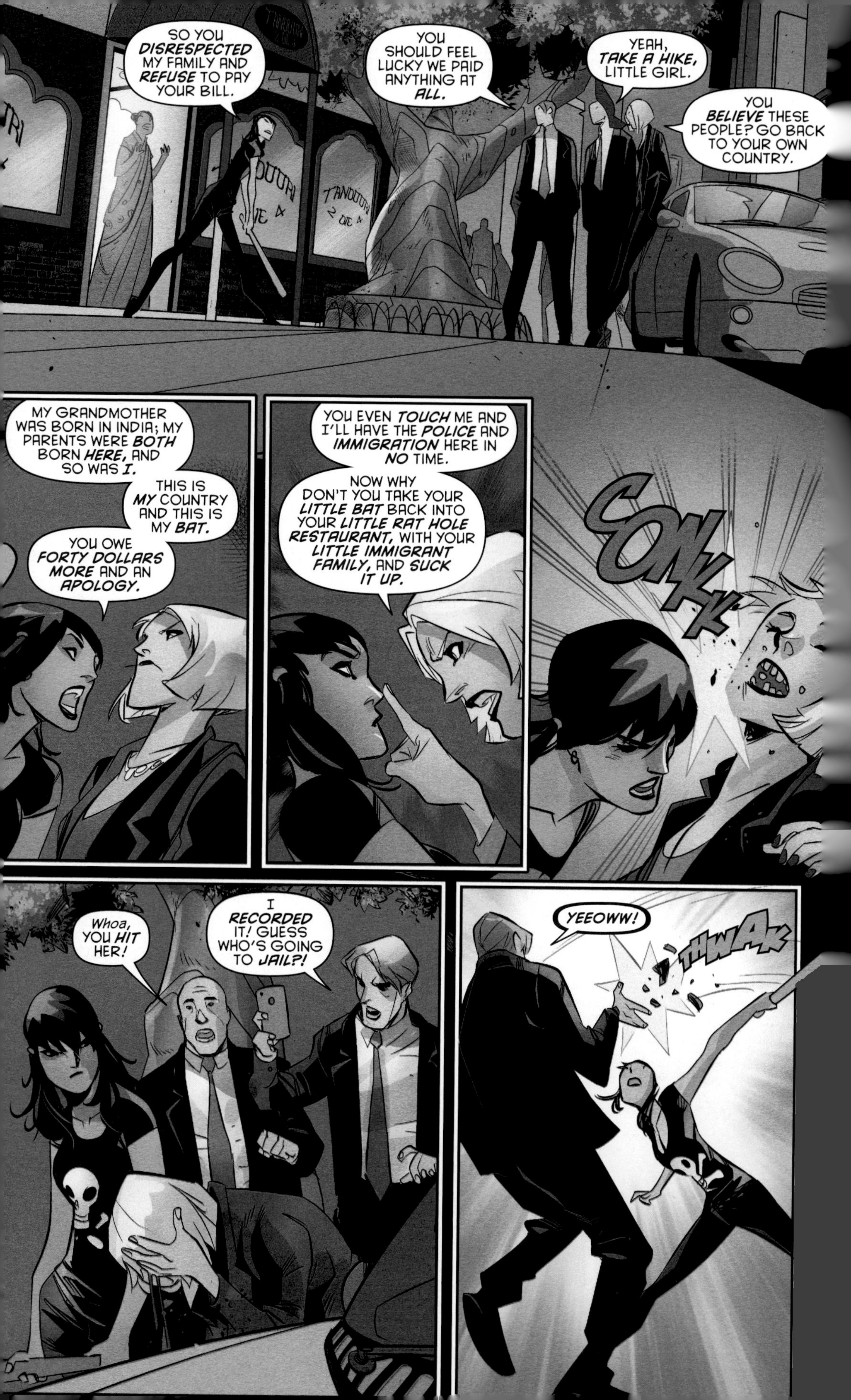
SO YOU DISRESPECTED MY FAMILY AND REFUSE TO PAY YOUR BILL.
YOU SHOULD FEEL LUCKY WE PAID ANYTHING AT ALL.
YEAH, TAKE A HIKE, LITTLE GIRL.
YOU BELIEVE THESE PEOPLE? GO BACK TO YOUR OWN COUNTRY.
MY GRANDMOTHER WAS BORN IN INDIA; MY PARENTS WERE BOTH BORN HERE, AND SO WAS I.
THIS IS MY COUNTRY AND THIS IS MY BAT.
YOU OWE FORTY DOLLARS MORE AND AN APOLOGY.
YOU EVEN TOUCH ME AND I'LL HAVE THE POLICE AND IMMIGRATION HERE IN NO TIME.
NOW WHY DON'T YOU TAKE YOUR LITTLE BAT BACK INTO YOUR LITTLE RAT HOLE RESTAURANT, WITH YOUR LITTLE IMMIGRANT FAMILY, AND SUCK IT UP.
CONKK
Whoa, YOU HIT HER!
I RECORDED IT! GUESS WHO'S GOING TO JAIL?!
YEEOWW!
THWAK

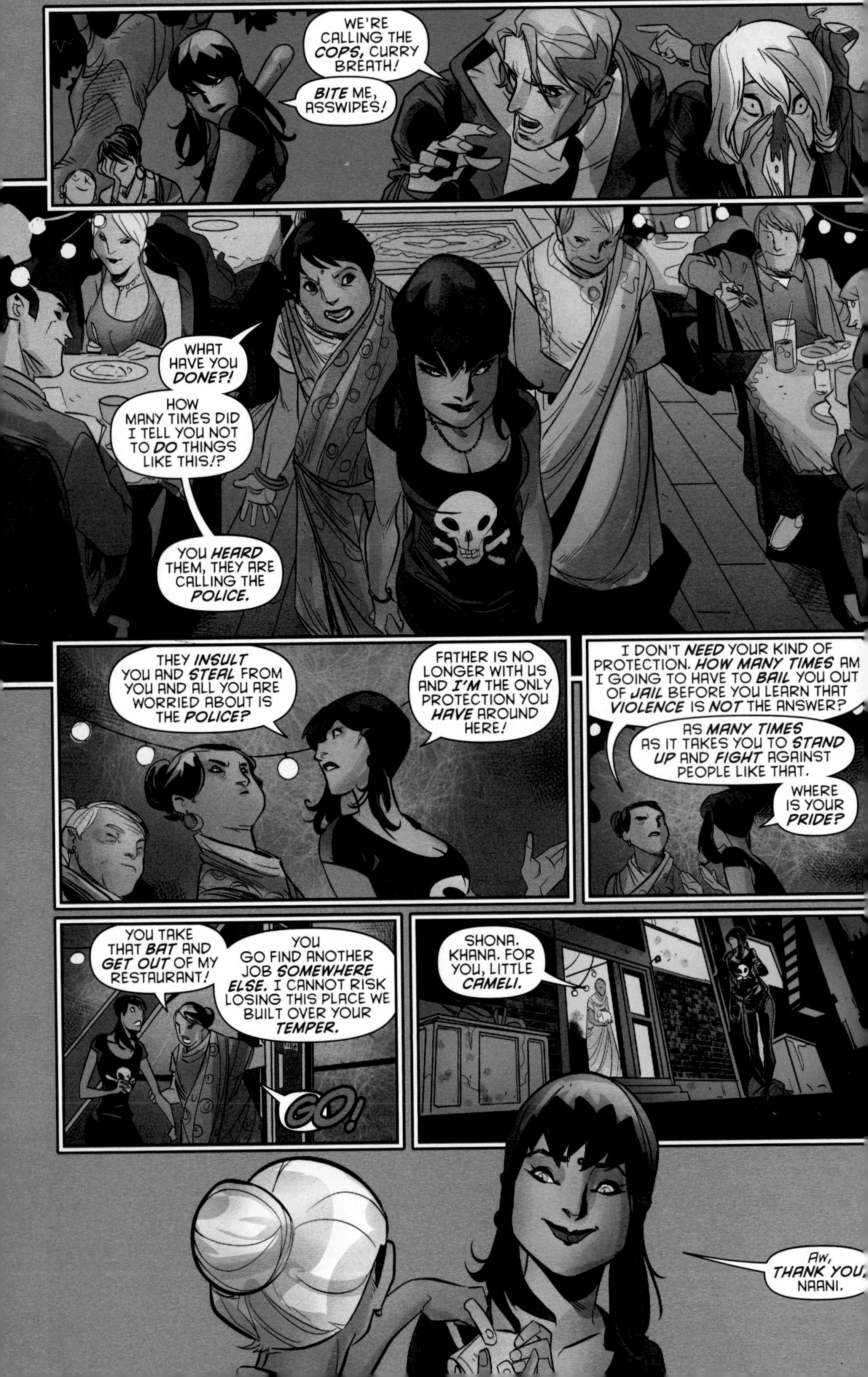
WE'RE CALLING THE COPS, CURRY BREATH!
BITE ME, ASSWIPES!
WHAT HAVE YOU DONE?!
HOW MANY TIMES DID I TELL YOU NOT TO DO THINGS LIKE THIS!?
YOU HEARD THEM, THEY ARE CALLING THE POLICE.
THEY INSULT YOU AND STEAL FROM YOU AND ALL YOU ARE WORRIED ABOUT IS THE POLICE?
FATHER IS NO LONGER WITH US AND I'M THE ONLY PROTECTION YOU HAVE AROUND HERE!
I DON'T NEED YOUR KIND OF PROTECTION. HOW MANY TIMES AM I GOING TO HAVE TO BAIL YOU OUT OF JAIL BEFORE YOU LEARN THAT VIOLENCE IS NOT THE ANSWER?
AS MANY TIMES AS IT TAKES YOU TO STAND UP AND FIGHT AGAINST PEOPLE LIKE THAT.
WHERE IS YOUR PRIDE?
YOU TAKE THAT BAT AND GET OUT OF MY RESTAURANT!
YOU GO FIND ANOTHER JOB SOMEWHERE ELSE. I CANNOT RISK LOSING THIS PLACE WE BUILT OVER YOUR TEMPER.
GO!
SHONA. KHANA. FOR YOU, LITTLE CAMELI.
AW, THANK YOU, NAANI.

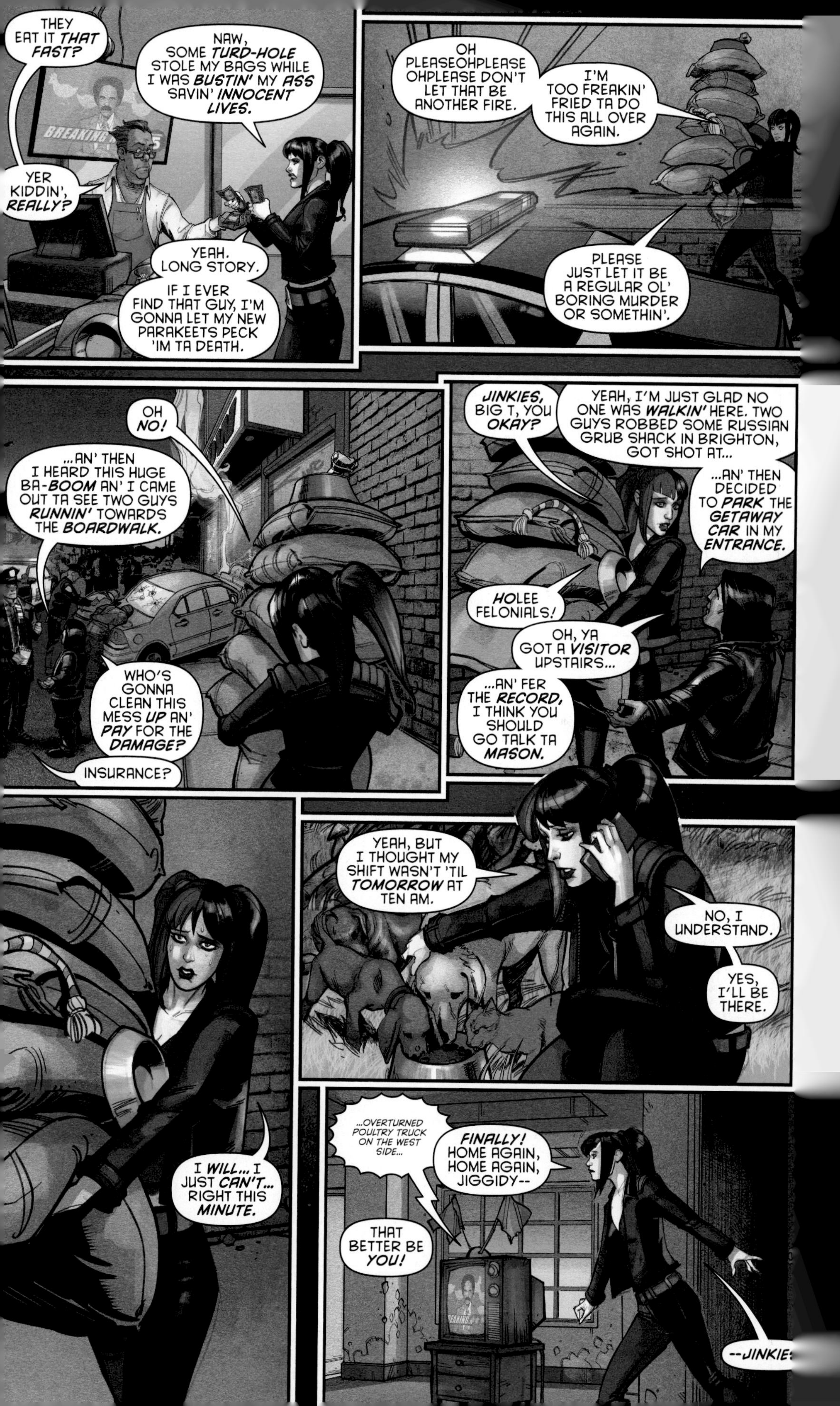
THEY EAT IT THAT FAST?
NAW, SOME TURD-HOLE STOLE MY BAGS WHILE I WAS BUSTIN' MY ASS SAVIN' INNOCENT LIVES.
YER KIDDIN', REALLY?
YEAH. LONG STORY.
IF I EVER FIND THAT GUY, I'M GONNA LET MY NEW PARAKEETS PECK 'IM TA DEATH.
OH PLEASEOHPLEASE OHPLEASE DON'T LET THAT BE ANOTHER FIRE.
I'M TOO FREAKIN' FRIED TA DO THIS ALL OVER AGAIN.
PLEASE JUST LET IT BE A REGULAR OL' BORING MURDER OR SOMETHIN'.
OH NO!
...AN' THEN I HEARD THIS HUGE BA-BOOM AN' I CAME OUT TA SEE TWO GUYS RUNNIN' TOWARDS THE BOARDWALK.
WHO'S GONNA CLEAN THIS MESS UP AN' PAY FOR THE DAMAGE?
INSURANCE?
JINKIES, BIG T, YOU OKAY?
YEAH, I'M JUST GLAD NO ONE WAS WALKIN' HERE. TWO GUYS ROBBED SOME RUSSIAN GRUB SHACK IN BRIGHTON, GOT SHOT AT...
...AN' THEN DECIDED TO PARK THE GETAWAY CAR IN MY ENTRANCE.
HOLEE FELONIALS!
OH, YA GOT A VISITOR UPSTAIRS...
...AN' FER THE RECORD, I THINK YOU SHOULD GO TALK TA MASON.
I WILL... I JUST CAN'T... RIGHT THIS MINUTE.
YEAH, BUT I THOUGHT MY SHIFT WASN'T 'TIL TOMORROW AT TEN AM.
NO, I UNDERSTAND.
YES, I'LL BE THERE.
...OVERTURNED POULTRY TRUCK ON THE WEST SIDE...
FINALLY! HOME AGAIN, HOME AGAIN, JIGGIDY--
THAT BETTER BE YOU!
--JINKIES

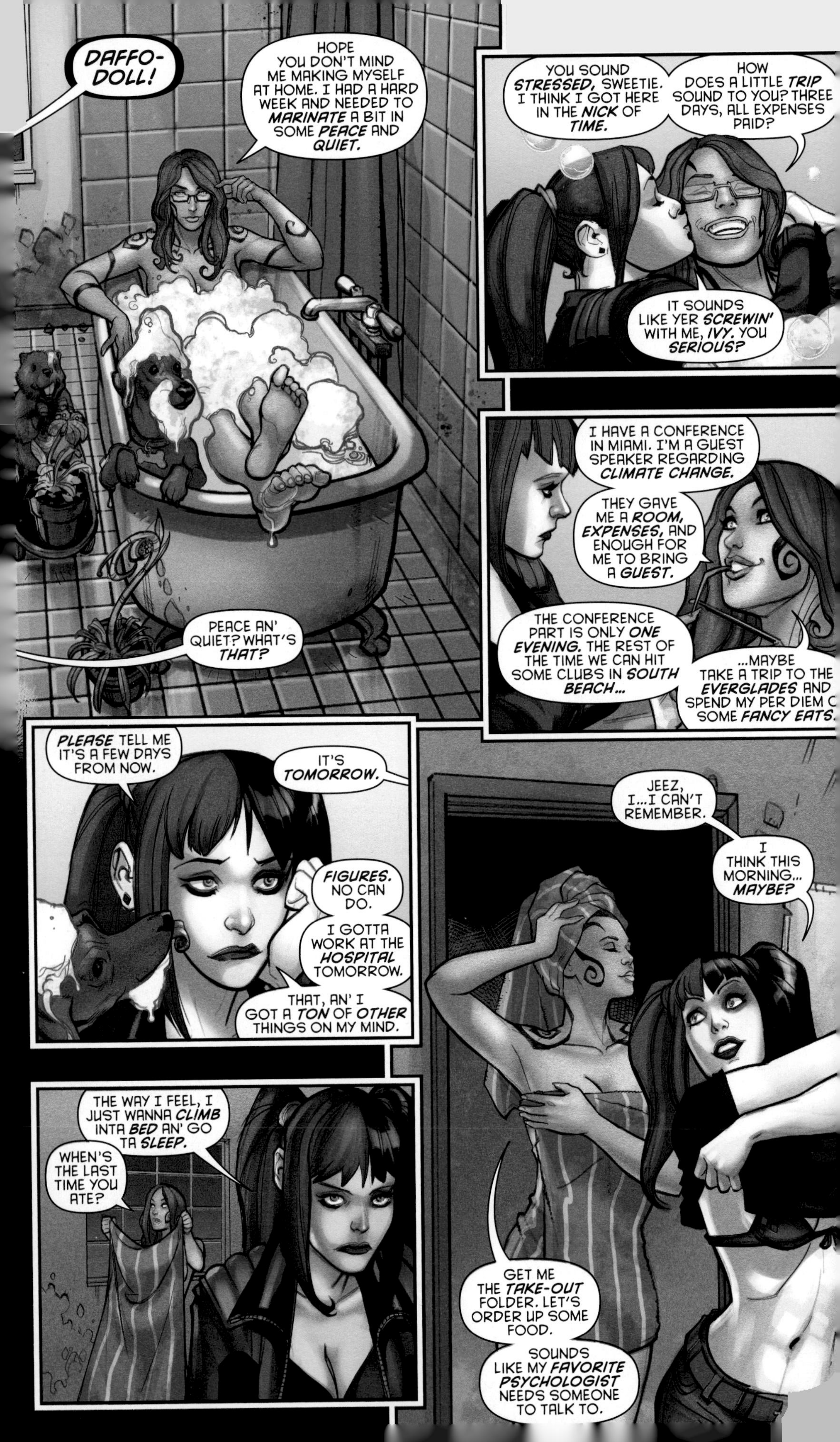
DAFFO-DOLL!
HOPE YOU DON'T MIND ME MAKING MYSELF AT HOME. I HAD A HARD WEEK AND NEEDED TO MARINATE A BIT IN SOME PEACE AND QUIET.
PEACE AN' QUIET? WHAT'S THAT?
YOU SOUND STRESSED, SWEETIE. I THINK I GOT HERE IN THE NICK OF TIME.
HOW DOES A LITTLE TRIP SOUND TO YOU? THREE DAYS, ALL EXPENSES PAID?
IT SOUNDS LIKE YER SCREWIN' WITH ME, IVY. YOU SERIOUS?
I HAVE A CONFERENCE IN MIAMI. I'M A GUEST SPEAKER REGARDING CLIMATE CHANGE.
THEY GAVE ME A ROOM, EXPENSES, AND ENOUGH FOR ME TO BRING A GUEST.
THE CONFERENCE PART IS ONLY ONE EVENING. THE REST OF THE TIME WE CAN HIT SOME CLUBS IN SOUTH BEACH...
...MAYBE TAKE A TRIP TO THE EVERGLADES AND SPEND MY PER DIEM O SOME FANCY EATS.
PLEASE TELL ME IT'S A FEW DAYS FROM NOW.
IT'S TOMORROW.
FIGURES. NO CAN DO.
I GOTTA WORK AT THE HOSPITAL TOMORROW.
THAT, AN' I GOT A TON OF OTHER THINGS ON MY MIND.
THE WAY I FEEL, I JUST WANNA CLIMB INTA BED AN' GO TA SLEEP.
WHEN'S THE LAST TIME YOU ATE?
JEEZ, I...I CAN'T REMEMBER.
I THINK THIS MORNING... MAYBE?
GET ME THE TAKE-OUT FOLDER. LET'S ORDER UP SOME FOOD.
SOUNDS LIKE MY FAVORITE PSYCHOLOGIST NEEDS SOMEONE TO TALK TO.

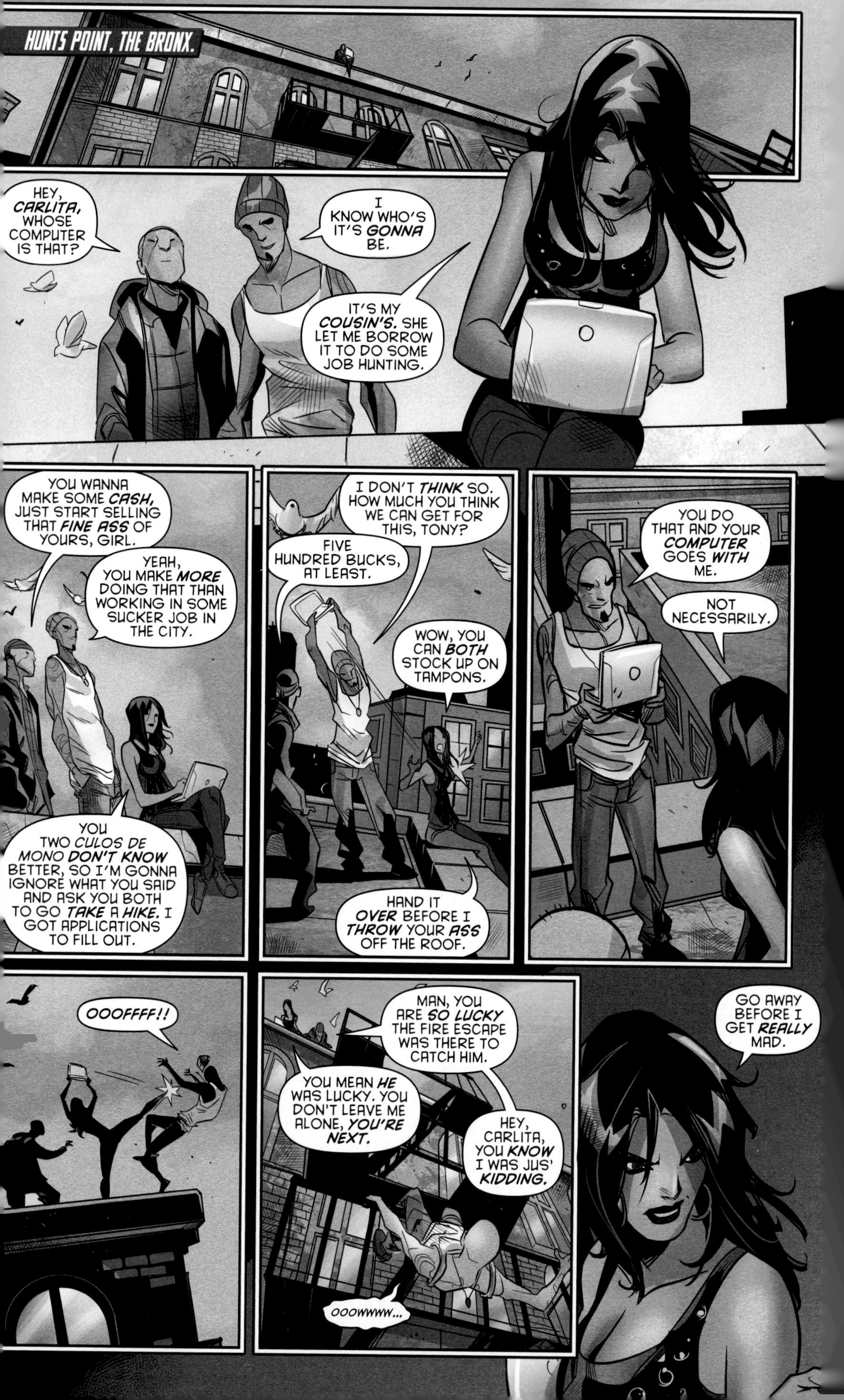
HUNTS POINT, THE BRONX.
HEY, CARLITA, WHOSE COMPUTER IS THAT?
I KNOW WHO'S IT'S GONNA BE.
IT'S MY COUSIN'S. SHE LET ME BORROW IT TO DO SOME JOB HUNTING.
YOU WANNA MAKE SOME CASH, JUST START SELLING THAT FINE ASS OF YOURS, GIRL.
YEAH, YOU MAKE MORE DOING THAT THAN WORKING IN SOME SUCKER JOB IN THE CITY.
YOU TWO CULOS DE MONO DON'T KNOW BETTER, SO I'M GONNA IGNORE WHAT YOU SAID AND ASK YOU BOTH TO GO TAKE A HIKE. I GOT APPLICATIONS TO FILL OUT.
I DON'T THINK SO. HOW MUCH YOU THINK WE CAN GET FOR THIS, TONY?
FIVE HUNDRED BUCKS, AT LEAST.
WOW, YOU CAN BOTH STOCK UP ON TAMPONS.
HAND IT OVER BEFORE I THROW YOUR ASS OFF THE ROOF.
YOU DO THAT AND YOUR COMPUTER GOES WITH ME.
NOT NECESSARILY.
OOOFFFF!!
MAN, YOU ARE SO LUCKY THE FIRE ESCAPE WAS THERE TO CATCH HIM.
YOU MEAN HE WAS LUCKY. YOU DON'T LEAVE ME ALONE, YOU'RE NEXT.
HEY, CARLITA, YOU KNOW I WAS JUS' KIDDING.
OOOWWWW...
GO AWAY BEFORE I GET REALLY MAD.

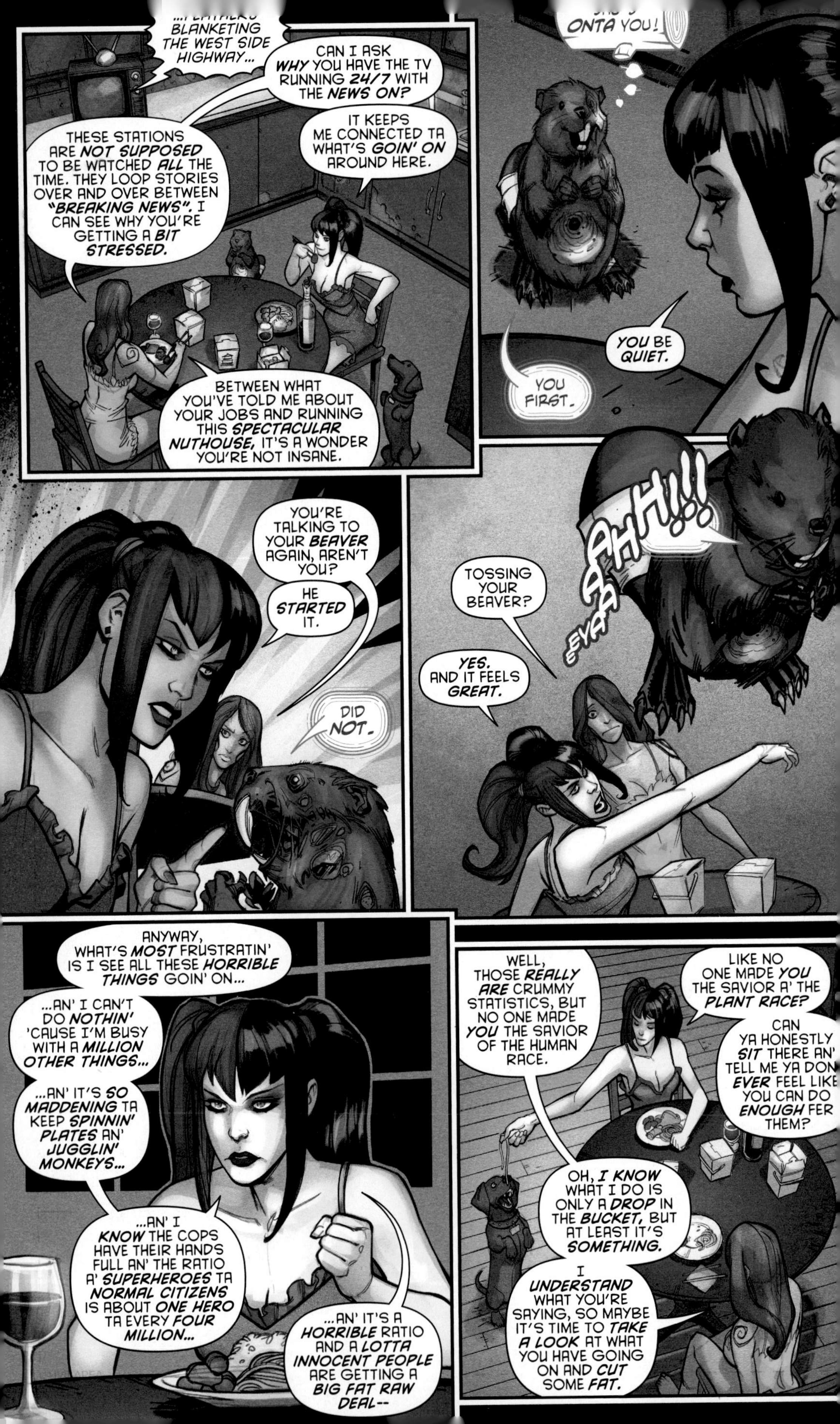
BLANKETING THE WEST SIDE HIGHWAY...
CAN I ASK WHY YOU HAVE THE TV RUNNING 24/7 WITH THE NEWS ON?
IT KEEPS ME CONNECTED TA WHAT'S GOIN' ON AROUND HERE.
THESE STATIONS ARE NOT SUPPOSED TO BE WATCHED ALL THE TIME. THEY LOOP STORIES OVER AND OVER BETWEEN "BREAKING NEWS". I CAN SEE WHY YOU'RE GETTING A BIT STRESSED.
BETWEEN WHAT YOU'VE TOLD ME ABOUT YOUR JOBS AND RUNNING THIS SPECTACULAR NUTHOUSE, IT'S A WONDER YOU'RE NOT INSANE.
ONTA YOU!
YOU BE QUIET.
YOU FIRST.
YOU'RE TALKING TO YOUR BEAVER AGAIN, AREN'T YOU?
HE STARTED IT.
DID NOT.
AHH!!!
EYAAA
TOSSING YOUR BEAVER?
YES. AND IT FEELS GREAT.
ANYWAY, WHAT'S MOST FRUSTRATIN' IS I SEE ALL THESE HORRIBLE THINGS GOIN' ON...
...AN' I CAN'T DO NOTHIN' 'CAUSE I'M BUSY WITH A MILLION OTHER THINGS...
...AN' IT'S SO MADDENING TA KEEP SPINNIN' PLATES AN' JUGGLIN' MONKEYS...
...AN' I KNOW THE COPS HAVE THEIR HANDS FULL AN' THE RATIO A' SUPERHEROES TA NORMAL CITIZENS IS ABOUT ONE HERO TA EVERY FOUR MILLION...
...AN' IT'S A HORRIBLE RATIO AND A LOTTA INNOCENT PEOPLE ARE GETTING A BIG FAT RAW DEAL--
WELL, THOSE REALLY ARE CRUMMY STATISTICS, BUT NO ONE MADE YOU THE SAVIOR OF THE HUMAN RACE.
LIKE NO ONE MADE YOU THE SAVIOR A' THE PLANT RACE?
CAN YA HONESTLY SIT THERE AN' TELL ME YA DON EVER FEEL LIKE YOU CAN DO ENOUGH FER THEM?
OH, I KNOW WHAT I DO IS ONLY A DROP IN THE BUCKET, BUT AT LEAST IT'S SOMETHING.
I UNDERSTAND WHAT YOU'RE SAYING, SO MAYBE IT'S TIME TO TAKE A LOOK AT WHAT YOU HAVE GOING ON AND CUT SOME FAT.

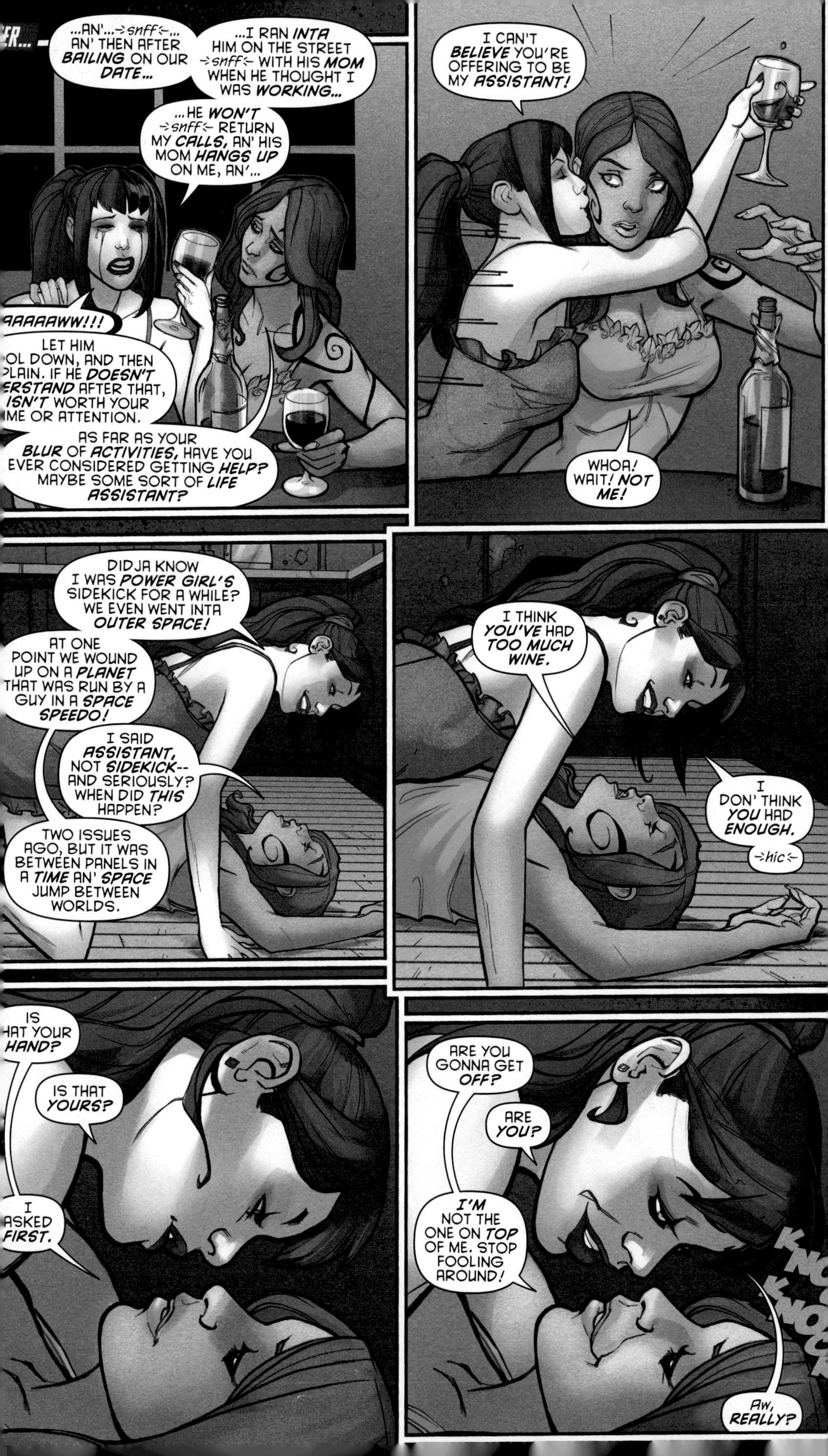

...AN'...→snff←... AN' THEN AFTER BAILING ON OUR DATE...
...I RAN INTA HIM ON THE STREET →snff← WITH HIS MOM WHEN HE THOUGHT I WAS WORKING...
...HE WON'T →snff← RETURN MY CALLS, AN' HIS MOM HANGS UP ON ME, AN'...
AAAAAAWW!!!
LET HIM OL DOWN, AND THEN PLAIN. IF HE DOESN'T ERSTAND AFTER THAT, ISN'T WORTH YOUR ME OR ATTENTION.
AS FAR AS YOUR BLUR OF ACTIVITIES, HAVE YOU EVER CONSIDERED GETTING HELP? MAYBE SOME SORT OF LIFE ASSISTANT?
I CAN'T BELIEVE YOU'RE OFFERING TO BE MY ASSISTANT!
WHOA! WAIT! NOT ME!
DIDJA KNOW I WAS POWER GIRL'S SIDEKICK FOR A WHILE? WE EVEN WENT INTA OUTER SPACE!
AT ONE POINT WE WOUND UP ON A PLANET THAT WAS RUN BY A GUY IN A SPACE SPEEDO!
I SAID ASSISTANT, NOT SIDEKICK-- AND SERIOUSLY? WHEN DID THIS HAPPEN?
TWO ISSUES AGO, BUT IT WAS BETWEEN PANELS IN A TIME AN' SPACE JUMP BETWEEN WORLDS.
I THINK YOU'VE HAD TOO MUCH WINE.
I DON' THINK YOU HAD ENOUGH.
→hic←
IS HAT YOUR HAND?
IS THAT YOURS?
I ASKED FIRST.
ARE YOU GONNA GET OFF?
ARE YOU?
I'M NOT THE ONE ON TOP OF ME. STOP FOOLING AROUND!
AW, REALLY?

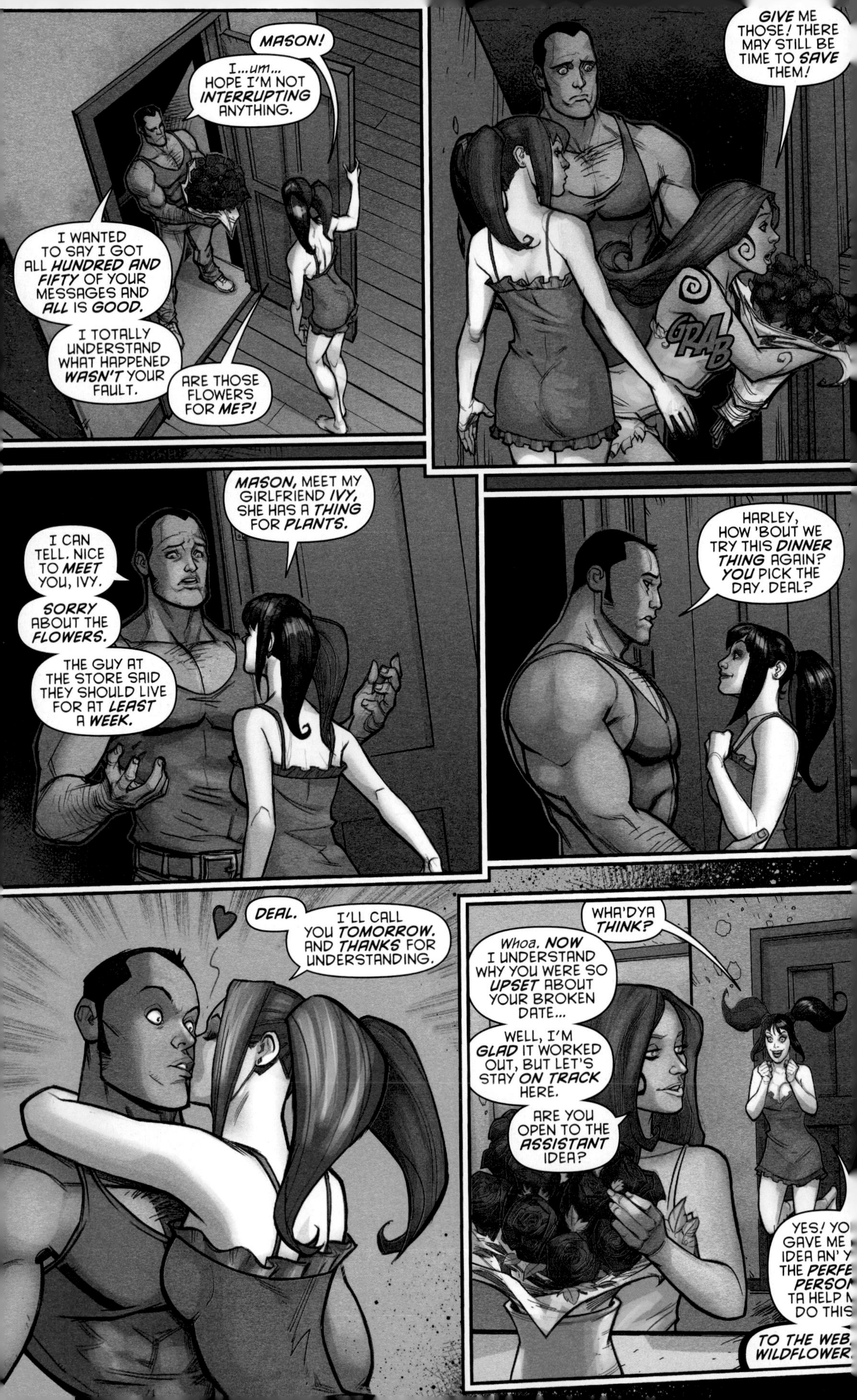
MASON!
I...um... HOPE I'M NOT INTERRUPTING ANYTHING.
I WANTED TO SAY I GOT ALL HUNDRED AND FIFTY OF YOUR MESSAGES AND ALL IS GOOD.
I TOTALLY UNDERSTAND WHAT HAPPENED WASN'T YOUR FAULT.
ARE THOSE FLOWERS FOR ME?!
GIVE ME THOSE! THERE MAY STILL BE TIME TO SAVE THEM!
GRAB
MASON, MEET MY GIRLFRIEND IVY, SHE HAS A THING FOR PLANTS.
I CAN TELL. NICE TO MEET YOU, IVY.
SORRY ABOUT THE FLOWERS.
THE GUY AT THE STORE SAID THEY SHOULD LIVE FOR AT LEAST A WEEK.
HARLEY, HOW 'BOUT WE TRY THIS DINNER THING AGAIN? YOU PICK THE DAY. DEAL?
DEAL.
I'LL CALL YOU TOMORROW. AND THANKS FOR UNDERSTANDING.
WHA'DYA THINK?
Whoa. NOW I UNDERSTAND WHY YOU WERE SO UPSET ABOUT YOUR BROKEN DATE...
WELL, I'M GLAD IT WORKED OUT, BUT LET'S STAY ON TRACK HERE.
ARE YOU OPEN TO THE ASSISTANT IDEA?
YES! YO GAVE ME IDEA AN' Y THE PERFE PERSON TA HELP M DO THIS
TO THE WEB WILDFLOWER

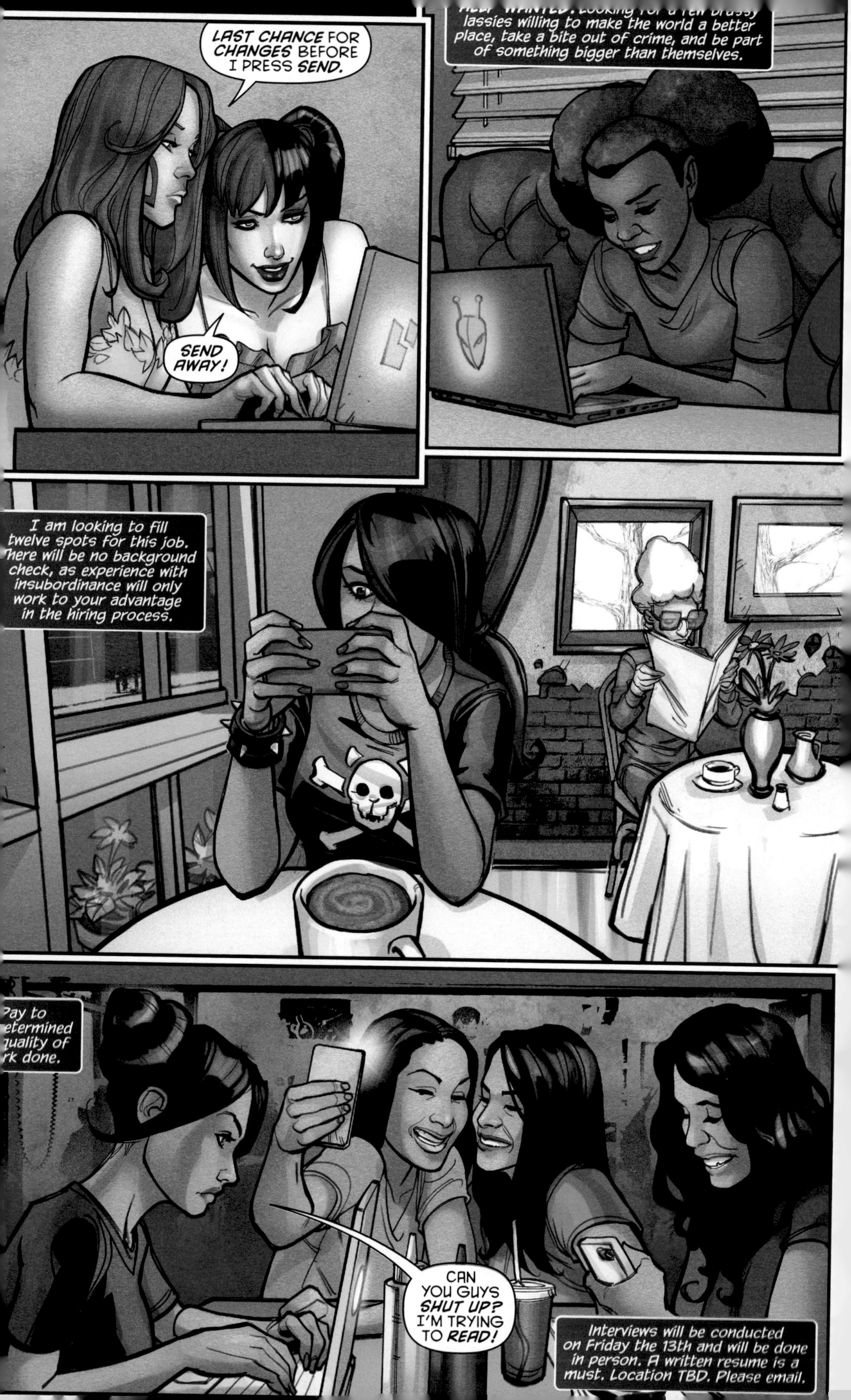
LAST CHANCE FOR CHANGES BEFORE I PRESS SEND.
SEND AWAY!
lassies willing to make the world a better place, take a bite out of crime, and be part of something bigger than themselves.
I am looking to fill twelve spots for this job. here will be no background check, as experience with insubordinance will only work to your advantage in the hiring process.
Pay to etermined uality of rk done.
CAN YOU GUYS SHUT UP? I'M TRYING TO READ!
Interviews will be conducted on Friday the 13th and will be done in person. A written resume is a must. Location TBD. Please email.

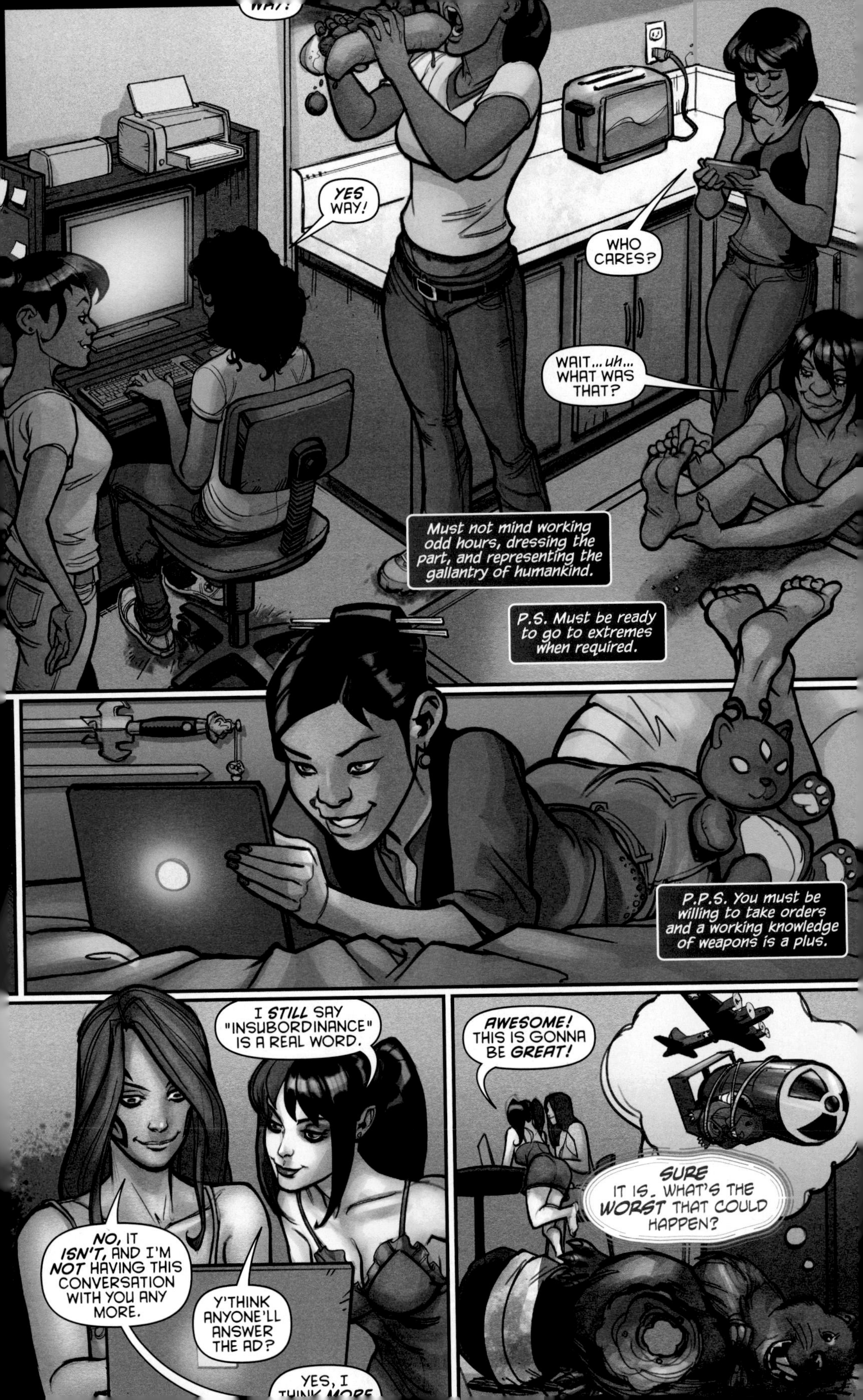
YES WAY!
WHO CARES?
WAIT... uh... WHAT WAS THAT?
Must not mind working odd hours, dressing the part, and representing the gallantry of humankind.
P.S. Must be ready to go to extremes when required.
P.P.S. You must be willing to take orders and a working knowledge of weapons is a plus.
I STILL SAY "INSUBORDINANCE" IS A REAL WORD.
NO, IT ISN'T, AND I'M NOT HAVING THIS CONVERSATION WITH YOU ANY MORE.
Y'THINK ANYONE'LL ANSWER THE AD?
AWESOME! THIS IS GONNA BE GREAT!
SURE IT IS. WHAT'S THE WORST THAT COULD HAPPEN?

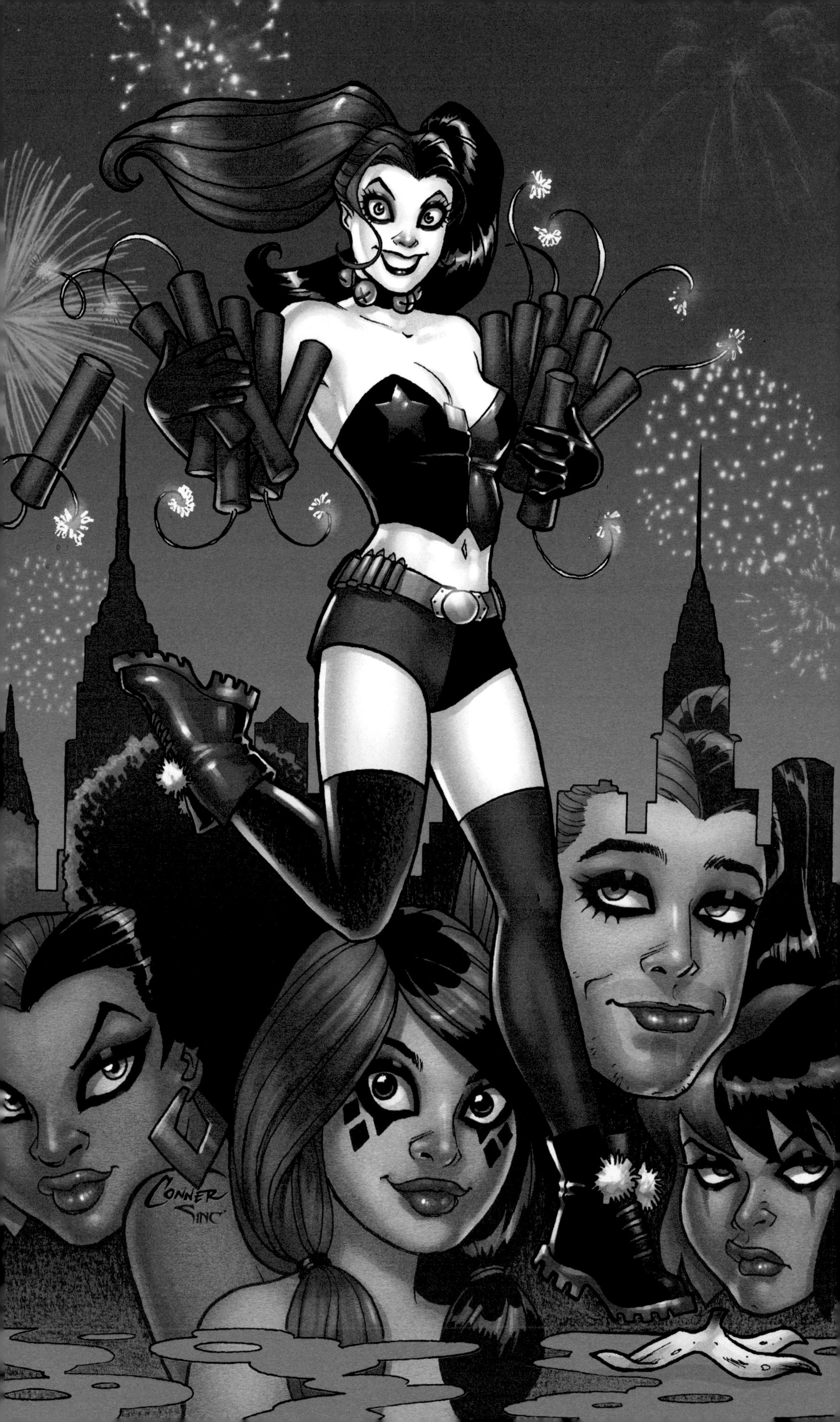
CONNER
SINC

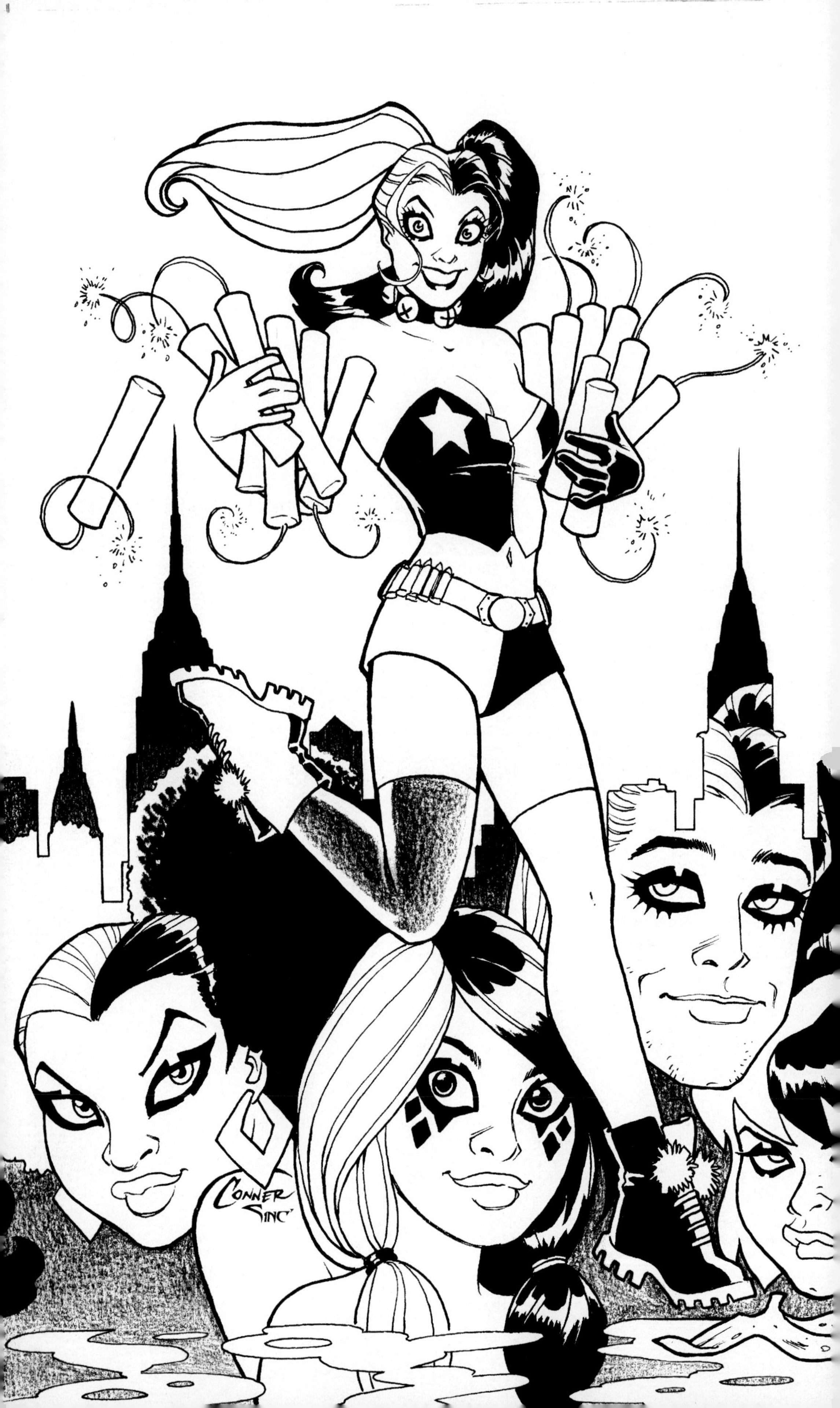
CONNER
SINC'

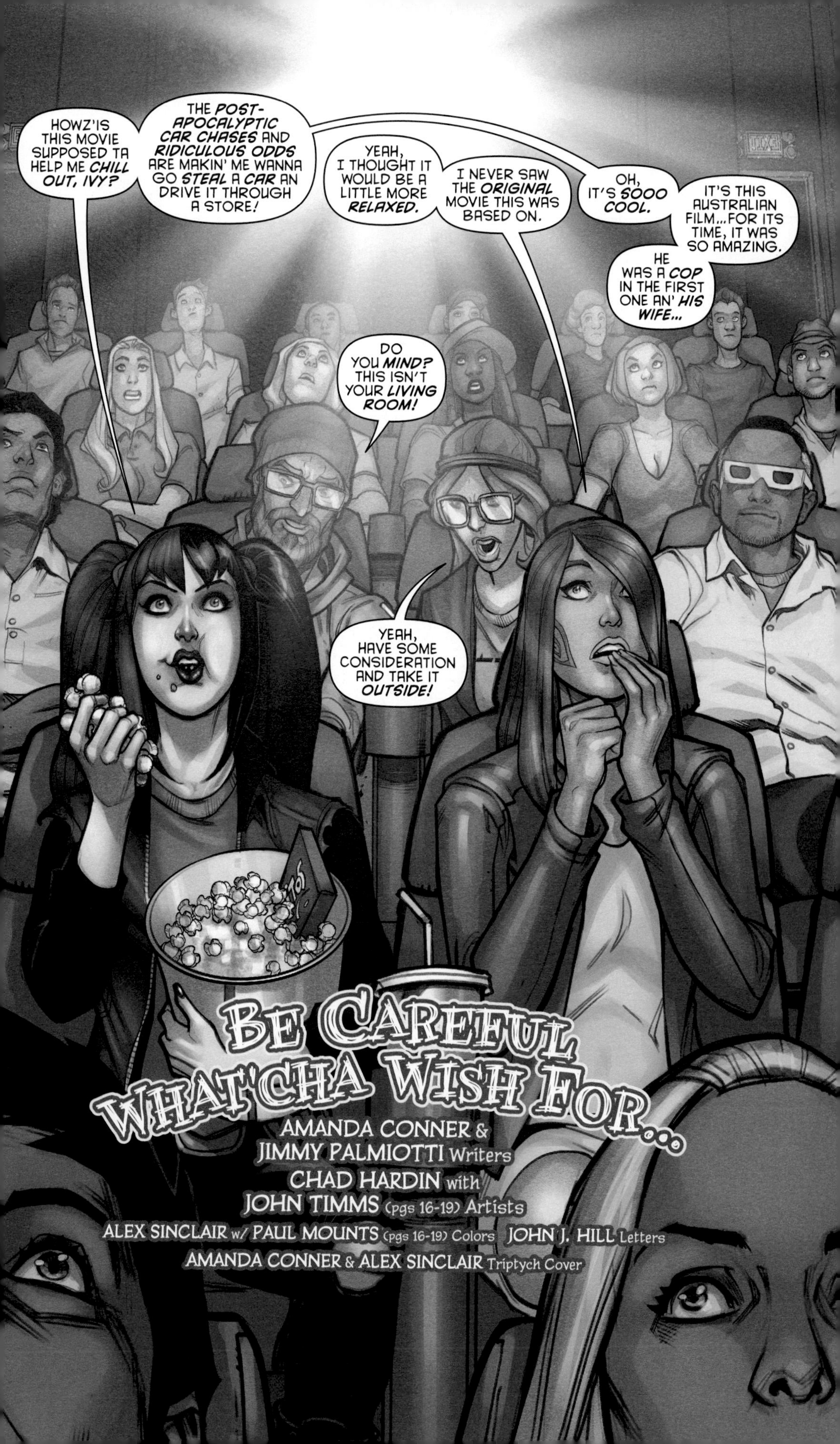
HOWZ'IS THIS MOVIE SUPPOSED TA HELP ME CHILL OUT, IVY?
THE POST-APOCALYPTIC CAR CHASES AND RIDICULOUS ODDS ARE MAKIN' ME WANNA GO STEAL A CAR AN DRIVE IT THROUGH A STORE!
YEAH, I THOUGHT IT WOULD BE A LITTLE MORE RELAXED.
I NEVER SAW THE ORIGINAL MOVIE THIS WAS BASED ON.
OH, IT'S SOOO COOL.
IT'S THIS AUSTRALIAN FILM...FOR ITS TIME, IT WAS SO AMAZING.
HE WAS A COP IN THE FIRST ONE AN' HIS WIFE...
DO YOU MIND? THIS ISN'T YOUR LIVING ROOM!
YEAH, HAVE SOME CONSIDERATION AND TAKE IT OUTSIDE!
BE CAREFUL WHAT'CHA WISH FOR...
AMANDA CONNER & JIMMY PALMIOTTI Writers
CHAD HARDIN with JOHN TIMMS (pgs 16-19) Artists
ALEX SINCLAIR w/ PAUL MOUNTS (pgs 16-19) Colors JOHN J. HILL Letters
AMANDA CONNER & ALEX SINCLAIR Triptych Cover

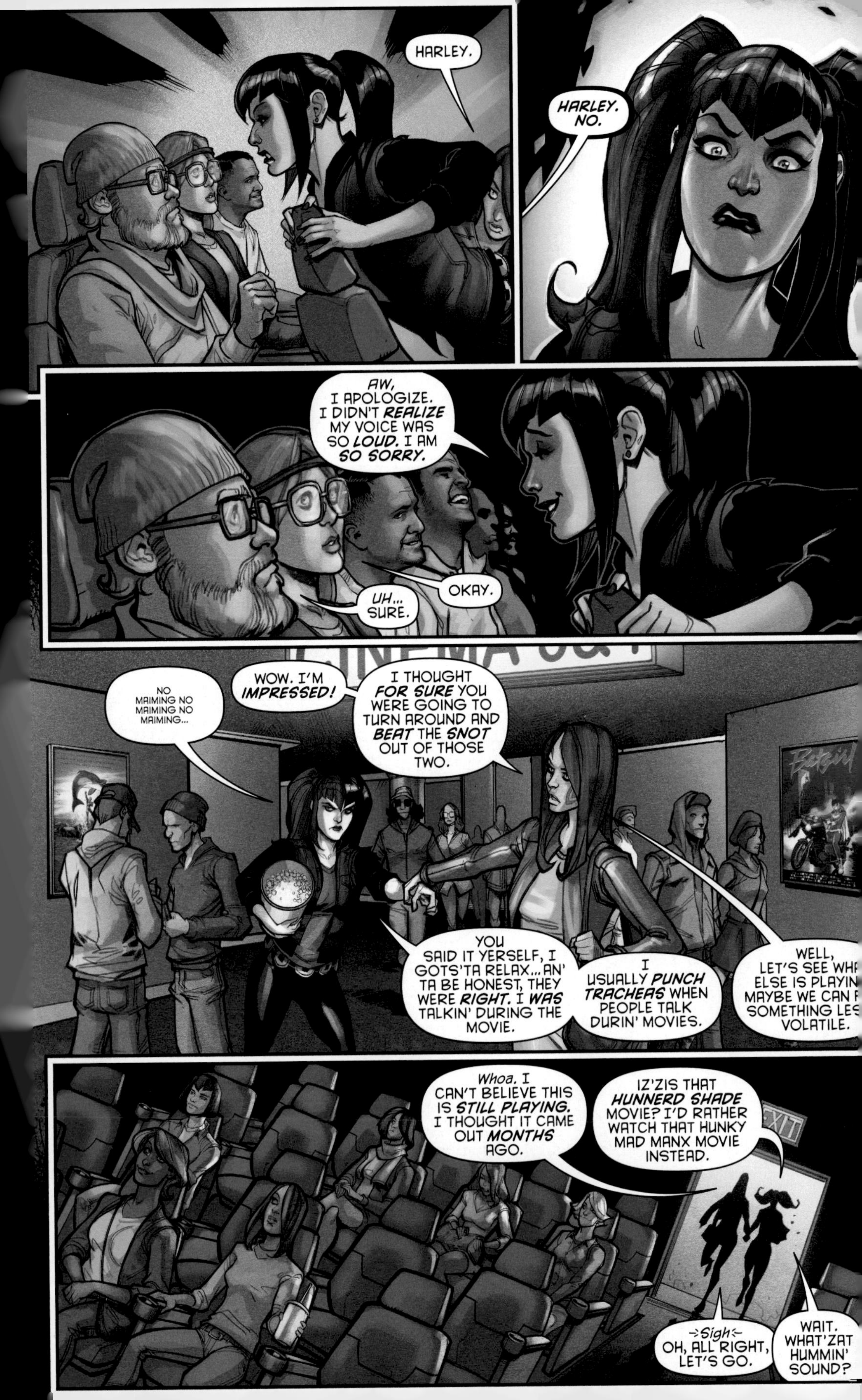
HARLEY.
HARLEY. NO.
AW, I APOLOGIZE. I DIDN'T REALIZE MY VOICE WAS SO LOUD. I AM SO SORRY.
UH... SURE.
OKAY.
NO MAIMING NO MAIMING NO MAIMING...
WOW. I'M IMPRESSED!
I THOUGHT FOR SURE YOU WERE GOING TO TURN AROUND AND BEAT THE SNOT OUT OF THOSE TWO.
YOU SAID IT YERSELF, I GOTS'TA RELAX... AN' TA BE HONEST, THEY WERE RIGHT. I WAS TALKIN' DURING THE MOVIE.
I USUALLY PUNCH TRACHEAS WHEN PEOPLE TALK DURIN' MOVIES.
WELL, LET'S SEE WHA ELSE IS PLAYIN MAYBE WE CAN F SOMETHING LES VOLATILE.
Whoa. I CAN'T BELIEVE THIS IS STILL PLAYING. I THOUGHT IT CAME OUT MONTHS AGO.
IZ'ZIS THAT HUNNERD SHADE MOVIE? I'D RATHER WATCH THAT HUNKY MAD MANX MOVIE INSTEAD.
EXIT
Sigh
OH, ALL RIGHT, LET'S GO.
WAIT. WHAT'ZAT HUMMIN' SOUND?

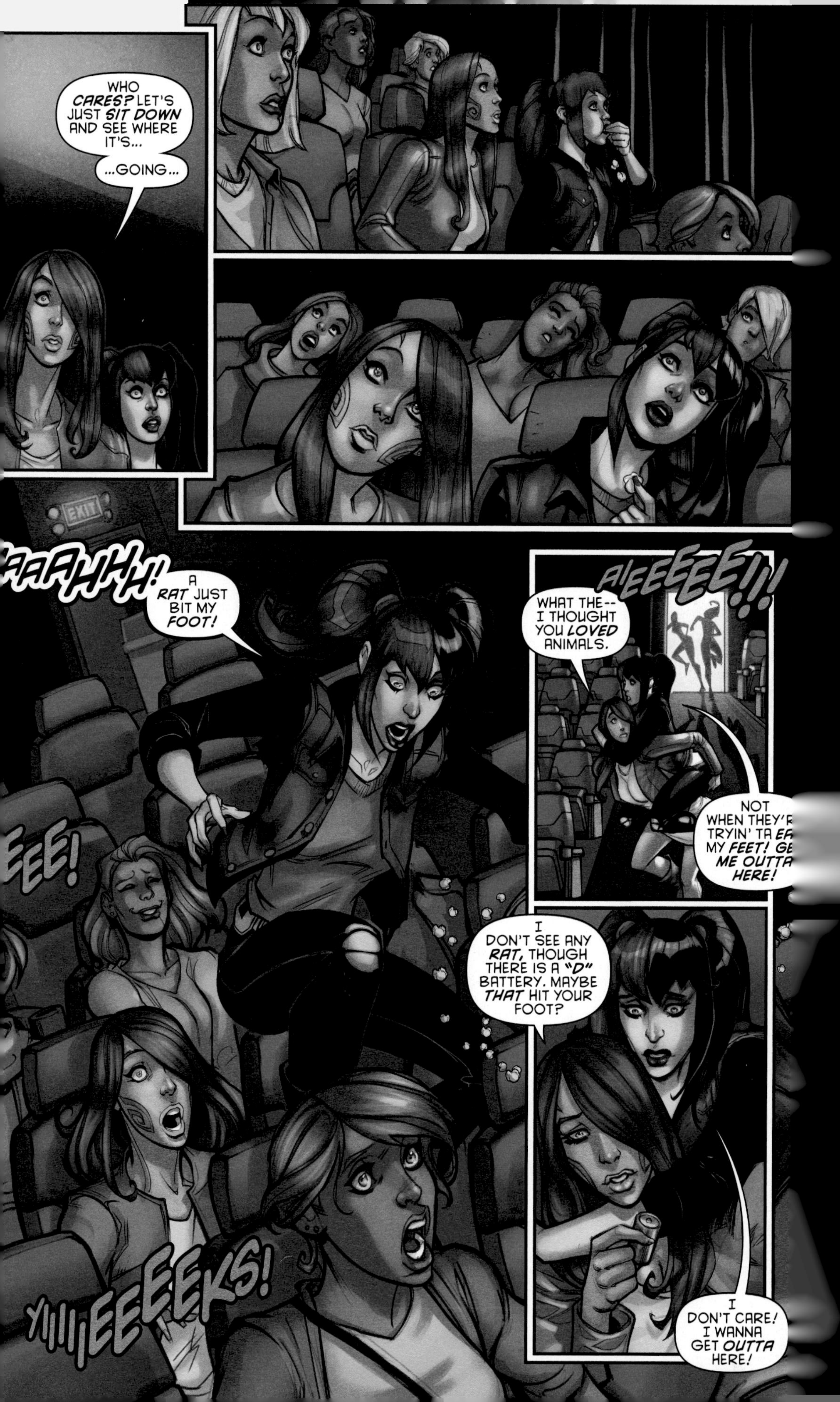

WHO CARES? LET'S JUST SIT DOWN AND SEE WHERE IT'S...
...GOING...
EXIT
AAAHHH!
A RAT JUST BIT MY FOOT!
EEE!
YIIIIEEEEKS!
AIEEEEEE!!!
WHAT THE-- I THOUGHT YOU LOVED ANIMALS.
NOT WHEN THEY'R TRYIN' TA EA MY FEET! GE ME OUTTA HERE!
I DON'T SEE ANY RAT, THOUGH THERE IS A "D" BATTERY. MAYBE THAT HIT YOUR FOOT?
I DON'T CARE! I WANNA GET OUTTA HERE!

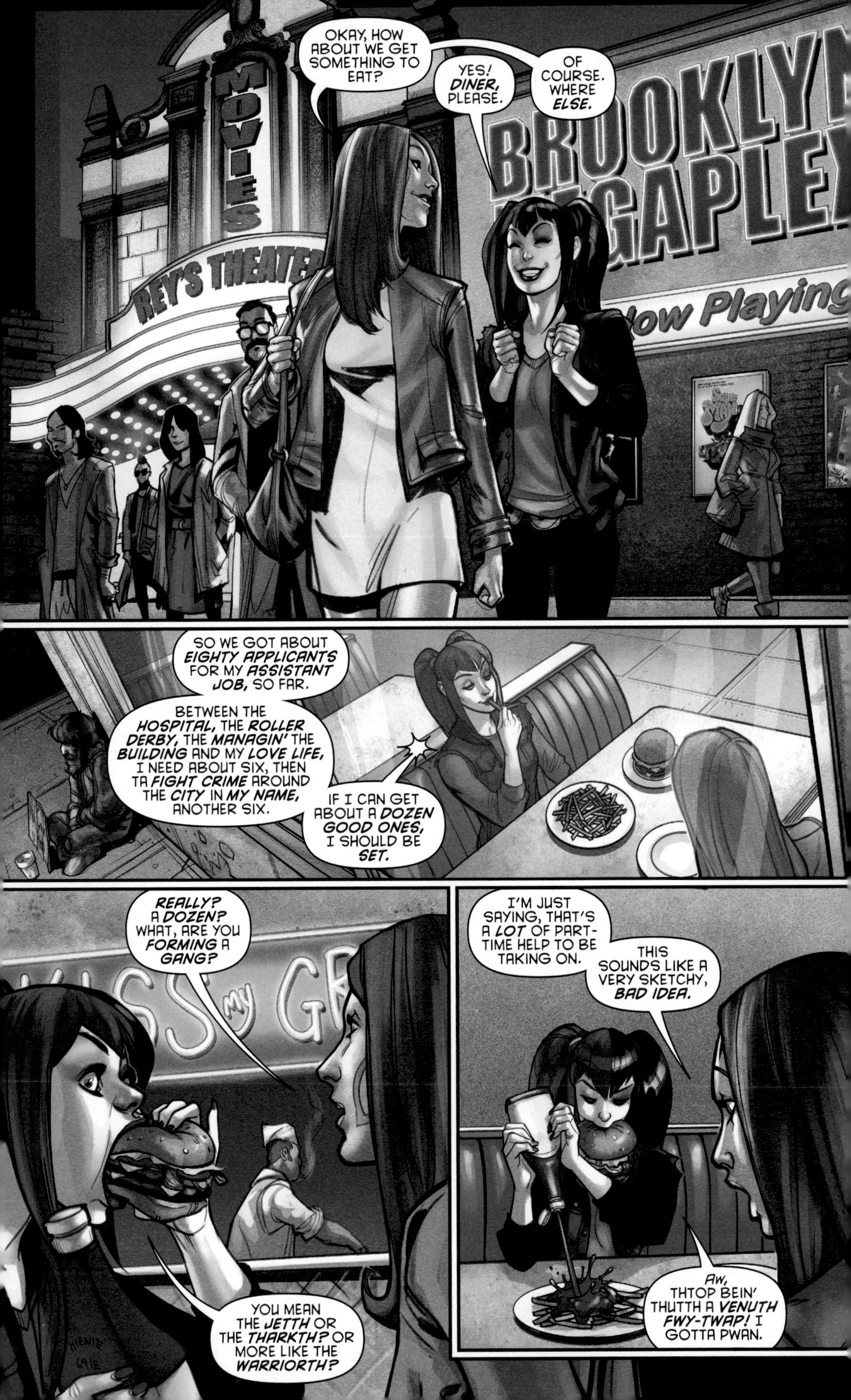

MOVIES
REY'S THEATER
BROOKLYN
GAPLEX
Now Playing
OKAY, HOW ABOUT WE GET SOMETHING TO EAT?
YES! DINER, PLEASE.
OF COURSE. WHERE ELSE.
SO WE GOT ABOUT EIGHTY APPLICANTS FOR MY ASSISTANT JOB, SO FAR.
BETWEEN THE HOSPITAL, THE ROLLER DERBY, THE MANAGIN' THE BUILDING AND MY LOVE LIFE, I NEED ABOUT SIX, THEN TA FIGHT CRIME AROUND THE CITY IN MY NAME, ANOTHER SIX.
IF I CAN GET ABOUT A DOZEN GOOD ONES, I SHOULD BE SET.
REALLY? A DOZEN? WHAT, ARE YOU FORMING A GANG?
YOU MEAN THE JETTH OR THE THARKTH? OR MORE LIKE THE WARRIORTH?
I'M JUST SAYING, THAT'S A LOT OF PART-TIME HELP TO BE TAKING ON.
THIS SOUNDS LIKE A VERY SKETCHY, BAD IDEA.
AW, THTOP BEIN' THUTTH A VENUTH FWY-TWAP! I GOTTA PWAN.

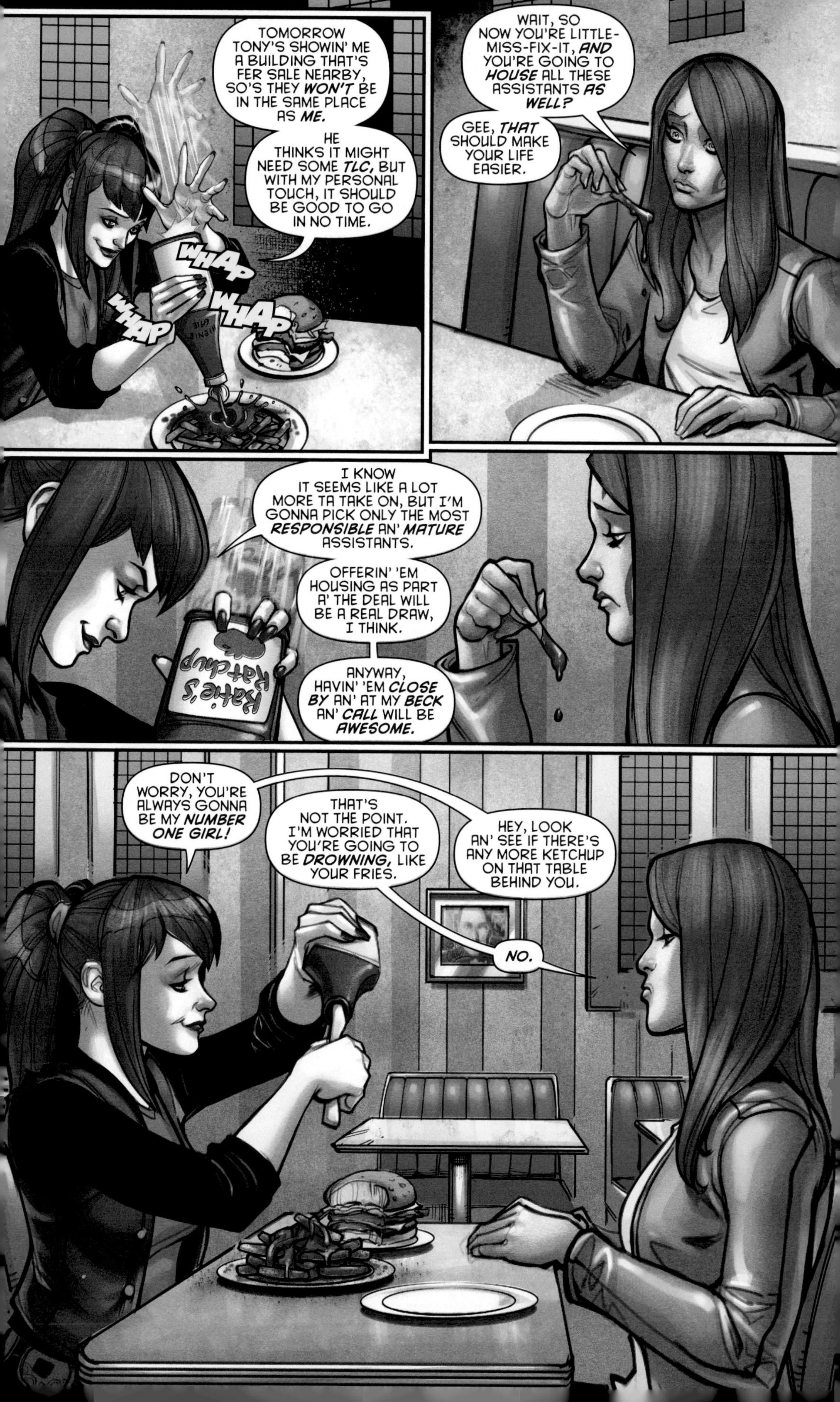
TOMORROW TONY'S SHOWIN' ME A BUILDING THAT'S FER SALE NEARBY, SO'S THEY WON'T BE IN THE SAME PLACE AS ME.
HE THINKS IT MIGHT NEED SOME TLC, BUT WITH MY PERSONAL TOUCH, IT SHOULD BE GOOD TO GO IN NO TIME.
WHAP
WHAP
WHAP
WAIT, SO NOW YOU'RE LITTLE-MISS-FIX-IT, AND YOU'RE GOING TO HOUSE ALL THESE ASSISTANTS AS WELL?
GEE, THAT SHOULD MAKE YOUR LIFE EASIER.
I KNOW IT SEEMS LIKE A LOT MORE TA TAKE ON, BUT I'M GONNA PICK ONLY THE MOST RESPONSIBLE AN' MATURE ASSISTANTS.
OFFERIN' 'EM HOUSING AS PART A' THE DEAL WILL BE A REAL DRAW, I THINK.
ANYWAY, HAVIN' 'EM CLOSE BY AN' AT MY BECK AN' CALL WILL BE AWESOME.
Katie's Ketchup
DON'T WORRY, YOU'RE ALWAYS GONNA BE MY NUMBER ONE GIRL!
THAT'S NOT THE POINT. I'M WORRIED THAT YOU'RE GOING TO BE DROWNING, LIKE YOUR FRIES.
HEY, LOOK AN' SEE IF THERE'S ANY MORE KETCHUP ON THAT TABLE BEHIND YOU.
NO.

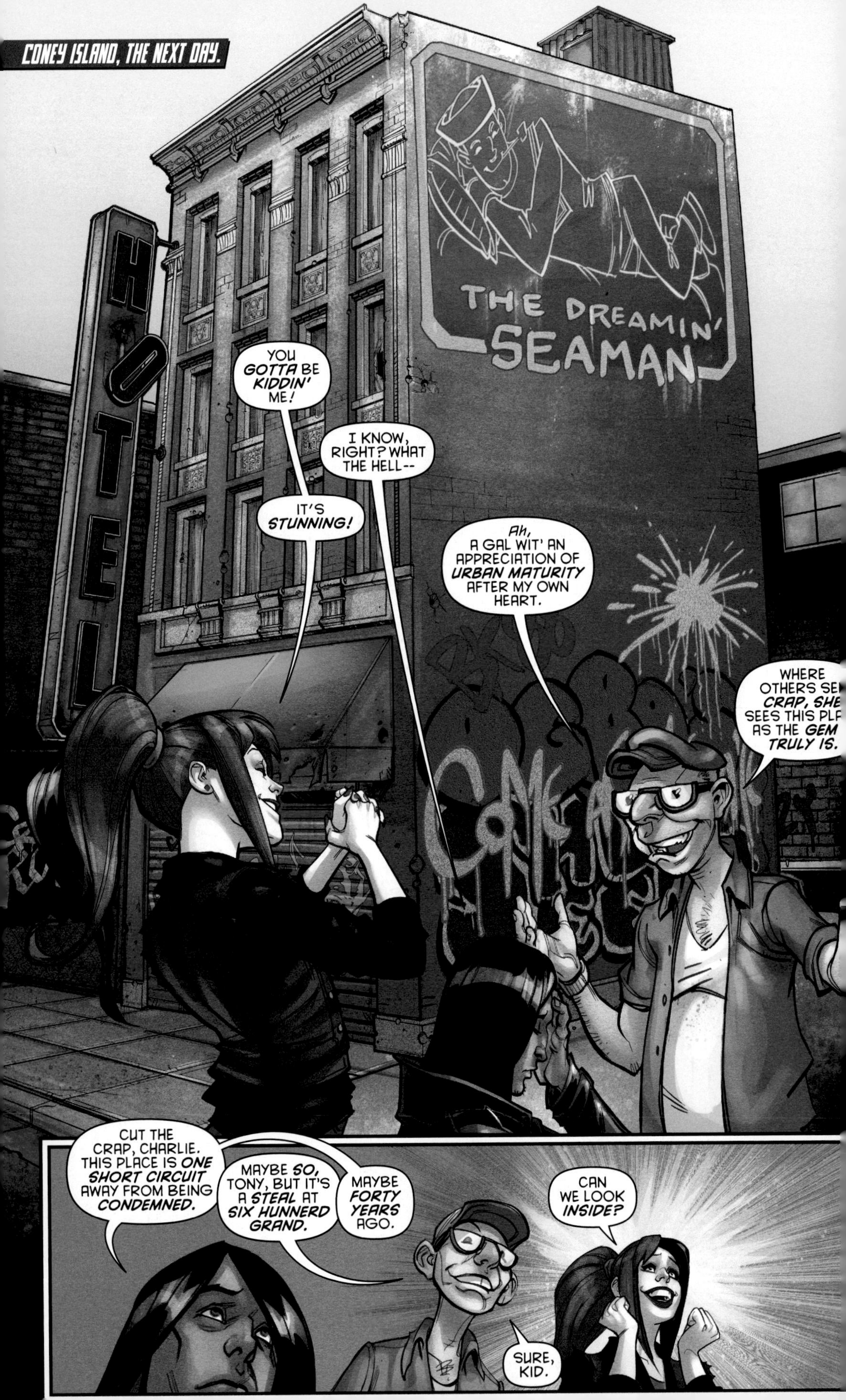
CONEY ISLAND, THE NEXT DAY.
HOTEL
THE DREAMIN' SEAMAN
YOU GOTTA BE KIDDIN' ME!
I KNOW, RIGHT? WHAT THE HELL--
IT'S STUNNING!
AH, A GAL WIT' AN APPRECIATION OF URBAN MATURITY AFTER MY OWN HEART.
WHERE OTHERS SEE CRAP, SHE SEES THIS PLA AS THE GEM TRULY IS.
CUT THE CRAP, CHARLIE. THIS PLACE IS ONE SHORT CIRCUIT AWAY FROM BEING CONDEMNED.
MAYBE SO, TONY, BUT IT'S A STEAL AT SIX HUNNERD GRAND.
MAYBE FORTY YEARS AGO.
CAN WE LOOK INSIDE?
SURE, KID.

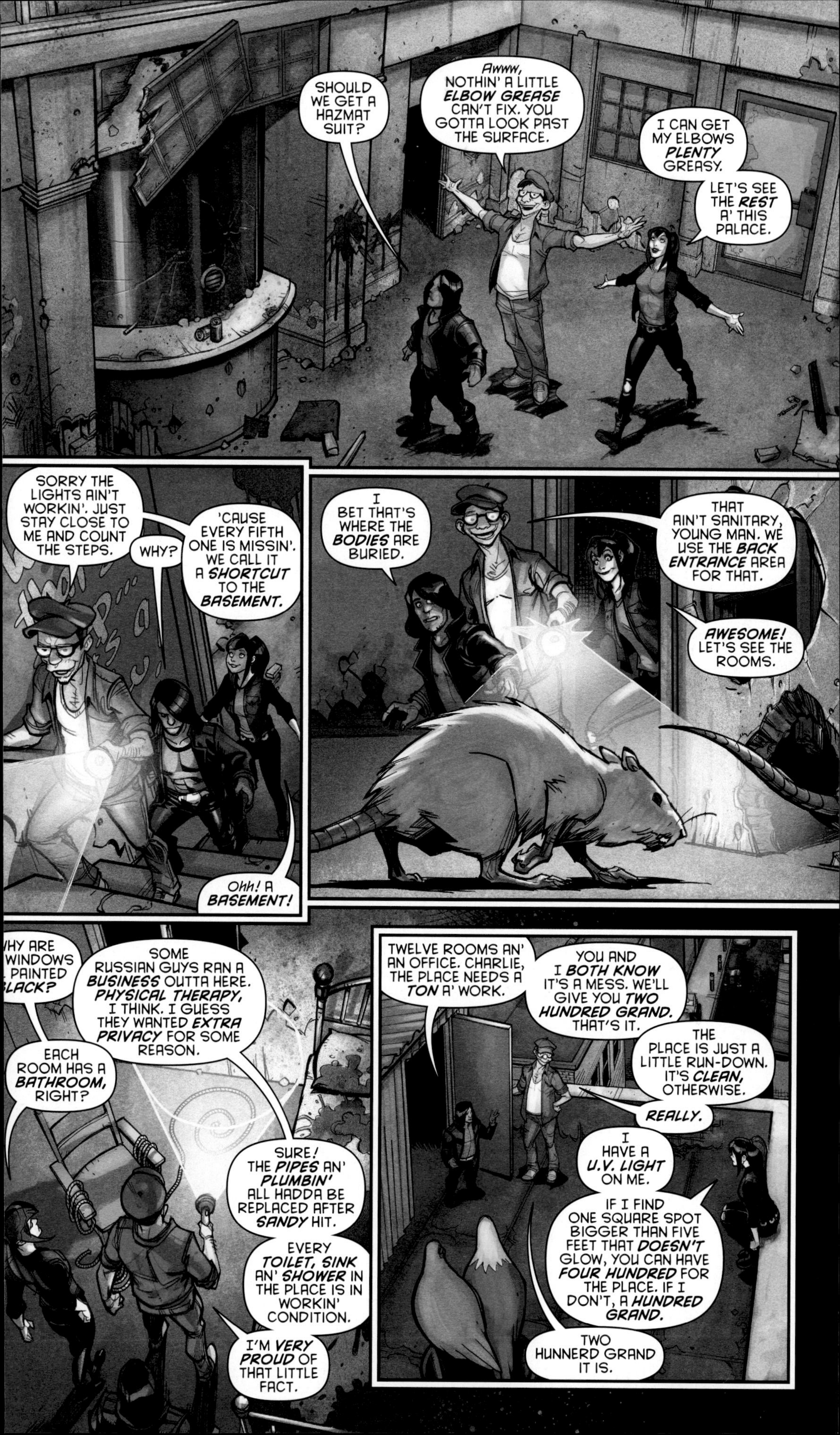
SHOULD WE GET A HAZMAT SUIT?
Awww, NOTHIN' A LITTLE ELBOW GREASE CAN'T FIX. YOU GOTTA LOOK PAST THE SURFACE.
I CAN GET MY ELBOWS PLENTY GREASY.
LET'S SEE THE REST A' THIS PALACE.
SORRY THE LIGHTS AIN'T WORKIN'. JUST STAY CLOSE TO ME AND COUNT THE STEPS.
WHY?
'CAUSE EVERY FIFTH ONE IS MISSIN'. WE CALL IT A SHORTCUT TO THE BASEMENT.
Ohh! A BASEMENT!
I BET THAT'S WHERE THE BODIES ARE BURIED.
THAT AIN'T SANITARY, YOUNG MAN. WE USE THE BACK ENTRANCE AREA FOR THAT.
AWESOME! LET'S SEE THE ROOMS.
HY ARE WINDOWS PAINTED LACK?
SOME RUSSIAN GUYS RAN A BUSINESS OUTTA HERE. PHYSICAL THERAPY, I THINK. I GUESS THEY WANTED EXTRA PRIVACY FOR SOME REASON.
EACH ROOM HAS A BATHROOM, RIGHT?
SURE! THE PIPES AN' PLUMBIN' ALL HADDA BE REPLACED AFTER SANDY HIT.
EVERY TOILET, SINK AN' SHOWER IN THE PLACE IS IN WORKIN' CONDITION.
I'M VERY PROUD OF THAT LITTLE FACT.
TWELVE ROOMS AN' AN OFFICE. CHARLIE, THE PLACE NEEDS A TON A' WORK.
YOU AND I BOTH KNOW IT'S A MESS. WE'LL GIVE YOU TWO HUNDRED GRAND. THAT'S IT.
THE PLACE IS JUST A LITTLE RUN-DOWN. IT'S CLEAN, OTHERWISE.
REALLY.
I HAVE A U.V. LIGHT ON ME.
IF I FIND ONE SQUARE SPOT BIGGER THAN FIVE FEET THAT DOESN'T GLOW, YOU CAN HAVE FOUR HUNDRED FOR THE PLACE. IF I DON'T, A HUNDRED GRAND.
TWO HUNNERD GRAND IT IS.

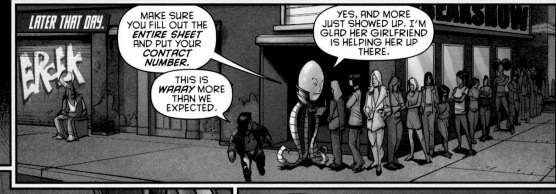

MAKE SURE YOU FILL OUT THE *ENTIRE SHEET* AND PUT YOUR *CONTACT NUMBER*.

THIS IS *WAAAY* MORE THAN WE EXPECTED.

YES, AND MORE JUST SHOWED UP. I'M GLAD HER GIRLFRIEND IS HELPING HER UP THERE.

TONY.

EGGY.

SEE YOU *MUCH* LATER.

WHAT? WHERE YA' GOING?

BACK TO GOTHAM. I HAVE THINGS TO DO, AND HONESTLY, THIS *WHOLE OPERATION* IS JUST *ONE BIG MISTAKE*.

YOU TELL HARLEY THAT?

A *HUNDRED TIMES*, BUT AS ALWAYS, SHE HAS TO FIND THINGS OUT FOR *HERSELF*.

I'LL BE BACK IN A WEEK OR SO TO SEE HOW IT'S COMING ALONG, THOUGH.

GOOD LUCK.

AW, MAN. I WAS HOPIN' SHE WOULD *STAY*.

ME TOO. I *LIKE* HER. SHE SMELLS NICE.

YOU CAN *SMELL* THINGS?

EVERYTHING BUT MYSEL[F]

UPSTAIRS...

SO YEAH, I'VE WORKED A FEW *TEMP JOBS* SINCE I WAS KICKED OUT OF HIGH SCHOOL, BUT NOTHING WORTH *STAYING* AT.

I STABBED MY STEPMOTHER AND SPENT SOME TIME *UPSTATE*, BUT IT'S WHERE I FOUND *RELIGION*.

I KNOW *EVERYONE BUT ME* IS THE *DEVIL*, SO THE CHANCE TO JOIN A GROUP LIKE THIS TO MURDER IN THE NAME OF, Y'KNOW, WHOMEVER YOU HAPPEN TO BELIEVE IN, IS *VERY COOL*.

I CAN ALSO SEE *GHOSTS*, SO IF YOU SEE ME STABBING WHAT SEEMS LIKE NOTHING, IT'S A *GHOST*.

I AM *SICK* OF WHAT'S GOING ON OUT THERE, Y'KNOW? THE COPS GOT THEIR *HANDS FULL* AND PEOPLE ARE GETTING AWAY WITH *MURDER* AND STUFF. I *DON'T* HAVE PATIENCE FOR BULLIES.

I'M *PRETTY GOOD* WITH *WEAPONS*. MY COUSIN TOOK ME TO SHOOTING RANGES 'TIL HE WAS STATIONED OVERSEAS. I HAVE *NO PROBLEM* WITH TAKING ORDERS...

WHAT'S WITH THE *BURNT BEAVER?*

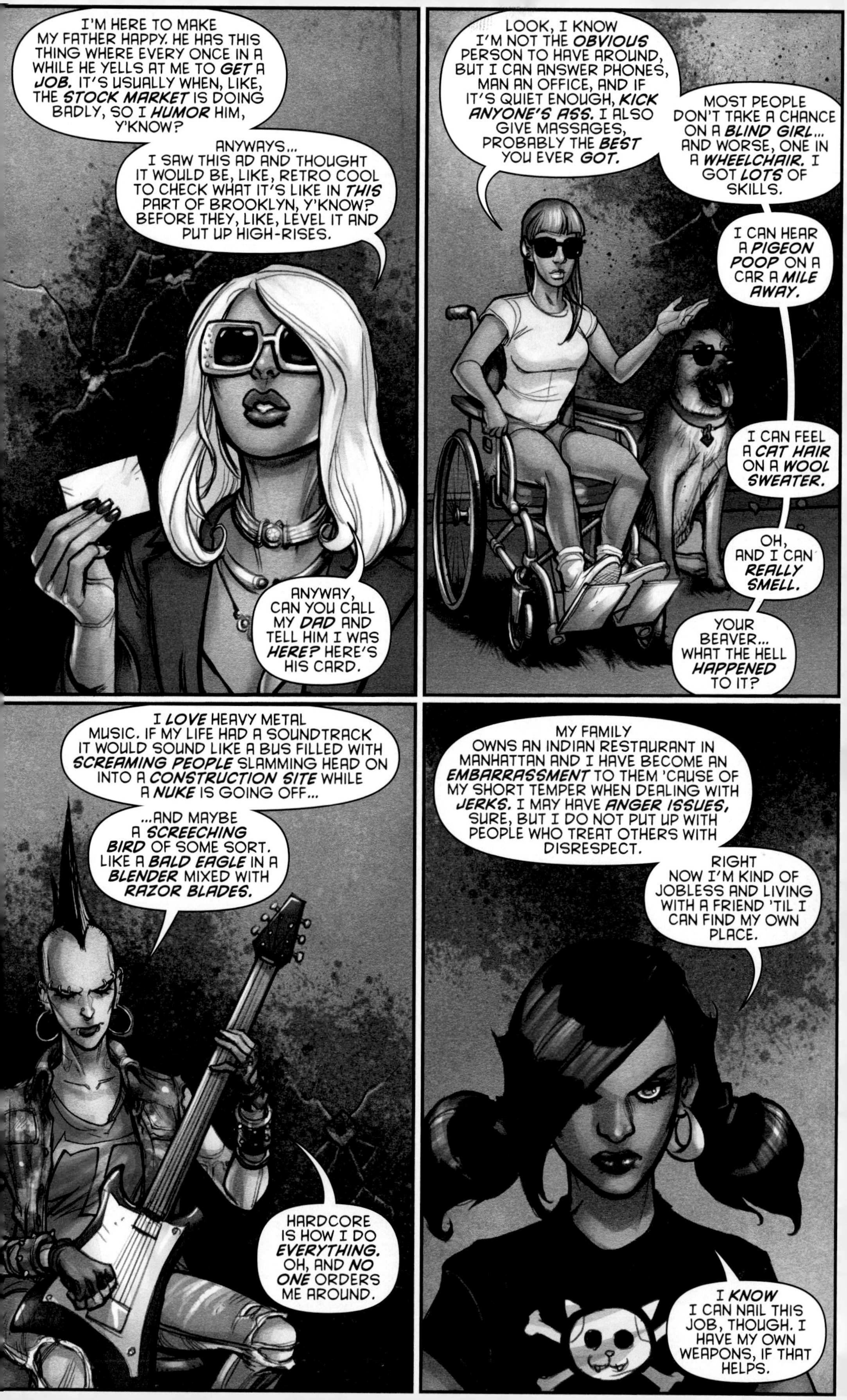
I'M HERE TO MAKE MY FATHER HAPPY. HE HAS THIS THING WHERE EVERY ONCE IN A WHILE HE YELLS AT ME TO GET A JOB. IT'S USUALLY WHEN, LIKE, THE STOCK MARKET IS DOING BADLY, SO I HUMOR HIM, Y'KNOW?
ANYWAYS... I SAW THIS AD AND THOUGHT IT WOULD BE, LIKE, RETRO COOL TO CHECK WHAT IT'S LIKE IN THIS PART OF BROOKLYN, Y'KNOW? BEFORE THEY, LIKE, LEVEL IT AND PUT UP HIGH-RISES.
ANYWAY, CAN YOU CALL MY DAD AND TELL HIM I WAS HERE? HERE'S HIS CARD.
LOOK, I KNOW I'M NOT THE OBVIOUS PERSON TO HAVE AROUND, BUT I CAN ANSWER PHONES, MAN AN OFFICE, AND IF IT'S QUIET ENOUGH, KICK ANYONE'S ASS. I ALSO GIVE MASSAGES, PROBABLY THE BEST YOU EVER GOT.
MOST PEOPLE DON'T TAKE A CHANCE ON A BLIND GIRL... AND WORSE, ONE IN A WHEELCHAIR. I GOT LOTS OF SKILLS.
I CAN HEAR A PIGEON POOP ON A CAR A MILE AWAY.
I CAN FEEL A CAT HAIR ON A WOOL SWEATER.
OH, AND I CAN REALLY SMELL.
YOUR BEAVER... WHAT THE HELL HAPPENED TO IT?
I LOVE HEAVY METAL MUSIC. IF MY LIFE HAD A SOUNDTRACK IT WOULD SOUND LIKE A BUS FILLED WITH SCREAMING PEOPLE SLAMMING HEAD ON INTO A CONSTRUCTION SITE WHILE A NUKE IS GOING OFF...
...AND MAYBE A SCREECHING BIRD OF SOME SORT. LIKE A BALD EAGLE IN A BLENDER MIXED WITH RAZOR BLADES.
HARDCORE IS HOW I DO EVERYTHING. OH, AND NO ONE ORDERS ME AROUND.
MY FAMILY OWNS AN INDIAN RESTAURANT IN MANHATTAN AND I HAVE BECOME AN EMBARRASSMENT TO THEM 'CAUSE OF MY SHORT TEMPER WHEN DEALING WITH JERKS. I MAY HAVE ANGER ISSUES, SURE, BUT I DO NOT PUT UP WITH PEOPLE WHO TREAT OTHERS WITH DISRESPECT.
RIGHT NOW I'M KIND OF JOBLESS AND LIVING WITH A FRIEND 'TIL I CAN FIND MY OWN PLACE.
I KNOW I CAN NAIL THIS JOB, THOUGH. I HAVE MY OWN WEAPONS, IF THAT HELPS.

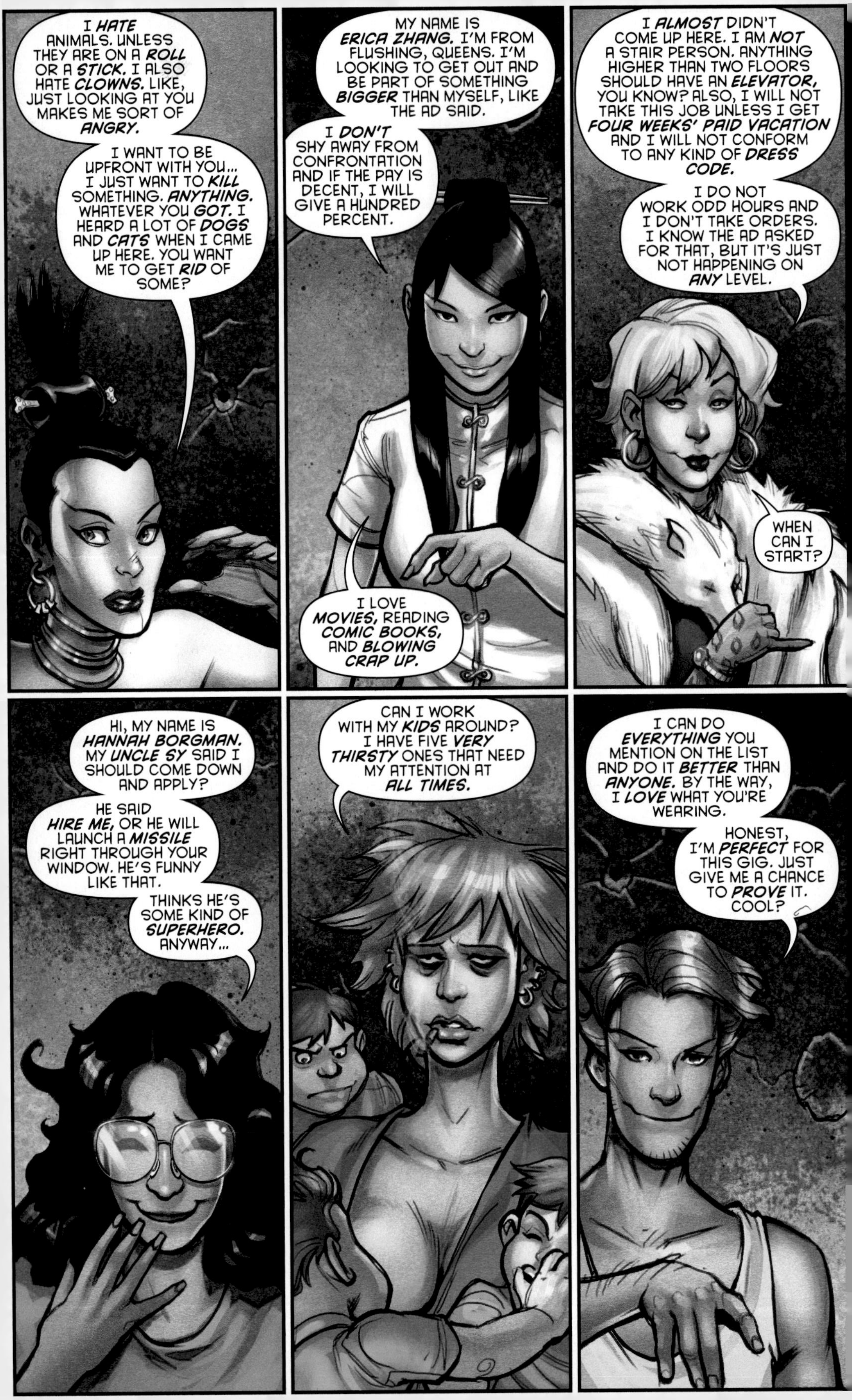
I HATE ANIMALS. UNLESS THEY ARE ON A ROLL OR A STICK. I ALSO HATE CLOWNS. LIKE, JUST LOOKING AT YOU MAKES ME SORT OF ANGRY.
I WANT TO BE UPFRONT WITH YOU... I JUST WANT TO KILL SOMETHING. ANYTHING. WHATEVER YOU GOT. I HEARD A LOT OF DOGS AND CATS WHEN I CAME UP HERE. YOU WANT ME TO GET RID OF SOME?
MY NAME IS ERICA ZHANG. I'M FROM FLUSHING, QUEENS. I'M LOOKING TO GET OUT AND BE PART OF SOMETHING BIGGER THAN MYSELF, LIKE THE AD SAID.
I DON'T SHY AWAY FROM CONFRONTATION AND IF THE PAY IS DECENT, I WILL GIVE A HUNDRED PERCENT.
I LOVE MOVIES, READING COMIC BOOKS, AND BLOWING CRAP UP.
I ALMOST DIDN'T COME UP HERE. I AM NOT A STAIR PERSON. ANYTHING HIGHER THAN TWO FLOORS SHOULD HAVE AN ELEVATOR, YOU KNOW? ALSO, I WILL NOT TAKE THIS JOB UNLESS I GET FOUR WEEKS' PAID VACATION AND I WILL NOT CONFORM TO ANY KIND OF DRESS CODE.
I DO NOT WORK ODD HOURS AND I DON'T TAKE ORDERS. I KNOW THE AD ASKED FOR THAT, BUT IT'S JUST NOT HAPPENING ON ANY LEVEL.
WHEN CAN I START?
HI, MY NAME IS HANNAH BORGMAN. MY UNCLE SY SAID I SHOULD COME DOWN AND APPLY?
HE SAID HIRE ME, OR HE WILL LAUNCH A MISSILE RIGHT THROUGH YOUR WINDOW. HE'S FUNNY LIKE THAT.
THINKS HE'S SOME KIND OF SUPERHERO. ANYWAY...
CAN I WORK WITH MY KIDS AROUND? I HAVE FIVE VERY THIRSTY ONES THAT NEED MY ATTENTION AT ALL TIMES.
I CAN DO EVERYTHING YOU MENTION ON THE LIST AND DO IT BETTER THAN ANYONE. BY THE WAY, I LOVE WHAT YOU'RE WEARING.
HONEST, I'M PERFECT FOR THIS GIG. JUST GIVE ME A CHANCE TO PROVE IT. COOL?

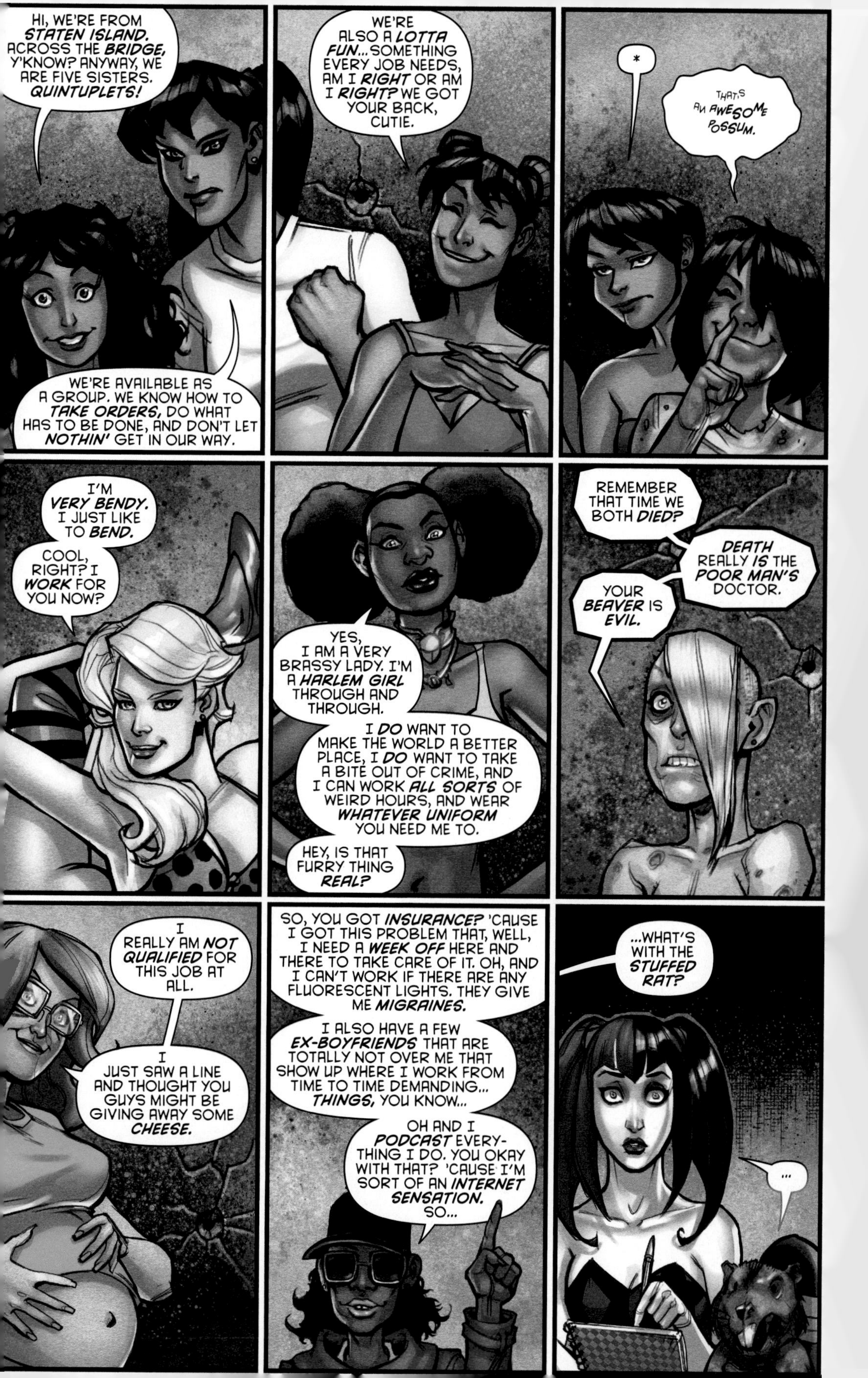
HI, WE'RE FROM STATEN ISLAND. ACROSS THE BRIDGE, Y'KNOW? ANYWAY, WE ARE FIVE SISTERS. QUINTUPLETS!
WE'RE AVAILABLE AS A GROUP. WE KNOW HOW TO TAKE ORDERS, DO WHAT HAS TO BE DONE, AND DON'T LET NOTHIN' GET IN OUR WAY.
WE'RE ALSO A LOTTA FUN... SOMETHING EVERY JOB NEEDS, AM I RIGHT OR AM I RIGHT? WE GOT YOUR BACK, CUTIE.
*
THAT'S AN AWESOME POSSUM.
I'M VERY BENDY. I JUST LIKE TO BEND.
COOL, RIGHT? I WORK FOR YOU NOW?
YES, I AM A VERY BRASSY LADY. I'M A HARLEM GIRL THROUGH AND THROUGH.
I DO WANT TO MAKE THE WORLD A BETTER PLACE, I DO WANT TO TAKE A BITE OUT OF CRIME, AND I CAN WORK ALL SORTS OF WEIRD HOURS, AND WEAR WHATEVER UNIFORM YOU NEED ME TO.
HEY, IS THAT FURRY THING REAL?
REMEMBER THAT TIME WE BOTH DIED?
DEATH REALLY IS THE POOR MAN'S DOCTOR.
YOUR BEAVER IS EVIL.
I REALLY AM NOT QUALIFIED FOR THIS JOB AT ALL.
I JUST SAW A LINE AND THOUGHT YOU GUYS MIGHT BE GIVING AWAY SOME CHEESE.
SO, YOU GOT INSURANCE? 'CAUSE I GOT THIS PROBLEM THAT, WELL, I NEED A WEEK OFF HERE AND THERE TO TAKE CARE OF IT. OH, AND I CAN'T WORK IF THERE ARE ANY FLUORESCENT LIGHTS. THEY GIVE ME MIGRAINES.
I ALSO HAVE A FEW EX-BOYFRIENDS THAT ARE TOTALLY NOT OVER ME THAT SHOW UP WHERE I WORK FROM TIME TO TIME DEMANDING... THINGS, YOU KNOW...
OH AND I PODCAST EVERYTHING I DO. YOU OKAY WITH THAT? 'CAUSE I'M SORT OF AN INTERNET SENSATION. SO...
...WHAT'S WITH THE STUFFED RAT?
...

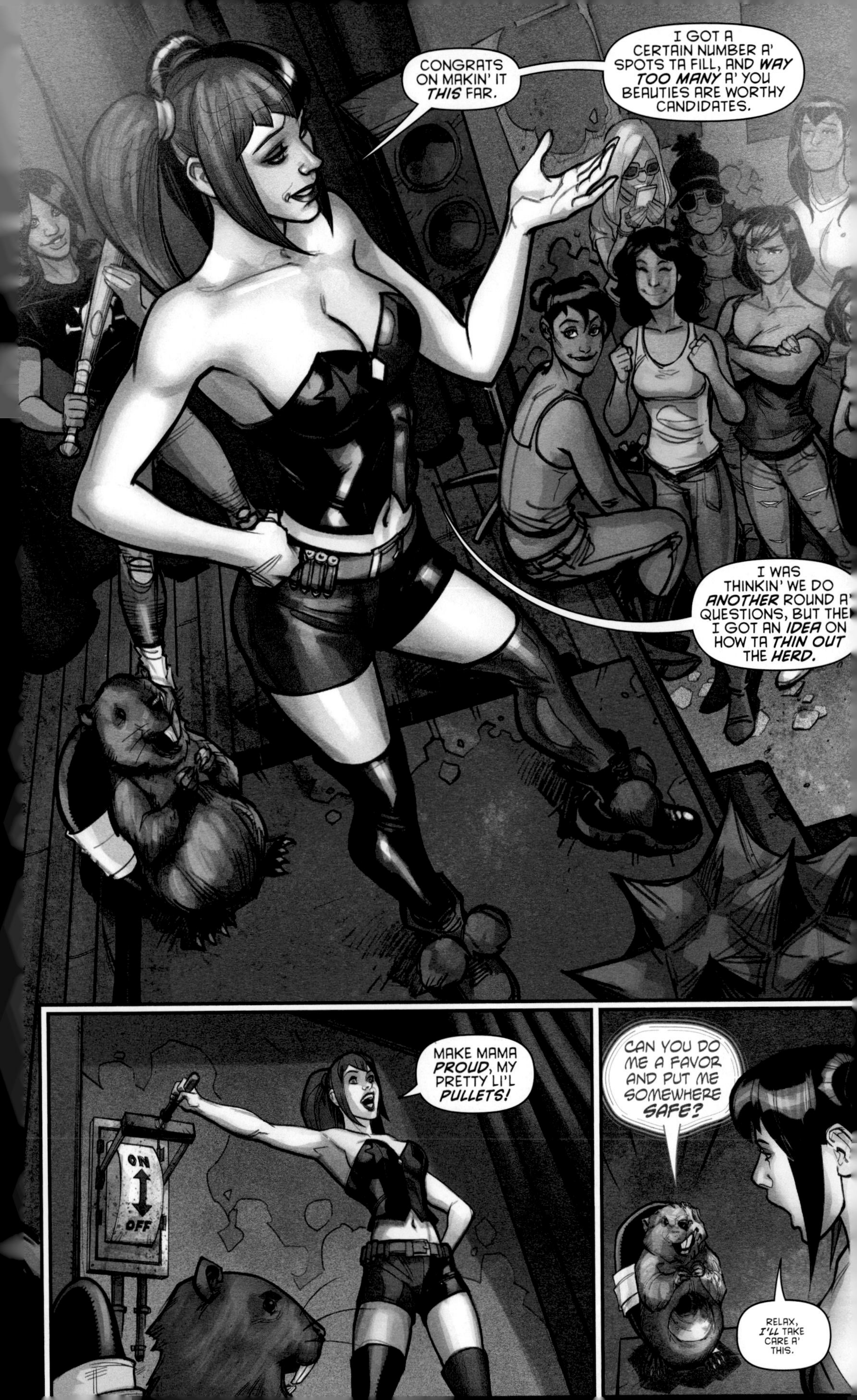
CONGRATS ON MAKIN' IT THIS FAR.
I GOT A CERTAIN NUMBER A' SPOTS TA FILL, AND WAY TOO MANY A' YOU BEAUTIES ARE WORTHY CANDIDATES.
I WAS THINKIN' WE DO ANOTHER ROUND A' QUESTIONS, BUT THE I GOT AN IDEA ON HOW TA THIN OUT THE HERD.
ON
OFF
MAKE MAMA PROUD, MY PRETTY LI'L PULLETS!
CAN YOU DO ME A FAVOR AND PUT ME SOMEWHERE SAFE?
RELAX, I'LL TAKE CARE A' THIS.

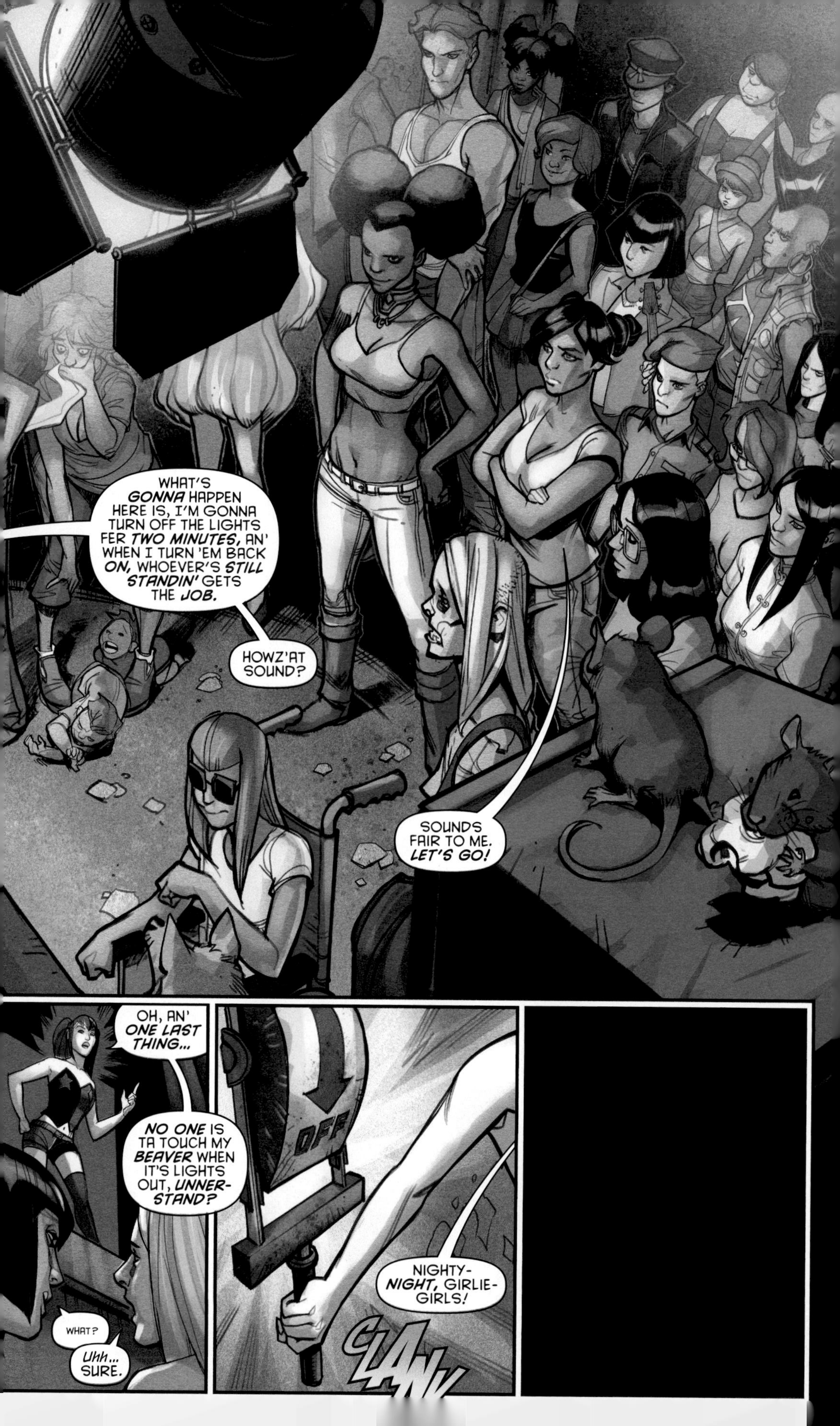
WHAT'S GONNA HAPPEN HERE IS, I'M GONNA TURN OFF THE LIGHTS FER TWO MINUTES, AN' WHEN I TURN 'EM BACK ON, WHOEVER'S STILL STANDIN' GETS THE JOB.
HOWZ'AT SOUND?
SOUNDS FAIR TO ME. LET'S GO!
OH, AN' ONE LAST THING...
NO ONE IS TA TOUCH MY BEAVER WHEN IT'S LIGHTS OUT, UNNER-STAND?
WHAT?
Uhh... SURE.
OFF
NIGHTY-NIGHT, GIRLIE-GIRLS!
CLANK

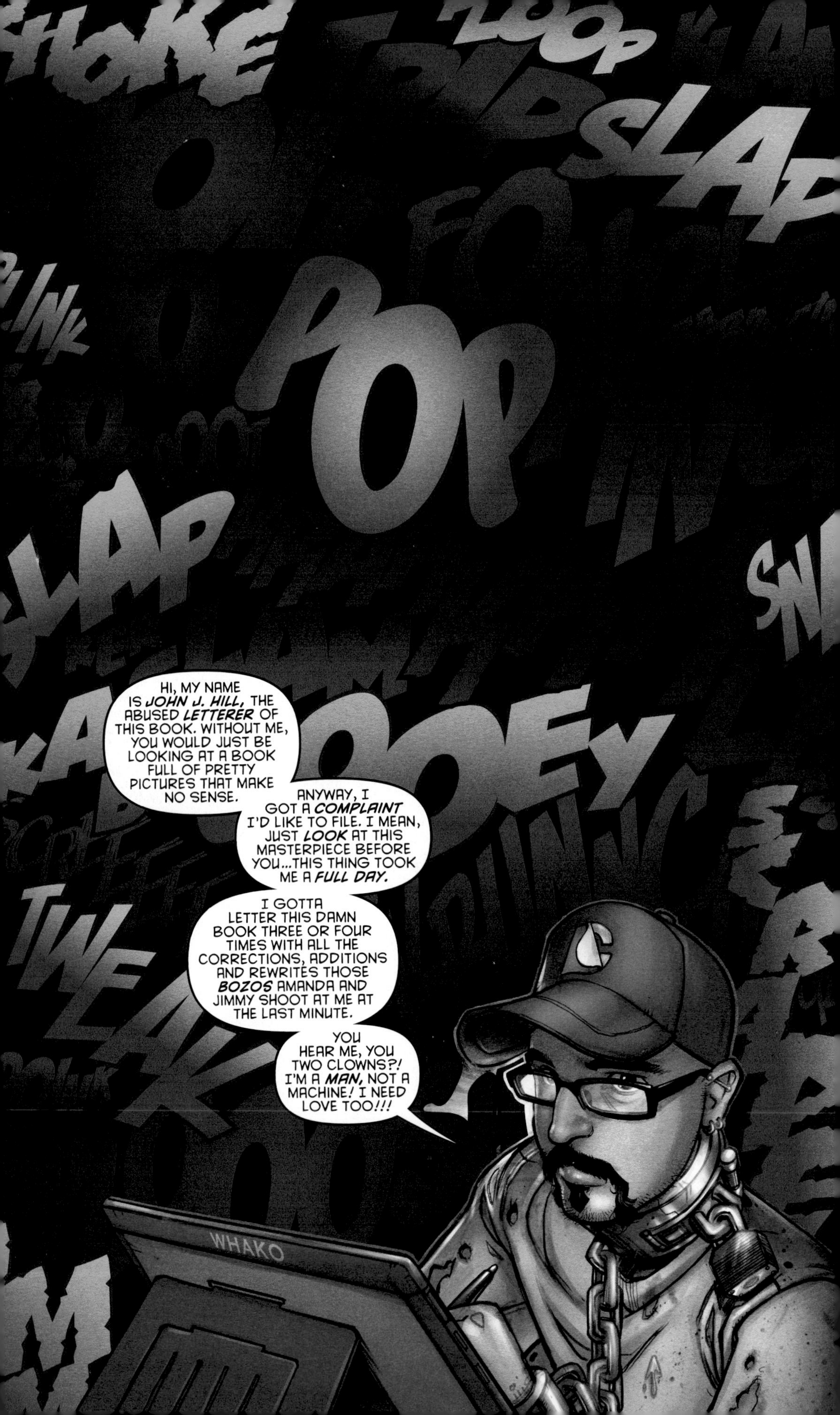
POP
HI, MY NAME IS JOHN J. HILL, THE ABUSED LETTERER OF THIS BOOK. WITHOUT ME, YOU WOULD JUST BE LOOKING AT A BOOK FULL OF PRETTY PICTURES THAT MAKE NO SENSE.
ANYWAY, I GOT A COMPLAINT I'D LIKE TO FILE. I MEAN, JUST LOOK AT THIS MASTERPIECE BEFORE YOU...THIS THING TOOK ME A FULL DAY.
I GOTTA LETTER THIS DAMN BOOK THREE OR FOUR TIMES WITH ALL THE CORRECTIONS, ADDITIONS AND REWRITES THOSE BOZOS AMANDA AND JIMMY SHOOT AT ME AT THE LAST MINUTE.
YOU HEAR ME, YOU TWO CLOWNS?! I'M A MAN, NOT A MACHINE! I NEED LOVE TOO!!!
WHAKO

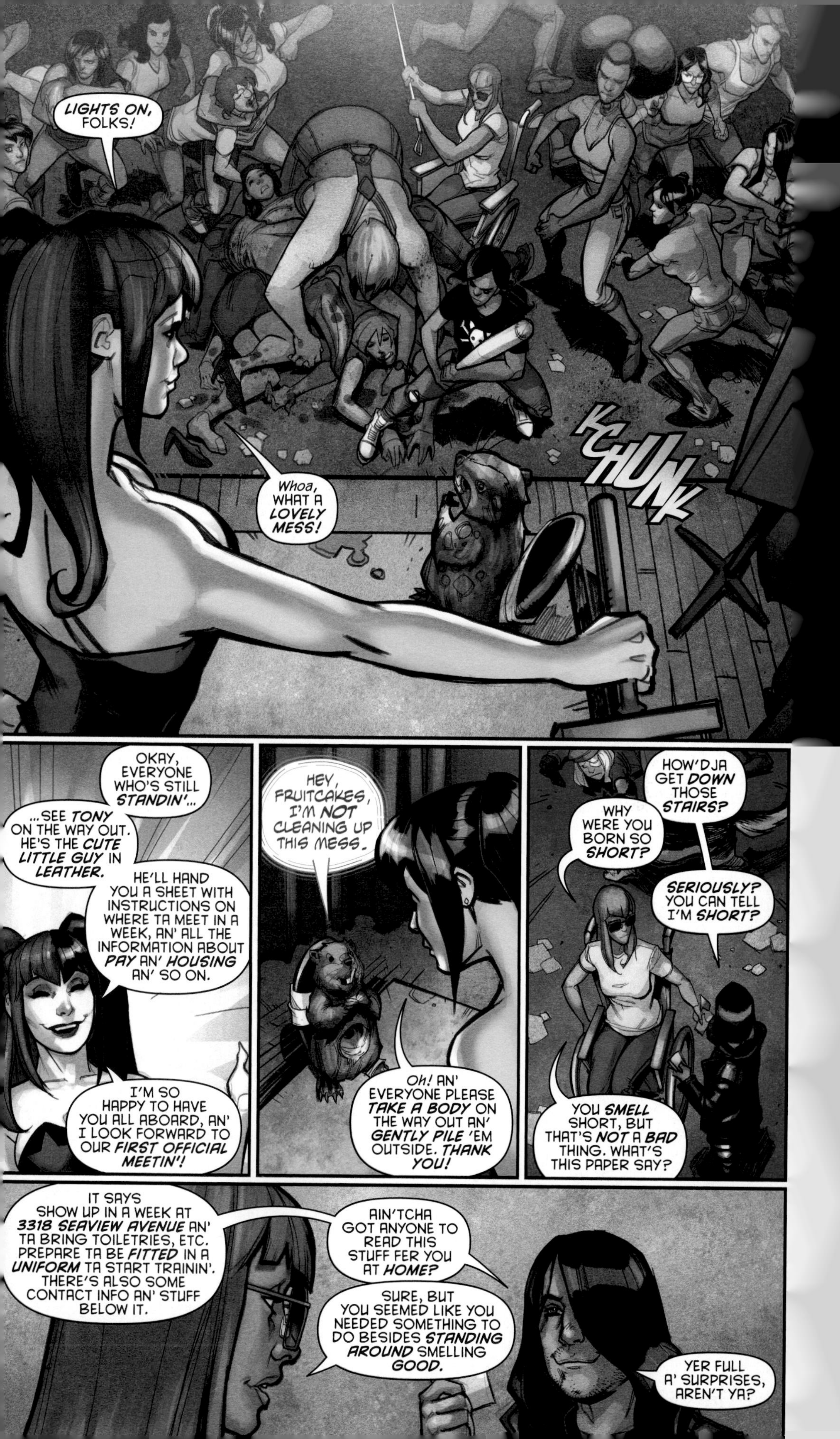
LIGHTS ON, FOLKS!
Whoa, WHAT A LOVELY MESS!
KCHUNK
OKAY, EVERYONE WHO'S STILL STANDIN'...
...SEE TONY ON THE WAY OUT. HE'S THE CUTE LITTLE GUY IN LEATHER.
HE'LL HAND YOU A SHEET WITH INSTRUCTIONS ON WHERE TA MEET IN A WEEK, AN' ALL THE INFORMATION ABOUT PAY AN' HOUSING AN' SO ON.
I'M SO HAPPY TO HAVE YOU ALL ABOARD, AN' I LOOK FORWARD TO OUR FIRST OFFICIAL MEETIN'!
HEY, FRUITCAKES, I'M NOT CLEANING UP THIS MESS.
Oh! AN' EVERYONE PLEASE TAKE A BODY ON THE WAY OUT AN' GENTLY PILE 'EM OUTSIDE. THANK YOU!
HOW'DJA GET DOWN THOSE STAIRS?
WHY WERE YOU BORN SO SHORT?
SERIOUSLY? YOU CAN TELL I'M SHORT?
YOU SMELL SHORT, BUT THAT'S NOT A BAD THING. WHAT'S THIS PAPER SAY?
IT SAYS SHOW UP IN A WEEK AT 3318 SEAVIEW AVENUE AN' TA BRING TOILETRIES, ETC. PREPARE TA BE FITTED IN A UNIFORM TA START TRAININ'. THERE'S ALSO SOME CONTACT INFO AN' STUFF BELOW IT.
AIN'TCHA GOT ANYONE TO READ THIS STUFF FER YOU AT HOME?
SURE, BUT YOU SEEMED LIKE YOU NEEDED SOMETHING TO DO BESIDES STANDING AROUND SMELLING GOOD.
YER FULL A' SURPRISES, AREN'T YA?

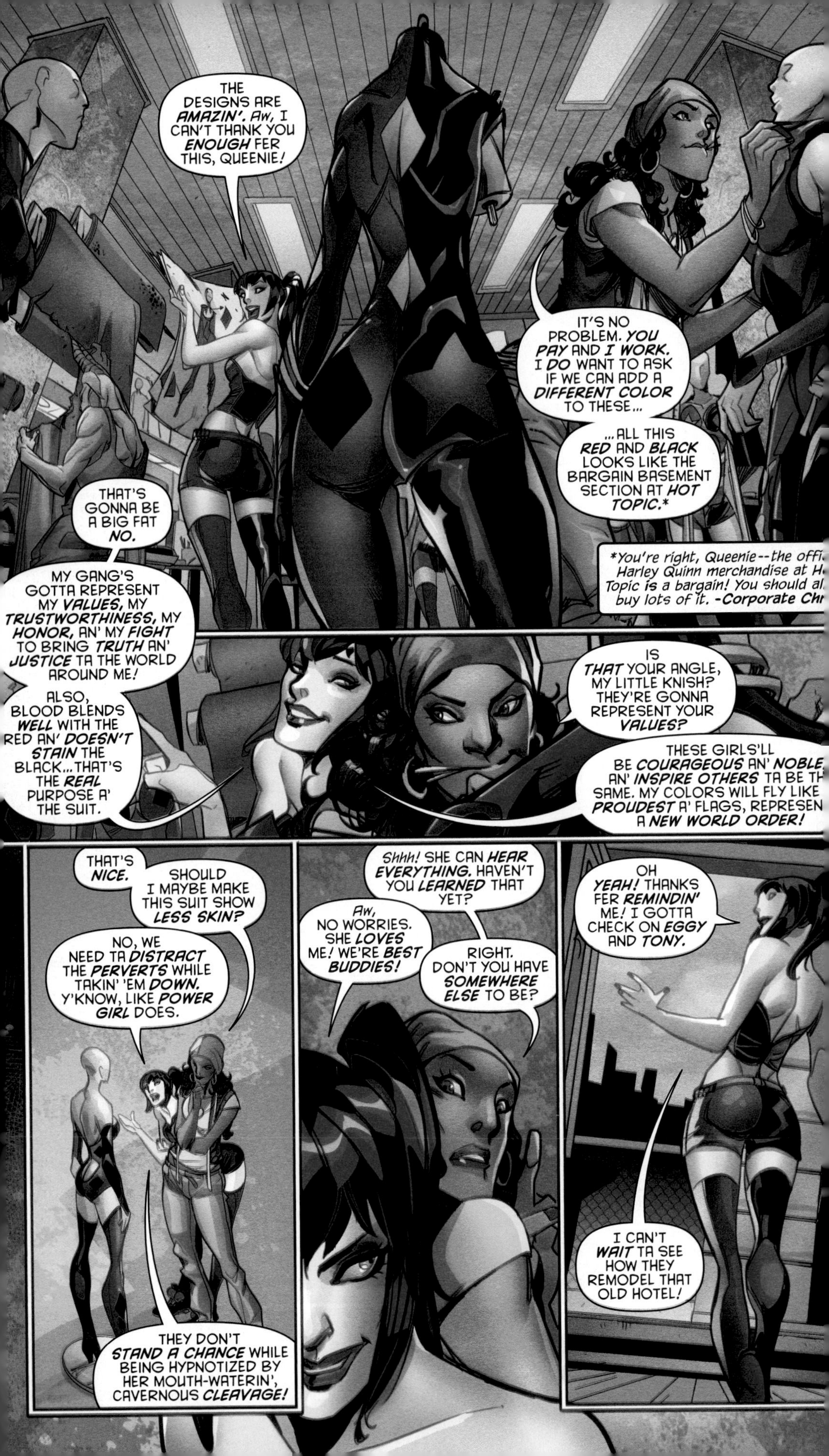
THE DESIGNS ARE AMAZIN'. AW, I CAN'T THANK YOU ENOUGH FER THIS, QUEENIE!
IT'S NO PROBLEM. YOU PAY AND I WORK. I DO WANT TO ASK IF WE CAN ADD A DIFFERENT COLOR TO THESE...
...ALL THIS RED AND BLACK LOOKS LIKE THE BARGAIN BASEMENT SECTION AT HOT TOPIC.*
THAT'S GONNA BE A BIG FAT NO.
MY GANG'S GOTTA REPRESENT MY VALUES, MY TRUSTWORTHINESS, MY HONOR, AN' MY FIGHT TO BRING TRUTH AN' JUSTICE TA THE WORLD AROUND ME!
*You're right, Queenie--the offi Harley Quinn merchandise at H Topic is a bargain! You should al buy lots of it. -Corporate Ch
ALSO, BLOOD BLENDS WELL WITH THE RED AN' DOESN'T STAIN THE BLACK...THAT'S THE REAL PURPOSE A' THE SUIT.
IS THAT YOUR ANGLE, MY LITTLE KNISH? THEY'RE GONNA REPRESENT YOUR VALUES?
THESE GIRLS'LL BE COURAGEOUS AN' NOBLE AN' INSPIRE OTHERS TA BE TH SAME. MY COLORS WILL FLY LIKE PROUDEST A' FLAGS, REPRESEN A NEW WORLD ORDER!
THAT'S NICE.
SHOULD I MAYBE MAKE THIS SUIT SHOW LESS SKIN?
NO, WE NEED TA DISTRACT THE PERVERTS WHILE TAKIN' 'EM DOWN. Y'KNOW, LIKE POWER GIRL DOES.
THEY DON'T STAND A CHANCE WHILE BEING HYPNOTIZED BY HER MOUTH-WATERIN', CAVERNOUS CLEAVAGE!
SHHH! SHE CAN HEAR EVERYTHING. HAVEN'T YOU LEARNED THAT YET?
AW, NO WORRIES. SHE LOVES ME! WE'RE BEST BUDDIES!
RIGHT. DON'T YOU HAVE SOMEWHERE ELSE TO BE?
OH YEAH! THANKS FER REMINDIN' ME! I GOTTA CHECK ON EGGY AND TONY.
I CAN'T WAIT TA SEE HOW THEY REMODEL THAT OLD HOTEL!

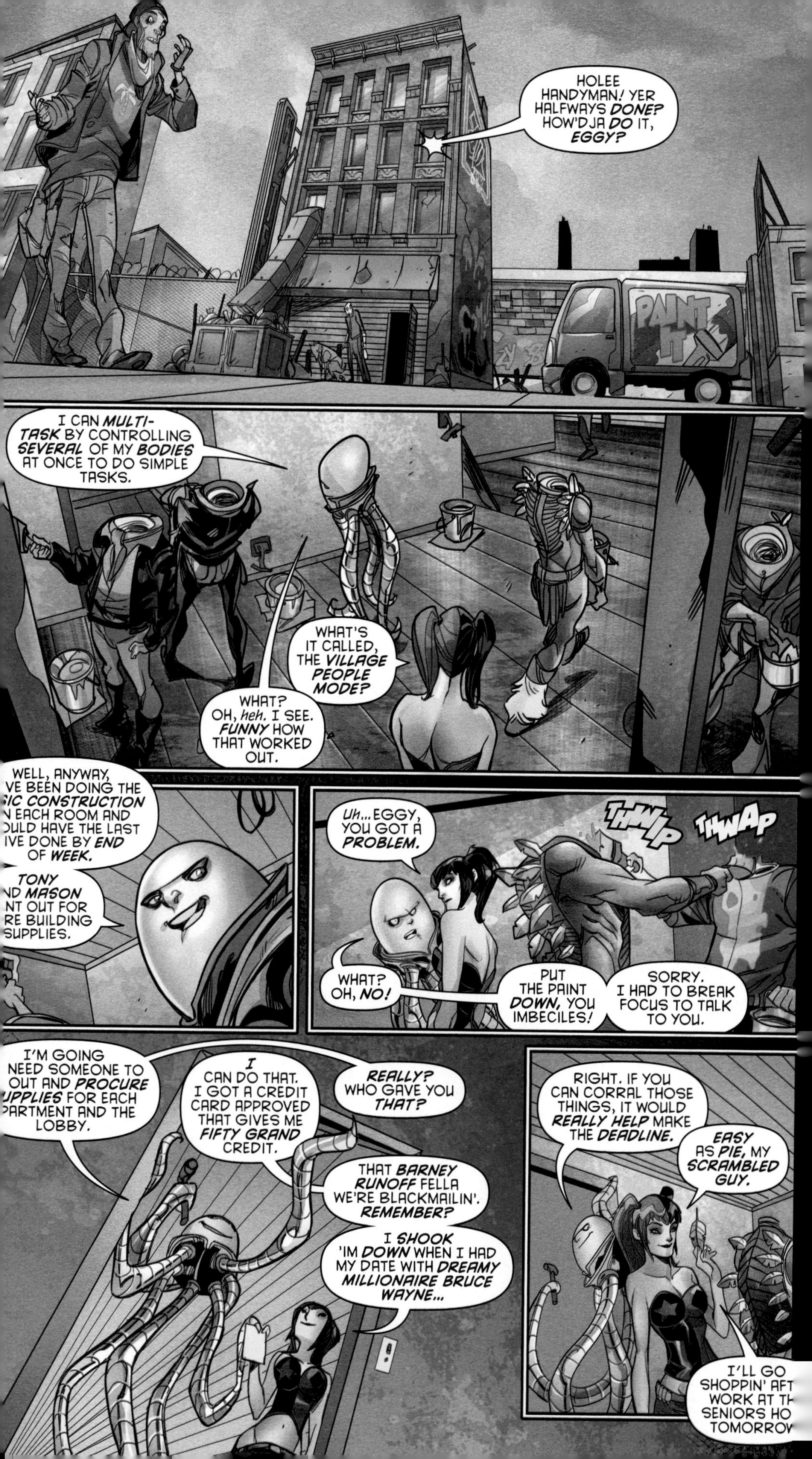
HOLEE HANDYMAN! YER HALFWAYS DONE? HOW'DJA DO IT, EGGY?
I CAN MULTI-TASK BY CONTROLLING SEVERAL OF MY BODIES AT ONCE TO DO SIMPLE TASKS.
WHAT'S IT CALLED, THE VILLAGE PEOPLE MODE?
WHAT? OH, heh. I SEE. FUNNY HOW THAT WORKED OUT.
WELL, ANYWAY, VE BEEN DOING THE SIC CONSTRUCTION N EACH ROOM AND OULD HAVE THE LAST IVE DONE BY END OF WEEK.
TONY ND MASON NT OUT FOR RE BUILDING SUPPLIES.
Uh... EGGY, YOU GOT A PROBLEM.
THWIP
THWAP
WHAT? OH, NO!
PUT THE PAINT DOWN, YOU IMBECILES!
SORRY. I HAD TO BREAK FOCUS TO TALK TO YOU.
I'M GOING NEED SOMEONE TO OUT AND PROCURE UPPLIES FOR EACH PARTMENT AND THE LOBBY.
I CAN DO THAT. I GOT A CREDIT CARD APPROVED THAT GIVES ME FIFTY GRAND CREDIT.
REALLY? WHO GAVE YOU THAT?
THAT BARNEY RUNOFF FELLA WE'RE BLACKMAILIN'. REMEMBER?
I SHOOK 'IM DOWN WHEN I HAD MY DATE WITH DREAMY MILLIONAIRE BRUCE WAYNE...
RIGHT. IF YOU CAN CORRAL THOSE THINGS, IT WOULD REALLY HELP MAKE THE DEADLINE.
EASY AS PIE, MY SCRAMBLED GUY.
I'LL GO SHOPPIN' AFT WORK AT TH SENIORS HO TOMORROW

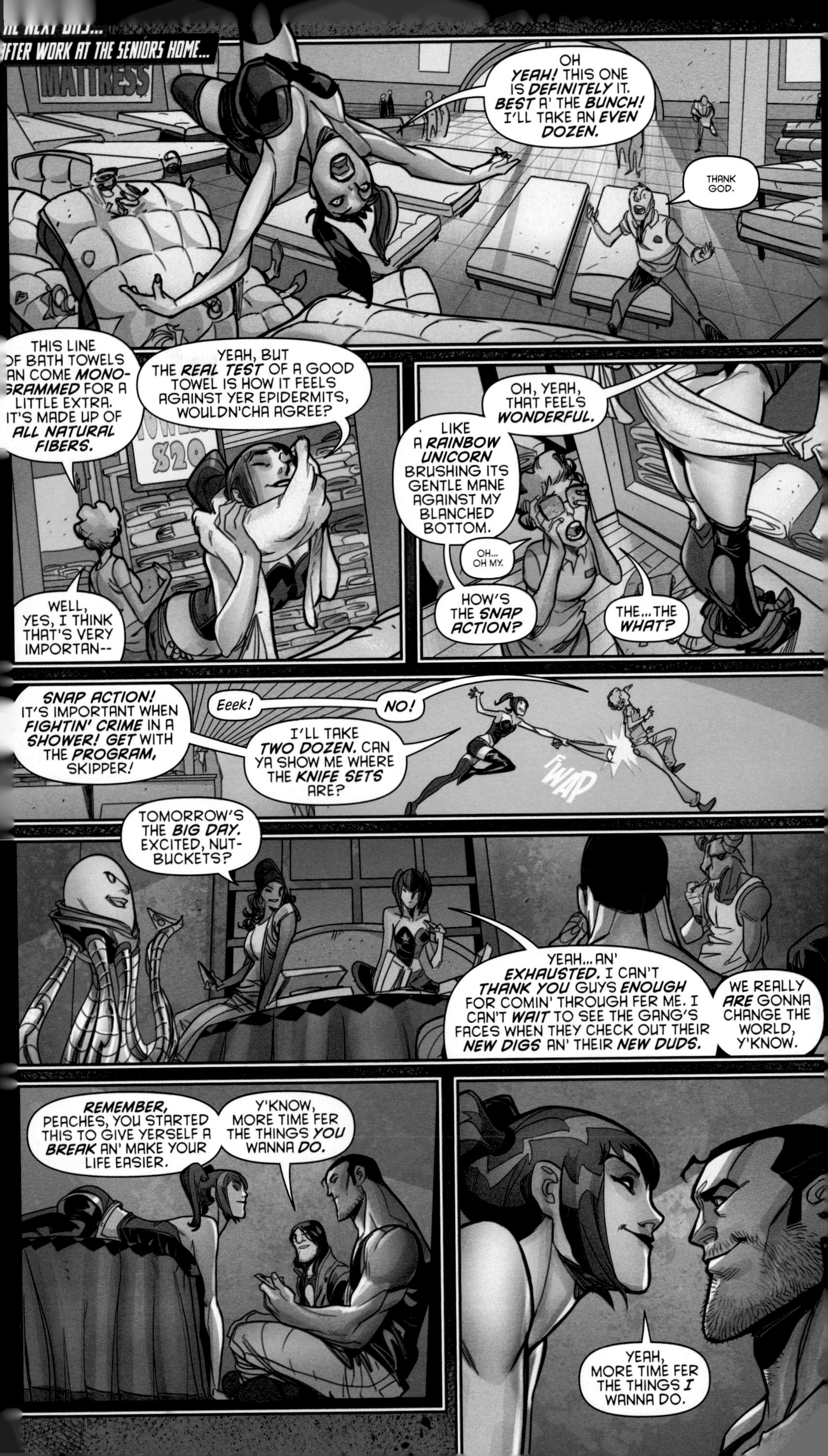

AFTER WORK AT THE SENIORS HOME...
MATTRESS
OH YEAH! THIS ONE IS DEFINITELY IT. BEST A' THE BUNCH! I'LL TAKE AN EVEN DOZEN.
THANK GOD.
THIS LINE OF BATH TOWELS CAN COME MONOGRAMMED FOR A LITTLE EXTRA. IT'S MADE UP OF ALL NATURAL FIBERS.
YEAH, BUT THE REAL TEST OF A GOOD TOWEL IS HOW IT FEELS AGAINST YER EPIDERMITS, WOULDN'CHA AGREE?
WELL, YES, I THINK THAT'S VERY IMPORTAN--
OH, YEAH, THAT FEELS WONDERFUL.
LIKE A RAINBOW UNICORN BRUSHING ITS GENTLE MANE AGAINST MY BLANCHED BOTTOM.
OH... OH MY.
HOW'S THE SNAP ACTION?
THE... THE WHAT?
SNAP ACTION! IT'S IMPORTANT WHEN FIGHTIN' CRIME IN A SHOWER! GET WITH THE PROGRAM, SKIPPER!
Eeek!
NO!
I'LL TAKE TWO DOZEN. CAN YA SHOW ME WHERE THE KNIFE SETS ARE?
FWAP
TOMORROW'S THE BIG DAY. EXCITED, NUT-BUCKETS?
YEAH... AN' EXHAUSTED. I CAN'T THANK YOU GUYS ENOUGH FOR COMIN' THROUGH FER ME. I CAN'T WAIT TO SEE THE GANG'S FACES WHEN THEY CHECK OUT THEIR NEW DIGS AN' THEIR NEW DUDS.
WE REALLY ARE GONNA CHANGE THE WORLD, Y'KNOW.
REMEMBER, PEACHES, YOU STARTED THIS TO GIVE YERSELF A BREAK AN' MAKE YOUR LIFE EASIER.
Y'KNOW, MORE TIME FER THE THINGS YOU WANNA DO.
YEAH, MORE TIME FER THE THINGS I WANNA DO.

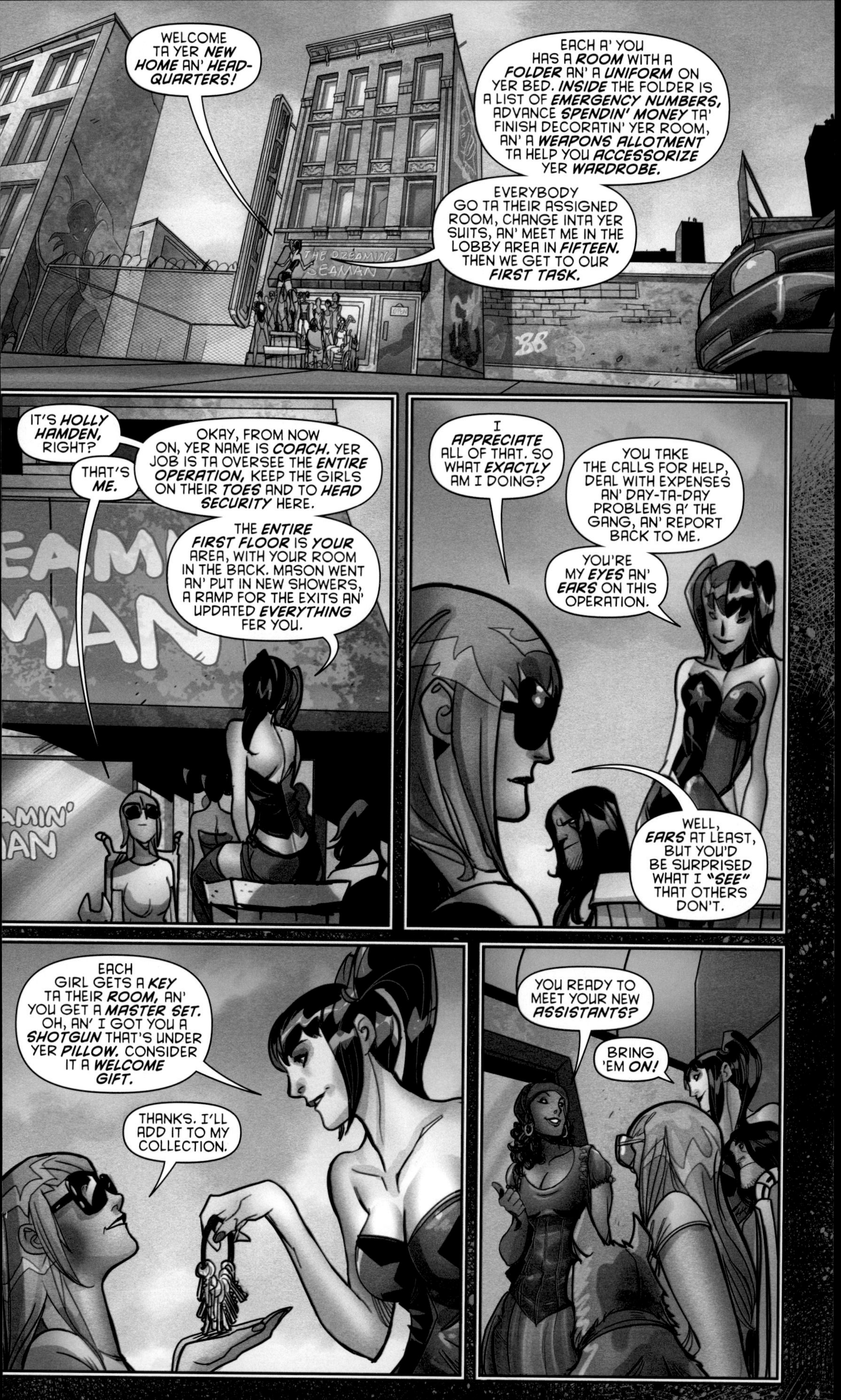

WELCOME TA YER NEW HOME AN' HEAD-QUARTERS!
EACH A' YOU HAS A ROOM WITH A FOLDER AN' A UNIFORM ON YER BED. INSIDE THE FOLDER IS A LIST OF EMERGENCY NUMBERS, ADVANCE SPENDIN' MONEY TA' FINISH DECORATIN' YER ROOM, AN' A WEAPONS ALLOTMENT TA HELP YOU ACCESSORIZE YER WARDROBE.
EVERYBODY GO TA THEIR ASSIGNED ROOM, CHANGE INTA YER SUITS, AN' MEET ME IN THE LOBBY AREA IN FIFTEEN. THEN WE GET TO OUR FIRST TASK.
THE DREAMING SEAMAN
IT'S HOLLY HAMDEN, RIGHT?
THAT'S ME.
OKAY, FROM NOW ON, YER NAME IS COACH. YER JOB IS TA OVERSEE THE ENTIRE OPERATION, KEEP THE GIRLS ON THEIR TOES AND TO HEAD SECURITY HERE.
THE ENTIRE FIRST FLOOR IS YOUR AREA, WITH YOUR ROOM IN THE BACK. MASON WENT AN' PUT IN NEW SHOWERS, A RAMP FOR THE EXITS AN' UPDATED EVERYTHING FER YOU.
I APPRECIATE ALL OF THAT. SO WHAT EXACTLY AM I DOING?
YOU TAKE THE CALLS FOR HELP, DEAL WITH EXPENSES AN' DAY-TA-DAY PROBLEMS A' THE GANG, AN' REPORT BACK TO ME.
YOU'RE MY EYES AN' EARS ON THIS OPERATION.
WELL, EARS AT LEAST, BUT YOU'D BE SURPRISED WHAT I "SEE" THAT OTHERS DON'T.
EACH GIRL GETS A KEY TA THEIR ROOM, AN' YOU GET A MASTER SET. OH, AN' I GOT YOU A SHOTGUN THAT'S UNDER YER PILLOW. CONSIDER IT A WELCOME GIFT.
THANKS. I'LL ADD IT TO MY COLLECTION.
YOU READY TO MEET YOUR NEW ASSISTANTS?
BRING 'EM ON!

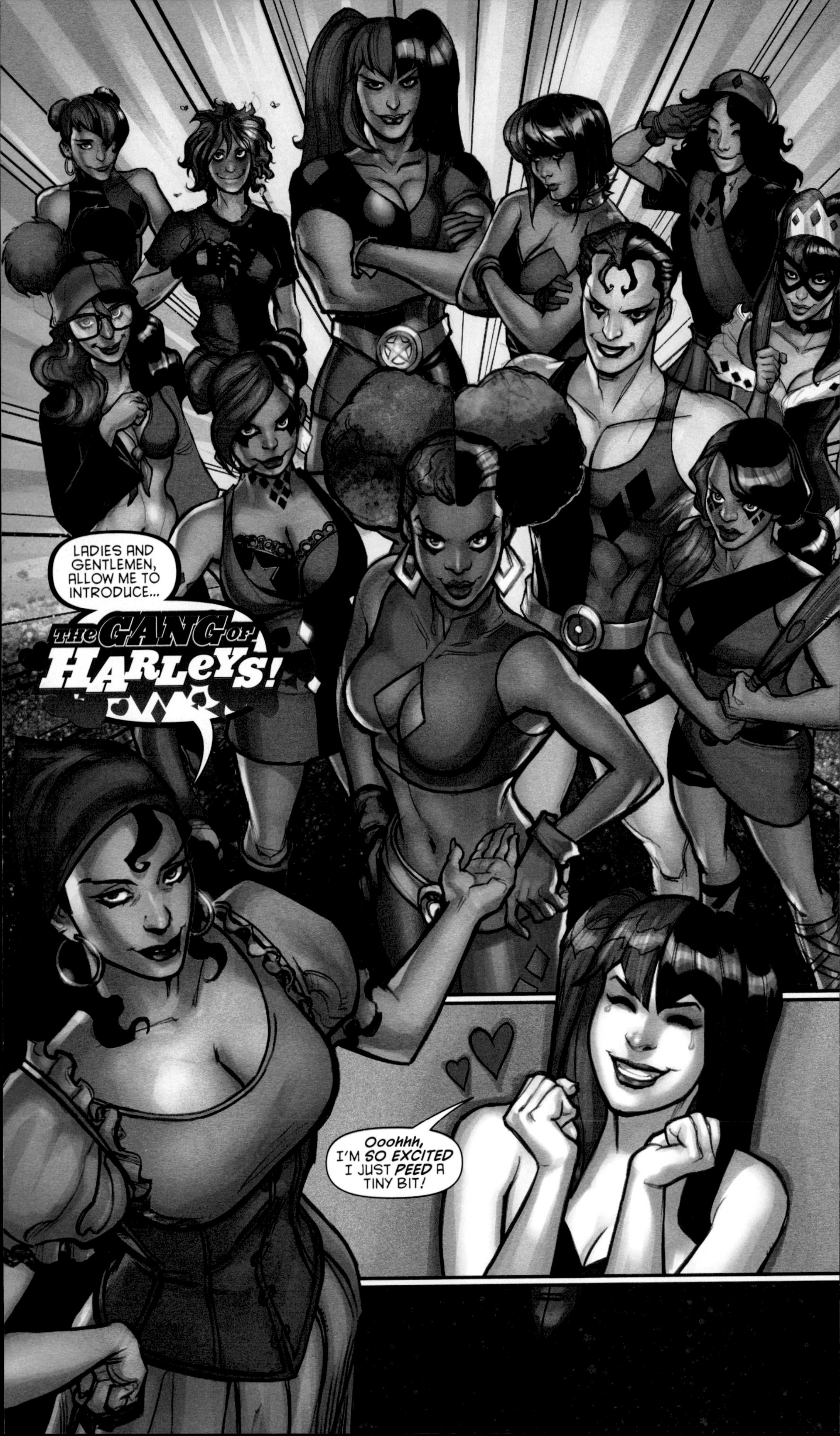
LADIES AND GENTLEMEN, ALLOW ME TO INTRODUCE...
THE GANG OF HARLEYS!
Ooohhh, I'M SO EXCITED I JUST PEED A TINY BIT!

ARLEY QUINN #14
iant cover by **AMANDA CONNER & ALEX SINCLAIR**

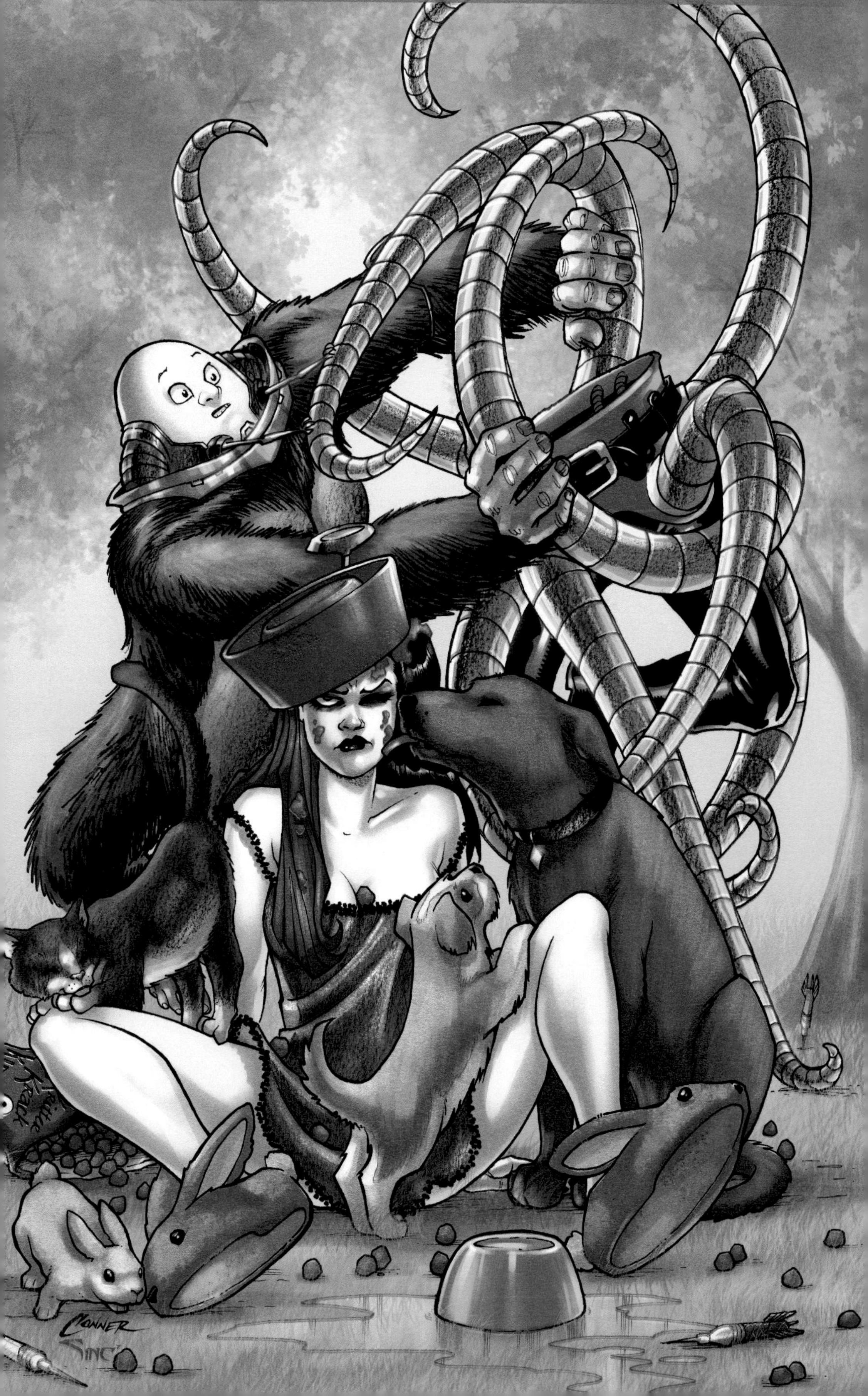

HARLEY QUINN #14
Flash 75th anniversary variant cover by **BRUCE TIMM**

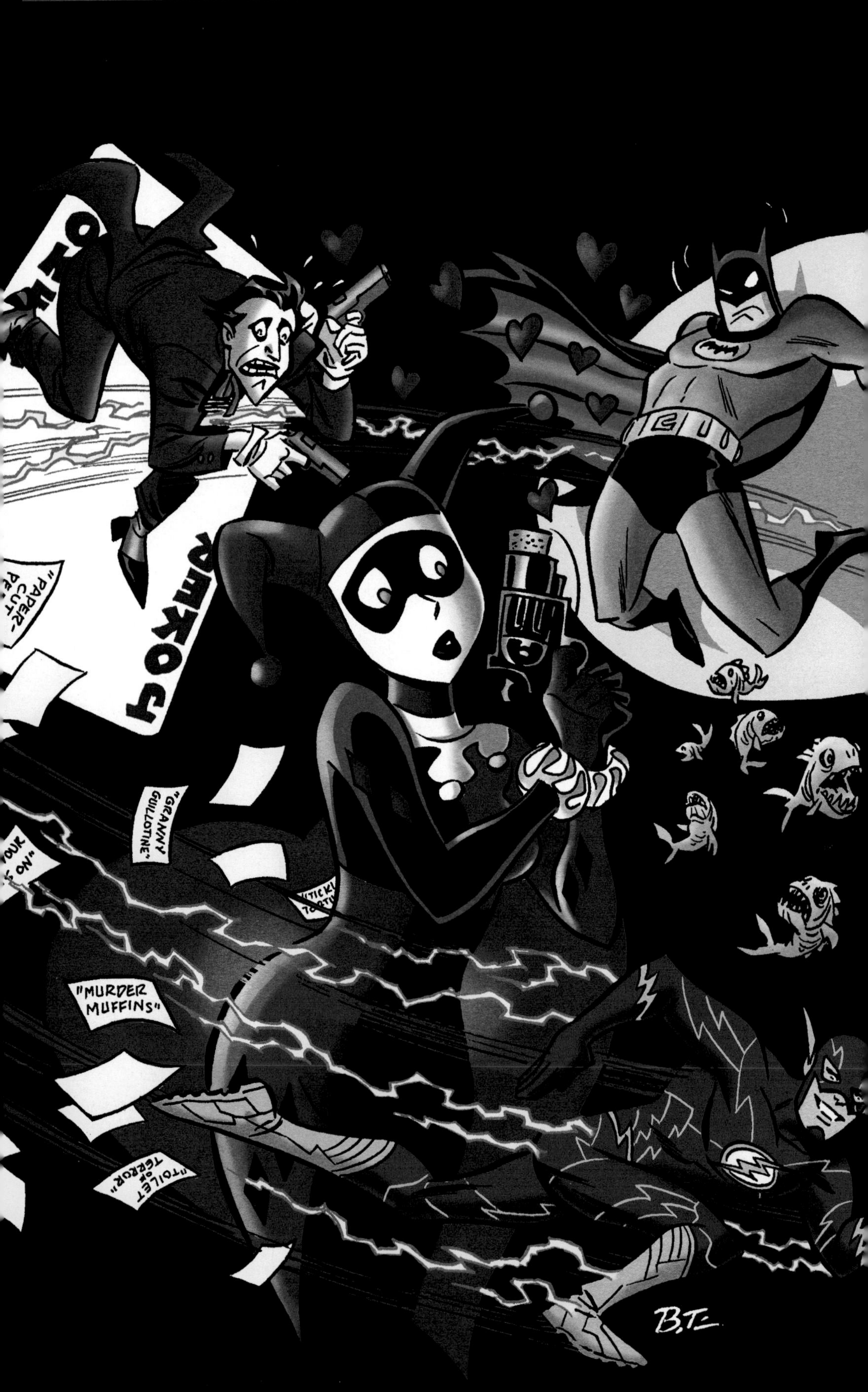
"GRANNY GUILLOTINE"
"MURDER MUFFINS"
"TOILET OF TERROR"
B.T.

HARLEY QUINN #15

Variant cover by **AMANDA CONNER, DAVE JOHNSON & ALEX SINCLAIR**

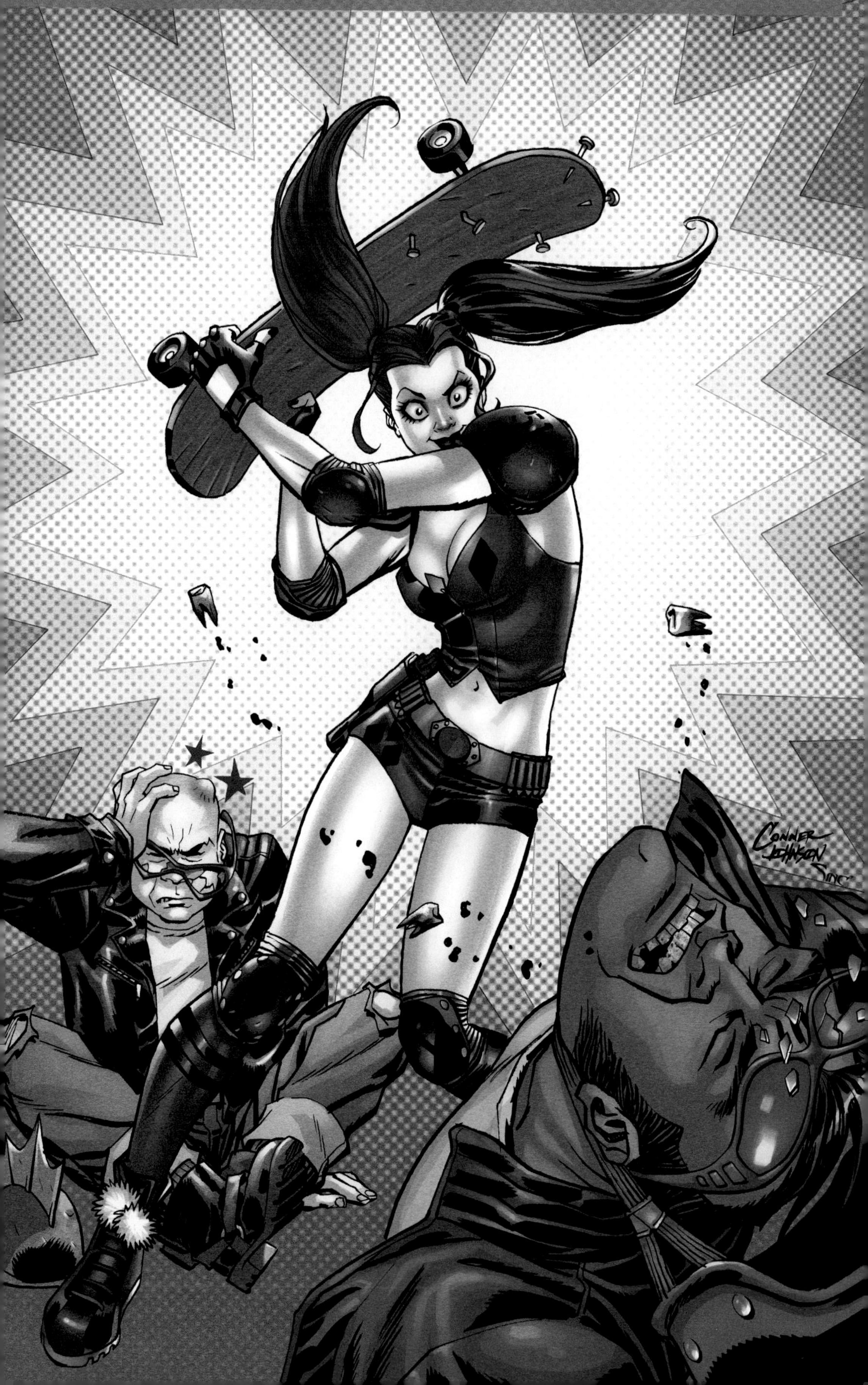
CONNER
JOHNSON
SINC

HARLEY QUINN #15
Harley Quinn Month variant cover by **MARCO D'ALFONSO**

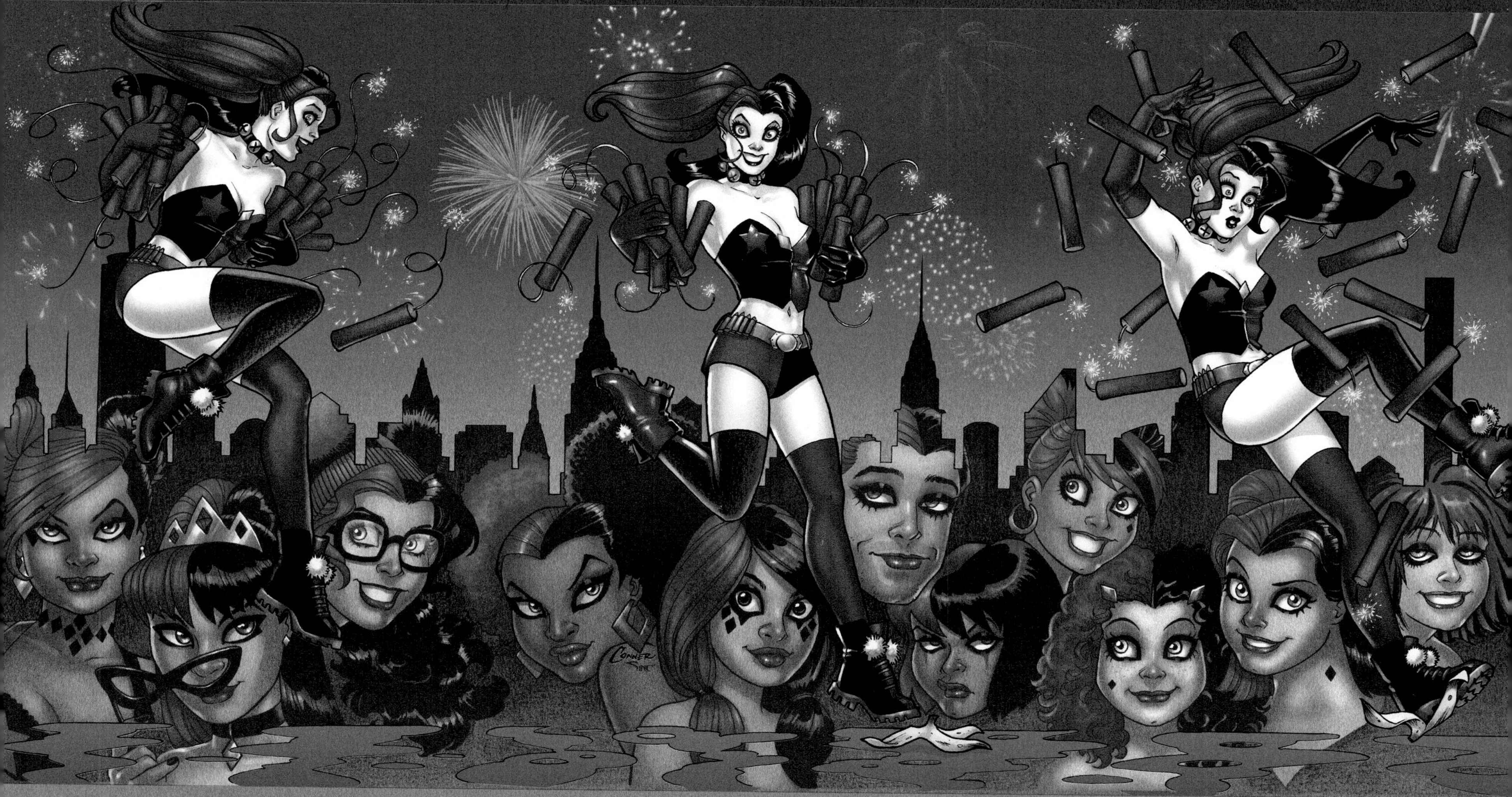
CONNER

HARLEY QUINN #16
Full triptych cover by **AMANDA CONNER & ALEX SINCLAIR**

HARLEY QUINN #16
Jailhouse Rock movie poster variant cover by **DAVE JOHNSON**

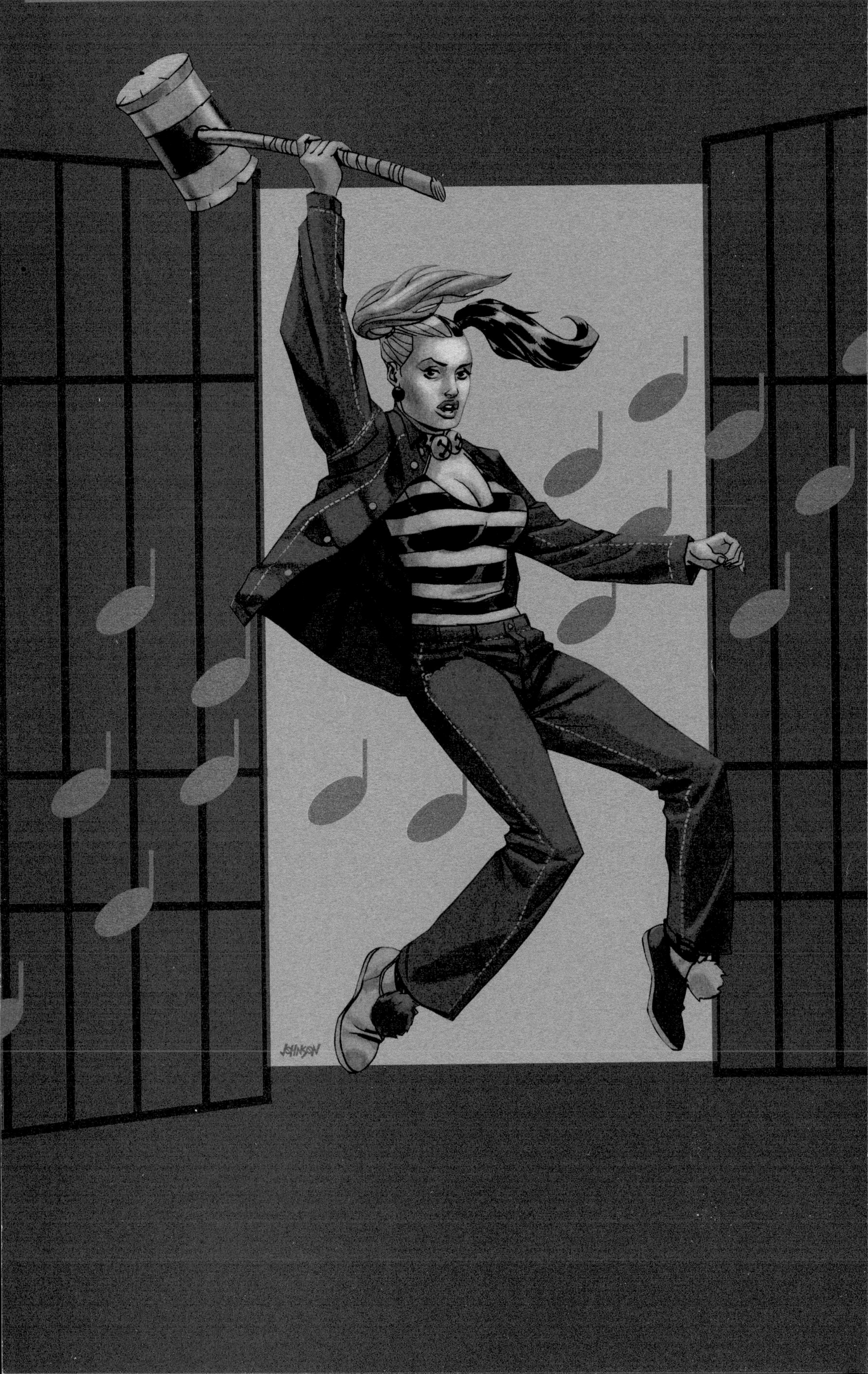
JOHNSON